לבי ער

הקדמות להגדה

Rav Dovber Pinson

THE
HAGGADAH

PATHWAYS
to PESACH *and the*
HAGGADAH

The Elbogen
Edition

Vol.1

Published by IYYUN Publishing
232 Bergen Street
Brooklyn, NY 11217

www.iyyun.com

Iyyun Publishing books may be purchased for educational, business or saless promotional usse. For information please email: contact@iyyun.com

Editor: Reb Matisyahu Brown
Editor: Reb Eden Pearlstein
Proofreading / Editing: Reb Yaakov Gershon
Cover and book design: RP Design and Development

pb ISBN 978-1-7367026-3-5

Pinson, Dovber 1971-
The Haggadah: Pathways to Pesach and the Haggadah
1. Judaism 2. Jewish Spirituality 3. General Spirituality

בס"ד

לבי ער

Rav Dovber Pinson

THE
HAGGADAH

הקדמות להגדה

PATHWAYS to PESACH
and the HAGGADAH

Vol.1

The Elbogen Edition

IYYUN PUBLISHING

DEDICATION

This book is dedicated and published
in honor of

REB YAAKOV ELBOGEN שיחי'

May the זכות */ merit of this Sefer*
be a source of blessing to his entire family.

ספר זה יוצא לאור לזכות והצלחת ידיד נפשי תלמידי חביבי
איש החסד אשר בו רוח חכמה ומוכתר בכל מידה נכונה
מקבל כל אדם בסבר פנים יפות
ואוהב ומוקיר תורה

הרה"ח אי"א נו"נ
ר' יעקב קאפיל עלבויגן שיחי'

זכות התורה תגן עליו ועל כל משפחתו

ויזכה למלוא חפניים נחת מילדיו מתוך בריאות ושמחה
אושר ועושר
מנוחת הנפש והרחבת המוחין

Contents

Part One
Aspects of Freedom

Part Two
Seder Night

Part Three
The Seder Plate

Part Four

The Haggadah

Note to the Reader:

Before delving into an exploration of the actual Haggadah, it would serve us well to first introduce the *Yom Tov* / Holy Day of *Pesach* / Passover and to probe the meanings and deeper understandings of enslavement, Egypt, and freedom. This is the purpose of the present volume; the first of two.

Part One
Aspects of Freedom

Chapter 1:
The Language of Freedom

PESACH AND FREEDOM ARE INTRINSICALLY BOUND. On these Holy Days, we celebrate both our people's freedom from Egyptian bondage as well as our personal freedom made possible in the present moment.

Indeed, 'freedom' is a loaded and powerful word in English, but what is the actual word for freedom in the Torah?

There are various words in the Torah that express the idea of freedom. The two basic words the Torah uses for 'freedom' are *Chofshi*, as in a slave going חפשי / 'free' (*Shemos*, 21:2), and דרור / *D'ror* / 'liberty', as in the earth being free, or again, slaves going free: וקראתם דרור בארץ / "Proclaim *D'ror* throughout the Land" (*Vayikra*, 25:10).

There is yet another word for freedom: חירות / *Cheirus*, which is the one we use most often in reference to the redemption of Pesach. In our liturgy, Pesach is called זמן חירותנו / *Zeman Cheiruseinu* / the Season of Our Freedom. This word connoting the simple idea of freedom is in fact not found in the Torah at all (although the Targum translates חפשי as בר חורין: Unkalus, *Shemos*, 21:2), rather it is from *Chazal* / our sages.

If all three of these words connote freedom, we then must ask: What are their differences?

The beginning of wisdom is the definition of terms. Therefore, we cannot begin to scratch the surface of what the Torah means by 'freedom' if we do not first clearly define the words the Torah itself uses to express freedom.

CHOFSHI. D'ROR. CHEIRUS. –
THE THREE WORDS OF FREEDOM

Chofshi is etymologically related to the word חיפוש / *Chipus* / search. D'ror is a contraction of the words דור דור / *Dor Dor* / 'generation-generation', as the Ramban writes (ועל דרך האמת דרור מלשון דור הולך ודור בא :Ramban on *Vayikra*, 25:10*), which implies a perpetual continuity and succession. Cheirus is related to the word חרות / *Charus* / engraved, as the Mishnah states, והלחת מעשה אלקים המה והמכתב מכתב אלקים הוא חרות על הלחת, אל תקרא חרות אלא חרות, שאין לך בן חורין אלא מי שעוסק בתלמוד תורה / "'The Luchos were the work of Hashem... *Charus* / engraved'

---

* Chazal understand the word *D'ror* to be connected with a home, with space (not time, as in generations). דכולי עלמא דרור לשון חירות מאי משמע דתניא אין דרור אלא לשון חירות אמר רבי יהודה מה לשון דרור כמדייר בי דיירא ומוביל סחורה בכל מדינה / "According to everyone, the term *d'ror* is a word meaning 'liberty'. From where may this be inferred? As it is taught, 'The word *d'ror* is a term meaning only liberty.' Rebbe Yehuda said: 'What is the meaning of the word *d'ror*? It is like a man who dwells (*Medayyer*) in any dwelling (*Dayyara*) and moves merchandise around the entire country (i.e., he can live and do business wherever he wants)': *Rosh Hashanah*, 9b. *Sifra*, Behar, 2:2. Rashi, *Vayikra*, 25:10. Space and time are linked; as *Dor* / generation represents timelessness, it also represents spacelessness, the ability to live anywhere. Note the teachings of Chazal, ארץ ישראל נמשלה לצבי לומר לך מה צבי זה אין עורו מחזיק בשרו אף ארץ ישראל אינה מחזקת פירותיה דבר אחר מה צבי זה קל מכל החיות אף ארץ ישראל קלה מכל הארצות לבשל את פירותיה / "Why is Eretz Yisrael likened to a *Tzvi* / deer? This comparison comes to tell you that similar to a deer, whose skin cannot contain its meat once it has been skinned, so too, Eretz Yisrael cannot contain its fruit once it has been picked, due to the great quantity of the produce. Alternatively, just as a deer is swifter than all the other beasts, so too, Eretz Yisrael is swifter to ripen its fruit than all the other countries": *Kesuvos*, 112a. In other words, abundance ('spacelessness') is connected to quickness ('timelessness').

(*Shemos*, 32:16); read it not as *Charus*, rather as *Cheirus* / freedom, for the only person who is truly free is one who occupies himself with Torah study" (*Avos*, 6:2).

And so we must ask: How do these ideas of 'searching', 'generations', and 'engraved' connect with the idea of freedom?

Everything within this world consists of three elements: *Olam* / 'world' or space, *Shanah* / time, and *Nefesh* / 'soul' or personal consciousness. These three concepts are connected to the three words employed for freedom, by means of their etymological roots and associations. Chofshi, and its inner quality of 'searching' is connected with the world of Olam, as 'searching' suggests a spatial investigation, looking at what immediately appears while trying to see beyond it. *D'ror* is connected with the world of time, as 'generations' alludes to what appears in the now, what has appeared in the past, and what will appear in future times. *Cheirus* is connected with the world of soul and consciousness, as 'engraving' is a term used to describe a quality of deep learning and integration of wisdom within one's psyche and soul.

מצרים / *Mitzrayim* / Egypt comes from the root word מצר / *Metzar* / constraint, constriction, or narrowness, implying stuckness. The natural limits of time, space, and personal consciousness set the stage on which a general state of 'constriction' can manifest. For example, constricted consciousness in the realm of time can appear as being obsessively tied to the current moment, to such an extent that one cannot see the big picture, including their past or future. In 'constricted space', a person can become stuck in their physical or geographical location without the freedom to move. In constricted personal consciousness, one can become so engrossed in their own life story that they cannot see or think about anyone else beyond themselves.

Let us go a little deeper and unpack these ideas. As it says, "All her pursuers overtook her בין המצרים / *Bein haMetzarim* / within the straits" (*Eichah*, 1:3). Egypt, from the root word מצר / *Metzar*, represents a place of 'narrow straits'; a place of total constriction and confinement, devoid of any possibility or movement. Indeed, for *Klal Yisrael* / the People of Israel, Mitzrayim was a place of stuckness, eclipsing their sense of freedom to choose and their ability to express themselves. In the most literal sense, no slave was allowed to leave.

Mitzrayim-Metzar is not a mere linguistic association, rather, the Torah itself infers that Egypt, in contrast to Eretz Yisrael, the Promised Land, was a place of constriction and narrowness. The *Pasuk* / verse says, "I have come down to rescue them from the Egyptians and to bring them out of that land to a ארץ טובה ורחבה / good and *spacious* land" (*Shemos*, 3:8). The Torah thus implies that Egypt was not spacious, but rather oppressive and claustrophobic. It was a society based on trauma and intractable stuckness. As a result, Mitzrayim represents any reality or condition of existential narrowness, any constriction of self-expression, or any sense of physical, emotional, mental, or spiritual enslavement.

In Egypt, Klal Yisrael was not only laboring under an external state of slavery, rather they were experiencing עבדות בעצם / *Avdus b'Etzem* / an 'essential' enslavement, an enslavement of their very essence. They thought and believed (especially those who were teetering on the fiftieth level of *Tumah* / impurity and stuckness, as will be explored) — as the Egyptian slave owners wished them to believe — that there was an absolute fixed class system, and that those who were currently slaves were meant to be, and would always be, slaves. This belief in the status quo permeated their experience of Olam, Shanah and Nefesh to the extent that their condition of constriction and slavery was not merely extrinsic, rather it was intrinsic and indispensable; they could not even conceive of themselves beyond its fanatical borders.

Then, suddenly from Above, with dramatic force, came Klal Yisrael's unprecedented liberation. This freedom was not merely a release from jail or bondage, rather Klal Yisrael was revealed to be חירות בעצם / free in essence. Our release from Mitzrayim brought us into an intrinsic freedom; we were no longer slaves by definition. No other people can ever truly enslave us again. Sadly, they are able to put us down, oppress, persecute, or abuse us, but we are eternally and existentially free. Ours is not just a freedom from being a slave and acting like a slave, it is an absolute freedom beyond the very context of enslavement and subjugation altogether (*Likutei Sichos*, 21, p. 68).

WHAT CREATES A HEBREW SLAVE?

חפשי / *Chofshi* is the most prominent word the Torah uses in reference to an actual slave or servant who has gone free. To understand the deeper significance of this concept, we will first explore the *Sugya* / topic of a 'servant' and how it is defined in the Torah.

Although for thousands of years this has not been practiced, the Torah provides the possibility for a person who has stolen money and cannot repay it to temporarily indenture themselves to another as a form of remuneration. Regarding the laws of owning a slave, the Torah opens with the words, "These are the laws which you shall set before them: if you buy an עבד עברי / *Eved Ivri* / a Hebrew indentured servant..." (*Shemos*, 21:1-2).

Normally, members of Klal Yisrael are referred to as *Bnei Yisrael* / Children of Israel, so why is a slave called an *Ivri* / Hebrew? Perhaps the phrase could have read, 'If you acquire a servant from among Bnei Yisrael etc.'

In fact, not only is it an unusual title, the term *Ivri* is never used explicitly for any member of Klal Yisrael after leaving Egypt and receiving the Torah (Because of this, the Even Ezra, on *Shemos*, 21:2, quotes a disputed opinion that *Ivri* may actually refer to a descendent of one of the other children of Avraham). We find the phrase *Elokei haIvrim* / "G-d of the Hebrews" used when Klal Yisrael is still enslaved in Egypt, but there is no reference to *Ivrim* after they go out of Egypt (Despite our sages' teaching that Klal

Yisrael is called *Ivrim* because they "passed through the sea": *Medrash Rabbah*, Shemos, 3:7). In general, it appears from these *P'sukim* / verses that the name *Ivri* in the Torah refers to an individual from Klal Yisrael who is a slave (although this is later in Tanach, not in the Torah itself. The descriptive *Ivri* is used outside the context of slavery, for example, *Yonah*, 1:9. However, perhaps Yonah was speaking this way to the sailors who 'knew' *Elokei ha'Ivrim*: see *Pirkei d'Rebbe Eliezer*, Chap. 10).

This is, then, the first question: why is a Jewish slave called *Ivri*?

Grammatically, there is another problem. It seems the text should have been written: "If you buy an עברי לעבד / *Ivri l'Eved* / a Hebrew *as* a slave….," since when the Pasuk says, עבד עברי / *'Eved Ivri* / slave-Hebrew', it is a rather ambiguous phrase. As Rashi notes, we don't know if it is talking about a Hebrew / Jewish slave or a slave that was previously *owned* by a Hebrew, meaning, a Hebrew's slave.

Beyond the ambiguity, let us assume that it is a clear statement meaning a Hebrew slave, still grammatically it should have said *Ivri l'Eved* / 'Hebrew for a slave', not *Eved Ivri* / 'slave Hebrew'. This hints at the idea that the indentured Jewish person was already a slave in their own consciousness.

SEEING AND SPEAKING: IMPRESSED AND IMPRESSING

Further on, the Torah teaches regarding a gentile slave, "If one (a master) hits the eye of his slave…to freedom he shall send him (the slave)…and if he takes out the tooth of his slave… to freedom he shall send him." (*Shemos*, 21:26). The own-er is forced to set his slave free if he injures his eye or knocks out his tooth.

Why does the Torah only mention the eye and the tooth in this discussion? What is unique about an injury to a slave's eyes or teeth? In truth, according to our Sages, the gentile slave is to be freed if the master injures any one of his *Roshei Eivarim* / main bodily organs (*Kidushin*, 24a, Rashi, *ad loc*). So, why does the Torah use these body parts specifically as examples of a more general principle? There is in fact a technical halachic reason why these two body parts are singled out (as Rashi explains), but our question is more philosophical.

Throughout the entire portion dealing with the laws of servants, whenever the Torah speaks about freedom, it is in the language of *Chofshi* — not *Cheirus* or *D'ror*. Why does the Torah use this particular term regarding the freedom of slaves? What does the idea of *Chofshi* have to do with a slave?

Let us go back to the eye and tooth. What is it about these body parts that if a master damages them the slave is to be freed? Says the Medrash (*Medrash Rabbah*, 36:8), the whole idea of slavery was introduced to humanity when Cham saw his father, Noach, lying naked, as it says: וירא חם אבי כנען את ערות אביו ויגד לשני־אחיו בחוץ / "And Cham, the father of Canaan, *saw* the nakedness of his father, and *told* his two brothers out-side" (*Bereishis*, 9:22). When Noach awoke from his drunken stu-por, he "knew what his youngest son had done to him. And he said: 'Cursed be Canaan; a *servant of servants* shall he be unto his brothers'.'* Since 'seeing' and 'telling' are the roots of the curse of slavery, when a master damages a slave's eyes ('seeing') or his 'teeth' ('telling'), he becomes freed from the predicament of slavery (*Rabbeinu Bachya*, Parshas Mishpatim).

Beyond the simple reading of this wonderful Medrash, which symbolically connects the eye and the mouth to slavery and freedom, there is something more profound going on. The Medrash is suggesting to us that there is an intrinsic bond between seeing, speaking, and slavery.

Let us delve a little deeper. It is known that the 'punishments' of the Torah are based on a system of cause and effect, as the Shaloh haKadosh writes. This means that they are objectively correlative to one's subjective actions. If a child does not put the milk back into the refrigerator, for example, and his parents withhold his allowance as a result, this punishment is not 'cause and effect' in the manner we are describing. There is no intrinsic relationship between putting back the milk and receiving an allowance. But, if the milk spoiled because he did not put it back, and therefore there is no fresh milk for the family to drink the next morning, this would be more of a cause and effect form of 'retribution'. Noach did not curse Cham to be poor, blind, or crippled. Rather, he cursed him that his descendants will be slaves to their brothers. So then, what is the intrinsic cause and effect connection between this form

---

* *Ibid*, 24-25. He cursed Cham's 'fourth' son (*Sanhedrin*, 70a), as he was not able to curse Cham himself: *Tosefos*, ad loc.

of 'punishment' and the act of seeing his father's nakedness and telling his brothers about it?

The reason Noach cursed Cham with slavery, under the control of his brothers, is that this was who Cham already was. Someone who 'sees and speaks' is already a slave to his environment and others' opinions. If what you see on the outside determines how you feel inside, then you are, at least subtly, a slave to your surroundings. And if you 'need' to tell others what you see and know, then once again you are enslaved to their validation and acceptance of your experience. If you see something, experience something, or learn something, and you must tell another person what you saw, experienced, or learned for it to be true in your eyes, you are mentally enslaved to others. And so, when Noach recognized this weakness in Cham, he said, 'Just as you are already acting as if you were a slave to your brothers, you will end up becoming literally enslaved to them. You will ultimately become the person who you are behaving as.'

When Cham 'sees' his father's nakedness, he straightaway goes to tell his brothers. He is easily impressed and immediately needs to impress. His father's curse to be a slave to his brothers is directly related to what he did: וירא...ויגד / *vaYar... vaYageid* / "he saw... and he spoke." This behavior showed that he was *already* a slave to his brothers, and the curse was merely a revelation of that fact; transparently revealing a dynamic of slavery that was already present within him.

Freeing a gentile ('Canaanite') slave because of the damage done to his eyes or mouth is now a little more understandable. He no longer has the *Kelim* / vessels or instruments that condition him to an internal life of slavery; he is thus no longer subject to that role.

Now let us return to the case of the Eved Ivri. To refresh our memory, the questions that we previously asked were: 1) why is he referred to as *Ivri*, an unusual and seemingly derogatory term, and 2) why is he called *Eved Ivri* / 'a slave that is a Hebrew', and not an *Ivri l'Eved* / 'a Hebrew for a slave', which would be a more conventional phrasing?

Indeed, *Ivri* is a term used for the people in Egypt who were living as slaves, and that is precisely why the Torah uses this term here. It hints at the slave mentality of this individual person who has legally become a slave.* He is therefore called *Eved Ivri* / 'slave, a Hebrew', even before he becomes an actual slave. He is already living with a slave mentality. The only reason he becomes an actual slave, by selling himself into slavery, is that in his mind and heart he already is a slave.

The Eved Ivri is a slave in his consciousness even before he sells himself. The way he thinks and lives his life is as if he were already enslaved. The process of becoming an actual slave is merely a manifestation of his internal reality. He was an *Eved* / slave to his lower self even before he actually became a slave

---

* Perhaps the words *Eved* and *Ivri* share a common root, as both words begin with an Ayin-Beis.

to someone else. This is the archetype of the *Ivri*, which is how we were referred to in Egypt.

The word *Yisrael*, on the other hand, comes from the word *Sar* / prince or master (Rashi, Bereishis, 35:9). Only after leaving Egypt did we become *B'nei Yisrael*, masters and free people: "We were not called Bnei Yisrael until we reached Mount Sinai" (*Chulin*, 101b). A person who becomes an actual slave is someone who is not living as a Yisrael, and as such is not called a 'Child of Yisrael'.

A free person is one whose life is not negatively entangled with or totally dependent on other people. To live as a master is to be the cause of your life, not the effect. You choose your path. You decide how you are going to live. 'Free' means not being dependent on outside influences. To live freely is to live your life outward from your deepest depths.

The Maharal (Rebbe Yehudah ben Betzalel Loew, 1521–1609), the illustrious 16th Century Rabbi of Prague, writes that simple Matzah (without any other ingredients, besides water and flour) is called "poor man's bread" (*Pesachim*, 36a), and precisely because it is "poor" is it also the bread of freedom. A free person is someone who is independent, alone, not 'mixed up' with others, just as poor man's bread is not mixed with 'added ingredients'. *Matzah Ashirah* / 'rich Matzah', by contrast, is mixed with other ingredients such as orange juice, milk, or sugar.*

---

* Although eating "rich Matzah" is technically allowed on all seven days of Pesach, it is not allowed for the Mitzvah of eating Matzah on Seder Night.

A free person's 'bread' or existence is simple and does not need other ingredients to create or sustain it.

Similarly, all types of Matzah bake very quickly. The original Matzah we ate when leaving Egypt did not have time to rise as we left in a rush, and the Matzah we eat today also bakes in a very short time so that it does not rise and become unkosher as Matzah. The entire process, from the mixing of flour and water until it is baked and removed from the oven, takes place in under 18 minutes. This idea of having 'little time' is also related to 'poor man's bread', as a poor person does not have the leisure to relax and eat slowly. Yet, as the Maharal points out, the issue of 'little time' also points to the fact that Matzah comes from a place beyond the flow of time, and beyond the need for time (*Gevuros Hashem*, 51). Matzah thus represents freedom from time.

Inwardly, to be free means to live your life from your deepest inner truth and core. The definition of a slave, on the other hand, is someone whose life is contingent upon and fused with his master: "Everything that an *Eved* / slave acquires, he acquires for his master" (*Pesachim*, 88b). A free person, on the other hand, is independent and autonomous.

Sadly, many 'free' people live as slaves. While they do not literally labor under a master, they do 'need' other people for validation, and in this way, they are 'enslaved' to them. Giving up their power of self-determination and identification, they must rely on the world outside of themselves to tell them who they are and how they should behave.

Living with a slave mentality is to continually be *impressed* by others and to live with a need to *impress* others. In this sense, 'seeing' is needing to be impressed, and 'telling' is needing to impress. Seeing means absorbing a truth from outside of one-self. A person looks outward, sees what others have or do, and then thinks he needs to have and do the same. In such a case, who decides what he wants or needs? Others do. In this state, one is dependent on others. One is psychologically and socially enslaved.

Why do some people have the 'need' to tell other people all about their lives and share every experience that they encounter? It is because of a lack of self-confidence and a need to find validity from others. Similar to the slavery of sight, this is yet another form of slavery characterized by speech, via 'telling'.

'HEARING' MEANS FREEDOM

One might be inclined to think that the sense of hearing must be just like the sense of seeing in terms of the possibility of becoming enslaved through it. Yet, hearing is in some ways 'beyond' seeing, with the power to open us up to real freedom, to that which transcends one's immediate circumstances.

There is, of course, a form of 'false hearing' or enslavement in relation to hearing. In the case of an Eved Ivri, if after a certain period of time he decides by his own free will to remain a slave, the master must pierce his ear. "If the slave says, 'I love my master, my wife, and my children. I will not go free,' his master shall bring him to the judges, and he shall bring him to the door or to the doorpost, and his master shall bore his ear" (*Shemos*, 21:5-6). "The ear that heard 'For the children of Israel are slaves to Me,' and then went and acquired a (human) master for himself, this ear shall be bored" (*Vayikra*, 25:55. *Kidushin*, 22b). Since it was the ear that heard at the giving of the Torah that we belong to *HaKadosh Baruch Hu* / the Holy Blessed One alone and to no mortal man — and still the person chooses to remain enslaved to another human being — his ear shall be bored.

There is a clear symbolic correlation between 'an ear that hears' and an ear that is not truly listening. Yet this is not merely a symbolic association. Rather, the state of freedom itself, our being lifted out of Egypt and slavery, and the essence of our receiving Torah, our hearing HaKadosh Baruch Hu say *Anochi Hashem* / "I am Hashem," are all connected with the ear and the sense of hearing.*

Hearing has a strong spiritual component corresponding to its ability to sense what is beyond the immediate. The eye can only see that which is in its immediate vicinity, but the ear can hear from a long way away.

The human ear is created for a specific purpose in that it "serves to receive, alone" (Maharal, *Be'er haGolah*, Be'er 3). Various orifices in the body have lids and coverings, such as the eyes

---

* The *Tikkunei Zohar* (130a) teaches that the shape of the ear is similar to the letter Aleph, and the Aleph is connected to *Anochi Hashem*, the opening of the revelation at Mount Sinai.

and mouth, and some do not, such as the nose and ears. The eyes and mouth have coverings because they both receive (e.g., sights and foods) and express or project (e.g., speak or visualize, as explored in the books *Visualization and Imagery*, and *Sounds and Vibrations*). We need to close these lids when we know we should not be ingesting the negative imagery or harmful foods before us. Similarly, we need to know when to stop talking or projecting outward when it does not serve us or others. This is the inner purpose for these coverings.

The nose is a channel for both inhalation and exhalation. Therefore, even though it does not have lids, it is functionally similar to the eyes and the mouth, which are interfaces for inward and outward transmission. The ear, on the other hand, is totally unique, in that it has no lids*, and it only receives and does not transmit. The ear is unidirectional — exclusively dedicated to taking in sound.

We proclaim at least twice every day, *Shema Yisrael...Hashem Echad /* "Hear, Israel... G-d is One." We do not say 'See, Israel...' because the way the world is today, we cannot yet 'see' that Hashem is One. It is not an 'immediate' and obvious reality. However, we can listen deeply and 'hear' the distant rumblings of the ever-approaching reality of Oneness, as it gradually reveals Itself.

---

* Although, the earlobe can serve as a covering, מפני מה אוזן כולה קשה והאליה רכה שאם ישמע אדם דבר שאינו הגון יכוף אליה לתוכה: *Kesuvos*, 5b.

When a person derives their sense of self and reality only by what they can observe with the naked eye, they are then living in a condition of inner slavery. Their life is defined and dictated solely by appearances and what can be immediately seen. Functioning from this state of mind, humans are like all other animals of the planet. It takes a refined and developed sense of listening and deep understanding to be truly human. Uniquely, human beings have the ability to truly listen, reason, and dialogue. Only humans can learn to actively reflect on and transcend themselves. The understanding gained through reflection is akin to listening.

Robotic, mindless doing is another function of slavery. A slave does exactly what the master instructs him, and he can do it well. A slave can do as told, but does not have the ability to deeply listen, to hear and consider other ideas and alternative ways of understanding. A slave can say *Na'aseh* / "I will do," but cannot say *Nishma* / "I will listen."

A slave can successfully do as he or she is told, but does not have the ability to listen to their heart, consider alternative courses of action, or reflect on their actions after the fact. They cannot hear the "still, small voice" (*Melachim* I, 19:12). They are therefore incapable of truly understanding the deeper purpose of their own actions. They do not have the capacity to make their own free-will decisions.

When a slave tells his master, "I like my life as a slave, I will not go free," he is declaring that he does not wish to listen and truly hear. He wants to continue to live in the place of 'seeing' and 'doing', alone, and not have to grow into the capacity of *Nishma* — hearing, inferring, dialoguing, and understanding.

By saying, "I like my life as a slave," he is denying the whole project of leaving Egypt and receiving the Torah. The whole point of Matan Torah is that we were able to hear *Anochi Hashem* / "I am Hashem," and thus to perceive the Oneness (the Aleph) of Hashem in order to fully understand our eternal bond with the One. By declaring, "I prefer to be a slave," he is closing himself off from the deep hearing and freedom we achieved by leaving Egypt. As such, his ear needs to be 'opened' by being bored through with a sharp instrument.

This helps us understand a specific detail regarding the idolatrous worship of the Golden Calf. When the people came to Aharon complaining and asking him to create an idol for them, Aharon said to them, "Remove the golden earrings from the ears of your wives, of your sons and your daughters, and bring them to me" (*Shemos*, 32:2). "Golden earrings" is a subtle reference to the pierced ears of willfully enslaved Jews. Aharon is intimating to them that making an idol means giving up the ability to truly hear and listen to the voice of the One. Idol worship, by definition, is focused on a visible 'image', while Matan Torah freed us from the world of image-obsession and connected us with the Imageless Infinite Creator.

PERSONAL & INNER ENSLAVEMENT

Of course, just as the rest of Klal Yisrael were freed from

Egypt, the Eved is always already free, since he too has חירות בעצם / freedom at the essence of his being. And yet, the Eved chooses not to live with free choice any longer, but rather to live and behave in limited and robotic ways. He chooses to surrender his human faculty of choice and live as a beast of burden. Without inner 'hearing', you are stuck in what you 'see' (with an added 'need' to broadcast what you see to the world), and are therefore living in a condition of slavery; enslaved to others, to society, to your own emotions and entrenched opinions.

While the laws of an Eved are no longer literally applicable, and already in the times of the Gemara all forms of slavery were almost completely obsolete among Klal Yisrael, the principles within those laws and verses are as relevant today as they were thousands of years ago.

Perhaps most people in our society are not physically bound by an enslaver, yet, sadly, many people are still enslaved to the world of 'impressions', to the paradigm of וירא... ויגד / vaYar vaYageid / "He saw and he spoke." So many are sadly enslaved to a world of imagery, billboards, and advertisements, allowing idealized images to define their sense of happiness and direct their actions. We are continually bombarded with countless unhealthy images and messages from the popular culture and mass media, whether through explicit advertisements or through subliminal imagery. After many years of this bombardment and stimulation, such images can accumulate in the storehouse of our subconscious mind. A need to 'be impressed' by images is also a need to impress, and so people publicly broadcast pictures of their vacation or even their meals. Upon making a beautiful looking egg salad, people immediately think of how a photo of it can impress the world. This is a modern form of Mitzrayim; not the technology itself, but the teleology of our awareness.

CHOFSHI AND CHIPUS

The world of images is about what you see on the surface of life. Therefore, the Torah tells us that to break the chokehold of inner enslavement, to 'see' beyond the facade of the trivialities and emptiness at the heart of the world of impressions, we need to 'seek' what is deeper. To be חפשי / *Chofshi* / free, we need to practice חיפוש / *Chipus* / seeking.

To be free we need to search, yearn, and dream for more; we must never be satisfied merely by what we see. We need to challenge any inner tendency within us to be mindlessly content or impressed with what appears to our immediate observation. We need to probe deeper than external images, and aspire to 'hear' the Presence of the Divine Utterance that gives rise to Creation. We need to be constantly in dialogue with the world around us, asking for and seeking the truth of things.

Chofshi is the most common, and arguably the most important, word for freedom in the Torah, as it implies the opposite of a slave *mentality*. It is freedom from the inertia of immediate appearances, as well as freedom to search and go deeper, beyond the level of images altogether. Cham saw and internalized only the image of shame and nakedness, because he did not attempt to look deeper and investigate, to probe and listen to what he beheld.

Chofshi is connected with the world of space; expressing a freedom from imagery and outer appearances, through an ability to search beyond. To be Chofshi is to be free to yearn for more; to search and look deeply, beneath the surface.

D'ROR: FREEDOM IN TIME

D'ror is a contraction of the phrase *Dor-Dor* / 'generation, generation', representing a sustained continuity through time, connecting what appears now to what will be in the future.

A slave does not own his time. His days are dictated and his schedule is set up by his master, and he is always pushed to move faster. He never has a choice of when to eat or sleep. Although he has no control over his time in general, he does have some control within each immediate moment. For example, when he is given his food, he may have a choice to eat with a fork or with his hands. When the hour to go to sleep arrives, he may have a choice to fall asleep or to lie awake, however, he has no ability to plan for the future or decide what he will do tomorrow.

The freedom of D'ror is a freedom of 'generations'; freedom from the way things are in the confines of the now. From a wider perspective, in time everything changes and evolves, and

you do not have to focus solely on the dictates of the immediate moment. In a state of D'ror, you can think about your
future, the future of your children and the coming generations.

A general principle of slavery is that עבד אין לו ייחום / "a slave
has no lineage." Of course a gentile slave is allowed to have
children, but his children are not considered 'his'. The meaning
of this is, although he is a slave, his children might not be slaves
(*Kidushin*, 69a). The slave loses his sense of self, and thus has no
past or future; no 'lineage' or 'offspring'.

Living freely includes the ability to think about your
future, your children and grandchildren. It is possible to think
about your future when you can remember and contemplate
your past. Individual memory answers the question of "Who
am I?" Collective memory answers the question "Who are we?"
Without a living memory of your past, you lose your individual
and collective identity in the present, and thus, who you can be
in the future.

Unique to humans is the natural love and attachment
between children and their grandparents, and between grandparents and their grandchildren. Parental love is found in the
animal kingdom, to lesser or greater degrees, but it does not
extend to grandparents. To contemplate your grandchildren is
to be free beyond the constraints of the 'immediate time' of
animals — and of slaves; it is to be in the expansive time of
'generations'.

Chazal tell us כל המלמד את בן בנו תורה מעלה עליו הכתוב כאילו
קבלה מהר סיני / "Whoever teaches his son's son Torah, the
Pasuk ascribes him credit as though he received it from Mount
Sinai" (*Kidushin*, 30a). If you are truly free, and truly 'remember'
that you left Egypt and received the Torah, you will be drawn
to create a bond and teach your grandchild Torah.

Chazal also tell us the reverse, that שכל השומע פרשה מן בן
בנו כאילו הוא שומעה מהר סיני / "Whoever hears Torah from his
grandchild, it is as if he heard it from Mount Sinai" (*Yerushalmi*,
Shabbos, 1:2). If you listen to words of Torah from your grandchild, it shows that you truly are a free person and you stood
at Sinai — because your consciousness extends beyond your
individual self, and even beyond your children. You are not
confined to the present moment and its circumstances; you are
openly connected to the past and the future.

CHEIRUS: FREEDOM OF SPIRIT, SOUL AND CONSCIOUSNESS

Another dilemma with slavery, whether literal or psychological, besides not owning your time and reality, is that everything in life seems to be forced upon you. Where you go
and what you do, how you spend your time and where the
trajectory of your life is going, are all dictated by external
forces, whether by a literal master, or by your surrounding
culture — enslaving you on the level of choice. This is
existential slavery of the spirit. Cheirus is the power of
freedom that comes to uproot this form of slavery.

Cheirus is related to the word *Charus* / engraved, a reference to the 'engraving' of the *Aseres haDibros* / Ten Commandments into the *Luchos* / Tablets. The Torah is the wisdom of life, guiding us in how to live morally, ethically, and spiritually. Everyone wants to live their fullest, emotionally, mentally, and spiritually. Yet, there are two ways we can relate to the Torah: a) we can feel like a slave performing the commands of his Master. This is, indeed, a popular approach. Instead of society dictating how to live, you feel commanded by a higher Being, and higher principles. While this is more liberating than living at the whim of society, it can still feel stifling. Or, b) we can have a more intimate relationship with HaKadosh Baruch Hu and the Torah, in which the commandments become "engraved" into us, an integral part of who we are.

Ink and paper are two separate objects, but as the Alter Rebbe explains, there is a level where the Torah is not just written 'upon' you as a separate object; it is not a prescription impressed into you from Above, it becomes one with you and appears within you, much like letters that are *Charus* / engraved into stone appear within the stone. In this higher-level freedom, an external force is not imposed upon you, but rather, a power emerges from within you. You recognize that Torah and its commandments are expressions of your very essence and your life.

Ultimately, when Torah is engraved within us, it is what 'I am'. This is the deepest realization; Torah is who we are, and it can even be called 'our Torah'. The Torah was transmitted to each one of us so that it can become *ours*, as phrased in the liturgy of Shavuos: *Matan Toraseinu* / "the giving of *our* Torah." When we live in active contemplation and 'master' Torah, it is referred to in our own name.

There is a spiritual movement upwards and inwards from a place of "I must" to "I am able," from "I have to" to "I desire to fulfill the Mitzvos because it is who I am." This is the level of Torah as it is engraved within us, the ultimate posture of true freedom.

Freedom is not merely being able to do what you want when you want. That is not real freedom. If a person is a brilliant scholar and one day he says, 'I am a free person, I can do whatever I want, I can be a plumber,' it is not freedom, it is foolishness. It is robbing yourself from who you can truly be. Freedom is to be your greatest, best and holiest self. Freedom is to be who you truly are, and to act from that place of spiritual authenticity.

NIGHT OF CHEIRUS / ENGRAVED GREATNESS

On Pesach night, we are gifted our highest potential, our own true *Gadlus* / greatness. Sitting before our Seder table, we are like kings and queens, and like the High Priest — sparkling with physical and spiritual greatness. "Through the leaving of Egypt we became masters and priests," as the Chinuch explains (*Chinuch*, Mitzvah 7-8, Mitzvah 15-16). This *Gadlus Ruchni* / spiritual expansiveness is expressed in the custom of many to dress in a *Kittel* / white garment, much like the *Cohen Gadol* / the High Priest, who was garbed in pure white as he served in the Holy of Holies (*Haggadah of the Maharal*, Divrei Negidim). As a further expression, on this night we dine while luxuriously reclining, "in the manner in which kings eat" (Rambam, *Pirush l'Mishnayos*, Pesachim, 10:1). This is our *Gadlus Gashmi* / physical expansiveness — this too puts us in touch with 'who we really are', and what we truly deserve.

On this night, we can soar into what we really are, and also lift others up. We can even become like the *Aron haKodesh* / Ark of the Covenant which held the Luchos: the Aron 'carried its carriers'. When it was lifted for transport, instead of the Cohanim 'carrying' the Aron, the Aron actually carried them (*Yalkut Shimoni*, Shmuel II, 5:142). As we ascend on this night, we are carried and we carry everyone and everything in Creation along with us.

Another allusion to the Gadlus of this night is its epithet, ליל שמרים / *Leil Shimurim* / Night of Guarding (*Shemos*, 12:42). This is connected with the terminology of ואביו שמר את־הדבר / *V'Aviv Shamar es haDaver* / "And his father (Yaakov) 'guarded' the thing (kept quiet and contemplated Yoseph's dreams of greatness)." Yoseph had dreams of greatness, of becoming a mighty ruler, but when he told his dreams to his father and brothers, "his father berated him." ויקנאו־בו אחיו ואביו שמר את־הדבר / "And his brothers were jealous of him, and his father 'guarded' the matter" (*Bereishis*, 37:11).

Yaakov 'guarded' the meaning of Yoseph's dreams because he was waiting for Yoseph to grow into himself and to start manifesting his true Gadlus. "He awaited and looked forward to the time when this would come to pass" (Rashi). So although Yaakov 'berated' him for speaking openly and causing his brothers to be jealous, still, he himself 'guarded' and 'protected' the dream and 'waited' for it to be manifest.

A short time later, after the dreams, when he encounters his brothers in the field, his brothers stripped away his special garment given to him by his father. They thought that it is the *Chitzoniyus* / the external layers or 'garments' of self that makes the man, and that the only reason Yoseph was dreaming of greatness was because of these garments. But this test, in fact, made it possible for Yoseph to let go of relying on his father's affection and any form of Chitzoniyus, and to own his dreams. This was precisely what Yoseph needed in order to begin to reveal his greatness and become who he really was.

Later on in the narrative, after being sold into slavery, Yoseph realized that he could not rely on his 'employers', Potifar and his wife, for his greatness, no matter how well Yoseph served them. And when Yoseph could not even rely on the Cupbearer whom he had comforted and befriended in prison, he was finally forced to accept that Gadlus is truly a gift from Above and that he needed to claim it himself. At that point, HaKadosh Baruch Hu sent dreams to Pharaoh and made Yoseph understand their interpretations, leading to his ascent to greatness and the fulfillment of his dreams.

On this ליל שמרים / Night of Guarding, we are gifted Gadlus from Above, the Gadlus that Hashem Alone 'guarded', 'protected' and 'waited' to gift us, although now on this night we must claim it ourselves and engrave it into our being.

We can be free on this night; we no longer need to try to be someone else. We can be our 'Torah-engraved' essential self; freedom is actually who we are, flowing with all our unique gifts and abilities. On Seder night, we can receive a taste of this Gadlus — what life could be — for on this night we are gifted a greater ability to see and receive the Gadlus that we really are; we are able to embrace and express our fullest potential.

Chapter 2:
Stages of Freedom:
Redeeming our Name, Voice, Speech, Song, and Silence

Y*ETZIAS MITZRAYIM* / THE EXODUS FROM EGYPT is mentioned in the Torah fifty times.* HaKadosh Baruch Hu asks us time and again to 'remember' this most formative experience of our lives, as our collective identity in the present is founded on our memory of our past. The fifty references to Yetzias Mitzrayim correspond to the fifty weeks and the fifty Shabbosim in every year (*Pirush haGra*, Tikkunei Zohar, p. 84). In this way, we are to remember Yetzias Mitzray-

---

* *Zohar* 2, 85b, and 3, 262a. *Tikkunei Zohar*, Tikkun 32. Rabbeinu Bachya, *Devarim*, 2:23. *Pardes Rimonim*, Sha'ar 13:1.

im throughout the entire year, and in fact every day, for every single day there is a Mitzvah of the Torah to remember the Going Out of Mitzrayim.*

A Mitzvah to 'remember' implies that there is a possibility of forgetting, and by repeatedly urging us to remember Yetzias Mitzrayim, the Torah is clearly warning us against this possibility. What type of 'remembering' or 'memory' is the Torah demanding of us? And what does it mean to 'remember Yetzias Mitzrayim'? Surely the Torah is not commanding us to merely have a nostalgic rumination about the past. Is the Torah interested in us memorializing a historical event to help us remain aware of where we come from as a people, and where we are heading? Is the point of 'remembering' to learn from the past for the sake of improving the present? What does the Torah want from us in the act of remembering, and what is the intended result?

GOING OUT OF EGYPT: HISTORICAL, PRESENT COLLECTIVE, PRESENT PERSONAL

Our sages say, "In every generation a person must regard himself as if he himself had gone out of Egypt" (*Pesachim*, 116b). This means that when recalling the Exodus from Egypt thousands of years ago, we should envision our own lives as if *HaKadosh Baruch Hu* / the Holy One, has taken us, in *our* generation, out of Egypt. Indeed, we were there in the past as well, because our ancestors' redemption is our redemption, and if not for their being redeemed we would not even be here in the present.

---

* Perhaps even women are obligated in this, and not just on Seder Night: *Sefer haChinuch*, Mitzvah, 21. Although see *Minchas Chinuch* and *Sha'agas Aryeh*, 12.

This remembrance thus relates to the historical past as it resonates in the present moment.*

---

* The Korban Pesach needs to be שה תמים זכר בן־שנה יהיה / "a lamb without blemish, a yearling male" (Shemos, 12:5). Yet, the Pasuk in Devarim says, וזבחת פסח לה' אלקיך צאן ובקר / "You shall slaughter the Passover sacrifice for Hashem your G-d, from the flock (sheep) and the Bakar / herd (bull)" (Devarim, 16:2). Chazal tell us clearly that a bull cannot be a Korban Pesach, and the reason the Pasuk mentioned Bakar is to tell us that מותר הפסח / the excess of Pesach (for example, a person dedicated more than one animal for the Korban) is brought as a Shelamim / peace offering, and a Bakar can be used: Zevachim, 7b. Menachos, 83b. Or that the Korban Chagigah that is brought with the Korban Pesach (so that the Korban Pesach can be eaten pleasantly, and not when a person is famished, as Rashi explains) can be offered from a Bakar: Pesachim, 70b. Reading the Pasuk literally, the Even Ezra (Devarim, ibid), brings down an opinion (by a Karaite), כי במצרים אמר כבש או עז ועתה בקר אם יוכל / "In Egypt they needed to offer a lamb, sheep or goats," but ever since then, the offering of the Korban Pesach can be offered also from a Bakar. This is an incorrect reading and is not the way our Mesorah / Oral Tradition understands this Pasuk, as Chazal clearly states. But what is the reason for this reading? Why is there a difference that in Egypt we specifically offered a sheep and since leaving Egypt we offer even a Bakar? This is because צאן / sheep were deities of the Egyptians, and offering a Korban Pesach was a way for Klal Yisrael to demonstrate our moving away from idol worship and commitment to HaKadosh Baruch Hu. But, since we left Egypt and moved away from the ways of the Egyptians, there is no longer any reason to bring a Korban Pesach specifically from צאן. This is the opinion of a Karaite, someone who does not believe in the living, vibrant tradition of Chazal, and he thus reads the Pasuk in the context of past events. Yet herein lies their great contrast with Chazal, who, with new authentic Chidushim / innovations and adaptations in every generation, are the living embodiment of the Oral Tradition. And thus, the Torah is alive in the present, the 'going out of Egypt' is not merely recounting a past, rather, "In every generation a person must regard himself as if he himself had gone out of Egypt." Going out of Egypt is not a past event, rather it is a continuous one, and moving away from idol worship, no matter how subtly, is a never-ending process.

On a collective level, remembering Yetzias Mitzrayim encapsulates all the minor redemptions of Klal Yisrael from their constant exiles and *Gezeiros Ra'os* / negative decrees throughout time. On the night of Pesach we raise up a cup of wine and declare, "And it is this (referring to the Torah, the Shechinah, and/or our resolute faith) that has stood by our ancestors and for us. For not only one (enemy) has risen up against us to destroy us, but in *every* generation they rise up to destroy us. But HaKadosh Baruch Hu, delivers us from their hands."

On a more inward level, *Mitzrayim* / Egypt represents any and all *Meitzarim* / constrictions and limitations that paralyze or silence the human spirit. Enslavement, in this context, represents a state of ambiguity, doubt, lack of clarity and focus, in which a person lives inauthentically, without direction, purpose or aim. The notion that each generation is taken out of Egypt by HaKadosh Baruch Hu implies that we must experience our own redemption, as if the Exodus is happening to us right now. Every generation has its own *Meitzar* / constriction, the principal Kelipah of that generation, be it secularism or communism, materialism or universalism, nationalism or globalism, or any other -ism. Every generation has its own challenges and unique struggles, and yet, if we would merely open our eyes and reclaim what is innately ours, we would recognize that Hashem is always giving us the power and the means to be lifted out of these exiles and constricted states of mind and spirit.

"Every generation" means not only every era, rather, each *day* a person must regard himself as if he had come out of Mitzrayim (*Tanya*, 47); on each day it should be as if you had personally left Egypt that very day (Rashi, *Shemos*, 13:4, as explained by the Chasam Sofer, *Derashos l'Pesach*, p, 521). Ultimately, Hashem is taking us out of our inner Egypt each and every *moment.**

Yetzias Mitzrayim is a continuous, ever-unfolding process. Ever since we left Egypt at the great Exodus, every generation has had its own exiles and redemptions, expulsions and revivals. Individually as well, every person throughout their life goes through stages of feeling small, constricted, empty, lifeless, or aimless — only to later experience breakthroughs, redemptions, and expansions, leading to greater openness, clarit,y and spiritual confidence. We all fall, and then Hashem gives us the strength to stand back up again.

To inwardly be in exile in Egypt means to live unauthentically, lacking direction, clarity, and focus. On a collective and personal level, in a state of consciousness called *Mitzrayim*, we forget who we are and what we stand for, whether as a people or as an individual. In order to go out of Mitzrayim, or at least to make the vessels to receive the gift of redemption that

---

* The Alter Rebbe teaches (as in Tanya above) in the name of Chazal, although Chazal only mention in every generation, that each *day* a person must regard himself as if he had come out of Mitzrayim הנה בכל נפש ישראל צ"ל בכל יום בחי' יצ"מ וקי"ס כמ"ש למען תזכר את יום צאתך מארץ מצרים וגו'. וכמארז"ל בכל יום יהיה בעיניך כאלו היום יצאת ממצ"ץ. *Torah Ohr*, Beshalach, 64a. See also, *Likutei Torah*, Emor. The Rebbe adds, although not quoting Chazal, that this means every moment of every day. *Sefer haSichos*, 5751, Shemos.

comes from Above, we need the clarity that begins to percolate in our consciousness through 'remembering' and 'understanding' such truths.

We begin to facilitate redemption when we 'remember' and become a channel for a flow of a deeper understanding of ultimate reality. This flow of understanding is described as the *Mei Binah*, the waters of *Binah* / understanding. (The numerical value of Mei - Mem (40) Yud (10) = 50. These are the 50 gates of Binah: *Tola'as Yaakov*, p. 102, corresponding to the 50 times the Torah mentions Yetzias Mitzrayim.) מצרים / Egypt is comprised of two words, מצר ים / 'constriction of water'. Egypt is a place where the Mei Binah, the waters of understanding and expansiveness, are restricted. In fact, in the paradigm of Mitzrayim, everything is stuck, and thus there is no flow at all. In Egypt, even the literal natural water was turned, for a period, into blood and death, which represents the great depth of the exile in Egypt. As we leave our inner Mitzrayim, there is a breaking open of the waters, like the splitting of the waters of the sea, and we achieve clarity and perfect faith. As the Torah declares, Klal Yisrael's state of mind at that moment was such that "they believed in Hashem and in Moshe his servant." They had steadfast faith in the Creator and Source of all Life, in Moshe, and by extension (see *Tanya*, 42) they had faith in themselves.

THE WORLD OF FORGETFULNESS

There are 50 'gates' or levels of understanding, and the fiftieth gate is Binah itself; absolute clarity and thus absolute openness and freedom.* As stated previously, the Torah mentions the idea of remembering Yetzias Mitzrayim exactly fifty times, as fifty represents the level of total freedom. In fact, when one has attained freedom on this fiftieth level, it is absolute; there is no possibility for its opposite.

Forgetfulness is connected to a type of brokenness in our perception of time. The world of *Pirud* / separation is where the past is considered separate from the present, and is thus forgotten. In the place of *Echad* / Oneness, the world of *Yichud* / unity, there is no forgetfulness, as the past is present in every moment. כל / *Col* / everything, is numerically 50. *Col* is the place of total recall, as in the world of all, the eternal now in which 'everything' is present.

'Exile' means separation, whether it is a geographical exile, separated from one's land, or an inner exile, in which one is alienated from their essential self. It is one thing to be in a literal and existential exile and, yet, still remember, and thus long for, home and authenticity. When one holds strong to the memory of where they came from or who they really are, they are still connected. Sadly, over time, if and when deeper levels of exile set in, one begins to no longer even recall that there is another place to go and a deeper self to reveal. Forgetfulness is a deeper, more traumatic state of stuckness and exile in which one no longer even remembers that their life could be bet-

---

* חמשים שערי בינה נבראו בעולם, וכולן ניתנו למשה, חסר אחד / "Fifty gates of understanding were created in the world, and all of them were given to Moshe, except for *Echad* / one": *Rosh Hashanah*, 21b. The 50th level is אחד / *Echad*, Oneness, the place beyond duality, and thus it is beyond an opposite and beyond forgetfulness.

ter. The situation is so dark that one mistakes the darkness for light, goodness and life.

Egypt was one such place, where Klal Yisrael was steeped in exile to the point of almost total forgetfulness of its past and destiny. Pharaoh, the king and master of Egypt, was the personification of the world of forgetfulness. The beginning of the descent of Klal Yisrael into slavery starts with ויקם מלך־ חדש על־מצרים אשר לא־ידע את־יוסף / "A new king arose over Egypt who did not know Yoseph (or recognize that he was the savior of Egypt)" (*Shemos*, 1:8). What does it mean "who did not know?" It means דהוה דמי כמאן דלא ידע ליה כלל / "He comported ed himself as though he did not know him at all" (*Sotah*, 11a). Pharaoh manages to *pretend* to forget what Yoseph had done for the Egyptians and for the king himself, and begins to enslave Yoseph's family.

Pharaoh is the paragon of forgetfulness. Even the name *Pharaoh* is connected to forgetfulness, as it is connected with the Hebrew word *Oreph* / neck, the back of the head. The back of the head is the place where things are forgotten,* while the front is the place of memory.

---

* The back side is connected to forgetfulness: See *Tanya*, Kuntres Acharon, 6. The Ten *Makos* / plagues undo this existential forgetfulness. For example, the Baal Shem Tov teaches that the first plague is דם / *Dam* / blood (numerically 44), which is the sacred Name *Mah* / 45 (also אדם), but missing an Aleph; the missing and 'forgotten' Aleph, Aleph being 'the One'. Through the water turning to blood, the Oneness of Hashem is remembered. The second plague is צפרדע / *Tzfardea* / frogs. In Hebrew the word can be divided into צפר / *Tzafar* / a revealing of דע / *De'ah* / awareness, which is the opposite of forgetfulness: *Toldos Yaakov Yoseph*, Beshalach, p. 53. צפרדע is also connected to the knowing that day is coming, as the frogs become quiet as the day is approaching.

The opposite of forgetting is *Binah* / understanding. כל / *Col* / everything, is a term signifying the Fiftieth Gate of perfect Binah, the world of ever-present clarity, openness and transparency, and thus total freedom of mind. As it is a place of perfect transparency, it is thus a world of freedom from physical mortality, which is a symptom of disunity and separation. Parenthetically, the Fiftieth Gate is also free of any *Yetzer haRa* / negative inclination: on the fiftieth day after leaving Egypt we received the Torah and were temporarily freed from death and from our *Yetzer haRa*.

RELATIVE VS. ABSOLUTE FREEDOM

In addition to the Fiftieth Gate of Understanding, the number 50 reflects 'the fiftieth year', what the Torah calls the *Yovel*, the Jubilee year. During the Yovel, slaves went free, debts were cancelled, and land returned to its original owner. In other words, in the fiftieth year, all people and things clearly 'remembered' and understood their own inner truth, their original source, and were thereby redeemed, returning to their origin.

This is brought down in the name of Rebbe Shalom, the Rebbe of the Maharil, *Sifrei Maharil*, Minhagim, Likutim, 635. The fact that *Tzfardea* is connected with the word *De'ah* is already found in the Medrash: *Pesikta Zutrasa*, Shemos, 7:29. See also *Pirushei haTorah l'Baalei Tosefos*, Shemos, 7:29.

Within the Name Hashem (the Yud-Hei-Vav-Hei), there are two 'active' or 'masculine', assertive letters: the Yud, a point, and the Vav, a line. There are also two 'passive' or 'feminine', receptive letters: the two Hei's.

Hei is the sound similar to an *'H'*. It can be used as a soft consonant, and can also be a 'silent letter', often at the end of a word. Sometimes the silent Hei is there to indicate a vowel, and sometimes it is just for syllabic or etymological emphasis. When Hei is sounded as a consonant, it mimics a person sighing from tiredness or relaxation, releasing a deep exhale: *Hhhh...* (*Amud haAvodah*, R. Baruch of Kasuv, Kuntreisim l'Chochmas Emes, p. 328). In any case, Hei represents rest and release.

Every seventh year in the Land of Israel is a *Shemitah /* Sabbatical year. We are instructed and empowered to work and toil the land for six years, but during the seventh year we need to release the land from production so it can rest and 'reset'. When the land is free from being planted and worked, the earth can replenish itself (Rambam, *Moreh Nevuchim*, 3:27). "Six years you shall sow your field, and six years you shall prune your vineyard and gather in its fruit. But the seventh year shall be a Shabbos of rest to the land" (*Vayikra*, 25:2-4). The six days, and more broadly the six years of work and toil, are connected with the active letters within the name of Hashem (and more specifically to the letter Vav, which equals six), whereas the seventh day and the seventh year are connected with the lower Hei within Hashem's Name.

The lower Hei of Hashem's Name symbolizes the resting of the earth that manifests with each Shemitah year. The earth corresponds to the *Sefirah* of *Malchus* / the Attribute of Sovereignty which is also the lower Hei. Within ourselves, the 'resting of the earth' means resting in the world of action — it is a state of non-doing.

Shemitah is a 'lower freedom', a freedom to stop working and recognize that the earth belongs to Hashem (*Sanhedrin*, 39a. *Sefer haChinuch*, Mitzvah, 84), and to focus more on spiritual work. In terms of "remembering," we remember that the earth and all it represents belongs to Hashem.

However, there is an even greater cycle: seven times seven years; after seven cycles of seven years there is a fiftieth year, the year of *Yovel*. Yovel is a manifestation of the higher Hei of Hashem's Name (the complete freedom of Yovel corresponds to the upper Hei in the Name of Hashem: *Zohar* 3:108a). Hei numerically equals 5. However, the upper Hei is called the 'full Hei' — the full or expanded 5, which is 50. In the fiftieth year, not only does the land (earth, Malchus, lower Hei) rest, but also "slaves go free." In ancient times, when most of the Jewish People lived in the Land of Israel, each in their designated tribal territories, "slaves" and those who needed to commit themselves to indentured service, were set free. This represents a higher form of "rest" — a rest not just of earth and actions, but of thought, consciousness, and identity.

As the upper Hei of Hashem's Name is *Binah* / understanding, this higher form of rest includes releasing our mind from all distracting thoughts and limited understanding. It is a state of existential rest, redemption and freedom from all forms of slavery, especially the worst form of slavery: the inner slavery of dependency, despondency, addiction, and constricted consciousness.

When in the Shemitah year the land is allowed to rest, the lower Hei of the Divine Name experiences a temporary degree of redemption. After the land rests from being planted and worked, it returns to its 'labors' and burdens.

In our own lives, this lower, relative type of freedom manifests as freedom from reactive behavior. If someone insults you, and you choose not to react but remain silent, you are refraining from 'planting new seeds' of conflict. Although you did not act in retribution, your mind and heart might still be upset. This is only a 'one-dimensional' form of freedom; it is a 'rest' from action alone. You have merely silenced your reaction, but you have not yet transformed your reactivity at its root — at the level of will and desire. Your mind and your heart may still 'want' to react and you have only temporarily controlled your outward actions, your level of Malchus. You did not yet redeem yourself on the level of Binah, of consciousness.

Yovel, however, brings transformational freedom for the entire human being — in 'thought' or consciousness, as well as in action. Binah contains seven permutations of each emotional attribute. This 'multi-dimensionality' has a balancing effect, freeing one from unconscious reactivity. In a state of clear understanding, our emotions are contained and balanced by a higher perspective sometimes called *Mochin* / intellect or mind. For example, if you are experiencing the expansive emotion of *Chesed* / loving-kindness and generosity from a higher perspective, you can be simultaneously in touch with the contractive emotion of *Gevurah* / strength and withholding. You are 'thinking out of the box' of your emotions, and are therefore free to respond with awareness, rather than merely reacting.

This is the deeper freedom that is spiritually available through the 50 times the Torah speaks of Yetzias Mitzrayim. It is a remembering of not only what we as a collective should or should not be doing, but more deeply remembering *who we are* as a people. To 'remember' in this sense is to free our minds and live freely and consciously.

When we as a people remember who we are, including our collective past, purpose, and destiny, we also remember ourselves individually, who we truly are, and can thus begin to live authentically. We are free from the chokehold of Pharaoh, the force of forgetfulness. Mitzrayim, and everything it represents, falls away.

On the night of Pesach, on the night of our collective and individual release from bondage, the more we 'remember' Yetzias Mitzrayim, the more we internalize the upper Hei of complete freedom of consciousness and Binah. On this cosmic night when HaKadosh Baruch Hu takes us out from all *Meitzarim* / constrictions and limitations, the more we recite the Haggadah and re-live the meta-narrative of the Going Out of Egypt, the more we become saturated with the *Koach* / power, and *Shefa* / flow, of Yetzias Mitzrayim.

On this night we are not to merely recall history, what happened in the past, but to experience memory, which is like a living organism, allowing the effects of the past to be felt in the present. This is the distinction between frozen history and living memory. Seder night is a night to remember.

HAGGADAH: THE BIRTHING OF SELF

In Egypt we were like fetuses within our mother's womb, without the freedom to be individuals. We were 'confined' to being an extension of someone else's agenda, owned by the state and simply defined as "slaves to Pharaoh in Egypt." We were a 'nameless' people — with no self-understanding. As a result, we had no voice. Our 'going out of Egypt' was our birth. Binah is sometimes called *Eim haBanim Semeichah* / 'the Mother that gives birth to joy' (*Tehilim*, 113:9), referring to the joy of birth and redemption. By attaining Binah and self-understanding, we can joyfully leave our inner exiles and experience life as if for the first time.

Throughout the Seder and the recitation of the Haggadah, we experience a reanimation of the Exodus, and thus the birth of selfhood. The story of this night is our birth as a people, and the birth of ourselves as distinct, authentic and conscious individual selves.

Haggadah means 'telling'. Through telling the story of Yetzias Mitzrayim, we remember that we too are going out of Egypt. Yet, the deeper meaning of the word Haggadah is connected to the word *Aggadah*, 'drawing out': "Words of *Aggadah* draw out."* By reciting *The Haggadah* with intention, passion and fervor, we relive the Exodus and draw down the waters of higher intelligence and expansive awareness from the inner world of Binah and beyond.

Therefore, *l'Sapeir* / to tell the story is essential on Pesach Night; not simply to 'remember' and 'reveal,' but to actively immerse in a living memory and to relish and revel in it. Every day and night of the year we need to remember Yetzias Mitzrayim by mentioning that Hashem took us out of Egypt in our daily prayers and recitations. While this is a Mitzvah to do every day, on Pesach Night the Mitzvah is more than simply stating the fact; it is to *tell* the tale (*Ma'aseh Nisim*, Pesichah. *Shevach Pesach*, Maggid, 1. *Siddur Maharid*, Inyan Mitzvah. *Malbim*, Bo, 13:8).

On Pesach night we are all storytellers. To be a storyteller, one needs to be proficient in crafting language and conveying nuanced expressions through subtle shifts in

---

* וכל משען מים אלו בעלי אגדה שמושכין לבו של אדם כמים באגדה / "And every support of water'; these are the masters of Aggadah, who draw people's hearts like water by means of Aggadah": *Chagigah*, 14a. The Mordechai writes that indeed, *The Haggadah* should be called *The Aggadah*, beginning with an Aleph, not a Hei: Mordechai, *Pesachim*, 117a.

tonality. This requires one to have conscious technique and patience to "draw out" the process of revelation. The deeper we go into our unique selves and into our collective narrative, and the more we draw out the "waters" of understanding, the more the story of Yetzias Mitzrayim has a psychosomatic effect on us. The more we are able to invoke and inhabit this living memory in the present moment, the more exile fades and redemption becomes real to us.

In this way, telling the story of the Exodus from Egypt, and then turning it inward and speaking about our own inner exiles, challenges, and hardships — and then giving thanks for all the miracles Hashem has shown us — all of this helps us rediscover our true collective and individual identities. We reclaim ourselves, becoming essentially free and spiritually liberated beings.

This process of redemption-through-storytelling is part of the very mechanism which empowered us to leave Egypt many centuries ago, as well as presently on this powerful night. In order to hone our storytelling abilities, let us review the story of Yetzias Mitzrayim, as transmitted to us in the Torah, and deepen our understanding of all the above discussions.

FROM A PROUD, 'NAMED' PEOPLE TO A NAMELESS PEOPLE

The proper title of the *Book of Exodus* is *Shemos* / Names, suggesting that it is a book primarily about names. Indeed, *The Book of Shemos* begins when the members of the household of Yaakov are still free people, proudly listing the names of each family who came down to Egypt: ואלה שמות בני / ישראל הבאים מצרימה... / ראובן שמעון לוי / "These are the Names of the children of Israel who came to Egypt...Reuvein, Shimon, Levi..." naming all the twelve tribes. They enter Egypt as a proud people, with distinct names and identities. However, as they descend deeper into the Egyptian exile, the Torah begins to refer to the children of Yaakov without names, but rather with pronouns. Immediately after naming them, the Torah continues, "*They* multiplied; *they* increased; the land was full of *them*..." (*Shemos*, 1:7). It does not say, 'And Reuvein became a huge tribe, and Shimon multiplied,' rather "...*they* multiplied."

ובני ישראל פרו וישרצו וירבו ויעצמו במאד מאד ותמלא הארץ אתם / "But the children of Yisrael / Israel were fertile and prolific; they multiplied and increased very greatly, so that the land was filled with them." The root of the phrase וישרצו, translated as 'prolific,' is שרץ / swarmed, like insects. The analogy of insects suggests a proliferation, multiplying and giving birth as animals do, which is typically in abundance and as many as six offspring per birth.*

The Seforno (the 16th Century Italian commentator) gives us an alternative meaning of "swarmed": נטו לדרכי שרצים / "(The people) veered to the ways of *Sheratzim* / creeping insects."

---

* In fact, according to the deeper teachings of the Torah [*Galei Raza*, see *Yalkut Reuveini* on the Pasuk] the souls of the Jews in Egypt were transmigrated souls from the sheep of Lavan, who in turn were the souls of the 974 generations before Creation: *Chagigah*, 13b. They are also the souls whom Yaakov brought to Egypt.

While the Torah is certainly hinting at their multiplying like insects, the term וישרצו can also be understood to mean that the people first reduced themselves, acting and feeling like lowly insects, and then they were reduced by their oppressors to being nameless, expendable creatures, disgusting creepy crawly things that swarmed the terrain. They first diminished themselves from being a proud, distinct, named people, to being a group that acted like roaches and pests. This self-degradation opened them up to being further diminished by their overlords as unworthy creatures; insects upon which to trample.

People may name their cats or dogs, but no one names the roaches that swarm their basement. To be viewed as a roach is to be reduced to nothing, with not even the respect given to a dog.

The children of Israel begin as proud people, with distinct, holy names and a strong sense of identity. Their names remind them of their past, of the patriarchs of each tribe, empowering them in their present mission, and signifying their glorious future (*Medrash Rabbah*, Shemos, 1:3-5). First they descend by their own commission, and then they are compelled by external forces into a mental and spiritual condition of slavery, a static state of stuckness, *Tumah* / impurity. Finally, they reach the lowest point of losing their names and sense of identity, struggling to live as debased, crushed, lowly forms of existence.

At this point there is a total eclipse of their humanity and selfhood. Nameless people with no access to authentic or meaningful expression. Exiled in a place of deep paralysis and silence, they say nothing.

Yet, as 'insects,' they proliferated, arousing Pharaoh to devise a plan to exterminate every newborn boy. ויאמר מלך מצרים / "The למילדת העברית אשר שם האחת שפרה ושם השנית פועה king of Egypt spoke to the Hebrew midwives, one of whom was named Shifrah and the other Puah" (*Shemos*, 1:15) and informed them of his diabolical decree. Here it seems that the two Hebrew midwives were clearly named, one Shifrah the other Puah. Chazal, however, reveal that these were not their actual names, rather descriptions of their work: שפרה שמשפרת את הולד.... פועה שהיתה פועה ומוציאה את הולד / "(Why is she called) 'Shifrah'? Because she would prepare (*Shaferes*) the newborn (for birth). And (why) 'Puah'? Because she would make a comforting, cooing sound (*Pu-ah*) as she would remove the child" (*Sotah*, 11b). In fact, Chazal go on to reveal that they were actually either Yocheved and Miriam or Yocheved and Elisheva (the wife of Aharon). Just at the very moment the Torah is seeming to give us the names of the two Jewish midwives, Chazal reveal to us that these were not their real names.

In another view, these *are* their proper names, but they were not Jewish women, rather Egyptians, as the Abarbanel writes: מילדת העברית means they were "midwives *to* the Hebrews," not "Hebrew midwives." This further supports the idea that Klal Yisrael are not named in Egypt; Shifrah and Puah, in this view, are not names of Jewish women, nor are they even pseudonyms based on their jobs.*

---

* ולא היו עבריות כי איך יבטח לבו בנשים העבריות שימיתו ולדיהן אבל היו מצריות מילדות את העבריות: Abarbanel, *Shemos*, 1:1.

How do Chazal know that these are not literal names? The Torah says clearly, "The name of one was Shifrah and the name of the other was Puah." Perhaps it is because in the very next episode, which talks about the birth of Moshe, the most important figure in the Torah, the Torah refers to his parents namelessly, and Moshe himself is not given a clear name. Unlike all the other very important characters of the Torah — Yitzchak, Yaakov and the Shevatim, for example, who are all named right at birth — Moshe is not given a name at birth.

When the Torah begins the story of the birth of Moshe, it says (*Shemos* 2:1), "A man from the house of Levi married a daughter from Levi." No names are given; he is just "a man from the house of Levi," who marries a likewise nameless woman. When Moshe is born, the Torah only says, "The woman conceived and bore a son, and when she saw how beautiful he was, she hid him for three months." A nameless couple has a nameless child (Chazal, in *Sotah*, 12a, tell us that his name was Tov or Tuvia, but he is not named clearly in the Torah itself. See also, *Megilah*, 13a). Only later is he named by his adoptive (albeit converted, *ibid*, 12b) step mother, Pharaoh's daughter.

Up until this point in the Torah, every time it speaks of the birth of a child, it tells us right away what the mother or father names the child. Now, in stark contrast, the greatest prophet and leader of Klal Yisrael is born in anonymity.

This is a deeper reason that Moshe, at the Burning Bush, asks Hashem, "What is Your Name?" Moshe says, "When I come to Bnei Yisrael and say to them, 'The G-d of your fathers has sent me to you,' and they ask me, 'What is His Name,' what shall I say to them?" (*Shemos*, 3:13) Enslavement is the reduction of named individuals into statistics, but redemption begins with a consciousness of the power of one's name. Moshe needs a "name" for Hashem in order to be able to transmit the vision of freedom to the, as yet, nameless people who seemingly do not even have names for their children, much less their Creator.

TO NAME / DEFINE / FRAME / CONTEXTUALIZE IS A BASIC HUMAN FUNCTION

Naming things is essential to the basic human project of survival and determining one's place in the world. One of the first acts Adam performs in the Garden is to name and define the animals: "And (Hashem) brought them (the animals) to the man to see what he would call them, and whatever the man called each living creature, that would be its name" (*Bereishis*, 2:19).

Naming things makes distinctions and contextualizes our reality. By naming the world around us, like Adam, we are able to navigate relationships, describe our experiences, and define our space. Without the ability to name and be named, one is trapped, perceptually cut-off from the world, from human reality and from all communication.

Personal interactions are based on having a personal name. Only free people have names, and having a name allows one to give names to others. A slave is a nameless statistic with no independent personal identity or existence, no power to speak, communicate, contextualize or define. The exile of Klal Yisrael was so deep that they could not even name themselves.

FROM NAMELESS TO NAMED

The transition from namelessness to possessing a name, representing the process of redemption, occurs with the emergence of the adult Moshe. He now appears as a named person, although his name Moshe was not given by his parents. Over time, Moshe gradually identifies with his people and begins to feel concerned about their plight.

Once Klal Yisrael has a leader who is one of them, and who sees them as individuals — as real people with honor and pride, not just as statistics or nameless slaves — the process of their redemption can begin. For this reason, in the *Book of Shemos* (6:14), while describing the hardships of slavery, the Torah begins reviewing the names of the households of the people of Israel. It is thus revealed that they had always kept their own names, at least among themselves: "The following are the heads of their respective clans. The sons of Reuvein, Israel's first-born: Enoch and Pallu, Hezron and Carmi; those are the families of Reuvein..." These *P'sukim* / verses seem totally out of context. In the middle of speaking about how Moshe and Aharon are going to Pharaoh, and while the plagues have already begun, the Torah suddenly begins to name the tribes, their children, and lineages.

For a redemption to occur, there needs to be 'someone' who can be redeemed. A person or people who feel like *Sheratzim* / creepy crawly things, who are broken and reduced to the point of not having a sense of self or *Tzuras Adam* / human form, cannot be redeemed. Klal Yisrael could not, at first, be lifted out of their enslavement, as there was 'no one' to uplift. And such, their process of redemption from this exile began with Moshe seeing them as real people. After experiencing that small but significant recognition, they were able to remember their names and tribal identities, as the Torah's narrative reveals. Once they had reclaimed their names, they could gradually regain their voice.

EXILE OF SPEECH

Naming is a function of speech; the ability to inwardly define and then outwardly express an idea. In the depths of slavery, Klal Yisrael lost its capacity to name and be named because, as the Zohar teaches, in Egypt *Dibbur* / speech itself was in *Galus* / exile (Zohar, 2:25b). The exile of speech and the inability to voice, even to oneself, one's needs and desires is the deepest exile possible. To be human is to be a *Medaber* / a 'speaking being' (Rashi, Bereishis, 2:7). When we cannot express ourselves inwardly, never mind articulate to others what we are thinking or feeling, we are exiled from our own humanity. To take away someone's ability to speak robs them not only of their own humanity but of their capacity for meaningful relationships with other humans.

A person who is in a state of personal exile speaks in a mode of broadcasting, like speaking about sports, the weather or any other trivial matter. They are just filling the void with empty noise. This is not real speech, nor an expression of human consciousness. It is like being a *Sheretz* / a swarming creature, like a cricket producing sound. In an even deeper level of exile, one loses their voice altogether. In Egypt, Klal Yisrael lost their name as well as their voice and self-expression.

Speech implies choice, for through language we define our reality*. We contextualize and navigate life linguistically. A slave does not have the choice to articulate or reveal who they really are, for their reality is imposed upon them. Nor can a slave listen to another; their ability to hear the possibility that their circumstances may change is completely absent. Even Moshe, who was essentially above slavery, born into the free Sheivet of Levi and raised as an Egyptian prince, could not easily speak. At the Burning Bush, Moshe says of himself, כי כבד־פה וכבד לשון אנכי / "I am not a man of words, and I have a hard (כבד / heavy) mouth" (*Shemos*, 4:10), and continues self-consciously, "the people will not listen to my voice" (*Shemos*, 4:1). These two statements are intricately related: Moshe 'did not have the choice' to speak because the people were not yet open to listen. At the same time, the people were unable to listen because there was no one to speak for them. There was no opening, no self-perception, no speech, and no conscious choice making.

---

* Dibbur is connected with De'ah / awareness: Rashi, *Bereishis*, 2:7. And without De'ah or Da'as there is no discernment and choice. *Yerushalmi*, *Berachos*, 5:2

A slave has no story to tell. As the devastation of their humanity robs them of their inner life, their dreams, aspirations, desires and longings, a slave has nothing to say, nothing meaningful to talk about or share. A slave is subjugated not only physically, but emotionally, intellectually and spiritually.

When, G-d forbid, a human being is reduced to a statistic, such as a prisoner under a dark regime, they are forced to think and dream of nothing but surviving the demands of the moment. They end up devoid of an inner life. They stop speaking because there is nothing inside to describe. Even if they can speak physically, there is no insightfulness, no warmth, no appreciation of life present in their words. And this is what occurred, on some level, to Klal Yisrael in Egypt; their voice was silenced until they lost their inner life. Physically, at least some of them could speak, but their words were shallow, superficial words and *Lashon haRa* / negative speech.

Reflecting on the predicament of Klal Yisrael, Moshe says, שהייתי תמה עליו, מה חטאו ישראל מכל שבעים אומות להיות נרדים בעבודת פרך, אבל רואה אני שהם ראויים לכך / "The matter I was wondering about, why Klal Yisrael are considered more sinful than all the seventy nations to be subjugated with back-breaking labor, has become known to me. Indeed, I see that they deserve it (because they speak *Lashon haRa*) (Rashi, 2:14, from *Medrash Rabbah*, Shemos, 1:30).

Klal Yisrael was silent until quite late in the exile, according to the Torah's account. We do not hear in the narrative that they complained or demanded to be treated better, nor that they rebelled or fought. Perhaps they were too overwhelmed to feel anything, or perhaps they had become so accustomed to their harsh subservience that they no longer noticed it or felt that it was foreign to who they truly were. They embraced their identity as slaves. Usually, when a community is oppressed, at least a couple courageous individuals arise to challenge the status quo and decry their internalized oppression. Before Moshe, there was no one who stood up.

Not only did they not speak about the possibility of becoming free, not only did they cease to recall their glorious past, they stopped speaking altogether; their Dibbur was completely in exile.

Their descent into silence and loss of choice was gradual, yet, at the end, there was a deeply devastating level of trauma, a total eclipse of their voices and self-recognition. They did not even dream or yearn for their freedom. In fact, they were so completely stuck and paralyzed that not even a cry or groan of conscious pain or sadness could escape their lips.

INNER PRACTICE:

When we are slaves to our emotions and reactions,
we have no independence from the stimuli or influences
in our lives. Look inward and ask yourself:
'Where in my life do I lack an independent identity?
Where do I react automatically to sensations, events, or other
people?'

Ask yourself: 'Where in my life have I silenced myself?
Where in myself do I accept my sense of exile?
Where am I unable to even conceive of being free?'

THE BEGINNINGS OF REDEMPTION

"Now it came to pass in those many days that the king of Egypt died, and the children of Israel sighed from the labor, and they cried out, and their cry ascended to Hashem from the labor" (*Shemos*, 2:23). The Chizkuni writes that when the King of Egypt finally died, the Jewish people realized that they might get an opportunity to rest briefly from their labors. Only when this thought crossed their minds did they become aware of their exhaustion and trauma, and when it did not happen and the slavery continued, a 'sigh', a groan finally emitted from their throats.[*]

---

[*] כל זמן שאותו מלך חי היו מצפין שמא כשימות זה יתבטלו גזרותיו ...וכשמת זה לא נתבטלו גזרותיו אמרו מעתה אין לדבר סוף לפיכך ויאנחו / "As long as the old king had been alive, they had hoped that with his death the harsh decrees against them would 'die' also. When they found out that they had hoped in vain, they groaned."

Perhaps when the king died, all the Egyptians were busy with the funeral and it was the first day, in many years, that there was a day off, as surely the Egyptian slave taskmasters did not show up to work (*Imrei Shefer*, Vanitzak). Or, perhaps they were even intentionally given a day off (*HaAmek Davar*, Shemos, 2:23). In any case, now that they had a moment of rest and a break from incessant labor, they now realized that there could be another way. They had the faintest glimmer of an insight that slavery was not their 'ontological' and permanent condition. As they rested, a buried memory arose: there was something called freedom, they were human beings and slavery had been imposed upon them from the outside — and so they sighed and cried out in grief.

People who are really stuck, physically, mentally, or emotionally can be so enmeshed in their condition that they stop remembering that there is even a possibility for an alternative. Even grief can be suppressed from awareness. Yet, once there is even an externally imposed pause in the oppressive conditions, the person can abruptly wake up and shake out of their stupor and listlessness.

With just a glimmer of understanding of where they were, and perhaps who they truly were — with just a hint of the possibility of freedom — a convulsive wave of grief arose. In its wake, a yearning to be free became palpable and real. The Torah says, "and they groaned...and Hashem heard their groan..." (*Shemos*, 2:23-24). The Ohr haChayim on this Pasuk notes that the "groan" was not an utterance of *Tefilah* / prayer, nor a cry to Hashem for help, rather it was a visceral, elemental cry of pain.* Similarly, when Hashem tells Moshe at the Burning Bush, "I have seen their plight," ואת־צעקתם שמעתי מפני נגשיו / "and I have heard their cries because of their taskmasters" (*Shemos*, 3:7), the Pasuk is saying clearly that their cries were not a form of prayer, rather a reaction to their being beaten; a visceral, instinctual scream from the pain of being abused. This is a very primal kind of cry, a cry coming 'from' pain, not a cry 'to' Hashem. It was simply a shout of "Ouch!" Yet because they were softened and opened enough for their voices to vibrate in some way, Hashem heard and received their groans as prayer. Hashem welcomed their groaning as a prayer, interpreted it as a reaching out, a yearning 'to', and a longing 'for'.

There is a distinction between *Kol* / sound and *Dibbur* / speech. Sure, every Dibbur is rooted in Kol, yet, Dibbur is an articulated, contextualized and defined Kol. In Egypt they cried out on the level of Kol, an inarticulate sound emitted in response to the hurt they were experiencing. Nonetheless, their Kol was heard on High as a Dibbur, a communicative expression directed toward Hashem, a prayer for help.

As they softened and opened, so too, in a manner of speaking, did Hashem 'soften and open', responsively opening the way for their Redemption. Hashem listened and 'felt compassion', so-to-speak, because they cried. There was an

---

* Although, later on the Torah does say, ונצעק אל ה' / "we cried to Hashem," *Devarim*, 26:7, this refers to the groans of the Tzadikim, who in fact did pray. ותפלת קצתם שהתפללו אז מצדיקי הדור. *Seforno*, Shemos, 2:24.

unshackling of rigidity and stuckness *Keviyachol* / as it were, in Hashem's Presence as well as in the people's perception.

צלך ה' / "Hashem is your *Tzel* / shadow" (*Tehilim*, 121:5). The simple meaning of this Pasuk is that Hashem protects us, but a deeper reading reveals that Hashem's Presence is literally like our shadow; moving and responding according to our actions, thoughts and words, much like a shadow reflects our movements (*Keser Shem Tov*, Hosafos, 60. *Shaloh*, Sha'ar haGadol, 22a). Whereas Hashem, Infinite Timeless Beingness, does not move or change (כי אני ה' לא שניתי: *Malachi*, 3:6), the emanation of Hashem's Divine Presence manifests in relation to us and our movements and changes.

When we are open and there is some positive movement on our part, even a simple cry can elicit a corresponding openness and movement 'Above'. There is a 'shadowing' or mirroring of our activity in the 'activity' of the Divine Presence. When we, 'below' in this world, cried out in Egypt, when we became open and softened enough to recognize where and who we really were, there was a corresponding opening and softening Above, initiating a Divine 'capacity' for listening: "And Hashem heard..."

In Egypt, the process of redemption, a movement away from slavery into freedom, did not begin until there was some percolation of movement, of vibration, a stirring of aliveness and human consciousness within Klal Yisrael. So long as we were stuck in the posture of slavery, without even a recognition of our own pain or a desire to cry out, there was a mirrored response Above of mute stuckness, as if the One Above did not recognize or desire to redeem us.

Today, more than ever, we too need a break in the monotony of day in day out work, a time to stop, to let go of doing and just 'be'. This is why Pesach, *Zeman Cheiruseinu* / the season of our release into freedom, is referred to in the Torah as *Shabbos*. To be free, we need Shabbos, a day of returning to ourselves, softening and expanding our consciousness. We also need a day of national mourning such as Tishah b'Av, when we can pause and feel, and open to the pain and bitterness of exile. In Mitzrayim, Klal Yisrael needed a break from *Avodah Kasha* / hard labor so that they could expand even slightly from the consciousness-narrowing effect of their *Meitzarim* / dire straits and stresses of exile. When we take such a rest, we can begin to entertain the thought of freedom. This is why Tishah b'Av is also known as the birth of redemption (Yerushalmi, *Berachos*, 2:4. *Medrash Rabbah*, Eicha, 1: 51). When the darkness of exile is seen for what it is, its opposite, the light of redemption, is paradoxically apprehended as well. Then we can realize, even minimally, that we are not essentially slaves but rather Hashem's People. And from this realization, when we are able to cry out to Hashem for help, Hashem manifests His Presence as עוזר דלים ועונה לעמו ישראל / "Helper of the destitute, Who answers His People, Yisrael" (*Siddur*).

In Egypt, once HaKadosh Baruch Hu heard the cries of 'His People' and received them as prayer, this receptivity rippled back downward and their voice raised their vibration and further opened their consciousness, allowing them to sense a relationship with something greater than themselves, something beyond and outside their predicament of slavery. Eventually they were able to remember and reclaim their true names, to speak and to dream of freedom.

PHARAOH: THE PERSONIFICATION OF STUCKNESS

There are three partners, as it were, in the Exodus story: Hashem, Klal Yisrael, and the *Mitzrim* / Egyptians. Once they groaned, the protective shell around Klal Yisrael softened, and they became open to change. Pharaoh, the antagonist of the narrative, is a self-absorbed, stubborn ruler, and he himself is the ultimate archetype of a stuck person, even to the point of self-destruction. Naturally, in the wider context, his state of consciousness needs to be shifted as well in order for change to occur on behalf of all the characters in the story.

Regarding the first five plagues in Egypt, the Torah states that Pharaoh 'hardened his heart' and refused to let Klal Yisrael go. However, referring to the next series of plagues, Hashem tells Moshe, כי־אני הכבדתי את־לבו / "I have hardened his heart" (10:1). Hashem is telling Moshe that Pharaoh has shut down his heart and closed himself off emotionally to the plight of his slaves to the extent that now it is as if the Creator created him with a hardened, sealed heart in place of self-directed will.

A person may be born, for example, with the free choice to drink or not drink alcohol, but sadly, once a person becomes habituated to having a drink every few hours, the force of addiction becomes all the more difficult to let go. This is not only true for obvious addictions; any type of behavior repeated over time becomes 'second nature', and almost impossible to stop. It may seem to the person that although they have free choice in other areas of life, regarding this issue in life, it is 'beyond' their capacity of free choice to do or not do. Once a person becomes stuck in this way, it feels to them as if they were simply born an addict and this is the way the Creator created them. They thus have no free choice at all.

Indeed, feeling stuck, paralyzed and without choice or power is itself part of the 'punishment' or consequence of willfully closing one's own heart. As the Rambam writes, if a person closes his heart down completely, whether through committing grave sins or through many smaller acts repeated over time, and refuses to make *Teshuvah* / a return to spiritual sanity, part of the punishment is that the gates of Teshuvah are 'closed' before him (ואפשר שיחטא אדם חטא גדול או חטאים רבים עד שיתן הדין לפני דין האמת שיהא הפרעון מזה החוטא על חטאים אלו שעשה ברצונו ומדעתו שמונעין ממנו התשובה ואין מניחין לו רשות לשוב מרשעו: Rambam, *Hilchos Teshuvah*, 6:3).

As Hashem is our shadow, and our actions below are mirrored by actions Above, if we close ourselves to Teshuvah, *Chas v'Shalom* / Heaven forbid, Hashem closes Teshuvah to us. Now, it is true that the path of Teshuvah is always available, and even when the door of Teshuvah is seemingly closed, one can always bang down the door if one chooses.* However, as long as one were to deliberately obstruct oneself from any desire for Teshuvah or acts of Teshuvah, that blockade will stand, and it will certainly appear to him as if the doors of Teshuvah are impenetrably sealed; meaning, it will appear to him as if he had no further choice in the matter.

Essentially, Pharaoh did not think that Teshuvah or a change of heart was possible. He was utterly mired in a static hierarchy of lords and slaves, and that was the only way, he believed, that the world could and should function. Spiritually, he believed in a hierarchy in the pantheon of gods in the cosmos, and as a result that was his experience of the social and economic world. In fact, not only did he believe in an absolute structure of higher and lower castes within society, he believed that he was a 'god' himself. Thus he ruled his people as if from above them. Aloof and immune to criticism, Pharaoh's heart and mind was bolted shut, paralyzed within his psychotic self-deification, and cemented within a belief in his divine right to enslave any human being.

Pharaoh was so stuck in his rigid mode of thinking that it penetrated his entire body. He proclaimed that, as a 'god', he consumed food but never needed to relieve himself (*Medrash*

* "The doors of Teshuvah are forever open": *Psikta d'Rebbe Kahana*, Parsha 45:8. Even when it says the doors of Teshuvah are closed, they are not completely sealed and if one really tries the doors can be opened: Rav Chasdai Cresces, *Ohr Hashem*, Ma'amar 3, Klal 2:2. Meiri, *Chibur ha Teshuvah*, Meishiv Nefesh, Ma'amar 1:3. *Tanya,* Igeres haTeshuvah, 11.

Rabbah, Shemos, 9:8). On the one hand, this supposed feat represents a form of self-control and self-sufficiency. On the other hand, it represents an absence of all natural movement from intake to output; no openness, no flow. This is the epitome of systemic exile. Both the slave and the slave owner are tied to being enslaved; they are both stuck in their narrow perspectives and their dependency upon each other. Up until the point at which the slave groans or the enslaver falls, neither is flexible or inspired enough to change the pattern or make a different choice.

THEY HAVE BECOME SOFT - HARDEN THEM!

Once the previous Pharaoh dies, whether this is literal or metaphorical, and once Klal Yisrael cries out, HaKadosh Baruch Hu hears their cry and a new kind of leader arises for and from the people. As Hashem beckons him to leadership, Moshe complains that he has a "hard / heavy mouth" and cannot speak and express himself correctly. Yet, he is commanded to challenge and speak to Pharaoh, the most powerful earthly ruler in the world at that time, and to tell him to set the slaves free.

Moshe, with the help of his brother Aharon, then begins to overcome his own speech impediment and to convey Hashem's words and message to Pharaoh. When Moshe's declarations and incitements toward freedom begin to have an effect upon the inner mindset of the slaves, Pharaoh reacts by telling his task masters, תכבד העבדה / *Tichbad haAvodah /* (from the word

Kaveid / hard or heavy) "*Harden* upon them the work" (*Shemos*, 5:9). He also snaps, "Make them work 'harder', because they are נרפים / *Nirpim* / lazy" (5:17). The word נרפים / *Nirpim* comes from the word *Rapheh*, 'soft'.

In other words, Pharaoh senses that the slaves have 'softened', and that as they are increasingly listening to and internalizing Moshe's words, they are being stirred to the possibility of freedom. Pharaoh, who is himself still very stuck in and functioning from the place of a hardened heart, cannot tolerate this softening of the soul. In order to prevent any redemptive 'opening', Pharaoh shouts at his taskmasters to make it even 'harder' on them. In contrast to *Nirpim*, he uses the term *Tichbad* — 'Harden their hearts, which are getting too *soft*!"*

A similar linguistic contrast is employed in Pharaoh's decree to use 'straw' for the 'bricks'. After Moshe and Aharon come to Pharaoh and demand that he let Klal Yisrael go, Pharaoh becomes agitated and decrees to the slave task enforcers: לא

---

* Chazal tell us (*Shemos Rabbah* on the Pasuk) that in Egypt, Klal Yisrael had scrolls which they would read on Shabbos telling them that HaKadosh Baruch Hu would one day redeem them. Thus Pharaoh says, *Tichbad haAvodah*, let them no longer read these scrolls. What are these scrolls? The *Shalsheles haKabbalah* and the Malbim (*Hakdama to Iyov*) bring down that it was *Sefer Iyov* / The Book of Job (see *Bava Basra*, 15a, משה כתב ספרו ופרשת בלעם ואיוב), a book that demonstrates that, despite horrific present conditions, there is always hope and salvation will come.

תאספון לתת תבן לעם ללבן הלבנים / "You shall no longer provide the people with straw for making bricks" (*Shemos*, 5:7). From now on, the slaves themselves have to gather the straw to form the bricks, all without reducing their productivity.

Straw is relatively soft and flexible, while bricks are hard and fixed. Pharaoh is saying to his enforcers, 'Stop letting the slaves become malleable and susceptible to change! Through my new decree I am going to תכבד / harden them. And I am going to demonstrate this to them in a tangible way: take soft straw and mix it with a solution that hardens it into inflexible bricks. I want you to take the softness of their heart and make it as hard as a brick.'

Softness and hardness of the heart are primarily psychological qualities; openness versus stuckness, the ability to speak and emote versus paralyzing self-censorship. Straw and bricks are those same qualities manifest in physical objects. Pharoah is telling them, 'This is how reality is; your hardening will not be a mere subjective psychological quality, it will be as objective as the bricks you will be making.'

Despite all Pharaoh's stubbornness, once the people cried out, the redemption of speech and thus their eventual redemption from enslavement was already inevitable. The snare had been broken, the rigidity had been softened, and Klal Yisrael had begun to listen to Moshe's exhortations about their imminent redemption, and they began to regain their own voice.

The redemption of the nameless, voiceless, stuck slaves began the very moment they cried out. The moment Hashem
heard their prayers was the moment they began to regain their
real voice and to articulate what they truly needed.

MOUTH THAT SPEAKS VS. NEGATIVE MOUTH

On Pesach we reenact and 'relive' the Exodus and the redemption of speech. The word פסח / *Pesach* can be split into
two words פה סח / *Peh Sach*, a mouth that speaks.* This stands
in stark contrast to the word *Pharaoh*. פרעה / Pharaoh can also
be broken into two words: פה רע / *Peh Ra*, meaning 'negative
mouth' (Arizal, *Sefer haLikutim*, Shemos 2). Pharaoh embodies and
symbolizes the force of negative speech, a reactive, rigid form
of expression that is meant to keep others stuck, hardened, deaf
and mute. On the holy day of 'Peh-Sach', the Torah wants us to
demonstrate our freedom by opening our mouths and speaking, raising our voices in retelling our story, the story of the
Exodus. Reciting the Haggadah allows us to accept and own
our history, our enslavement, as well as our future, redemption,
in the present moment.

---

* Although *Sach* / 'speaks' is with a Shin שׂ, not a Samach as in ס (and *Pesach* is spelled פ ס), yet, in the language of the Gemara, Chazal refer to
pleasant speech as סיחה נאה, with a Samach: *Bava Basra*, 78b. Also, the word
Peh / mouth within the word *Pesach* is missing the final Hei (פסח instead
of פה-ס). The missing Hei represents the five places of articulation in the
mouth, which need to be revealed through actual speech, and were thus
'missing' from Klal Yisrael's experience while enslaved.

In Egypt the slaves were forced to do עבודת פרך / *Avodas Perach* / harsh labor. The word פרך / *Perach* can be broken down into the two words, פה רך / *Peh Rach*, 'weak mouth' (*Sotah*, 11b). This refers to the exile's diminishment of Klal Yisrael's power and potential to authentically express themselves; even when the yearning for freedom was awakened, Klal Yisrael were not able to articulate their thoughts, dreams, and yearnings. Their mouths were in a weak condition. The *Ra* / negative, harsh, en-slaving mouth of Pharaoh imposed this condition of a weak-ened mouth.

Klal Yisrael, as slaves, were tasked to build the cities of פתם and רעמסס / Pisom and Ramses (*Shemos*, 1:11). The names of these two cities are also indicative of this enslavement: פתם can be split into two, as in פי תום / *Pi Tom*, closed or sealed mouth (or פי תהום / the mouth of the abyss: *Sotah*, 11a), and Ramses can be split into רע ממס / *Ra Moses* (דבלשון מצרי תיבה זו כצורתה משמעו ילד, 'Moses,' or *Mezes* / son in the Egyptian language is Moshe: *HaAmek Davar*, Shemos, 2:10. Note, *Likutei Torah*, and *Sefer HaLikutim*, Arizal, Shemos. את פיתום הוא הפה...כי אומר הב הב...והתהום בולע לעולם. ואת רעמסס שהוא הממס לעכל המאכל והוא ממס רע).

Ra Moses can mean 'negative Moshe', indicating a constric-tion of the person and idea of Moshe, who would eventually become the great 'speaker' on behalf of both Hashem and Klal Yisrael.

Parenthetically, it should be noted, there is the possibility that רע ממס is also actually the name of the Egyptian ruler at the time of Yetzias Mitzrayim, Ramesses or רעממס, and the city is called by his name (unless the Egyptian ruler at the time was Thut-Mose III). *Ra* is also the name of the 'sun deity' that the Egyptians worshiped. The ruler of Egypt claimed to be the son of a god, and thus was called *Ra Meses* / the Son of Ra.

Essentially, there are three levels of speech discussed here: פה רע / *Peh Ra* / negative mouth, פה רך / *Peh Rach* / weak mouth, and פה סח / *Peh Sach* / a mouth that speaks (*Zohar Chai*, Tazria). The Peh Ra caused a Peh Rach. The Lashon haRa of the *Mitzrim* / Egyptians constricted and weakened the capacity of the people to speak, until they descended into a place of utter voicelessness. In contrast to this state of estrangement, Geulah comes about through Peh Sach, recounting and reflecting on the miracles and wonders of our collective going out of Egypt.

However, despite the liberatory potentials of speaking and storytelling, sometimes the best form of 'speech' is transcending the story altogether and in self-control and inner master; remaining silent. The middle letters of מצרים / Egypt is יצר / inclination, generally referring to our negative inclination. The first letter is an open Mem, מ, representing an open mouth, whereas the final letter is a closed Mem, ם, representing a closed mouth, a mouth that is silent.* A spiritually, emotional-

---

* A closed Mem is similar to a closed womb: *Sha'ar haPesukim*, Tehillim, 18. See also *Sefer haBahir*, 84. Whereas an open Mem represents giving birth: *Sefer haBahir*, 85. An open Mem represents a state of 'giving' and expressing: *Pardes Rimonim*, Sha'ar haOsyos, Mem. Tzemach Tzedek, *Sefer haLikutim*, Mikvah, p. 1458.

ly and mentally healthy person is one that knows the balance of when to open their *Peh* / mouth (פ is numerically 80) and when to keep the it closed (two Mems also equal 80). The exile in Egypt represents a separation, a divide, a disunity between the two possibilities of the mouth. There, *Peh Ra*, negative speech, which would be best unspoken, was expressed and this led to a weak and powerless mouth. The redemption of Pesach brings about a healthy, balanced mouth, which knows when to speak and when to remain silent.

In Egypt, our mental, emotional, physical and spiritual state of פה רך / weakened mouth, eventually devolved into פה רע / a negative, lifeless, hopeless mouth. In this hopeless state, we submissively went along with Pharaoh's agenda, and occupied ourselves with building the city of פי תום / *Pi Tom* / Closed Mouth, which was a פי תהום / *Pi Tehom* / opening of the abyss, a gateway into a bottomless spiritual void known as the 49th gate of impurity. Surrounded by such self-reinforcing structures of רע / negativity and brokenness, we did not even have the will to return to ourselves and leave this gate, which stands before the eternal abyss of despair and enslavement.

At some point after we groaned, a miracle occurred, and the space that was once *Pi Tom* (closed), was transformed — all the buildings they constructed sunk, one by one, into the mouth of the earth (*Sotah*, 11a). In fact, once we set off to leave Egypt, we immediately chanced upon a place called פי החירת / *Pi haChiros* (*Shemos*, 14:2). Says Rashi, הוא פיתום, ועכשיו נקרא פי החירות על שם שנעשו בני חורין / "This place was actually *Pi Tehom* but now it was called פי החירת / the Mouth of Freedom, as they had now become a free people." *Pi Tehom*, the mouth of the abyss, the energetic quality of chaos, had been transformed into *Pi haCheirus*, 'the mouth of freedom'. Our closed and misdirected mouth was opened, and that same mouth became a mouth of freedom.* From Mitzrayim we were liberated forever to use constructive, positive, holy language, words of freedom, aspiration, hope, possibility and positive movement. There were, of course, subsequent exiles, oppressions and censorships, but after Yetzias Mitzrayim, our *Peh Sach*, our liberative ability to speak, will never fully leave us; we became free people *b'Etzem* / in our essence, and "Etzem is unchangeable" (כל עצם בלתי משתנה: See *Ma'amarei Admur haZaken*, Shemos 2, p. 474. *Toras Chayim*, Va'era 1, 78b). This is why we will inevitably leave behind our current exile, as well, already equipped with holy, authentic, positive words and songs of Torah and *Tefilah* / prayer.

INNER PRACTICE:

Notice the pain you have caused yourself through any reactive tendencies. You might want to imagine how it would sound and feel to groan from this pain. Now, soften any tension you're holding in your body. What is it like to let go of your complacency or stuckness? Freedom is possible, even if it still seems far off.

---

* Indeed, the ultimate transformation and elevation occurred even within the mouth of Pharaoh himself. In the language of Chazal — as quoted by the *Panim Yafos*, Haggadah, VaYa'avidu Mitzrayim — הפה שאמר לא אשלח

FREE SPEECH IS NOT ONLY WHAT WE SAY,
BUT HOW WE SAY IT

A truly free person is not only redeemed physically, but in speech as well. There is a difference between the speech of an inwardly enslaved person, chained to his whims and instincts, and the speech of someone who has control and mastery over his consciousness and behavior.

Redeemed speech is more than being able to express yourself when needed. It is more than an ability to express your deepest desires and yearnings. It is even more than having the refined awareness to honestly express who you really are. Redeemed speech also has a certain quality, tone and vocabulary.

You can hear in someone's voice if he is inwardly free or enslaved, in control of himself or bound tightly to his whims, rigidities, and instinctual behaviors. The wise Shlomo haMelech / King Solomon says, דברי חכמים בנחת נשמעים מזעקת מושל בכסילים / "Words spoken softly by wise men are heeded sooner than those shouted by a ruler in folly" (*Koheles*, 9:17). Not only are words spoken softly more effective, as in the simple reading of this Pasuk, but in general, a wise person naturally speaks softly, without screaming (Rambam, *Hilchos De'os*, 2:5), and you can tell a wise, inwardly free person by the gentleness of their speech (*Otzar Medrashim*).

אתה אמרת וגם את הוא הפה שאמר צאו מתוך עמי. Although, the actual quote is, בני ישראל לא אשלח חייך למחר אתה אוחז ביד כל אחד לשלחו: *Yalkut Shimoni,* Shemos, 175.

Beyond the tonality of the voice is the refinement of the voice. A free and truly empowered individual speaks בלשון נקיה / clean language, whereas an unredeemed, unrefined individual speaks coarsely and with foul language. This is the deeper reason why Chazal's teaching about speaking בלשון נקיה is recorded in the beginning of *Tractate Pesachim* (3a), the tractate dedicated to the laws of Pesach — it is a mark of a truly free and empowered person.

Furthermore, a 'redeemed' person consciously chooses words that frame the Divine goodness in a given situation, or which have a relatively positive effect on the consciousness of others as well as themselves. For instance, instead of saying 'This publication has a deadline...' the (Lubavitcher) Rebbe, of righteous memory, would say, 'This publication has a due date....' In this way, even the slight negativity of a (non-literal) reference to death is replaced by the positivity of a (non-literal) reference to birth. The positive effects of such elegant word choices could be subliminal or obvious, depending on the situation. When expressed in this way, one's speech is not only redeemed, but redemptive.

REDEMPTION OF SPEECH & THE HIDDEN EIGHTH PLAGUE

Moshe began his journey as an individual with a "heavy" or "hard" mouth. Much like all of Klal Yisrael, Moshe too had a compromised capacity for speech. Whereas the actual slaves were laboring under the harsh, 'hard' conditions of *Peh Ra* / negative speech and *Peh Rach* / weak speech, Moshe, who was not enslaved, could still speak but his mouth was heavy. Words did not come easy to him and it was difficult for him to openly emote or speak assertively in front of Pharoah.

Redemption, as explained, began when the people finally cried out, and it continued to unfold when Klal Yisrael was able to really hear Moshe. Prior to the initiation of this process, Moshe was 'unable' to speak because the people were not yet open to hear; speaking and listening are interdependent. As such, the more the people and Pharaoh listen to Moshe speaking, the fuller and clearer Moshe's expression becomes. The more open and receptive the listener, the more eloquent and articulate is the speaker. In place of a heavy mouth, along with the opening of Klal Yisrael's hearts and ears, Moshe gains a fluent mouth and an ease with language and direct communication.

This phenomenon of Moshe's metamorphosis helps us explain a perplexing event within the story of *Yetzias Mitzrayim* / the Going Out of Egypt.

In the beginning of the Torah portion Bo, before the eighth plague, the portion opens, ויאמר ה' אל־משה בא אל־פרעה כי־אני הכבדתי את־לבו ואת־לב עבדיו / "Then Hashem said to Moshe, 'בא / *Bo* / Come to Pharaoh, for I have hardened his heart and the hearts of his courtiers.... ולמען תספר באזני בנך ובן־בנך את אשר התעללתי במצרים / "So that you tell over, to the ears of your sons and of your sons' sons how I made a mockery of the Egyptians...'" (*Shemos*, 10:1-2). Unlike the other nine plagues, here Moshe is not told what exactly the next plague will be. Yet, when he comes before Pharaoh he says, "Thus says Hashem...'How long will you refuse to humble yourself before Me? Let My people go, that they may worship Me. For if you refuse to let My people go, tomorrow I will bring ארבה / locusts on your territory'" (10:3-4).

Moshe is never told that the eighth plague will be locusts, all he is told is בא אל־פרעה / *Bo El Paroh* / Come to Pharaoh. How does he know that the next plague will be ארבה / locusts? There are deeper reasons why this plague was not overtly and clearly articulated to Moshe,* but the question remains: how does Moshe know what the plague will be?

It is possible in this instance, as the Chasam Sofer suggests (*Toras Moshe*, Bo), that Hashem allows Moshe to freely choose what he desires or thinks the next plague should be, and in that case a great swarm of locusts was Moshe's choice. We also know from the teachings of the Arizal that the Ten Plagues correspond to the Ten Utterances of Creation and express the Ten Sefiros, but in an imbalanced way. Counting from the bottom up, the eighth plague is connected to unbalanced *Binah* / understanding, which is manifest in the idea of locusts. Perhaps this also comes into the spiritual intuitive equation of Moshe.

The Medrash (*Shemos Rabbah*, 13) suggests that Moshe knew that the next plague would be locusts from Hashem's descrip-

---

* ארבה בגי׳ יצחק סוד הדין...כדי שלא יתעורר הקטרוג והגבורה והדין ...לא דברו הקב״ה בפירוש רק ברמז: *Agra d'Pirka*, 273.

tion: the next plague will inspire people to "tell the story to their children and grandchildren." As the Maharal (*Gevuros Hashem,* 34) explains, only a 'natural' event, but one that is extreme, like a plague of locusts, would be told generation after generation. Every time in the future locusts would swarm, and this occurs frequently in Egypt, they would remember that there was once a locust plague of extreme proportions. A 'supernatural' event, such as blood or the death of the firstborn, would not be told for generations, as there would be no constant reminders, whereas every locust swarm would remind Egypt of this event.*

In this way, Moshe intuited what type of plague it would be from Hashem's description of its intended effects.

In addition to the above answers, there is a cryptic teaching by the saintly student of the Megaleh Amukos, Rav Shimshon of Ostropoli, the great *Mekubal* / Kabbalist who was massacred together with his community in the devastating Cossack uprising in the year 1648. Rav Shimshon teaches (*Likutei Rav Shimshon Ostropoli.* See also *Ohev Yisrael,* Bo) that in the words בא אל־ פרעה / *Bo El Paroh* Hashem is hinting to Moshe what the next plague will be. Based on a hyper-literal reading of those words, one can bring the letters Beis-Aleph from the word בא / *Bo,*

---

* Ramban, *Shemos,* 10:14, writes that never has a locust swarm, and such are frequent, destroyed all the crops in Egypt, and regarding this it is said, "Sing praises to Him; speak of all His wondrous acts"— *Tehilim,* 105:2: וכתב רבינו חננאל בפירוש התורה שלו מעת עתרת משה רבינו ועד עכשיו אין ארבה מפסיד בכל מצרים, ואם יפול בארץ ישראל ויבא ויכנס בגבול מצרים אינו אוכל מכל יבול הארץ כלום עד עכשיו, ואומרים כי זה כבר ידוע הוא לכל...ועל זה נאמר שיחו בכל נפלאותיו.

and put them into the word פרעה / *Pharaoh*, spelling ארבה *Ar-beh* / locust. This is accomplished by employing the art of interchanging letters. In both the word פרעה and the word ארבה there are two similar letters, the ר ה. In the word פרעה there is a Pei / פ and Ayin / ע, and in the word ארבה there is an Aleph / א and Beis / ב. Moshe thus reveals the plague from within Pharaoh himself.

There are five places of articulation in the mouth: the lips, tongue, throat, teeth, and palate. The letters Beis and Pei both come from the lips, and are for this reason considered interchangeable. The letters Aleph and Ayin both come from the throat, making them interchangeable as well. Hashem thus tells Moshe, בא אל-פרעה: "Take the letters Beis and Aleph, and put them into the name *Pharaoh*; the Pei will be replaced by Beis, and the Ayin will be replaced by Aleph, and then instead of פרעה it will read ארבה.'

Superficially, this seems to be a sophisticated linguistic trapeze act. This teaching is nevertheless hinting at something very profound, and that is the transformation which is occurring within Moshe throughout this process. It means that Moshe is becoming an adept linguist, a master of words and letters, and this represents a metamorphosis of his capacity to speak. Moshe who, like all of Klal Yisrael, began with a *Kaveid Peh*, is now able to manipulate language in a lucid, creative way. This is a sign of redemption, which must begin with the redemption of speech and language. From a stutterer, he becomes a great orator, and eventually his speech impediment is totally healed (at Matan Torah: *Medrash Rabbah*, Devarim, 1. *Zohar* 2, 25a. *Agra d'Pirka*, 166).

In fact, while the letters of *Pharaoh* can be transformed into those of ארבה / *Arbeh*, the letters of the word ארבה can be re-arranged to spell the phrase ברא-ה / create five. Moshe is now able to create new words using the five places of articulation in the mouth, and thus was able to intimate and tell Pharaoh that the next plague would be locusts.

Significantly, it was at the eighth plague when this unprec-edented fluency of speech appeared within Moshe. Eight rep-resents going beyond the natural cycle of sevens, beyond nature as it were, and Moshe is in this moment breaking free of his natural limitation, his personal constriction of speech. In the process of his own personal redemption, Moshe miraculously becomes a master of language and communicator par excel-lence. Hashem never clearly instructed Moshe to announce the plague of locusts, yet Divine speech spontaneously flowed through him and he was able to deduce the word 'locust' out of the coded information Hashem had given over to him.

Indeed, this eighth plague inspired Klal Yisrael למען תספר / "so that you will tell over," to become storytellers, and to relate the story of exile and redemption "to the ears of your children and grandchildren."

Klal Yisrael, who have descended into a condition of en-slavement and lost their names, identities and voices, must regain their voice to the extent that they become storytellers and masters of language.

TELL THE STORY OF THE MITZVOS OF THE NIGHT

On the night of Pesach, as we sit down to remember and tell over the story of Yetzias Mitzrayim, we mirror the process of Klal Yisrael going from a nameless, voiceless people to a people possessing a clear, confident voice. Therefore, we must conduct our Seder with a full, empowered voice as well.

Yet, before we begin to recite the Haggadah in a proud, passionate voice, we break the middle Matzah, the poor man's broken bread, representing a pre-verbal state of brokenness. And even before this, we wash our hands before the Seder without making a blessing. This too represents, among other things, our inability to speak at this early stage of the Seder. Then we take a bitter or bland vegetable, an onion or potato for example, dip it in salt water and bite off a piece. This reflects the state of exile and enslavement, with all its bitterness, brokenness and voicelessness. Only after tasting of this salty bitterness do we begin to recite the Haggadah and redeem ourselves through holy, vital speech.

The Mishnah in *Pesachim* (116a-b) teaches, "Rabban Gamliel would say, 'Anyone who did not mention these three matters on Pesach night has not fulfilled his obligation (...fully: Ran, *ad loc*) — *Pesach*, *Matzah* and *Maror*... the Pesach is brought because the Omnipresent Passed Over the houses of our forefathers in Egypt, as it is stated: 'That you shall *say* it is the sacrifice of

Pesach to Hashem, for He passed over the houses of the Children of Israel in Egypt when he smote the Egyptians, and delivered our houses'" (*Shemos*, 12:27). The source of this *Halachah* / law of *saying* the words Pesach, Matzah and Maror, and mentioning at least briefly what they are referring to, is based on the above Pasuk: "That you shall *say* it is the sacrifice of Hashem." From this Pasuk about the *Pesach* / Paschal Lamb offering, we learn that we need to 'say' something, and not only about our larger story, but specifically about Matzah and Maror as well. This teaching of Rabban Gamliel is recorded in the Haggadah: "This *Pesach* / Passover sacrifice that we are eating is for the sake of what? To commemorate that the Omnipresent *passed over* the homes of our ancestors in Egypt… (One lifts the Matzah and says,) 'This Matzah that we are eating is for the sake of what? To commemorate that the dough of our ancestors did not have enough time to become leavened before the Holy One, blessed be He, revealed Himself and redeemed them immediately…' (Then he lifts the *Maror* / bitter herbs and says,) 'These bitter herbs that we are eating are for the sake of what? To commemorate that the Egyptians embittered the lives of our ancestors in Egypt'."

---

* As Tosefos, *Pesachim*, 116a, explains: ואמרתם זבח פסח הוא פי' באמירה, שצריך לומר פסח זה שאנו אוכלין, ואיתקש מצה ומרור לפסח, וצריך לומר נמי – מצה זו מרור זה. "Has not fulfilled his obligation" simply means that one's full obligation in telling over the story of the Going Out of Egypt: *Meiri*, ibid. Or perhaps it means his full obligation in the actual eating of the Pesach, Matzah and Maror: Ramban, *Milchemes al haRif*, Berachos, 2b. See also Ran, *Ibid*.

Why do we need to 'say' the words *Pesach, Matzah* and *Maror* and mention what they are about? Besides the fact that the Pasuk commands us, "You shall *say*…," what is the 'technical' reason for this command, as it were? When we put on Tefillin, for example, there is no Mitzvah to *say*, 'These are Tefillin and we put them on because of such and such'. Additionally, why do we 'say' these things about Pesach, Matzah, and Maror in a question and answer format, asking "…for the sake of what?" Why not just simply say, for example, 'We eat the Pesach because our homes were passed over.'

We are told to answer that we eat the Pesach offering because Hashem "passed over" our doors, we eat the Matzah because we left in haste, and we eat the Maror to be reminded of the bitter exile in Egypt. These are actually puzzling responses to our three questions. The reason we ate the Pesach offering during the time period that we offered it, is that it is a Mitzvah to *eat* a Korban Pesach. This was a Mitzvah that Klal Yisrael received even before the night that HaKadosh Baruch Hu passed over their homes. Similarly, we eat Matzah today, just as we ate it on the night of Yetzias Mitzrayim, because there is a Mitzvah to "eat Matzah in the evening." Again, this Mitzvah was given days before we left Egypt in haste. And the reason we eat Maror is because there is a Mitzvah to eat Maror together with the Korban Pesach. In this way, it seems that we do not actually eat the Pesach offering due to the fact that "Hashem passed over us," nor Matzah because "we did not have enough time," nor Maror because "they made our life bitter."

Again, the simple answer given by the sages for this question is that the Pasuk says, "that you shall *say* it is the (Pesach) sacrifice of Hashem who passed over the houses of the Israelites in Egypt..." The Torah is saying that we *eat* the Pesach sacrifice because Hashem passed over the houses. But what does the Torah mean when it makes it a Mitzvah to "say" something, when in fact, the Torah clearly states that it is a Mitzvah to "eat" the Pesach?

Every Mitzvah contains both the element of *Chok* / a decree that is transcendent of human reasoning and *Mishpat* / a decree that relates to human reason. Each has dimensions of *Na'aseh* / doing and *Nishmah* / listening, obedience and inspiration, 'prose' and 'poetry', the letters and the trope.

We relate to the Creator as servants to a king; Hashem commands and we obey. But we also relate to HaKadosh Baruch Hu as a child to a parent. Hashem gives us the means to connect to Him as our Beloved Parent, and we lovingly 'participate' in Mitzvos by decoding and understanding their deeper 'reasons'.

On Seder Night, as we ourselves are experiencing a departure from our own inner Egypt, and becoming a holy people, we are asked to actively participate and creatively engage our full selves in this process. Similar to Klal Yisrael, we are beckoned to become storytellers: למען תספר. The Mitzvah of this night is in fact *Sipur* / to tell the Exodus as a story — not just to *mention* Yetzias Mitzrayim, as we do all the days and nights of the year, but to illustrate, infer, and elaborate.

There is a primary element of *Chok* / 'mysterious command' in the Mitzvos of Pesach, Matzah and Maror: we do them simply because we are commanded. The core of the Mitzvos and the 'real' reason why we do them is that they are the absolute will of HaKadosh Baruch Hu. Hashem commands and we do; there is no 'poetry' in this, and in a sense, no questions to be asked. Yet, on the night of Pesach we also need to think about these Mitzvos in terms of their historical unfolding and their inner significance. In this way, not only do we eat the Pesach, Matzah and Maror because we were so commanded, but we also need to immerse, embody, and participate in the stories related to them. Pesach is thus the 'headquarters' of actively attempting to more deeply understand and express the inner depths and meanings of our actions and Mitzvos; the *why* and *how* behind the *what, where*, and *when*. And it is this very process of speaking and listening and singing that we too may become free from all that constricts us.

Hashem wants us to be storytellers on this night; passionate, poetic transmitters of the narrative. Hashem wants us to get involved, to ask provocative questions and offer evocative answers, to excavate the deeper meanings of the Mitzvos, to sing, to use *our* voice. Thus, as we are personally and collectively going out of Egypt on this night, we must *say* the stories of Pesach, Matzah and Maror. And we do not merely pronounce that on this night we eat these items because of the given reasons, but we dramatize the questions and verbally flesh out the history, the narratives, and the spiritual implications for our own lives.*

On this night we activate the *Geulah* / redemption of our authentic voices. Through poetically intermingling our people's history with our own personal stories and inner life, expressing it all vocally and vibrationally, Yetzias Mitzrayim becomes real to us in the present. We *participate* in it. We are no longer slaves with muted self-awareness. We have a voice, and Hashem hears us.

Stories are sometimes the only medium through which we can fully express ourselves. The more relaxed mode of expression makes us feel more comfortable, warm and open. If we only dealt with 'cold', detached ideas and pronouncements on this night, we would never be able to identify with the narratives and experience ourselves as if *we* were actually leaving Mitzrayim on this very night. Stories take us beyond the domain of intellectual ideas.

---

* Every year before the Seder, Reb Chayim Brisker would gather his family and explain to them that on this night the remembrance of going out of Egypt is different from the Mitzvah to remember the going out of Egypt every day of the year. 1) On this night we need to remember in the form of a question and answer. 2) On this night we need to tell the entire story, not just the moment of leaving Egypt, including our entire history, beginning with an invocation of our idol worshiping ancestors. 3) On this night there is a Mitzvah to ruminate on and relay the 'reasons' for the Mitzvos of the night, and thus, the teaching by Rabban Gamliel and the reason for these Mitzvos: *Reshimas Talmidim*, Maran haGriz, Shemos, 13:8.

FROM STORYTELLERS TO SINGERS

When we *feel* the story of our own Yetzias Mitzrayim unfolding within us, we naturally burst out in song.

On this night, we go beyond even the level of storytellers — to become singers.

Throughout this process our voice, language, self-understanding and identity have been regained and forged on a higher level. In fact, even while we were still in Egypt, when the Mitzvos of eating Pesach, Matzah and Maror, were revealed to us, we were raised to the level of Matan Torah — the revelation of Divine speech and an outpouring of Divine commandments and communications.

We were 'first-hand witnesses' of the miracles and wonders displayed in Egypt and are thus empowered to tell these stories and miracles in vivid detail to our children, spouses, friends and communities, for all of history. Finally, having left Egypt and having miraculously crossed the Sea of Reeds, together with Moshe himself, we break out in songs of praise and sing the Great Song, the *Shiras haYam* / Song of the Sea.

When we look back upon this night, we see how far we have come in just a few hours. Mirroring the birth of Klal Yisrael from the 'Land of Constrictions,' we began with a broken Matzah, with salty water and humble acknowledgments of our state as slaves. As we gradually moved through the Haggadah, we felt and expressed the bitterness of our past and realized that Hashem always hears our voice and story and sees our afflictions. Increasingly, our name and true identity emerged. We miraculously left behind our inner enslavement and reactive behavior; we became independent, free. We became empowered to articulate ourselves, and to actively *create* the story of our lives to the point that Divine speech began resonating to us and through us, revealing our true purpose and reason for existence.

A REDEEMED VOICE SINGS PRAISE

At the end of Maggid, the bulk of the 'speaking' part of the Haggadah, we begin singing the first part of Hallel, which speaks about the miracles and wonders that occurred at Yetzias Mitzrayim. Then we lift up a cup of wine and declare, "*Therefore, it is our duty to thank, laud, praise, glorify, exalt, adore, bless, elevate, and honor the One who did all these miracles for our ancestors and for us!*" At this moment our speech is fully redeemed, as we speak openly and clearly, with a refined, confident voice, and we begin to sing praises to Hashem.

Praise and thanksgiving are the highest form of speech and expression, they are in fact the very reason our mouths were created. In the words of the Arizal and later Poskim, הפה נברא להודות לה' / "The mouth was created to offer thanks and praise to Hashem" (*Kaf haChayim, Shulchan Aruch*, Orach Chayim, 60:4, in the name of the Arizal. Chida, *Midbar Kedeimos*, Zayin).

We sing praises not only for all the miracles that occurred during Yetzias Mitzrayim, but also for all the miracles that continue to occur throughout our history. And not only do we sing for all of the many miracles throughout our glorious, albeit often tragic history, but we sing for the greatest miracle of all, the survival of our people (Siddur, *Ya'avetz*, Hakdamah*).

We offer thanks for the miracle of our own lives, for the myriad gifts within each of our individual stories. On Seder Night we are moved to speak "about all the kindness and miracles Hashem has done for us, both collectively and individually — and one who does so fulfills a Mitzvah" (*Peleh Yoetz*, Erech Dibbur).

Seder Leil Pesach / 'The Order of the Night of Passing Over' is a template for liberation, guiding us deftly through the depths of our alienation to acknowledge the manifold miracles

---

* In the words of the Ya'avetz, מי שיעיין ביחוד עניננו ומעמדנו בעולם, אנחנו האומה הגולה שה פזורה. אחר כל מה שעבר עלינו מהצרות והתמורות אלפים מהשנים, ואין אומה בעולם נרדפת כמונו. מה רבים היו צרינו, מה עצמו נשאו ראש הקמים עלינו מנעורינו, להשמידנו לעקרנו לשרשנו, מפני השנאה שסיבתה הקנאה רבת צררונו. גם לא יכלו לנו לאבדנו ולכלותינו. כל האומות הקדומות העצומות אבד זכרם, בטל סברם, סר צלם... חי נפשי כי בהתבונני בנפלאות אלה, גדלו אצלי יותר מכל נסים ונפלאות שעשה השי"ת לאבותינו במצרים ובמדבר ובא"י. וכל מה שארך הגלות יותר, נתאמת הנם יותר ונודע מעשה תקפו וגבורתו: *Siddur Sulam Beis Keil*, Hakdamah. A similar idea is expressed already in the Rishonim. The *Chovos HaLevavos*, (Sha'ar HaBechinah, 5) writes, והגדולה שבטובות שהיטיב בהם הבורא לאדם והראיה החזקה עליו התורה הנתונה למשה והראות האותות על ידו...ואם יבקש אדם בזמן הזה לראות מה שהוא דומה לעניינים ההם יביט בעין האמת עמדנו בין האומות מעת הגלות וסדור עניינינו ביניהם. Rabbeinu Menachem ben Aaron Ibn Zerach writes, מי שיש בלבו אמונה ודעת נכונה, יראה כיום הזה בעיניו ניסים ונפלאות בכל מקומות נפוצותינו שהם יותר מקריעת ים סוף, למי שלא ידחה האמת הנראה שבכל יום ויום עומדים עלינו לכלותינו והקדוש ברוך הוא מצילנו מידם...היש פלא כיוצא בו *Tzeidah LaDerech*, 4, Klal 7, 1.

and kindnesses that Hashem has shown us, in such a way that we open ourselves up to receiving even greater wonders and goodness. With this powerful, initiatory template, we can begin to fill all the other nights and days of our lives with thanks and praise.

The *Kli* / vessel to receive Hashem's infinite kindness, blessings and miracles beyond imagination, is humble gratitude. Continually thanking Hashem, and joyfully singing about all the *Chasadim* / kindnesses and miracles that HaKadosh Baruch Hu does for us every moment — this is what forms the vessel that draws down and receives even more Divine kindness, miracles, and salvations.

After singing the first part of *Hallel* / Praises at the end of the Maggid section of the Seder, we eat and physically internalize the Mitzvos, and then proceed to enjoy a royal meal. After reciting the *Bentching* / Blessings and Thanks After the Meal, we continue with the second part of Hallel, which speaks of the future Ultimate Redemption. As the Haggadah crescendos with the final praises of Hallel, there arises an almost spontaneous, free-flowing of song up until the final stage of the Haggadah, *Nirtzah* / Acceptance. As we have reached a sense of clarity and mastery over our articulation, our speech is thus elevated to the level of joyful song. We are now a liberated nation singing at the Splitting of the Sea of Reeds, celebrating our birth into Redemption, and pouring out our hearts in overwhelming praise and gratitude. We have evolved from nameless slaves, to prophetic storytellers, to angelic singers, and a cascade of beautiful, enlightened tunes comes tumbling out of our mouths.

FROM PASSIONATE SINGERS TO TRANSCENDENT SILENCE

At the peak of Yetzias Mitzrayim, as Klal Yisrael is standing at the banks of the Sea with the Egyptian army in hot pursuit, Hashem asks Moshe, "Why do you cry out to Me? Speak to the people of Israel and they shall journey forward!" (*Shemos*, 14:15). After the long process of the redemption of their speech and dignity, from dark silence to brilliant stories and glorious praises, now, at the climax of their redemption, the people are told to remain silent. This seems counterintuitive. The Zohar remarks on this Pasuk that this event expresses the Divine mystery of *Atik Yomin* / Ancient of Days, also known simply as *Atik* / the Primordial, the place of Pure Transcendence (בעתיקא תלייא מלתא: *Zohar* 2, 48a).

Experientially, the level of Atik corresponds to the 'silence beyond sound'. This is in profound diametric contrast to the 'silence before sound', the silence that mutes all sound, which was the condition of Klal Yisrael as slaves in Egypt. Now we have attained a level that is *beyond* all expression. When words fail, we sing, and when even song fails, we fall into ecstatic silence.

This is a rich inner quietness, like the warm blanket of silence that descends after riding the final crescendo of a magnificent symphony, when all the music, and noise, emotion and movement, suddenly cease. Beyond sound, beyond expression, is silence of pure *Deveikus* / unity. It is a sense of effortless expiration within the Infinite One.

Much like Klal Yisrael in the historical Yetzias Mitzrayim, we began the night of the Seder in a place of 'silence' before sound. That silence came from an exile of speech, an inability to express ourselves. In fact, even when one is able to physically speak, but all that comes out are empty words — weather, politics, sports, emptiness — this too is a form of silence, 'noisy silence', which fills one's inner void with meaningless static.

Now, at the end of the Seder, almost miraculously, we find ourselves at the other end of the spectrum, the paradoxical pinnacle of meaningful self-expression. Having drunk three cups of wine, having songs, melodies and infinite light flow from our mouths, now a happy exhaustion envelopes us, and we sink into the world of Atik, transcendent silence. This is the stage of *Nirtzah* / Acceptance. Suddenly there is nothing to do and nothing needs to be said. All is complete and accepted. We are home, free.

We have spoken and sung until there is nothing else to say or sing. We have reached a point of silence beyond words, song beyond sound. This is the level of Atik Yomin, the same silence that Klal Yisrael reached at the Sea.

Indeed, מצוה לספר ביציאת מצרים / the Mitzvah to tell and talk about the tale of Yetzias Mitzrayim is to do so until שתתחטפנו שינה / *Shetichatfenu Sheinah* / sleep takes hold of you, even after the Seder is complete (Tosefta, *Pesachim*, 10:8. Rosh, *Pesachim*, 10:33. Tur and *Shulchan Aruch*, Orach Chayim, 481:2). The obligation on this night includes continuing to speak of the wonders and miracles of Yetzias Mitzrayim until we fall asleep.*

After silence, sleep is somehow the crescendo of the Going Out of Egypt. This total surrender is not simply a demarcation, the point at which we stop telling the story. "Until sleep overtakes you" means that we need to tell the story until we reach the level of sleep.

The root letters of שינה /*Sheinah* / sleep are the same letters as ישן / *Yashan* / old, hinting at the level of *Atik* / ancient. Through sleep you take leave of 'this world' as it were, and enter into more inner worlds. In sleep, you let go of the world of noise, commerce and activity, and enter a world of subtlety, silence and, potentially, self-transcendence.

On the night of Pesach, at the culmination of the Seder, the apex of leaving all forms of Mitzrayim, all shackles of limitation, restriction and constriction, we move from the place of sound, song, and even praise, into the utter Transcendence of Atik Yomin. We slip into an easeful consciousness of unity with HaKadosh Baruch Hu, 'the Ancient One', a subtle, quiet

---

* Note that the obligation is to לספר ביציאת מצרים / "tell over the story of the Exodus from Egypt" all night, even after the Seder, but if you fall asleep after the Seder you become absolved of the obligation because you simply cannot continue. The obligation is 'up until the point' of falling asleep; as such, if you doze off and wake up again, you can go to bed and return to sleep, and you do not need to continue speaking about Yetzias Mitzrayim.

Deveikus of having arrived. At this point we simply let go and give ourselves over to Hashem.

REALIZING WE ARE CHOSEN

On this night, it is as if we are all undergoing the process of becoming a Jew again for the first time. We start off as 'idol worshipers', as we proclaim in the beginning of Maggid, and conclude with HaKadosh Baruch Hu taking us out of Egypt to become His people. We are each like a convert, thus we recite the blessing on the Haggadah — *Asher Go'al* / "...Who has redeemed us" — only after we read the Haggadah, not before (as we do with all other Mitzvos; the blessing is customarily recited before the performance of a Mitzvah). This is much like how a person undergoing conversion recites the blessing of conversion only after converting (*Chasam Sofer*), as before conversion one cannot accurately recite the blessing of "...Who has commanded us." Therefore, when we reach Nirtzah, we quietly celebrate our *Bechirah* / chosenness, Hashem's choosing us.*

וצריך להתחיל בגנות ולסיים בשבח, כיצד, מתחיל ומספר שבתחלה היו אבותינו בימי תרח ומלפניו כופרים וטועין אחר ההבל ורודפין אחר עבודת אלילים. ומסיים בדת האמת שקרבנו המקום לו והבדילנו מהאמות וקרבנו ליחודו. / "One must begin with disgrace and conclude

---

* Perhaps this is the reason for the *Meshech Chochmah's* ruling, (*Bamidbar*, 9:7, *Ohr Sameach*, Hilchos Mechesurei Kapara, 1) that a Ger/convert fulfills his obligation to bring a Karbon for his conversion if he brought a Korban Pesach, since the Korban Pesach is in fact a type of Korban for conversion. It is a Korban through which we enter into a Bris with HaKadosh Baruch Hu. Thus, Korban Pesach is similar to an actual Bris, in that these are the only two positive Mitzvos which *not* performing them causes Kares.

with praise. How is that? He begins and narrates that in the beginning, our ancestors at the time of Terach, and before, were heretics, erring after emptiness and pursuing idolatry. And he concludes with the true religion — that the Omnipresent brought us close to Him, *separated* us from the nations, and *brought us close* to His unification (Rambam, *Hilchos Chametz uMatzah*, 7:4).

It is not merely a night to מספר / tell the story of Yetzias Mitzrayim and of how Hashem has brought us closer, but also to declare, and מודיע / 'Let it be known', that we were slaves and Hashem chose us and freed us with great and wondrous miracles.

We do not just simply say, 'This night is special', rather, 'This night is different from all other nights': *Mah Nishtanah haLailah haZeh.* We contrast it with all other nights of the year, as on this night we were, and are, Divinely chosen. And this choice is not 'because' of anything, it is just because that is what Hashem desires, so to speak.

Just as Hashem chooses us and 'takes' us for no 'rational' reason, we choose Hashem for no rational reason, beyond causality, beyond 'Seder', beyond Da'as. On this night we have *Mochin d'Gadlus* / expanded mind and total clarity, above the Tree of Da'as paradigm, above deliberations and decisions. Whereas decisions on the level of the Tree of Da'as take time, good and bad are intermingled and nothing is clear, on Seder Night we make decisive actions from a space of timeless clarity; this quality of thought and action is also called alacrity or 'haste'.

BEYOND SOUND, BEYOND SEDER

Experientially, this transcendent silence is experienced as the melding of two into one, like the comfortable silence that comes about when you are so intimate with another person that you can walk for twenty minutes with them and not say a word. Walking side by side in silence with someone you are less comfortable with can be awkward and unsettling; you are not 'at one' with them, and are therefore not able to share a space 'beyond words'.

Ultimately, the whole point of the *Seder* / order of the night is to arrive at this place 'beyond Seder'. It is essentially an 'order that transcends order'. After all the steps, all the work and words, all the *Haggadah* / storytelling, all the Mitzvos we have done and the praises we have sung, we reach a pinnacle 'beyond' all effort or activity, beyond all Avodah / spiritual work. All of it vanishes like smoke into the repose of *Nirtzah* / complete acceptance. In this loving embrace of silence, we become aware of a perennial Divine reverberation that constantly calls to us saying, "I want you for 'you', not for what you do, say, think, feel or sing. I love you just for who you are, My child."

We have come full circle, from silence to sound to speech to song, and back to silence. But now, we are suspended in the blissful silence of two lovers in a deep embrace. There are no more questions. There is only silence. And that silence is itself the answer, it is Redemption, the eternal acceptance of Nirtzah.

SONGS BIRTHED IN SILENCE & SOUNDS THAT INCLUDE SILENCE

For many, the Seder concludes with the drinking of the fourth cup of wine, the joy-filled declaration, "Next year in Jerusalem," the final step of Nirtzah, and then, sleep. Yet, many have the custom to continue the night with a post-Seder recitation of *Shir haShirim* / Song of Songs, and various other *Piyutim* / symbolic hymns and poems.

In a semi-drunk, semi-asleep state, late at night, after four cups of wine, those with *Koach* / strength keep singing what on the surface might sound like (*leHavdil*) 'bar tunes': "Who knows one? I know one…! Who knows two, I know two…," and the like. Yet, in truth, these seemingly frivolous songs* contain tremendous hidden depth and are rooted in a world of quietness, *Sheinah* / sleep, and Atik. Piyutim and songs such as these give voice to the innocence that emerges from within stillness — they are the childlike sounds of mature silence. The songs sung in this hypnagogic Atik state are songs of such depth and mystery that they remain deep and mysterious despite being expressed and exposed.

---

* No sage regards these particular Piyutim as seemingly frivolous, but some sages do question Piyutim that are written in encrypted language, as was the custom of the Ashkenaz writers of Piyutim (unlike the Spanish) and some earlier writers, and especially the Piyutim that some inserted into the Davening: see Even Ezra, *Koheles*, 5:1 — אם כן אין ראוי להתפלל אלא על דרך פשט, ולא על דרך שיש לו סוד, או הוא על דרך משל, או הוא כעניין שאין הלכה כמותו, או שיתפרש לעניינים רבים.

There are plain words, rooted in the world of noise and sound, and there is the higher expression of sound, from within the world of poetry and song. And yet, interestingly, songs produced on this level are still birthed within the world of noise. They are higher vibrations that are created out of a lower context of noise. Thus, in a way, they are just another form of noise, albeit a more subtle, harmonious manipulation of noise. And while they are indeed a more beautiful vibration from within the external world of sound, there is a deeper type of sound that emanates from the inner world of silence.* There is a type of Shirah that emanates from the deepest recesses of the soul, from the place of utter transcendence, a place of silence beyond noise, beyond words, and from that deep quiet place, a song effortlessly flows. This is a song that, even while emanating from the deepest depths, always remains deep.

The great singer of Israel, Dovid haMelech, says in *Tehilim*, למען יזמרך כבוד ולא ידם / "For my whole soul will sing to You and not remain silent" (30:13). He is referring to a level of song that emerges from the place of utter *Dom* / silence, inwardness and stillness, and from there pours forth into the world.

---

* Similarly, after reaching the level of Atik, there was the *Shiras haYam* and six weeks later the revealing of Matan Torah, *Anochi Hashem* / I am Hashem. Anochi is the level of *Keser* / Crown (the letters of *Anochi* rearranged spell *k'Ani*, suggesting *Keser, Ani* / I). Chazal tell us in *Medrash Rabbah*, Shir HaShirim, 1:2, 4 — when Klal Yisrael heard *Anochi Hashem*, נתקע תלמוד תורה בלבם, והיו לומדים ולא היו משכחין / "the Torah was imprinted upon their hearts so that they would learn and not forget." נתקע comes from the root תקע the same letters (with the Yud) as עתיק. The Torah is a revelation of the Ten *Dibros* / words that are rooted within Keser, the utter Transcendence of HaKadosh Baruch Hu.

Re-enacting the cosmic, historical Yetzias Mitzrayim narrative, we hear the Divine challenge: "Why do you cry out to Me? Speak to the People of Israel and they shall journey forward!" The response to this mandate is the key to attaining the Transcendent level of Atik. When Klal Yisrael emerged on the other side of the splitting Sea of Reeds, they all, together with Moshe, sang the great *Shirah* / song, the Song of the Sea. On the night of Pesach, we do the same.

This *Shirah* is a song that emanates from within the depths of a profound inner quietude. In that redemptive moment on the other side of the sea, Klal Yisrael sang out from their deepest *Penimiyus* / interiority. Their highest song was an echo of their deepest silence. The Shirah is thus a song that emerges from a place deep within, a place beyond "crying out to Me," beyond all noise and even beyond all prayer.

In the world of duality, sound contradicts or cancels silence, yet, on the deepest level, such opposites are not mutually exclusive. The songs that emerge from the depths of Atik at the end of the Seder are so deep that nothing holds them back or eclipses their inward or even outward expression. This is the level we all, G-d willing, reach on the night of Pesach; a measure of the level that Klal Yisrael attained at *Kriyas Yam Suf* / the Splitting of the Sea, when they burst into spontaneous song from the deepest point of inner stillness. This is the song of redemption.

KAVANAH

To make the Seder more personal, think about your own inner stuckness, feel the "Ouch!" of your life, take a few moments during the Seder to pray quietly about your life. Open up and converse with the Master of the Universe. You can ask for whatever you want. You can express your spiritual, physical, emotional and mental yearnings, your complaints, or even just 'explain' to Hashem what's going on with you, and then sit for a moment in a comfortable silence.

Speak openly about the hardships of life, also about the personal *Galus* / exile, alienation, disconnect, that you may have or are currently experiencing. Voice the things that are bothering you, anything and everything.

Tell your story to Hashem, your loving Parent who is with you at the Seder; tell over *your* story, and all the miracles of your life. Speak about the kindness and miracles Hashem has done for you and for us, collectively as well. Then give thanks to HaKadosh Baruch Hu for all these miracles, all the blessings that Hashem has revealed; be grateful and thankful for the infinite Divine kindness, beyond all imagining.

The main *Mitzvah* / 'Divinity-infused act' of the Seder is *l'Sapeir* / to tell the story and pass it on to our children. As the Haggadah itself says, "Anyone who elaborates in speaking about Yetzias Mitzrayim, he is certainly praiseworthy." When we have 'a mouth that speaks' not only can we liberate ourselves from our own 'weak mouth' and 'negative mouth', we can merge our mouth with the Divine Mouth, as it were, 're-vealing' through our storytelling the truth of our exodus and redemption, and eventually, the truth of the Final Exodus and the revealing of Moshiach, speedily in our days.*

INNER PRACTICE:

Where in your life has an opportunity for freedom or choice come to you, but you were so stuck in your story that you couldn't listen?

Where can you begin now to define your own reality, and articulate who you are and what you need?

---

* As the word *Moshiach* is related to the word *Me-Siach* / one who speaks.

Chapter Three:
Exile and Redemption of Dibbur/Speech

MATZAH IS CALLED לחם עוני / 'BREAD OF AN *ONI*'. What does *Oni* mean? Say our sages, עני כתיב מה שדרכו בפרוסה / "*Oni* is actually written without a Vav, meaning 'a poor person'; it is the manner of a poor person to eat a small piece of bread, for lack of a whole loaf." In this way, *Lechem Oni* means 'poor man's bread'.

Alternatively, say our sages, לחם עוני is called bread of *Oni* / 'of answering': לחם שעונין עליו דברים הרבה / "bread over which one answers and speaks regarding many matters" (*Pesachim*, 115b).

Clearly, these two interpretations are linked; a 'poor person' might speak of דברים הרבה / many matters or 'lots of words' over his piece of Matzah. Indeed, in the context of the Haggadah, we speak of "many matters" and say lots of words over the broken, poor man's Matzah. *Haggadah* means 'speaking', as does *Maggid*, the longest section of the Haggadah in which we recount and discuss our movement from slavery to redemption at length.

'MANY WORDS' HEAL INNER ALIENATION

Speaking 'many words' can be viewed as a form of verbal catharsis that brings inner healing. When a 'poor person', whether literally, mentally or emotionally poor, is stuck or paralyzed in their muteness and unable to speak and express himself, he is deep in inner exile. The process of his healing and redemption is activated by speaking many words about his situation. Just saying דברים הרבה, and allowing for a cascade of words to tumble out of the mouth, can facilitate a sudden flash of self-expression and self-awareness that opens one to inner transformation and redemption.

In other words, on the night of Pesach, we hold or display a piece of poor man's bread, a broken (middle) Matzah and recite "many matters," the "many words" of the Haggadah over it, and through this recitation and discussion, we, the 'poor people', are moving from the historical Egypt and inner Egypt, toward historical and personal redemption.*

---

* דברים הרבה can refer to the Haggadah: Ran, *ad loc*. Tur, *Orach Chayim*, 473. It can also refer to certain passages within the Haggadah [Rabbeinu

In this way, the experience of speaking "many words" is the remedy for the symptom of עָנִי / poverty.

LOTS OF WORDS INDICATE SCATTEREDNESS

It also seems logical to conclude that both the idea of עָנִי and דברים הרבה are part of the same idea of mental, emotional, spiritual poverty. "No one is poor except one who lacks *Da'as* / awareness and knowledge" (*Nedarim,* 41a), and often a person without self-awareness speaks "many words." From this perspective, דברים הרבה is not the remedy for such inner poverty, rather, it can also be seen as an expression of the problem and syndrome.

דברים הרבה literally means 'lots of words'. When a person is conveying a coherent thought they might use 'many' words, but not 'lots' of words. הרבה suggests an unnecessary, disconnected overabundance of words. This is because the person is poor in Da'as or proper self-awareness.

When a person needs to say a 'lot of words' to transmit a thought, it shows that the idea is not securely assimilated within him. It shows a lack of Da'as; the ideas are not fully formulated and understood by the speaker himself, and he is still an *Oni* / poor man in this regard.

Chananel, *ad loc*], or the Haggadah and Halel [Rashi, *ad loc*], or the Haggadah and the first part of Halel [Meiri, *ad loc*]. Just as Kiddush is said over wine, the Haggadah needs to be said over Matzah. This is a *Din* / principle in the laws of Haggadah: *Brisk Haggadah,* Mah Nishtanah.

As such, Chazal are telling us that when a person is still in a state of mental or emotional poverty, stuck or immature, and he is asked to speak, he will speak דברים הרבה / many empty, indirect words. In the case of Klal Yisrael, when they finally gained a voice but were still mentally, emotionally and spiritually 'enslaved' and immature, at least some of them (*Medrash Rabbah*, Shemos, 1:7. *Tanchuma*, Shemos, 10) spoke לשון הרע / *Lashon haRa* / negative speech, as will be explored (Chapter 4, regarding the reasons for Galus).

While Klal Yisrael was in a state of lack of Da'as, redemption did not seem to be a possibility. Moshe was the embodiment of Da'as, and as such, only when Moshe appeared did redemption appear to Klal Yisrael as an actual possibility. When they began to listen to Moshe, it means Da'as began to seep into their consciousness. In this way, they were beginning to move from *Peh Ra* / 'a bad mouth', toward *Peh-Sach* / 'a mouth that speaks', as there cannot be correct speech without Da'as (*Ohr haChochmah*, Rebbe Uri Feivel, student of the students of the Baal Shem Tov, Beha'alosecha. Thu,s איוב לא־בדעת ידבר: *Iyov*, 34:35).

Before this integration of Da'as, they merely spoke דברים הרבה / many words for no reason or purpose, which by nature leads to Lashon haRa. Lacking Da'as is a state of exile, the condition of being an *Oni* / impoverished person.

Not only was Klal Yisrael without Da'as in Egypt, leading them to speak Lashon haRa, but it was Lashon haRa that led them into the Galus of Mitzrayim in the first place. The Galus begins with the sale of Yoseph and his being taken down to Egypt. Yoseph's brothers sold him because they were upset at him. Why were they upset? ויבא יוסף את־דבתם רעה אל־אביהם / "And Yoseph brought bad reports about them to their father" (*Bereishis*, 37:2), meaning, whatever he saw wrong in his brothers, the sons of Leah, he reported to his father (Rashi, *ad loc*). In their anger, they sold him, and subsequently he was sold into slavery in Egypt. Years later, he came to power, reconciled his family and brought them all down into Egypt to save them from famine. In this way, the whole foundation of the exile of Egypt began with Lashon haRa, Yoseph speaking "lots of words."

On this night, and each day and moment, all of us need to work on regaining our own distinct, authentic voice. We need to redeem our true sense of speech in order to reach a redemptive state, in which our words are consciously directed, meaningful and purposeful. The special gift of this night is freedom through illuminating expression and speech.

SHORT BREATH

A human is defined as a creature of speech, a *Medaber* / speaker. In the story of the creation of the human being, it says Adam was given a נשמת חיים / living soul (*Bereishis*, 2:7). According to the *Targum* / translation, this refers to a רוח ממללא / 'speaking spirit'.

Ruach means 'spirit' and also 'wind' or 'breath'. Speech is precisely formed, projected and contextualized breath. First breath rises from the lungs, passes through the vocal cords and fills the mouth, and then various powers of the mouth shape it into particular sounds in sequences that are understood as words. The undifferentiated sound, essentially the vibrating 'wind' of breath, is filtered through the five 'powers' of the mouth: the lips, throat, teeth, palate, and tongue becoming distinct words.

In this way, breath is the root of speech. As such, talking too much, needlessly using "lots of words," or being unable to speak, both reflect a misalignment in the world of *Ruach* / wind. Either there is too much wind and no filter or limiting factors, or there is too little wind and not enough movement to carry thoughts and feelings to the world outside the self. Being 'short of breath' renders a person stuck within himself, without the tools or ability to move outward. This also creates a stuckness in communication that also does not allow one to hear others. There is very little movement inward or outward.

In the unfolding narrative of Yetzias Mitzrayim, the Torah says, ולא שמעו אל־משה מקצר רוח / "They did not *listen* to Moshe because of their shortness of *Ruach* / Breath" (Shemos, 6:9). This means that in their anguish their breath only came in short gasps and they could not draw in long breaths (Rashi, *ad loc*). And just as Klal Yisrael were unable to speak and their speech was in exile, they were also unable to hear or listen; there was an overall immobilization in both directions.

קצר רוח / CUT BREATH

קצר רוח / *Kotzer Ruach*, most often translated as 'short of breath', literally means 'cut breath'. It can thus refer to a deficiency of breath, or a type of breath, along with its expression as speech, that is cut up or that cuts something up. In both cases, קצר indicates that the breath is detached from its source within, as is its expression in speech.

To better understand this idea, let us digress and explore the nature of the words גלות / *Galus* / exile and גאולה / Geulah / redemption. These terms share the same root, גל — which also spells *Gal* / wave or 'revealing'. How can *Galus* and *Geulah* in their root mean the same thing? They are complete opposites.

At the end of *Vayikra*, the Torah uses the word *Geulah* / redemption repeatedly. In those chapters, the Torah speaks of various legal types of Geulah. For example, it reveals legal rights around a Mitzvah to 'redeem' properties and slaves that were sold out of desperation and thus the field, house or person, is brought back to its original owner or family. In this way, Geulah means a return of objects or subjects, things or people, back home to their original state. In this way, the historical Exodus and Geulah from Egypt is a returning of the children of Israel to their homeland, their own original state and space.

Exile, then, means being separated, estranged or alienated from one's homeland, whether physically or spiritually.

In the Torah, there is one particular category of person whose punishment — meaning, his or her form of recuperating, healing, and *Tikkun* / correction for their actions — comes through a type of exile. That is the מצורע / *Metzora* / (loosely) 'leper', although this is incorrectly translated, as it was primarily a spiritual disease. A Metzora בדד ישב מחוץ למחנה / "must sit alone, outside the camp" (*Vayikra*, 13:46). They are exiled from their home, and they must live for a duration of time outside their camp, and furthermore, within their exile they must live alone, in solitude.

Specific changes in skin pigmentation and 'leprous' marks are the physical manifestations of the *Tzara'as* of the Metzora, but the real disease behind these manifestations is a spiritual defect and malady. *Chazal* / our sages reveal to us that leprous marks appear because of *Lashon haRa* / evil, harmful speech: כל המספר לשון הרע נגעים באים עליו / "Anyone who speaks malicious speech will be afflicted by leprous marks coming upon him" (*Erchin*, 15b). In the Torah we find that Moshe's sister Miriam is speaking ill about her brother and immediately she is inflicted and becomes a Metzora (*Bamidbar*, 12:1-16).

In fact, the Hebrew word מצורע / Metzora, says Reish Lakish, is from the words מוציא שם רע / *Motzi Shem Ra* / 'emitter of negative, evil speech' (*Erchin*, 15b). A person becomes a *Metzo-ra* because they are a *Motzi* Shem *Ra* and speak evil or malicious words against others.

MEASURE FOR MEASURE

As mentioned, not only does the Metzora need to live separately outside the camp, but he needs to live there alone. Moreover, the actual translation of the word *Metzora* is 'secluded' or 'closed up' (Unkalus translates *Metzora* as סגירו: *Vayikra*, 13:2. See also *Zohar* 3, 48b: סגירו דנהורא עלאה. *Derech Mitzvosecha*, Mitzvas Tumas haMetzora).

The Metzora is ostracized and isolated from his community, and within his exile he must remain secluded and kept away from others. In this way, the definition of a Metzora is 'one who is separated'.

All ritually unclean people need to live outside the camp and community, but why does the Metzora need to 'live alone', in addition? "Why is he different from other unclean people, that he must remain completely isolated? Since, with his slander and Lashon haRa, he caused a separation and a rift between a man and his wife or between a man and his fellow, he too, shall be separated" (*Erchin*, 16b. Rashi, *Vayikra*, 13:46). In the Torah, punishments are meted out *Midah K'neged Midah* / 'measure for measure'. Hence, since he caused separation he needs to be separated.

Sitting alone and contemplating his lot will allow him to heal his inner malady. As he sits there in utter isolation he will come to recognize the error of his actions, and how his words caused a devastating sense of separation between himself and friends or family. He will be moved to do *Teshuvah* / 'return to a life of benefit' through genuine regret and resolutions for the future; he will commit himself to be much more cautious and conscientious with the power of his words.

OBJECTIVE CORRELATIVE

On a deeper level, *Midah K'neged Midah* / 'measure for measure' means not merely that the 'consequences' you receive are a reflection of what you put in, as in separation for separation — rather, you actually create the objective correlative experience through your actions, words, and thoughts.

According to this deeper understanding of reward and punishment, through your every action, word and thought in this world you project a 'vibrational template' into your surroundings. What you then experience are the objective correlations of your subjective actions, words and thoughts. Your subjective state is projected onto your objective reality, and as a 'consequence' you live in the very 'place' you yourself created.*

In the Torah, the first 'punishment' is that Adam and Chavah become mortal. They are first told that they are allowed to eat from every tree in the Garden besides the Tree of

---

* You are simultaneously living your life and creating your afterlife experiences — ענין שכר העה"ב שהוא מעשי ידי האדם עצמו שאחר פרידת נפשו מהגוף הוא העולה להתעדן ולהשביע נפשו בצחצחות האורות והכחות והעולמות הקדושים שנתוספו ונתרבו ממעש' הטובים. אבל האמת שהעה"ב הוא הוא מעשה ידי האדם עצמו שהרחיב והוסיף והתקין חלק לעצמו במעשיו... וכן עונש הגיהנם ענינו גם כן שהחטא עצמו הוא עונשו: *Nefesh haChayim*, Sha'ar 1:12.

Knowledge Good and Evil, and if they eat from that Tree they will become mortal and die. They eventually make that decision and become mortal. Through their actions, namely eating from the Tree of Duality (good and evil), they create an objective correlation: a world of duality, in which there is life and the opposite of life. As a result, their lives eventually end and they die.

With all of this in mind, we need to dig a little deeper to understand how the actions and words of the Metzora, which caused alienation and distance between people, created an objective reality of isolation in which they too must dwell.

CHITZONI / EXTERNAL & PENIMI / INTERNAL

Within the Creation narrative, the Torah describes two different ways that HaKadosh Baruch Hu 'creates the world'. First, there is a creation of the world through Divine speech, as in "Elokim said, let there be light," and "Let the earth sprout vegetation," and so on. And then there is the creation of man, in which Adam is fashioned from the dust of the earth, and then Hashem blows into his nostrils "a breath of life."

Chapter One of *Bereishis* tells the tale of Creation, until after the Seventh Day of Shabbos. Notably, this narrative only mentions the Name *Elokim* as the Creator of nature. Thus, all creations that are generated via Divine speech are associated with the Name Elokim. In contrast, at the beginning of Chapter Two, the section where Torah describes HaKadosh Baruch Hu blowing a breath of life into the nostrils of the human being, the Name *Hashem-Elokim* is introduced. *Hashem* (the Yud-Hei-Vav-Hei) is the Name of G-d that represents Infinity, the aspect that is beyond nature and all of Creation.

Olam / the world, nature and physicality, is connected with the "speech" of Elokim, while the soul and animating force of the human being is linked to the "breath" of Hashem. This means that our outer reality, the world of nature around us, is connected with Divine speech, while our inner reality, the world of Souls, is connected with Divine breath, a creative force which is deeper than speech, and is in fact the root of speech. This world of souls is intricately bound with the deepest 'interiority' of Hashem, so to speak. For מאן דנפח מתוכיה נפח / "One who blows (breathes) does so from within himself — from his innermost being" (*Tanya*, 2. See also Ramban, *Bereishis*, 2:7. *Emek haMelech*, 127, 3. Hakdamah, *Shefa Tal*). Therefore, when Hashem blows a breath of life into our nostrils, it comes from the deepest 'place' from within Himself.

Speech is a form of 'externalization' or outward expression. Everything in the outer world — plants, stones, rivers and animals, are rooted in the *Chitzoni* / external dimension of reality, which arises from 'speech'. The human being, on the other hand, exists on a deeper plane of existence. His external body is created through the speech of Elokim, the 'external dimension' of HaKadosh Baruch Hu, while his soul comes from the *Penimi* / inner dimension of reality, the 'innermost being' of HaKadosh Baruch Hu, *Keviyachol* / so to speak.

All of Creation is in the aspect of Chitzoni, except for the human being who alone has the potential to live from either the Penimi dimension or the Chitzoni dimension. As our body is related to the realm of Chitzoni, we have the choice to live like an 'animal', meaning reactively and instinctually, but we can also cultivate an inner freedom from circumstantial reactivity and live more deeply from a place of our Divine soul. This is what it means to be a true human being, a person rooted in the Divine Breath. In life, we can place primary value on the externals of empirical reality, the physicality of the world, or we can appreciate the inner, subtle, spiritual aspects of our deepest Divine life-force. The choice is ours.

Our sages tell us (*Erchin*, 6b) that עובדי כוכבים / idol worshipers generally speak a lot, blabbering and screaming to make themselves heard, whereas Klal Yisrael do not, as we prefer to keep silent (וטעמא דעובד כוכבים הוא דפעי אבל ישראל דלא פעי). The Gemara also says (*Chulin*, 133b), סתם עובד כוכבים מפעא פעי / "An ordinary idol worshiper yells." The connection between idol worship and speaking loudly is obvious. Idol worship is an extreme obsession with the world of Chitzoni, worshiping what is observable, as literally, the sun or moon. An idol worshiper only values and identifies with what can be 'seen', the Chitzoni world. He is disconnected from the internal mystery which lies far beyond the façade of what is seen. Basing his existence solely in the external physical world, his speech lacks subtlety and he cannot 'listen'; he merely turns up his volume and chatters like an animal without human awareness or restraint.

In speech itself, there are different levels. The Chitzoni of the Chitzoni, the most external of external forms of speech, is mindless, insensitive or crude yelling. The Penimi of the Chitzoni of speech includes speaking in a nicer, gentler tone. Idol worship is connected with the Chitzoni of the Chitzoni, an automatic reaction to the world as it appears on the surface. The idolator sees something, believes it, and then rushes to shout about it and broadcast his 'insights' to everyone.

There are seventy nations in the world. The letter that represents the number seventy is Ayin, which also means 'eye'. As such, the Maharal teaches (*Derush al haMitzvos*), there are seventy nations connected to the world of the 'eye', to the world that can be seen and observed. This superficial, external, reactive way of seeing — and worshiping what is seen — is also related to superficial forms of speech. Shallow seeing produces an urge to speak superficial words, a need to 'chat' and 'post a comment' about what was seen, to make the ego heard and gain 'followers' or promote one's opinion. In this state, there is no moment of mindful self-awareness between seeing and speaking.

Of course, many people from the 'Seventy Nations' are not 'idol worshipers', and do speak of their perceptions and ideas conscientiously, mindfully, discretely and intelligently. However, there is a powerful trend around the world to observe the surface of issues and events, and to compulsively broadcast that superficial image with shouting, imbalanced emotions and crude language.

Recall the discussion above, about how the existential nature of a person who lives enslaved to the superficiality of the world is someone who functions in a dynamic of ...וירא וַיַגֵד / vʾYar... vʾYagid / "He saw...and he spoke." When there is no buffer between the eye and the mouth, unfiltered seeing becomes unfiltered speaking, and there is no control or healthy boundaries in it.

There is a deeper way of living that is possible, connected to the art of truly listening, as explained. In touch with the inner world of hearing, we resonate with the Life Force of Creation, in harmony with the Creator of Creation. Klal Yisrael are the Children of Avraham, the disrupter and destroyer of idols and the revealer of the underlying Divine Unity. Through ancestry, Klal Yisrael is inherently connected to the Breath of Life, the inner world, the *Sod* / secret, the mystery of the hidden world, the world of *Shemia* / listening — as in *Shema Yisrael* / "Listen Israel..." As such, Klal Yisrael is blessed with refined, subtle, lucid speech, with a sense of restraint and quietude.

A person who chooses to focus mainly on the external, the obvious, and what can be seen, speaks impulsively about what is being seen. In the world of eyes, where there is nothing hidden as everything is observable, speech tumbles out of the mouth smoothly, in an uncomplicated movement from seeing to revealing to others what has been seen.

In contrast, a person who has a very deep inner life, and one who does not look at things simply as they appear, but rather probes beyond appearances and seeks to part the curtains and touch the hidden — speech may not come as easily or smoothly. Still, when such a person does find words, a revelation of deeper thinking occurs. This is completely unlike the conventional speech which merely parrots what is easily observed, and moves sound waves about through the air without pointing to any substantial meaning.

Moshe Rabbeinu, in his deep *Penimiyus* / inwardness had difficulty speaking, but when he did speak, it was a substantial revelation from within, a clear expression of Divinity and redemption.

Indeed, the deeper and more *Penimi* / inward one is, the more difficult it is for him to express what he perceives and understands. Wise people have said that the illustrious scholar and Rebbe, the Chidushei haRim, was a 'hidden Tzadik', as he concealed his true greatness in his scholarship. He hid behind the external persona of a great scholar, but his inner righteousness was beyond what can be revealed. In this way, a more superficial revelation (scholarship) served to conceal a deeper reality.

ANIMAL VS. HUMAN SPEECH

An animal, to the best of our estimation, barks or twitters with more fluency than humans can speak, even when they are speaking gibberish or repeating empty sounds. 'Animal' in Hebrew is בהמה / *Beheimah*, and this word can be subdivided into two, בה מה / *Bah Mah* / 'in her is *what?*'. A human being is called an *Adam*, which is numerically 45 / מה, which means 'What'. To be human is to ask questions, to probe; not to be satisfied with 'what is', or what merely seems to be real. What is irrefutably true? What am I really? A literal animal, or a person living from an extremely Chitzoni perspective, has swallowed his or her 'what'. Her powers of asking and listening for a deeper answer are suppressed and buried 'in her'.

A person who lives like a בהמה speaks easily, making general statements boldly and in a loud tone, as he feels confident that he is an authority and sees everything objectively. The more 'human' and Penimi a person is, the more reticent he is to make broad generalizations. He is aware of the fact that things are very often not what they appear to be. When he does express an idea, it is with humility, curiosity, and thoughtful softness: דברי חכמים בנחת נשמעים מזעקת מושל בכסילים / "The words of the wise are spoken softly, and are heeded sooner than those shouted by a lord in folly" (*Koheles*, 9:17).

Additionally, when a Penimi person speaks, there is a sense of mystery; even when he is revealing something of his inner life, it remains clear that there is still a deeper level of meaning or perception that remains hidden and unrevealed.

EXILE BEGINS & CONTINUES WITH CHITZONI SPEECH

On the Pasuk, "Indeed it has become known" (*Shemos*, 2:14), Rashi quotes the Medrash (*Shemos Rabbah*, 1:32) in which Moshe wonders to himself, מה חטאו ישראל מכל שבעים אומות להיות נרדים בעבודת פרך... / "Why are Klal Yisrael considered more sinful than all the Seventy Nations, that they should be subjugated with such back-breaking labor?" The answer he arrives at is somewhat surprising: אבל רואה אני שהם ראויים לכך / "However, now I see that they deserve it (because they speak Lashon haRa)."

The Galus of Klal Yisrael began with Yoseph speaking ill about his brothers, as discussed. Yoseph was sent to Egypt and thrown in prison as a result, and then the people as a whole were later afflicted with back-breaking labor, as they too continued to speak nonsense, and did not express their Penimiyus within their Chitzoniyus. Their speech was exiled, since it became exclusively connected to the world of the Chitzoni, thereby eclipsing their Penimi. As a mirror of this, they were externally forced to live in a world of pure Chitzoniyus, a world of exile.

WHY DOES A PERSON SPEAK LASHON HARA?

Now we can understand why people are prone to speak *Lashon haRa* / negative speech about another person, or merely just blabber nonsense about others. People who tend to speak about other people, instead of about ideas and deeper questions, are people who have very shallow inner lives.

What our sages call בעלי לשון הרע / 'masters of slander', of negative speech, are people who live in a very *Chitzoni* / superficial level of consciousness. Nothing deep is going on internally, intellectually or emotionally, and they choose to ignore the possibility of living deeper lives, to be truly human and connect with their soul, their Penimi. With no taste for things of the soul, they take interest instead in banter about their reactions to the surface appearances of other people.

Bigger people, those with vibrant inner lives and inquiring minds, speak about ideas, while small people, those with 'constricted' inner lives, speak about other people.

When people with smaller minds are chattering about other people, casually tossing words to the wind, it sounds like the sound of chirping birds. In Torah, נגעים / *Nega'im* / 'lesions' are physical symptoms of a spiritual defect that appears on the body, clothes or home of a person who has spoken Lashon haRa. Appropriately, the purification of this afflicted individual comes about through a spiritual ritual that involves birds: אמר הקב"ה הוא עושה מעשה פטיט לפיכך אמרה תורה יביא קרבן פטיט / "The Holy One, Blessed be He says: 'He acted with an act of chatter; therefore he is to bring an offering of birds, who chirp and chatter all the time.'" (*Erchin*, 16b. *Rashi*, Vayikra, 14:4. *Medrash Rabbah*, Vayikra, 16:7). This is another example of *Midah k'Neged Midah* / measure for measure, as discussed previously.

EVERY PERSON HAS BOTH PENIMI & CHITZONI

Now we can begin to understand the idea of נגעים. Every person has both an internal reality and an external one, a Penimi and Chitzoni.

On a more mental level, every person, no matter how they choose to live their life, has a 'soul', an inner *Sod* / 'secret' dimension behind immediate appearances — even if it is sometimes difficult to discover. This is the way a person exists for himself; the hidden place of his dreams, hopes, longings, yearnings, aspirations, even fantasies and worries. And every human being also has an outer, revealed expression of their life, the way they project themselves out into the world around them. The primary medium for this outward expression is the world of speech.

This dichotomy between inner self and outer expression is found overtly in human beings, whereas in the animal kingdom, the outer dimension is an uncomplicated expression of the inner dimension — there is no divide. This difference between humans and animals again reflects the nature of the creation of the human being, as discussed.

Hashem created the world through Divine Utterances, with speech being an external expression of Hashem's will. Accordingly, the inner and outer dimensions of non-human beings — the physical blade of grass and its 'vegetative soul', and the physical body of the lion and its 'animating soul' — were simultaneously created as they were spoken into being. Only the human being was created in a two stage process: 1) Adam / Chavah's body was created through Divine Speech, and then, 2) as the lump of clay lay on the ground, Hashem "blew into his nostrils a breath of life" (*Torah Ohr*, Bereishis, 3d). Whereas the human being's body, the 'clay' of the outer self, is connected with the world of Speech, his deeper self, his soul, is connected to Divine 'Breath'. Every person is part animal and part soul.

One's 'clay', his body and physical senses, is the medium through which he interacts with the world around him, the way he apprehends, navigates and functions in the natural world. One's internalized 'Divine Breath' is present in experiences and realities that cannot or should not be spoken about with words, for they are the existential ingredients of one's creation as an individual, one's personal secrets. Your unique, intimate world of *Sod* / sacred mystery is not designed to be shared with anyone outside of you. Only with your soul-mate — who is not 'outside of you', insofar as you actually share a 'single' soul — might your indescribable inner dimensions be consciously transmitted and shared, however even that cannot be a full sharing.

WHITE EXTERIOR REVEALING RED INTERIOR

Within the body itself there is a physical reflection of our dual nature of Chitzoni and Penimi. Our inner life is represented by the blood within the body, which, when exposed to oxygen, is an extremely vibrant red color. Our outer life is represented by the skin, a duller or less vibrantly colored aspect of the body.

A healthy person's *Ohr* / skin is subtly tinged with red and other colors that 'glow through' from under the skin. In this way, the 'outer self' reveals a hint of the inner reality that lies within it.

When a person dies, the skin loses the ruddiness of the life-blood within. A light skinned person's appearance turns white or gray when there is no longer a vivifying soul glowing within the body.

Similarly, in one who speaks Lashon haRa and is afflicted with נגעים, the pigmentation of the נגע becomes white and life-less. One who suffers with נגעים on the body, say our sages, is likened to one who is 'dead' (*Nedarim*, 64b). The color white and the idea of death are interconnected (*Sheim miShmuel*, Tazria, 672). On the part of the person who speaks Lashon haRa, there is a loss of inner vitality and connection to his Penimi life; a loss of soul. He thus dies a little, as his aspect of 'Divine Breath' is disregarded and obscured. In times past, this literally showed up as a deadening and whitening of his skin.

A Metzora was someone who had emptied himself of his Penimi reality and inner world of Sod, keeping nothing with-in. And thus the defining symptom of being a Metzora is to develop white spots on the skin; the colorlessness of death appears, as his inner reality is obscured by his superficiality, effectively displaying a form of decay.

A person became a Metzora because he spoke Lashon haRa, giving up his 'breath', the soul of his speech. As he chose to live as a Chitzoni, his body is disconnected from his Penimi, and he no longer reveals that which lies deep within.

When the Torah introduces the laws of the Metzora, it says, אדם כי־יהיה בעור־בשרו שאת / "An Adam who has upon his skin a swelling" (*Vayikra*, 13:2). *Adam* is the highest description used in characterizing a person.* Only an Adam, a human being in the fullest sense, could become a Metzora. An idol worshiper, connected only to the world of Chitzoniyus and disconnected from the inner world, cannot become a Metzora. Only someone who is consciously connected to their inner life, and then chooses to speak Lashon haRa, can 'lose' his Penimi and become afflicted with the symptoms of Tzara'as. A Metzora is someone whose Chitzoni is disconnected from the glow of his Penimi and his 'skin' obscures what lies 'beneath the skin'. His speech no longer reveals the life-giving Divine Breath within.

In fact, as the Alter Rebbe (*Likutei Torah*, Tazria) writes, it is not just any member of Klal Yisrael who can become a Metzora, only a Tzadik might contract such a psycho-spiritual condition. This is because only a person with a true and holy Penimi can experience a discernible *Siluk* / departing of their Penimiyus. People who anyway live their life on a Chitzoni level, with no glow of an inner life, like any animal, cannot become a Metzora.** Only a person who has a very vibrant and holy Penimi life, can lose his Penimiyus by speaking Lashon haRa.

Consequently, a Metzora must sit alone since he caused an alienation and separation between his inner life and his outer life. As he chose to live in *Galus* / exile from his inner life, he now needs to physically be alone in Galus, until he recovers his

---

* *Zohar* 3, 48a. See also *Yevamos*, 61a. This is the same even regarding a child: *Niddah*, 44a. אדם is thus always singular, and never in the plural as in אישים or אנשים.

** This is the reason why there is no longer any נגעים — sadly, today most people are living on the level of Chitzoni, as the Alter Rebbe explains.

inner-outer unity. He therefore lives in the objective place that he has subjectively created for himself. The *Makif* / projected reality in which he dwells is the one he generated by exiling his own inner self.

REVEALING THROUGH PARTIAL CONCEALMENT

Proper self-revelation and communication avoids over-exposure and 'wearing your soul on your sleeve'. There is a way of living and speaking in which you partially reveal something, yet simultaneously conceal much more.

In *Maseches Pesachim*, Chazal teach at length on how a person should speak with *Lashon Nekiah* / pure speech, and not speak negatively or superficially, even when the information is true. For example (3b): "Rav Kahana fell ill, and the Sages sent Rebbe Yehoshua, son of Rav Idi, as their emissary to him. They said to him: 'Go and assess what Rav Kahana's condition is at present.' Rebbe Yehoshua, son of Rav Idi, went and found that Rav Kahana had passed away. He rent his garment and turned his garment around so the tear would be behind him and would not be immediately apparent, and he was crying as he was coming. They said to him: 'Did Rav Kahana pass away?' He said to them: I did not say that, as the Pasuk states: 'And he who utters slander is a fool.'" Rebbe Yehoshua had already revealed, in a subtler, deeper way, that Rav Kahana had passed away. There was no reason to spell it out, much less to use a 'negative' statement such as 'He has died.'

In addition, even a subtle hint in one's speech can reveal hidden realities of the soul within them.

The Gemara (*Pesachim*, 4b) says, שמע. אמרי: דונו דיני. ההוא דאמר: דונו דיני. אמרי: שמע מינה מדן קאתי, דכתיב: "דן ידין עמו כאחד שבטי ישראל". ההוא דהוה קא אזיל ואמר: אכיף ימא אסיסני בירואתא. בדקו ואשכחוהו דמזבולון קאתי, דכתיב: "זבולן לחוף ימים ישכן" / "A certain man would regularly say, whenever involved in conflict, 'Adjudicate my case (*Dunu Dini*).' The Sages commented: Learn from this that he descends from the tribe of Dan, as it is written: 'Dan will judge (*Yadin*) his people like one of the Tribes of Israel.' Another man would regularly take a walk and say, 'The bushes on the seashore are cypresses; (items located by the sea) are more beautiful than those found in other places.' They examined his lineage and found that he descended from the Tribe of Zevulun, as it is written: 'Zevulun shall dwell by the seashore.'"

DIFFERENCE BETWEEN גאל / REDEEMED AND גלה / EXILED

As mentioned above, גאל / redeemed and גלה / exiled share the same root word: גל, which also means 'to reveal' or 'a wave'. Earlier, we began to explore the question of how redemption and exile can share the same root word. Now we need to examine the connection between 'revelation', 'exile' and 'redemption'.

One marked difference between the word גלה and גאל is that גאל / 'redeemed' has the letter Aleph within it. In redemption, there is a revelation of the *Aleph*, the 'Oneness' of Hashem. To be redeemed is to reveal the Penimi, the semi-hidden Oneness of reality, within the Chitzoni, the apparent multiplicity of reality — while paradoxically allowing it to remain Penimi.

There are two types of revelation: revealing exile and revealing redemption. Galus is the Chitzoni with no Penimi
presence; 'everything is revealed' because there is an absence
of anything deeper. This is the world of *Akum* / idolatry, and
the world of *Ayin* / the eye, of seeing and rushing to conclusions and loudly chattering about them like a bird, just creating
more noise.

Again, the faculty of speech was in exile in Egypt. Slaves
have no authentic voice as they have no inner story, no Penimi,
to express. The devastating crushing of their humanity robs
them of their inner life, their dreams, aspirations, wants, and
longings. Over time, a slave begins to have nothing to say, they
have no story to tell and nothing to share.

When, G-d forbid, a human being is reduced to a statistic,
they are robbed of their inner personal uniqueness and experience. If all a person can do is focus on their immediate physical
survival, they may end up losing their inner life, and eventually
their speech may begin to resemble the chattering of animals.

REVEALING THE WONDER AND INNER MYSTERY

Geulah / redemption is when there is an Aleph within the
Gal / revealing. The letter Aleph spelled out, as in אלף, has
the same letters as the word פלא / *Pele* / wonder and mystery.
Aleph is the 'mystery', the hidden, the Penimiyus of every existence and situation.

To be in a redemptive state of mind means to reveal our inner Pele, and to experience ever-deeper mysteries and wonders within Creation. Redeemed consciousness is sensing the *Aleph* / the 'Oneness' and Pele of HaKadosh Baruch Hu within everything and everyone at all times.

When a person in a state of inner redemption speaks, he reveals what is really on his mind and heart. The words he speaks are דברים / words that are יוצאים מן הלב / emanating from his inner heart (and thus they can enter another person's heart: דברים היוצאים מן הלב נכנסים אל הלב — *Sefer haYashar*. See *Shaloh*, Sha'ar Osyos, Lamed). Instead of simply speaking דברים הרבה / 'lots of words', or פטפוטי דברים / chirping words (Rashi, *Vayikra*, 14:4), the more redeemed an individual is, the more his words come from the depths of his heart.

Gal with an Aleph, as in *Ga'al* / redeemed, means 'to reveal' when and what is needed; to speak when one must not remain silent, and to do so with a sense of deeper meaning, positivity, and purpose. When a person living a more redemptive life does speak, he is never cheap with his words, and does not denigrate the sacred power of speech. His words are connected to a more Penimi reality, the mystery and the inner life of that which is being expressed, yet not fully revealed. The Sod is revealed while still remaining Sod. Whatever is expressed is only a hint to a much greater mystery that remains concealed, even to the one speaking. A Sod is not simply 'secret' because it has not yet been revealed, rather it is in essence a Sod, something that can never actually be fully revealed or comprehended.

When someone just exposes all of their thoughts in a torrent of words, the listeners become aware that there is no sense of mystery in him. There is only *Chitzoniyus* / superficiality, only 'what the eye can see'. And this is the *Bechinah* / concept of an idol worshiper — meaning human consciousness when it is completely limited and endarkened by the world of the 'observable', the world of superficial images and desires.

And so, when the Penimi, the Tzadik / *Adam*, slips spiritually and reveals what he shouldn't reveal, becoming a Motzei Ra, a Peh Ra, he then loses his Penimiyus. He loses the red color of his internal Chayus, and thus his 'skin', his Chitzoni, turns 'white'. He takes on the appearance of 'death', as there is no longer true vitality beneath the surface of what he is saying. And thus he becomes a Metzora whose consequence is to live for a time in Galus and isolation.

Exile is the loss of inner life, represented by the loss of the Metzora's home, his homeland, his identity or his life force. Only someone who has an inner life can lose it and be exiled from it. Only someone with real authenticity can lose touch with their authentic self, and eclipse their inner light with an external expression.

Galus is a state of Chitzoniyus in which there is no Penimiyus, and 'everything is revealed' because there is nothing behind the facade. This is the reason why *Galus* is connected with the word *Gal* / 'wave' or 'to reveal'. When a person reveals just their superficial, external self, for example in the over-exposure of the body, the soul is eclipsed and isolated 'outside the camp'. Total exposure is cheap and signals a loss of mystery. This is the epitome of exile, and it is emblematic of the exile we are living in currently: over-revelation and exposure of the 'skin' of superficial life, without leaving any mystery or possibility for imagination.

REVEALING HASHEM'S PRESENCE EVEN IN EXILE

Although many people are in an inner state of redemption, we still find ourselves in a historical, collective exile. We need to know that there is a deeper purpose and intention in this: Hashem wants us to be in this collective state in order for us to complete a certain task that can only be achieved in exile.

Again, *Galah* / גלה / exiled, and *Ga'al* / גאל / redeemed, share the same root, Gimel-Lamed, גל / *Gal*, which means revealing. Both exile and redemption are about revelation; we reveal Hashem's Presence in this world whether we are in a state of exile and dispersion, or redemption and unity.

In גלה / exile, we are Gal-Hei, 'revealing the Hei'. The letter Hei is made of a Dalet with a Yud (as the Maharal explains). Dalet (4) refers to the four corners of the world to which Klal Yisrael is dispersed in exile. The Yud is the *Nekudah* / 'point' of Divinity that is revealed in Galus, in our survival within exile.

The Yud is also the Yid, who by the mere act of survival, and more so when he is spiritually proactive, reveals the Yud within the four corners of the world. This is a central *Tachlis* /

purpose in our being in exile, yet this is only the 'lower unity'. The higher level of unity is when we will reveal that there is *only* Hashem; *Ein Od Milvado* / "There is nothing else but The One" (*Devarim*, 4:35). This higher unity will be revealed with the coming Geulah, when there will be a *Gal* / revelation of the *Aleph* / Oneness of Hashem.

MOSHE REVEALING THE HIDDEN ONE

Moshe, whose name means 'drawn from the water', is the one whom Hashem chooses to facilitate the process of the Redemption from Egypt. This is because Moshe is the one who draws from the בלב ...עמוקים מים / deep waters in the heart" (*Mishlei*, 20:5), and properly reveals these depths to the 'outside'. He is the one to bring the Geulah — *Gal* with an Aleph — Aleph being the silent letter, the ineffable interior point of redemption and perfection within Klal Yisrael.

By revealing the Aleph within his people, Moshe also reveals the *Alufo shel Olam* / Master of the Universe to the world. Moshe's mother's name was יוכבד / Yocheved. The letters in this name, say the authors of Tosefos, spell the word כבודי / My glory (*Pirushei haTorah, l'Baalei Tosefos*, Shemos, 6:20. *Asarah Ma'amaros*, Ma'amar Chikur Din, 3:4). Moshe is the one who subtly yet publicly reveals the *Kevod Hashem* / Glory and Honor of Hashem that is hidden within all human beings.

By revealing the essence of Klal Yisrael, Moshe returns them from their exile and frees them to be who they are: a holy people, a people of the Aleph. The early Rishonim call Moshe

אדון המאיר / the Master who Illuminates (Rabbeinu Nissim ben Yaakov (Gaon), *Chibur Yafeh me-haYeshua* (Israel, 1970) p. 11). Moshe is personally illuminated, and he thus is able to illuminate Klal Yisrael, empowering them to attain their highest, deepest potential.

This is Geulah—to live authentically in such a way that is consciously connected with the *Aleph* / the Divine spark and mystery within; and to reveal it outward, into the world, in proper, positive ways. The ultimate Geulah is a time when the Kevod Hashem, the deeper Aleph, will be revealed in all places, at all times, and within all living beings.

Chapter Four:
Was the Exile Inevitable or Due to Our Actions?
THE EGYPTIAN EXILE AND ITS MACROCOSMIC & MICROCOSMIC REASONS

EVERYTHING IN THIS WORLD OCCURS ON MULTIPLE levels and due to multiple intersecting purposes. There is a scientific, natural explanation for an earthquake, for example, while our sages tell us (*Berachos*, 59a, in the name of a necromancer who told Rav Ketina) that the source of earthquakes is that when HaKadosh Baruch Hu remembers His children who are suffering among the nations of the world, Hashem sheds two tears into the Great Sea. Their reverberations are sensed from one end of the earth to the other, and that is an earthquake. The rainbow has a natural explanation, yet, it is also a sign of the covenant that Hashem made with mankind. There are outer and inner reasons for all events and phenomena, and each is true on its level; they are thus not mutually exclusive but collaboratively comprehensive.

What, we must then ask, were the reasons and purposes of the Exile in Egypt, and the painful experience of enslavement? Yes, on the surface, Pharaoh observed that Klal Yisrael was multiplying and increasing, and he was afraid for political reasons, but what was the deeper reason? And, from the perspective of the enslaved, why did Klal Yisrael 'deserve' this harsh treatment?

Why was Avraham told that his descendants would be oppressed in a land that was not theirs? Why couldn't we have become a holy people without a traumatic past? Why, in particular, did we need to begin our collective history as slaves, or even earlier, as idol worshipers, in Egypt? It is fascinating that the Torah itself does not tell us why Klal Yisrael had to go through this ordeal, nor of any collective sins preceding the descent into Egypt that might have caused it. Such questions of deeper meaning beneath the surface of the text and of our history requires elucidation.

As the Zohar (Shemos, 14b) teaches, אמר רבי אלעזר לרבי שמעון אבוי, מה חמא קודשא בריך הוא, לנחתא ישראל, למצרים בגלותא. אמר ליה חדא שאלתא את שאיל, או תרין. אמר ליה תרין. גלותא למה, ולמצרים למה / "Rebbe Eliezer said to his father, Rebbe Shimon, 'What did Hashem observe (that caused Hashem) to lower Klal

Yisrael to the Exile of Egypt?' Replied Rebbe Shimon, 'Are you asking one or two questions?' 'Two,' said Rebbe Eliezer, 'why exile, and why in Egypt?'"

Regarding this complicated issue, we must look to the Arizal, who offered numerous reasons for the Exile (*Sha'ar haPesukim*, Shemos).

GOSSIPERS AND INFORMERS

In order to understand the reasons for Galus, let us begin with Rashi's simple *Peshat* / literal interpretation of the *P'sukim* / verses in the Torah. Rashi aspires to interpret the text in the simplest possible manner, albeit based on the words of the sages, and rarely his own ideas.

In the Pasuk where Moshe kills the Egyptian slave-beater, and then discovers that people know about it, Moshe says, אכן נודע הדבר / "Indeed, the matter has become known" (*Shemos*, 2:14). Rashi comments, in Moshe's words "Now it is known to me the matter about which I have been puzzled: namely, in what way has Klal Yisrael sinned more than all the Seventy Nations, that they alone should be oppressed by this crushing servitude? But now I see that they do in fact deserve this [for they have been speaking and gossiping'" (*Medrash Rabbah*, Shemos, 1:30).

In other words, Moshe sees that there are informers and gossipers among Klal Yisrael, as his actions have become known to everyone, and he says, "Now I understand why Klal

Yisrael deserves such harsh punishment — because they are informers and gossipers." Thus, Rashi is seemingly suggesting that they have come to 'deserve' Galus as a consequence of their Lashon haRa.

Yet, upon closer reflection, it is clear that Rashi is not saying that this is the reason for Galus itself, but, rather, the reason they were oppressed and subjected to crushing servitude within that Galus (as Sifsei Chachamim writes, אף ע"פ שגזר עליהם ועבדום וענו אותם, מ"מ בעבודת פרך לא נגזר עליהם, וזה הי' תמוה בעיניו). Alternatively, it is also possible that Rashi is explaining why they were not worthy of redemption. On the other hand, the Medrash does say it clearly: היה משה מהרהר בלבו ואומר מה חטאו ישראל שנשתעבדו מכל האומות, כיון ששמע דבריו אמר לשון הרע יש ביניהן היאך יהיו ראויין לגאולה / "Moshe was pondering in his heart what sin Israel had done, that they, among all nations, should be enslaved. Since people had heard of his deeds, it means there was Lashon haRa between them, and this is how they had deserved to be exiled" (*Medrash Rabbah*, Shemos, 1:7. *Tanchuma*, Shemos, 10, has the exact same account).

However, we need to look beyond the Medrash to uncover the actual reason for the exile and enslavement, because already at the *Bris Bein haBesarim* / the great covenant that HaKadosh Baruch Hu entered with Avram (Avraham), Hashem tells him, ידע תדע כי־גר יהיה זרעך בארץ לא להם ועבדום וענו אתם ארבע מאות שנה / "Know well that your offspring shall be strangers in a land not theirs, and they shall be enslaved and oppressed for four hundred years" (*Bereishis*, 15:13).

Avraham is told that his offspring will be exiled and oppressed for four hundred years, starting from the birth of Yitzchak (Rashi, *ad loc*. See *Megilah*, 9a, Rashi, *ad loc*). It thus appears that hundreds of years before Klal Yisrael was enslaved in Egypt, there was already a Divine decree for exile. This does not answer the question of *why* the exile, but it does trace the root and 'reason' for the exile to an event a couple of hundred years prior to Moshe Rabbeinu's observation of widespread Lashon haRa. We too must go deeper.

THE RAMBAN'S REASON

The Ramban (*Bereishis*, 12:10) writes a big *Chidush* / novel interpretation regarding Avraham's descent to Egypt in a time of famine. Avraham tells the *Mitzrim* / Egyptians that his wife Sarah was his sister, thinking that if they knew she was his wife, they would kill him in order to take her for themselves.

"You should know that our father Avraham committed a חטא גדול בשגגה / great unintentional sin, when he brought his righteous wife to stumble into (the possibility of) transgression because of his fear of getting killed, and he should have trusted Hashem to save him and his wife and all that was his, because Hashem has power to help and to save. Also, his leaving the Land of Israel due to famine, (even though) he had originally been commanded to do so, was the commission of a transgression. Hashem would have saved him from dying (even) in a famine. And because of this deed, it was decreed that his offspring would be exiled in Egypt under the hand of Pharaoh, במקום המשפט שמה הרשע והחטא / 'In a place where there is judgment, there was negativity and sin.'"

Yet, as the Maharal asks (*Gevuros Hashem*, 5), besides the fact that לא יומתו אבות על בנים / "Children should not be put to death (nor punished) for (the sins of their) parents" (*Devarim*, 24:16), this interpretation is quite puzzling. For, a little later on in the Torah, we find Avraham *again* tells people that Sarah is his sister (*Bereishis*, 20:2), and this is *after* the Bris Bein haBesarim, when he received the news about the four hundred years of exile. If deceiving the Mitzrim about Sarah triggered the exile, and he was informed of this consequence at the Bris Bein haBesarim, surely Avraham would not have made the same mistake again?!

Another reason why the Ramban's interpretation is such a tremendous Chidush, is that this is not one of the reasons that Chazal offer*. And in general, as the Akeidas Yitzhak asks, א"כ היה עונש כבד ועצום על חטא קל כזה / "If so (if the deception regarding Sarah was the cause of the exile), the devastating harsh punishment was brought on by an apparently very light transgression. In other words, the punishment does not fit the crime (*AkeidasYitzchak*, Sha'ar 36:1, 6). And so, we must still go deeper.

THE THREE REASONS OF CHAZAL

HaKadosh Baruch Hu tells Avraham, the first 'Jew', that his offspring will be oppressed as strangers in a foreign land

---

* Although, the Ramban customarily offers interpretations in the Peshat of the Pasuk that are not consistent with Chazal.

for 400 years. This Pasuk refers to a *Galus* / exile but not an enslavement, certainly not an enslavement of brutally "harsh work." Hence there are two questions: why Galus and why specifically in the hard conditions of Egypt? To explore these questions, let us begin with the words of *Chazal* / our sages.

Chazal (*Nedarim*, 32a) offer three reasons for Klal Yisrael's enslavement in Egypt: אמר רבי אבהו אמר רבי אלעזר מפני מה נענש אברהם אבינו ונשתעבדו בניו למצרים מאתיים ועשר שנים מפני שעשה אנגרייא בתלמידי חכמים שנאמר וירק את חניכיו ילידי ביתו / "Rebbe Avuah said that Rebbe Elazar said: For what reason was Avraham our Patriarch punished and his children enslaved to Egypt for two-hundred and ten years? This is because he made a military draft (*Angarya*) of Torah scholars, as it is stated: 'He led forth his trained men, born in his house'" (*Bereishis*, 14:14). These 'trained men' that he enlisted to battle were his disciples, Torah scholars.

ושמואל אמר מפני שהפריז על מדותיו של הקב"ה שנאמר במה אדע כי אירשנה / "And Shmuel said, '…It is because he overly examined (*Hifriz*) the characteristics of the Holy One, Blessed be He, as it is stated: "Whereby shall I know that I shall inherit it?" (*Bereishis*, 15:8).

ורבי יוחנן אמר שהפריש בני אדם מלהכנס תחת כנפי השכינה שנאמר תן לי הנפש והרכוש קח לך / "And Rebbe Yochanan said: He was punished because he distanced people from entering under the wings of the Divine Presence (converting them to Monotheism), as it is stated that the king of Sodom said to him: 'Give

me the people and take the goods to yourself'" (*Bereishis* 14:21).
If he had not listened to the king of Sodom and had kept the
prisoners of war with him, he would have brought them under
the wings of the Divine Presence.

These are the three reasons offered by Chazal in
Gemara / the Talmud. But the real question is, what is the
Midah-Kneged-Midah / measure-for-measure 'reason'? Why
would Galus be a punishment for drafting Torah scholars into
battle, examining the characteristics of the Holy One, or fail-
ing to convert idolatrous prisoners to Monotheism? What is
the connection between these three mistakes and Galus?*

REASONS OFFERED BY THE MEKUBALIM

Above are the reasons offered in Gemara. The other major
reason is offered in the 'inner sources' — in the *Zohar*, Arizal,
and other *Mekubalim* / Kabbalists. It seems from these sources
that the whole purpose of Galus Mitzrayim is to 'refine' Klal
Yisrael and to 'remove' the dirt that was attached to mankind

---

* לעולם אל ישנה אדם בנו בין הבנים, שבשביל משקל שני סלעים מילת שנתן יעקב ליוסף
יותר משאר בניו, נתקנאו בו אחיו ונתגלגל הדבר וירדו אבותינו למצרים / "A person
should never distinguish one of his sons from among the other sons, as
due to the weight of two Sela of fine wool that Yaakov gave to Yoseph
beyond what he gave the rest of his sons (in making him the striped coat),
his brothers became jealous of him and the matter unfolded and our forefathers descended to Egypt": *Shabbos*, 10b. Says Tosefos, ואע"ג דבלאו הכי
נגזר דכתיב ועבדום וענו אותם שמא לא היה נגזר עליהם עינוי כ"כ / "Even though at
any rate it (slavery) was decreed, as it says 'And they will enslave them and
oppress them,' perhaps such *great* oppression was not decreed upon them."
This is therefore not a *reason* for the exile, rather, for the *hardship* of exile.

from the *Cheit Eitz haDa'as* / sin of eating from the Tree of Knowledge. To cleanse away the *Zuhama* / impurity that became attached to the human race, Klal Yisrael needed to be refined through harsh exile, much like gold becomes refined through fire. Then they could accept the Torah and begin to raise up the rest of the world.

For example, the Ramak, Rebbe Moshe Cordovero, writes the following (*Pardes Rimonim*, Sha'ar 13:3) — ענין גלות מצרים להיות
שער שזרח אור אברהם היה הקב"ה משפיע שפע נשמותיו בהמובחרים
שבין האנשים כי כן היה ראוי. כ"א לא חטא אדה"ר היה לו כתנות אור
באלף שהוא רומז לאחדות השם ויחודו. אבל כשחטא וערבב קדש בחול
וחול בקדש ובא נחש על חוה והטיל בה זוהמא, נתערב הקדש והוליד
לקין קינא דמסאבותא והיה העולם הולך ומתקלקל והפת מתעפש ולכן
נתלבש בכתנות עו"ר שהוא שבעים אומות [כמניין ע' שבעור]. ולא חלקם
הקב"ה לכבוד שמים שעדיין לא זרח אור אברהם עד דור הפלגה וחלקם
הקב"ה כאו"א לפי מקומו הראוי לו. ונטיל לחלקו אברהם שהוא אור ונתקן
כתנות אור באלף ולא תיקון גמור כי עדין היו סיגים מעורבים בכסף וכסף
בסיגים, שבין האומות היו נשמות קדושות ובין הקדושה היתה עדיין זוהמא
/ "The matter of the exile from Egypt was that until the light of Avraham shone, HaKadosh Baruch Hu was bestowing the abundance upon His souls, the chosen ones among the people, because it was appropriate. For if Adam haRishon had not sinned, he would have had his cloak of light which hinted at the Oneness (Aleph) of Hashem, and (Adam's) unification (with Hashem). However, when he sinned, there was a mingling of the holy with the profane, and the profane with the holy, and the Snake came to Chavah and cast impurity on her

and (her) holiness was mixed (with it), and jealousy and impurity was produced (in her child) Kayin, and the world began to be more and more spoiled and the bread (true spiritual nourishment) more and more stale, and thus we were clothed in the garments of skin, which is the Seventy Nations, corresponding to the numerical value of the letter Ayin (70) in *'Ohr* / skin (which replaced the Aleph in *Ohr* / Light). And in Divine honor, HaKadosh Baruch Hu did not divide (disperse) them, for the Light of Avraham did not shine until the Generation of the Tower of Bavel. And then HaKadosh Baruch Hu did divide them, with each and every one of them appropriate to his place (spiritual level). And He cast His portion upon Avraham, who was Light, and repaired his cloak of Light with an Aleph (and not an Ayin, as in skin). However, this was not a complete repair, for there was still slag mixed into the silver and silver mixed into the slag, for among the (idolatrous) nations there were still holy souls, and within holiness there was still spiritual impurity and pollution" (See also Shaloh, *Meseches Pesachim*, Derush 6).

In the words of the Arizal (Sha'ar haKavanos, Derushei Pesach, Derush 1): One should know that *Neshamos* / souls are like gold that is formed in the belly of the earth and when the gold is extracted, the gold is filled with dirt and slag until you cannot call it gold — until the wise refiner of the gold removes the slag again and again, and purifies it over and over until gradually the slag is separated from the gold, and the existence of pure gold is recognized.... The same is with Neshamos. Since the *Cheit* / sin of Adam, the *Tov v'Ra* / good and evil are mixed together.... and reality needs refining to remove the *Ra* / negative and impure from the Tov / positive and pure. Thus, the Pasuk says, ויוצא אתכם מכור הברזל ממצרים להיות לו לעם נחלה כיום הזה / "He took them/us and brought out of Egypt, that iron furnace (refinery), to be His very own people, as is now the case" (*Devarim*, 4:20). The gold is thus refined and becomes pure through such a process.

From these sources in the Sod of Torah, it seems that the root of *Galus* / exile *precedes* Avraham and goes back to the *Cheit Eitz haDa'as* / the sin of the Tree of Good and Evil. In addition, Galus is not seen as a micro-cosmic event stemming from one person and affecting one nation, rather it is a cosmic event, involving the whole of humankind, and rooted within humanity's common primordial ancestors, Adam and Chavah.

While the Gemara relates the Galus to Avraham, the first Jew, the Penimiyus sources relate the Galus to the Cosmic event of the Eating from the Tree of Good and Evil, to Adam and Chavah, the first human beings. Furthermore, the reason for exile is thus to cleanse the dirt, remove the impurities, and refine the spiritual gold — for the entire human race.

FIRE AND EXILE REDUCING EXISTENCE & ALLOWING FOR A NEW BIRTH

Another way of saying this (see *Si'ach Yitzchak*, Derush l'Shabbos haGadol), is that through the breaking down of Klal Yisrael's existence and identity in the depths of exile, their *Tzurah* /

form was reduced and broken apart, and thus they were able to be re-birthed into a new, higher, and miraculous reality. This is much like Avram himself, who was first thrown into a fire and only then emerged as Avraham — one who can speak with HaKadosh Baruch Hu and enter into a covenant with Him.

Avraham's passing through fire alive means that he shed his old identity, allowing it to be consumed, and then emerged in a miraculous state of being, one that defied nature. This is connected with the fact that even though it had been written in the stars that he could not have children with Sarah, he was able to rise above nature, 'above the sky', and was thus able to have a child with her, Yitzchak.

This is similar to the journey of Klal Yisrael. We needed to go through the 'seven gates of Gehenom' — the fires of exile and harsh labor — in order to emerge cleansed, refined, and divested of our limited identity, marred nature and spiritual decay, and to become an eternal, infinite, miraculous people.

To become a 'people of miracles', so that we could survive and thrive despite all odds, we too needed to go through a 'furnace', to burn off all the natural effects of the Tree of Knowledge of Good and Evil, in order to become miraculous.

Human beings are partly composed of dust; laboring under the forces of nature. Through the breakdown of our humanity during our exile, we reached a higher, more refined level, beyond 'nature'. We became collectively a בריה חדשה / 'new creation'.

According to this perspective, Galus began with the birth of the first born Jew, Yitzchak. Yitzchak is born despite all odds, despite his parents being advanced in age, and despite 'fate' predicting that they would not have a child together. To counteract these 'natural forces' of physicality and fate, Hashem took Avraham outside his tent and said, "Look toward heaven and count the stars, if you are able to count them." And He added, "So shall your offspring be" (*Bereishis*, 15:5). Says the Medrash (*Bereishis Rabbah*, 44:12), "Hashem took him outside his perceived limitations and said, 'Go forth from (give up) your astrological speculations that suggest you will not raise a son.'" In other words: Rise above the stars, the world of static predictability, elevate yourself beyond the natural world and connect yourself to the miraculous world of Faith, of Emunah, and of Deveikus with the Infinite One. Have faith and you can transcend all 'fate'.

As such, the very beginning of the Jewish people is a miracle, something that by all available evidence should not have come to be. This is true of the first born Jew, Yitzchak, whose name means 'Laughter', suggesting some kind of cosmic 'joke' or anomaly, and even more so with Klal Yisrael, who were born as a people from within the womb of an oppressive empire. The forging of Klal Yisrael into Am Yisrael / the nation of Israel was achieved under the harsh conditions of deep enslavement and exile on all levels. Such conditions are normally and naturally are unconducive to the forming of a unified people, however, in this case they were applied specifically in order for Klal

Yisrael to model and manifest a miraculous, nature defying connection to the Infinite Eternal One, and thus become Infinite, Eternal. Indeed, the greatest miracle of all of history is Klal Yisrael, the miracle of the Jewish people (Siddur Sulam Beis Keil, *Ya'avetz*, Hakdamah).

Our very lives testify to the presence and possibility of the miraculous, and in that we are able to reveal the Infinite One within the midst of the many. As such, our collective mission and purpose as a people is to reveal the *Achdus Hashem* / Oneness of Hashem within this manifold world.

DUAL META-SOURCE OF EXILE

In this way, the microcosmic or national roots of our exile, as well as the power to rise above it, are connected with Avraham, the first 'Jew', while the macrocosmic or global roots of more general existential exile are connected to Adam and Chavah. Yet, we still might ask, which of these reasons is the most defining of our experience? Is it one of the three 'national' reasons offered by the Gemara or the one 'global' reason offered by the Zohar and the Mekubalim?

Every experience in life is simultaneously part of global and macrocosmic events and effects, as well as individual, tribal and microcosmic events and effects. Macrocosmic influences are for the most part beyond our individual choice, as they are general expressions of the way the world functions from the place of Hashem's *Yediah* / knowing. The Divine Yediah is characterized by *Hanhagas haYichud* / the pathways of Unity, meaning, the universe is always being guided toward the direction of unity, always progressing and evolving spiritually, no matter how chaotic the world might appear. This is the root of faith. Microcosmic events stem from our place of *Bechirah* / choice, the dimension in which we are co-creators of our lives. This level of reality is governed more by the *Hanhagas haMishpat* / the pathways of justice, or cause-and-effect. This is the field of action.

There is a 'big story' and a 'small story', a place of Yediah or general foreknowledge, and a place of Bechirah and specific human choice.*

THE NARRATIVE / PLACE OF CHOICE & THE META-NARRATIVE / THE PLACE OF DIVINE KNOWING

There is a bigger story of history, a meta-narrative, in which we are just 'pawns' of the 'cosmic events' that are playing out through us. From our limited perspective, this is an unstoppable, and perhaps unconscious, force of the universe. Really, HaKadosh Baruch Hu is moving and evolving Creation toward *Yichud* / unity, irrespective of whether or not our actions are consistent with the grand plan. This is the idea of Hanhagas haYichud and Divine providence.

An example of this kind of Divine providence is played out

---

* Yet, it should be pointed out that both these paradigms are simultaneously true, although comprehension of this paradox is beyond the reach of logic.

in the sale of Yoseph, and the subsequent descent of Yaakov with his family into Egypt. From a microcosmic perspective, certainly the brothers were guilty of selling Yoseph and they needed to do Teshuvah. In fact, even today, Klal Yisrael carries the burden of this wrongdoing, and we are collectively involved in making Teshuvah for their action. The Mitzvah (which technically could only be achieved when there was a *Beis haMikdash* / Holy Temple in Jerusalem) to give a half *Shekel* / coin each year was an atonement for this wrongdoing, as each of the ten brothers had received a half Shekel from the sale of Yoseph (Yerushalmi, *Shekalim*).

Yet, from the macrocosmic narrative, Yoseph needed to be sold into Egypt so that he could become the second in command of Egypt, so that he could give food to his family, so that the entire exile into Egypt could begin, and so that Klal Yisrael could eventually be refined and rebirthed as an eternal people.

As Yoseph tells his brothers, ואתם חשבתם עלי רעה אלקים חשבה לטבה / "You thought to do me harm, but Elokim thought to do good" (*Bereishis*, 50:20). From the place of your distinct, individual microcosmic Bechirah, you did something terrible. Yet, there is a bigger picture and a deeper vision: the Divine unfolding of events exactly how Hashem wanted them to be. You were just pawns.

THE "SIN" OF EATING FROM THE TREE OF KNOWLEDGE

Such a double-layered story, with an overt narrative and an inner meta-narrative, also occurs within one of the most cosmic of events in the Torah, the apparently free-choice sin to eat from the Tree of Knowledge. Yet, Chazal read this too as part of Yediah, and Hanhagas HaYichud. The Medrash (*Tanchuma*, Vayeshev, 4) speaks of the eating from the Tree of Knowledge Good and Evil, as follows:

לכו חזו מפעלות אלקים נורא עלילה על בני אדם. אמר רבי יהושע בן קרחה, אף הנוראות שאתה מביא עלינו, בעלילה את מביאן. בא וראה כשברא הקדוש ברוך הוא את העולם, מיום הראשון ברא מלאך המות. מנין, אמר רבי ברכיה, משום שנאמר: וחשך על פני תהום זה מלאך המות המחשיך פניהם של בריות. ואדם נברא בששי ועלילה נתלה בו שהוא / הביא את המיתה לעולם, שנאמר: כי ביום אכלך ממנו מות תמות.

"Come and see the works of Hashem: He acts circuitously in His dealings with the children of Adam.' Rebbe Yehoshua the son of Karcha declared: 'Even the fearful experiences that You inflicted upon us You brought about circuitously.' For example, when the Holy One, blessed be He, created His world, He fashioned the Angel of Death on the first day. How do we know that? Rebbe Berechiah said: We know it from the Pasuk, 'And darkness was on the face of the deep.' 'Darkness' refers to the Angel of Death, for he darkens the face of man. Adam was created on the Sixth Day and Hashem informed him in a roundabout way that he had brought death into the world, as it is said: 'For in the day that you eat thereof, you shall surely die....'"

ועלילה נתלה בו שהוא הביא את המיתה לעולם / "An *Alilah* / false accusation was placed on Adam, when it was implied that he had brought death to the world" by eating from the Tree, when in fact, the Angel of Death was created on the First Day of Creation, and Adam did not eat from the Tree until after he was created on Day Six. Death was already a part of life from Day One, and Adam had no hand in that.

On a macrocosmic level, נורא עלילה על בני אדם / "He acts circuitously in His dealings with the children of Adam," means that the death sentence incurred through the eating from the Tree of Knowledge was a 'set up' and beyond Adam and Chavah's capacity of choice. They *had* to eat from the Tree, and they were compelled to do so in order for the hidden force of the universe to express itself, according to the Divine plan. Yet, on a microcosmic level, Adam and Chavah did commit a terrible misdeed and they needed to do Teshuvah for it. From a human perspective, they did act from their Bechirah and caused their own demise.

These are two opposite paradigms in life; both are true simultaneously, and the same pattern plays out in the Galus of Egypt. The Mekubalim emphasize the macrocosmic narrative, and the function of Exile in terms of world history from Adam and Chavah in the Garden of Eden to Matan Torah, and from Klal Yisrael entering Eretz Yisrael to the future redemption of all Creation. History is but a series of stages in the grand narrative of the great unfolding of Creation. Every detail of it needs to happen as it is part of the Divine plan and our destiny of Yichud.

Part of the grand narrative involves the gradual refining of souls after the eating from the Tree of Knowledge, and that narrative could not occur without the eating itself. It too was part of the original plan of evolution toward Divine Yichud. And for this refinement to occur, Klal Yisrael needs to enter כור הברזל / the iron furnace of Mitzrayim in order to let go of all negative attachments.

In the words of the Kli Yakar, המנקה הכסף מכל סיג ופסולת עד שיהיה נקי וזך ברה כחמה כך נזדכך חומר שלכם בעינוי מצרים עד שנעשה ברור כשמש / "As heat cleanses the silver from all dross and waste matter until it is clean and well purified, so did (exile) purify their material existence in the suffering of Mitzrayim, until they were made as clear as the sun."

Again, Chazal are talking about the microcosmic justifications for exile; what Klal Yisrael or our patriarch Avraham did to deserve it, and leaving aside the Penimiyus reasons. As such, Chazal answer their three reasons for exile according to the three 'sins' that Avraham committed.

In the words of the Maharal, "The *Sibah* / cause of exile is *Cheit* / sin — yet, the *Sibas-haSibah* / 'primal cause of that cause' is hidden from us" (*Netzach Yisrael*, 2: סבת הגלות הוא מבואר בעצמו בכתוב שהוא החטא שגרם כל זה. אך סבת הסבה נעלם ממנו).

Cheit is a *Chitzoni* / 'external' reality to Klal Yisrael (Rashab, *Sefer haMa'amarim Ranat* (5659), 88. *Likutei Sichos*, 6, p. 54), so whereas Cheit is the Sibah of Galus, there must also be a deeper *Penimi* / 'inner' reason. This is the reason that the Mekubalim reveal.

DEATH IS PART OF THE FABRIC OF A CREATED, FINITE WORLD

From an elevated perspective, the Cheit of eating from the Tree of Knowledge, and even deeper, the idea of 'sin' in general, was actually only a נורא עלילה / circuitous act, a magnificent ruse, a necessary trick. Man *needed* to eat from the Tree of Knowledge because he needed to experience death.

Death is part of Creation, woven into the fabric of a created world that has a 'beginning'. Anything that 'begins' must mature and eventually end. Also, in a world of duality, everything is created with its opposite: where there is birth, there is eventually death — and this dual design is a necessary part of the Divine purpose of Creation.

The desire to create the universe first emerges from within a primordial state of *Ein Sof* / Infinite Unity. For a finite world to exist, however, the Infinite One needed to 'create space' within which creation could manifest. This is the Divine *Tzimtzum* / contraction of the Infinite in order for the finite to exist. This cosmogenic concealment is what makes possible the experience of Cheit and death. However it also makes possible the path of Teshuvah and redemption, through which the 'contracted', individuated self can return and unite itself back within the Ein Sof from which it originally emerged.

Before Creation there was a simple Singularity, and then a dualistic Creation appeared, but the ultimate Divine purpose is to return and include duality within a greater Unity. This is possible because once a finite individual life has 'turned back' toward its Source and 'loses' itself within the context of Infinite Unity, it can reemerge as an individual with the indelible imprint of that Unity. We can call this 'inclusive transcendence'; a state of limitlessness and Unity that includes and does not eclipse the limited individual.

For this cosmic purpose of greater unity, there needed to be the possibility of Cheit and free choice, implying a duality of good and evil. And this is the Divine root of Galus Mitzrayim: the inevitability of the Cheit gave rise to the inevitability of exile — "...and they descended by Divine decree."

Galus Mitzrayim needed to happen according to the Yediah and Hanhagas haYichud. Klal Yisrael needed to go through this process as part of the cosmic plan of moving from Transcendent Oneness to individuation, and finally back to Unity in a mode of 'inclusive transcendence'.

THREE STEPS: A) SINGULARITY, B) TZIMTZUM-ENSLAVE-MENT, AND C) INDIVIDUATION WITHIN UNITY

Necessary to the unfolding of Klal Yisrael was this descent from Divine Singularity — אחד היה אברהם / *Echad Hayah Avraham* / "Avraham was 'one' (a manifestation of Singularity)" (*Yechezkel,* 33:24) — to a world of separation, hardship and slavery. In such a 'death' or reduction of selfhood, life becomes completely dependent and broken. The *Yesh* / individual existence becomes *Ayin* / 'non-existent' in itself, so there can finally be a new birth and building of an authentic self, a new Yesh that transcends itself while paradoxically remaining itself.

Yetzias Mitzrayim is likened to a birth, the birth of the new Yesh of Klal Yisrael, which is both a oneness and a community of unique individuals. The process of birth includes the infant's first cry as it emerges from the silence of the womb. As Klal Yisrael leaves the 'womb' of Mitzrayim, they break their silence. All at once they acquire the ability to express themselves, and their power of speech is redeemed. We, too, during the Seder, cry out, gain a voice, and spontaneously become expressive storytellers and singers. This newly birthed individual self is included within the Oneness, which is palpably felt through the culminating praises and finally the completely redeemed state of Nirtzah.

So whereas Avraham and Yitzchak were in an elevated state of Singularity, Yaakov and his household needed to depart from this state, descend to Egypt, and be splintered apart, enslaved. Silenced within this Tzimtzum, as it were, they were dissolved into Ayin, so they could emerge anew with redeemed individual and collective voices, singing praises at the Sea; only to finally rest in the 'Nirtzah' of Matan Torah, consciously at One with the Ein Sof. In this way, Klal Yisrael is an image of the purpose of Creation, a unity of many, with each individual an expression of the One.

SPEAKING NEGATIVELY AGAINST EACH OTHER

The fact that the slaves suddenly had a voice and were speaking — even though it was לשון הרע / Lashon haRa — shows the beginning of the emergence of individuation. In this way, their Lashon haRa was also part of a greater cosmic plan.

Rashi is thus alluding to what Moshe says, "Indeed it is known": 'I now know why they are in exile. The purpose of exile is to develop a voice and individual expression. But the silence of Ayin must come before the new expression, the new Yesh. And this Lashon haRa is not yet the new Yesh; it is clear to me, says Moshe, that they are progressing but are not yet ready for redemption.'

Redemption is possible when we each have an individual voice, yet even when we use it to argue and give voice to our differences and uniqueness, it does not lead to Lashon haRa, for our underlying oneness shines through our individuality.

And so, Moshe is encouraged, in a way, that his people are starting to speak, showing that redemption is beginning. They were in the process of emerging from the voiceless Ayin or Tzimtzum state, but, since they were speaking ill of each other, it was obvious that their time had not yet come. They still needed to develop and mature in their individuality, their speech and self-expression.

EXILE IS THE LOSS OF ONE'S SPACE

A simple principle given by the Maharal (*Netzach Yisrael*, 1) is that Galus is a loss of one's מקום / *Makom* / space; one's place in the world. A person's Makom is connected with their very

Kiyum / existence. When a person loses their Makom, either literally or inwardly, they lose touch with who and what they *really* are.*

THE REASONS OF CHAZAL

Each of the three reasons for Klal Yisrael's exile that the Gemara offers is connected with one of Avraham Avinu's moments of lacking awareness of מקום / *Makom* / the proper 'place' of things:

מפני שעשה אנגרייא בתלמידי חכמים / "Avraham made a military draft of Torah scholars."

שהפריז על מדותיו של הקב"ה / "He overly examined the characteristics of the Holy One, Blessed be He."

שהפריש בני אדם מלהכנס תחת כנפי השכינה / "He distanced people from entering under the wings of the Divine Presence."

Making a "draft of Torah scholars" was problematic since the 'place' where a *Talmid Chacham* / Torah scholar belongs is in the Yeshivah, in a place of learning and contemplation. Making such a person a soldier — in this case, Eliezer — was not being *Makir* / cognizant of his Makom.

The Gemara (*Sanhedrin*, 49a) tells us that King Dovid and his general, Yoav Ben Tzeruya, complemented each other, as

---

* הגלות הוא שנוי ויציאה מן הסדר, שהשם יתברך סדר כל אומה במקומה הראוי לה... והגלות מן מקומם הוא שנוי ויציאה לגמרי. וכל הדברים כאשר הם יוצאים ממקום הטבעי, והם חוץ למקומם, אין להם עמידה במקום הבלתי טבעי להם, רק הם חוזרים למקומם הטבעי.

Dovid was immersed in the study of Torah, while Yoav went out to battle. "If it weren't for Dovid's Torah study, Yoav would not have succeeded in war; and if not for Yoav's effort in battle, Dovid would not have been able to study Torah." Each person needs to know their position, their Makom in life.

And so, making a אנגרייא בתלמידי חכמים / military draft of Torah scholars is not to be Makir of who they are and where they belong.

The third reason offered in the Gemara was that Avraham did not allow others to enter under the *Kanfei haShechinah* / wings of the Divine Presence, meaning that he did not allow them to 'enter their true Makom', where they truly belonged in relationship to HaKadosh Baruch Hu.

This is similar to when Adam was not *Makir Mekomo* / aware of his own place in relationship to Elokim, and he ate from the Tree of knowledge in order to become (in his own self-estimation) "*like* Elokim." As a result, ויגרש את־האדם / "Hashem ejected Adam from his Makom" from Gan Eden, and he entered a world of exile.

Adam is to this day not allowed to re-enter his Makom until he is truly ready: "…and Hashem stationed the cherubim and the fiery, ever-turning sword to the east of Gan Eden to guard the way to the Tree of Life." The human being will finally leave this primordial exile, and humbly re-enter its true place in relation to Divine Power, with the coming of Moshiach.

The middle reason, that Avraham "overly examined the characteristics of the Holy One, Blessed be He," seems to suggest a lack of Emunah and awareness of Hashem's 'place'. Also, the term of Chazal, הפריז, is similar to the word for 'scattered' or 'spread out'. This suggests a type of misaligned relationship with Hashem that was distinct from Adam's. Namely, on the extremely refined level of Avraham Avinu, there was some sense of scattering or 'misplacement' of the מקומו של עולם / Mekomo shel Olam / Hashem, the "Place" or Context of the World.

Hashem told Avraham that he would inherit the Promised Land and have a Makom in this world for his descendants, and yet he asked, במה אדע כי אירשנה / "How will I know that I am inheriting it?" He did not trust himself completely to achieve his life's mission, and at that moment, on some level, he was internally *Hifriz* / scattered in relation to the Divine space.

Avraham, who represents the foundational 'space' of Klal Yisrael, is in general deeply connected with Makom; we stand and flourish in his 'space', in the Makom he carved out for us. Thus, for instance, Chazal tell us that – כל הקובע מקום לתפלתו אלקי אברהם בעזרו / "Anyone who establishes a set place to pray, the G-d *of Avraham* will help him" (*Berachos*, 6b). However, in these three instances it is *K'ilu* / as if Avraham (however we can understand this) slipped from his place, and introduced an element of disconnection from Makom into the experience of his progeny.

Looking closely at these three reasons, it is clearly the middle one, the loss of Emunah, which is the 'source' of the first and third reasons. When Avraham takes Eliezer out of his Makom and makes him join the army, and when he does not bring others into their true Makom in Hashem's Presence, it is due to his own 'scattered' relationship with HaKadosh Baruch Hu, as it were, on his level. His historical effect on his progeny is sourced in this loss, on some *Dak* / subtle level, of a clear awareness of מקומו של עולם / the Ultimate Space within which all space exists. And because he was in some moments not 'holding his own space', nor honoring the place of other souls — in some way not honoring the true 'space' occupied by HaKadosh Baruch Hu — his children eventually lost their Makom and were exiled from their true Makom, the Land of Israel. They needed to live in other peoples' space, the place of Egypt, an idolatrous 'foreign land'. And there, exiled from their true land, from others and from Hashem, they lost their very selfhood, their inner space.

There are two levels of Galus revealed in the story of Adam. The first level is *VaY'garesh* / "And Hashem ejected him," and the second level is ...וישכן מקדם לגן־עדן / "And Hashem stationed (obstacles) to the east of Gan Eden" to prevent him from re-entering his true place. And this is the reason for the two great exiles, the Galus from Gan Eden and the Galus of Mitzrayim. The cosmic Tikkun for the Cheit in Gan Eden required a second great Galus. In Mitzrayim, the Children of Avraham needed to refine all of the seemingly harsh obstacles to their own Geulah. This second level of exile planted seeds of Geulah so that millennia later, the Children of Adam could fully return to The Makom, to Gan Eden, the Essential Divine Presence.

WHAT IS HAMAKOM / THE SPACE?

Hashem is the Source of all Makom and is Himself 'The Makom', ממקומו של עולם / *Mekomo shel Olam* / the Space within which all Space exists (*Medrash Rabbah*, Bereishis, 68:9). Metaphorically, as space accommodates others, so does Hashem make space and accommodate all of Creation. Hashem is, so to speak, the Space in which existence emerges.

המקום ינחם אתכם / *HaMakom Y'nachem Es'chem* / "May the Space comfort you..." begins the expression of empathy that we pronounce when taking leave of one who has lost a family member. When a child loses a parent, *Chas v'Shalom* / Heaven forbid, on some level they (can) lose their Makom, their place in the world. One's parent is in many ways one's 'context', one's space of life. It can seem as if the ground under oneself has collapsed. As such we tell a mourner that the Creator is המקום, the Source of 'Place', Who makes room for you. You shall ultimately have a sense of place again, because the Ever-Present is the unchanging Place of your life.

In this physical world, the essence of space is the place of the Beis haMikdash (*Yuma*, 54b. *Yalkut Shimoni*, Koheles, 2:967), the space which is a manifestation, *Keviyachol* / so-to-speak, of the Mekomo shel Olam.

ויפגע במקום / "And he encountered the place" (*Bereishis*, 28:11). When Yaakov "encounters HaMakom," say Chazal, this means he encounters the Har haBayis, the place of the future Beis haMikdash (לא הזכיר הכתוב באיזה מקום אלא במקום הנזכר במקום אחר, הוא הר המוריה: Rashi, *Pesachim*, 88a). This encounter represents the beginning of a return to the Essential Makom.

Eventually, all the world, all souls, all people will be refined, and all good people will return to their true Makom. Everyone will ascend to the essential Makom, when the prophecy is fulfilled — *Ki Beisi Beis Tefilah, l'Chol haAmim* / "For My House will be a house of prayer for all nations."

Now, the state of the world still corresponds to *Shema Yisrael, Hashem Elokeinu* / 'Listen, *Yisrael*, the Eternal is the Divine Context of *your* life.' But in *leAsid* / the future, the true Oneness of Hashem will be realized by all peoples in the aspect of *Hashem Echad* / 'the Eternal is the Divine context of *all* life', may we experience this speedily, in our days, with the coming of our righteous Moshiach.*

---

* ה' אלקינו ה' אחד: ה' שהוא אלקינו עתה ולא אלקי האומות, הוא עתיד להיות ה' אחד, שנאמר [צפניה ג, ט] כי אז אהפוך אל עמים שפה ברורה לקרוא כולם בשם ה' ונאמר [זכריה יד, ט] ביום ההוא יהיה ה' אחד ושמו אחד / "'Hashem is our Divinity, Hashem is One' means: Hashem who is now our Divinity and not the Divinity of the other peoples of the world, He will at some future time become 'the One Divinity', as it is said [*Zephaniah*, 3:9], 'For then I will turn to the peoples a pure language that they may all call upon the name of Hashem', and it is further said [*Zechariah*, 14:9], 'On that day Hashem will be One (אחד) and His name One'": Rashi on *Devarim*, 6:4.

Chapter Five:

Remembering Our Names:
CONNECTING WITH OUR PAST, PRESENT & FUTURE

A NAME IS SOMETHING THAT TIES US TO OUR PAST; one is often named after an ancestor, or after a narrative that occurred at or around the time of the birth. Yitzchak was named after Sarah's laughter at the prospect of having a child in her old age, and Yaakov, from the word for 'heel', was born holding onto his twin brother's heel. All of the *Shevatim* / Tribes were named after narratives, as well. When a person named Levi, for example, thinks about his name, he connects to his past, to figures from previous generations and perhaps notable events around the time of his birth.

In a sense, all names are 'narrative names'. In the beginning of *Shemos*, which means 'Names', Klal Yisrael is still connected, consciously, with its past.

FROM NAMES TO NAMELESS

The first Pasuk in the Torah which describes the beginning of the exile and harsh slavery, begins with the words, "These are the 'names' of the people who are coming to Egypt" (*Shemos*, 1:1). After this, the Torah goes on to list all the names of the Shevatim of Israel, the sons of Yaakov. This book, *Sefer Shemos* / 'The Book of Names' begins when the Children of Israel were still free people with proud names. From *Shemos*, 1:7 until the birth of Moshe, however, the Torah mostly just uses pronouns for Klal Yisrael: "*They* multiplied; *they* increased...the land was full of *them*...." When specified, they are merely called "the Children of Israel." They no longer have their own names.

Even when it does name the two Hebrew midwives as Shifrah and Puah (1:15), Rashi writes that these are not their 'real' names, rather descriptions of their work: beautifying the child, and cooing to the child (*Sotah*, 11b). Later, leading up to the birth of Moshe, it says, "A man from the house of Levi took a daughter from Levi to marry" (2:1). Moshe's parents' names are missing. When she gives birth, the Torah reveals no name given to him by his mother.

"And they saw that he (the baby) was *Tov* / good." Say Chazal, this was his name — 'Tov' or 'Tuviah' (*Sotah*, 12a). Moshe is not named by his mother in the Torah, and even the name that Chazal specify is not really a 'narrative name', it is just a description, like Shifrah and Puah.

Then, the nameless daughter of Pharaoh — we only learn her name from *Sefer Divrei haYamim* — finds the boy, and takes him home and calls him Moshe. "And she called his name Moshe; and said, 'Because I *drew him out* of the water'" (2:10). This, finally, is a true 'narrative name'.

Only free people have names. A slave is a nameless statistic, with no independent personal identity or existence. Likewise, when we are slaves to our emotions and reactions, we have no independence from the stimuli or influences in our lives.

Similarly, Chazal tell us, *Eved Ein Lo Yichus* / "A slave has no family lineage" (*Kidushin*, 69a).

He has no 'past', only the now, and he has no self-sovereignty, as he is the 'property' of someone else.

Yishretzu / "(the People) became a swarm" (1:7). They started acting like *Sheratzim* / swarming creatures, writes the Seforno — and animals have no *Yichus* / parental lineage. Sheratzim generally abandon their babies as soon as they are born, but even with the animals that do care for their children, there is no indication that they have any concept of grandparents or grandchildren. Shifrah and Puah tell Pharaoh, "The Hebrew women are like *Chayos* / animals." In other words, they have no historical memory, no back story, no narrative, and because of this, there is no need to worry about them being a threat to your regime.

ELIMINATING OUR INNER EGYPTIAN

During the *Shibud* / oppression in Mitzrayim, the first person to receive a name connected to a story was Moshe — but even then, he was given an Egyptian name, not a Hebrew one. Later, when he grew up, Moshe saw an *Ish Mitzri* / "Egyptian man" hitting an *Ish Yisraeli* / "Hebrew man"— neither one having a name. ויפן כה וכה וירא כי אין איש / "He looked here and saw that there was no man there," ויך את־המצרי ויטמנהו בחול / "...and he hit the Mitzri and buried him in the sand" (*Shemos*, 2:12. כל היכא דאיכא הכאה סתם לאו מיתה הוא: *Sanhedrin*, 84b). Says the Shaloh, the word המצרי / *haMitzri* has a numeric value of 345, the same value as the name *Moshe* (*Shaloh, Torah Ohr*, Parshas Shemos).

In a deeper reading, it seems Moshe is killing off and burying his own inner 'Egyptian', eliminating his superficial, assumed identity in order to reveal his true identity. Moshe the 'Jew' was brought up as an 'Egyptian'. He goes out and sees an external conflict between an Egyptian slave owner and Hebrew slave, and inwardly he discerns a lethal conflict between his own two identities, as such, ויפן כה וכה וירא כי אין איש / he looks "this way" and "that way" and sees there is no איש / "person"— he sees that *he himself* is neither a Jew nor an Egyptian. Who is he? He looks inward and does not find a "man"; he feels his lack of identity, and so he proactively takes a stand as a Jew, a Hebrew, and defends the oppressed. In defending an oppressed Jew, Moshe finally finds himself. He becomes a Jew and brings an end to the Mitzri oppressor within himself; when he buries the Mitzri in the sand, Moshe covers that negative aspect of his superficial conditioning and is able to wholly identify with this true nature, his birthright as a part of Klal Yisrael.

MOSHE AS YOSEPH

Moshe had been hidden for three months after he was born, and then placed in a basket in the Nile. The daughter of Pharaoh went down to bathe and saw this basket and she opened it up and "saw the *Yeled* / baby, and the *Na'ar* / youth was crying." She had compassion and said, "This Na'ar is from the Hebrews!" *Na'ar* suggests an older child. The Megaleh Amukos says she sees two children; not physically, but she sees the image of Yoseph haTzadik with Moshe, and *Na'ar* refers to Yoseph: "When Moshe was born, the *Diyokna* / image of Yoseph was with him" (*Megaleh Amukos*, Shemos, Derush, 4:2). This is what it means when she finds Moshe מילדי העברים זה / *Mi-Yaldei haIvrim Zeh* / "This is one of the Hebrew children." *Mi-Yaldei* / children is plural, hinting that she sees that with Moshe is the Diyokna of Yoseph.

This is also seemingly connected to her spotting at first a "*Yeled*" / child, but when she actually looks at him, the text says she sees a *Na'ar* / youth. One could say the term *Na'ar* here subtly refers to the last person in the Torah who is called a *Na'ar*: Yoseph. And in this sense, she sees 'two' people; the Yeled Moshe and the Na'ar Yoseph.

Both Moshe and Yoseph were born as part of Klal Yisrael, but raised and matured in Egypt. "The daughter (Bitya or Batya: *Divrei HaYamim* I, 4:18) of Pharaoh brought the child and raised him in her house." Moshe was raised as an Egyptian prince. Yoseph matured in Egypt* and became a powerful person there, although he was raised as one of the *Shivtei Kah /* Divine Tribes, a son of Yaakov.

By subtly drawing a parallel between the life of Moshe and the life of Yoseph, the Torah hints to Moshe's deep issue of remembering and claiming his true identity. Just as Yoseph, at the end of his life, reconnected with his 'past' — his father and family — Moshe too needs to embrace his past as a Jew in order for the redemption to occur. He and Klal Yisrael need to have a 'history' in order to have a future. We need to know our past in order to realize our future.

At the Burning Bush, Hashem begins by telling Moshe, "I am the G-d of your father, the G-d of Avraham, G-d of Yitzchak and the G-d of Yaakov" (*Shemos,* 3:6). This is not just identifying G-d, it is identifying his lineage. Did Moshe need to be reminded of his Yichus, and who his father and ancestors were? It seems as though he is still, to some extent, insecure about who he is within, and needs to be affirmed as a Jew,

---

* On all levels, including physically — e.g., he did not have a beard before he was sold, and when the brothers met him in Egypt, he had a full beard.

a prophet, a redeemer. As Hashem reveals Himself, He also reveals to Moshe who he is, giving him the missing link in his past and his identity. This is what Moshe really needs to hear.

Moshe's name means 'extracted', pulled out of the water, and indeed, it becomes his mission to 'extract' Klal Yisrael from Egypt, and 'pull' them through the water of the Sea of Reeds. Similarly, although Klal Yisrael have no names, Hashem tells Moshe to tell Klal Yisrael that they need to know that 'I (Hashem) made a promise to their grandparents,' etc. They have a story, a history, and because they have a past, they will also have a future. And most of all, they will have a mission.

Individual memory answers the question of 'Who am I?' Collective memory answers the question of 'Who are we?' Without a living memory of our past, we lose our individual and collective identity of who we are in the present. Through Moshe, Hashem tells Klal Yisrael, "...Your G-d and the G-d of your fathers...." You have Yichus, and because of this past you will have a future.

THREE TIMES THE NAME OF HASHEM

The Medrash (*Shemos Rabbah*, 3:6) says that Hashem tells Moshe to tell His people, "I, Hashem, am the One who was, I am the One who is, And I am the One who will be in the future. For this reason, the name Eh'yeh appears three times (in the narrative)." As the Ramban elaborates, "Hashem is always the same, and always *is*." It seems Hashem is saying, 'My Name is there in the Past, in the Present and in the Future. And the same is true with your name, your identity; you *are*. You exist as a distinct People, and not only are you here now, but you have a past and a future. You have a name.'

On one hand, the names of the Shevatim refer to the past, what happened at their birth. On the other hand, the name Reuvein, for example, also means, 'Look… at the difference between my son and Eisav.' In other words, it refers to the present and to his future and to life in general, not only his birth. Our name, as well, not only tells us about where we came from, but who we are now and where we are going.

Chazal tell us the names of the Shevatim also refer to their future Geulah from Egypt. For example, Reuvein means, 'I *see* their suffering (and will redeem them),' and Shimon similarly means, 'I *hear* their cries'. This is a tool that Moshe reveals to the people so that they can be redeemed; they ask, 'In whose Name do you speak?' The answer is *'Eh'yeh Asher Eh'yeh* — the One Who will be with you now (to redeem you), is the One Who will be with you in the future (to redeem you from every subsequent exile).'

Our name is not only our identity, it also indicates something about our soul journey and our future. There is a Rashi in Tanach (*Michah*, 6:9) that tells us that after our earthly life, one is asked their name, and the Torah spares them from the torments of Gehenom if they remember their name by reciting a *Pasuk* / verse connected to their name (see *Zohar*, Acharei. *Zohar Chadash*, Rus, 84a. *Reishis Chochmah*, Sha'ar haYirah, 12:2). If we remember our name after our death, it means we remembered our purpose during our life.

Chazal tell us that in Egypt, Klal Yisrael "did not change their names." What does this mean? As mentioned, a name has three dimensions: past, present, and future. It is clear that they did not remember their past, nor did they hope for their future, and this was a missing dimension in the names that they kept. It could be that they knew who they were in the present, and this was reflected in the names that they 'kept'. Hashem tells Moshe to speak in the Name of the Divinity of the past (as above), and also of the future: "Thus shall you say to the Israelites, 'Ehe'yeh / "I Will Be" sent me to you'" (3:14). The Medrash says that the Name Ehe'yeh is revealed three times in this episode to point to the past, present, and future.

Eh'yeh is paralleled by the name 'Yoseph', which is a 'future' conjugation of *Hosafah* / addition. When he was born, his mother said, ותקרא את־שמו יוסף לאמר יסף ה' לי בן אחר / "And his name will be called Yoseph, which is to say, 'May Hashem add to me another son'" (*Bereishis*, 30:24).

The *Kelipah* / dark side of this forward-looking approach to life is to forget about the past and only think about the future. This seems to happen to Yoseph, as he names his son, Menasheh, which means *Nashani* / 'I was made to forget' my father's home.

When he was first thrown into a pit, Yoseph may have thought that his father was part of the plot, since Yaakov sent him to Shechem to find his brothers who did not like him and were jealous of him. In contrast, it is Pharaoh who 'takes him out of the pit' — the Torah calls the prison "the pit." Pharaoh believes in Yoseph, and in his dream interpretations, unlike his brothers who did not believe his dreams. Pharaoh even gives him a new name and places him in charge of the land, almost like a son and inheritor. Yoseph had a whole new life, and he named his children after the present moment: Menasheh — he is in a place of forgetting his father and his past, and Ephraim, from the word *Hefrani* / 'I have become prosperous' in my new life.

After many years, Yoseph reconciles with his family, and becomes part of it again. In fact, at the end of Yaakov's life, Yoseph even dares to place his allegiance with Yaakov, his real father, over his allegiance to Pharaoh: Yoseph asks Pharaoh to allow him to fulfill his oath and bury his father in Kena'an — rather than embalming him in Egypt.

After Yaakov passes away, Yoseph speaks to "the House of Pharaoh" and says, 'Please speak in the ears of Pharaoh and tell him that my father made me promise that I should take his body out of Egypt and I should bury him in the land of Kena'an.' In this instance, Yoseph speaks to the House of Pharaoh, meaning, to the ministers of Pharaoh, to ask permission to take his father's body to Kena'an; why doesn't he speak directly to Pharaoh? We do not find mention anywhere that Yoseph has a strained relationship with Pharaoh, in fact, he's second in command and he certainly has Pharaoh's ear.

Yoseph understands that Pharaoh is like his father; Pharaoh made Yoseph into the great person he has become. He named him and he gave him a wife. Yoseph realizes that if he goes to Pharaoh and tells him, "My father told me to take his body and bury him in Kena'an," it would be a terrible blow to Pharaoh. The Egyptians were obsessed with the afterlife and understood the mummification of the dead as a way to preserve the corpse for transit to the next world, enabling them to remain in contact with the world of the living. This 'honor' was preserved exclusively for royalty, the rich and respected. Everyone in Egypt regarded Yaakov as a Tzadik; blessings came to Egypt because of Yaakov. Certainly the Egyptians felt that they should mummify Yaakov's body and bury him in Egypt, so that they could use him as a deity. Of course Yaakov didn't want to be buried there for that very reason.

Yoseph thus has a quandary — who am I? Where is my allegiance? I'm returning to my people, but I still owe much gratitude to Egypt. If not for them I wouldn't have my sons. Yes, one is Menasheh because 'I forgot my father's home', although I tried to remember — but Hashem made me prosperous here; I lived in a way that was Ephrayim, 'fruitful', on all levels, in this land. There was thus a Kavanah and even purpose in my living here; I was meant to raise up certain sparks, including the land itself.

If Yoseph were to go to Pharaoh and say, 'My real connection is with my biological father — *Avi Hishbi'ani* / my father made me promise to do this,' he knows that Pharaoh is going to be hurt and their future relationship will be compromised. Therefore, he goes about it in a roundabout way: 'Please speak gently to Pharaoh and tell him that my real father is Yaakov, and I need to take him to be buried in Kena'an because that's where he belongs.' Yoseph is placing his allegiance with Yaakov and rejoining his true people, in a most diplomatic way. As a result, not only is Pharaoh not offended, but many others recognize the importance of Yaakov and give him honor.

As the burial entourage is bringing Yaakov's body to Kena'an, the Torah says they came "to the threshing floor of the thorn bushes" (*Bereishis*, 49:10). Say Chazal, this means the people of Kena'an and the princes of Yishmael came to wage war on the sons of Yaakov. When they saw Yoseph's crown hanging on Yaakov's coffin, they all stood up and hung their own crowns on it, surrounding it with crowns until it looked like a threshing floor surrounded by a fence of thorns (*Sotah*, 13a).

Why did Kena'an and Yishmael change their minds? Kena'an and Yishmael originated with two children who were rejected by their parents. Kena'an was cursed by his grandfather Noach to be a slave, and Yishmael was sent away, much like Yoseph by his brothers (again, perhaps in Yoseph's own thinking he was maliciously sent away by Yaakov, *Chas v'Shalom* / Heaven forbid). The answer is, Yoseph was sent away, yet he was able to make peace with his past. When Kena'an and Yishmael saw Yoseph's crown on his father's coffin displaying his allegiance and forgiveness, they too felt some peace, and thus dropped their anger and laid down their arms to give honor to Yaakov. The resolution of intergenerational trauma brought peace within and between the warring tribes.

And so too, at the *Sneh* / Burning Bush, Moshe needs to remember and make peace with his past.

REMEMBRANCE THROUGH ACTION

Zechirah means memory of the past, yet it comes from the word *Zachar* / male, symbolizing an active force or activity, which in turn is an allusion to the future. In this way, *Zechirah* signifies a type of memory that enlivens the past in such a way that it actively ensures a future. Rambam (*Hilchos Chametz uMatzah*, 7:1) writes, "It is a positive commandment of the Torah to relate the miracles and wonders wrought for our ancestors in Egypt on the night of the Fifteenth of Nisan, as *Shemos*, 13:3 states: 'Remember this day, on which you left Egypt' — just as *Shemos*, 20:8 states: 'Remember the Shabbos day.'" Why does the Rambam need to say this? Why does he need a proof text for recalling the events of our redemption on Pesach night from the commandment to "Remember the Shabbos"?

Rambam is telling us it is not enough to passively 'remember' our going out of Egypt, rather it is an active form of memory, to remember *l'Kadsho* / "to sanctify it" — the way we actively remember Shabbos. On Shabbos, the Mitzvah is to "remember Shabbos" as it enters and exits, through actions such as Kiddush and Havdalah. We need to *remember* the past, but we need to *do* something in the present in order to *create* a future. Zechirah is a form of active memory that sanctifies the present as it moves into the future.

The idea of a mirror is to 'look back' in history, and yet the Jewish women in Egypt used mirrors to create the future. Following the pronouncement of the death of all firstborn boys, husbands separated from their wives in despair. But the righteous women did not give up on the possibility of a brighter future, no matter how bleak. The Medrash mentions how the women would take their copper mirrors with them out to the fields, where they would beautify themselves after work in order to seduce their husbands in the orchards. They thus became pregnant and gave birth to the future of Klal Yisrael. It is this 'mirror' of memory that is both *Mechayev* / obligatory and motivational, in the present, in such a way that it creates a future. The *Hemshech* / continuation of Klal Yisrael came from these righteous, inspired women taking mirrors and looking into the past in order to give birth to a future. Klal Yisrael needed to reclaim their 'names' and their history so that they could move forward toward their redemption.

Names are thus not only about our past, but also our present and future. While Reuvein is named for how Hashem *saw* Leah's suffering, she is also saying *Reu-Ben* / "*see* my son" — look how he acts differently than his cousins. His way of behavior shows that he will be a Tzadik, an inwardly redeemed person.

"Rebbe Meir was *Medayek* / precise in using a person's given name." We have Ruach haKodesh when we name a child, as the name is an expression of the child's mission throughout their life. A name not only tells a story of the present, but it also hints to the future. Chazal say (*Shemos Rabbah*, 1:3-5) that the names of the Tribes are Reuvein, Shimon and Levi, etc., as they are *Al Shem Geulasam* / named after their redemptions:

"These are the names of the Children of Yisrael." They were remembered according to their exiles: Reuvein, as it is said, "I have marked well the pain of My People (in Egypt);" Shimon is named after "And Elokim heard their cries;" Levi is named after the fact that HaKadosh Baruch Hu 'joined' in their distress from within the *Sneh* / Burning Bush in order to fulfill what is written in *Tehillim* (91:15), *Imo Anochi b'Tzarah* / "I am with him in his distress;" and Yehudah is named after the fact that they thanked HaKadosh Baruch Hu at the Sea, after being redeemed (ואלה שמות בני ישראל: על שם גאולת ישראל נזכרו כאן: ראובן

שנאמר [שמות ג, ז]: "ראה ראיתי את עני עמי". שמעון על שם [שמות ב, כד]: וישמע אלקים

את נאקתם. לוי על שם שנתחבר הקדוש ברוך הוא לצרתם מתוך הסנה [שמות ג, ב] לקים

(מה שנאמר [תהלים צא, טו]: "עמו אנכי בצרה". יהודה על שם שהודו להקדוש ברוך הוא).

Thus, their names were a narrative of their past and their roots, an indication of who they were in the present, and also a prophetic narrative of their future. We too need to remember our names — where we come from, who we are, and where we are going. We too need to be awakened by the revelation at the Sneh: 'I am the Divinity of your Ancestors... I am with you here and now in your exile...and *Eh'yeh* / I Will Be What I Will Be — in the future.'

Chapter Six:
Gal as Galus / Exile
or Gal as Geulah / Redemption

GEULAH / גאולה AND GALUS / גלות SEEMINGLY SHARE the same root, גל / *Gal* / revelation, or 'flow', as in *Galgalim* / waves. What is the difference between the ideas of revelation and flow as they relate to Geulah and Galus?

When he first returns to Egypt from Midyan, Klal Yisrael does not listen to Moshe because of *Kotzer Ruach* / shortness of breath: ולא שמעו אל־משה מקצר רוח ומעבדה קשה / "And they did not listen to Moshe, from shortness of *Ruach* / breath, and hard labor" (*Shemos*, 6:9). Says Rashi, כל מי שהוא מיצר, רוחו ונשימתו קצרה ואינו יכול להאריך בנשימתו / "Whoever is under stress, his wind and his breathing are short, and he cannot take a deep breath." All of this shows that when Klal Yisrael were under the most intense stress of slavery, they still had Ruach, but it was קצר / cut short; they were not able to breathe deeply.

What are the deeper implications of having short or cut off Ruach?

Interestingly enough, Matzah, poor man's bread, the bread of affliction, contains the element of fire (in the baking of the Matzah), the element of earth (in the flour, which grows from the ground), and the element of water (which is mixed with the flour). The only element that is, in a certain sense, 'lacking' in Matzah is *Ruach* / wind or air. This is because we do not let the flour and water mixture rise and form air-pockets. In this way, Matzah is connected with the notion of 'shortness of breath', a lack of air or wind.

When being charged with the mission to take Klal Yisrael out of Egypt, Moshe tells Hashem, "The people will not listen to me." One might assume that they did not listen because Moshe had a כבד־פה / *K'vad Peh* / 'hard mouth' or speech impediment.* However, we can also say it was the other way

---

* There is a כבד־פה hard mouth, and there is also a כבד לשון / hard tongue or difficulty with the tongue — what is the difference? Says Rabbeinu Chananel: זה שהזכיר שני דברים כבד פה וכבד לשון יורה כי משה רבינו לא היה צח (הדבור) [הדבור] באותיות זשצר"ס שהן אותיות השינים זהו שאמר כי כבד פה גם לא באותיות הלשון שהם אותיות דטלנ"ת. ועל זה אמר וכבד לשון / "The very fact that

around: since they would not listen due to their קצר רוח, he was unable to speak to them properly. The prophetic flow of influence is from the people to Moshe.

The Zohar writes that after Matan Torah, Moshe was no longer *K'vad Peh* / 'heavy of mouth', afflicted with a stuttering speech impediment (*Zohar* 11, p. 25a. *Agra d'Pirka*, 166). The Medrash Rabbah, too, comments on the Pasuk (*Devarim*, 1:1), "These are the words of Moshe," that once he received the Torah, Moshe was healed and no longer stuttered; he formed "words" fluently. The truth is that Matan Torah was only the beginning of this healing, and only after revealing the entire Torah, until the last Mitzvah at the end of the forty years, did Moshe become a completely fluent orator. Indeed, in the Pasuk (*Mishlei*, 15:4), "A healing tongue is a tree of life," the phrase "tree of life" refers to the Torah (*Erchin*, 15b). The Torah brings healing, particularly (though not exclusively), to one's capacity for creative expression.

The *Sheim miShmuel* (beginning of *Devarim*) asks a basic, simple, question: Why does the Medrash say this Derasha on this Pasuk in *Devarim*? If he was healed at Matan Torah, the Medrash should attach the above Derasha to the event of Matan Torah, 40 years earlier in the narrative. However, by saying the Derasha on the Pasuk in the beginning of Devarim,

---

Moshe mentioned both these deficiencies of his separately, is a clear indication that he had difficulty in formulating certain words which are articulated with the teeth. The consonants he had difficulty with were ז,ש,ר,צ,ס, and when he referred to his difficulty as כבד פה, he had in mind the letters ד,ל,ת,ט, which are made with the לשון (lingual consonants).

which is at the end of the 40 years, the Medrash seems to be teaching us that Moshe was only healed after his 40 years of teaching Torah in the Desert. Revelation was just the beginning.

With this in mind, Moshe said to Hashem at the *Sneh* / Burning Bush, "I am K'vad Peh," and Hashem responded, 'That is true now, and it will take 40 years to heal it, but right now you have the *potential* to become a great *Medaber* / speaker.' This would mean that, on a certain level, Moshe was already a Medaber and orator even at the *Sneh*, but he did not yet know this about himself.

Many times, other people know things about us better than we do. The Medrash says (*Tanchuma*, Balak, 3. *Bamidbar Rabbah*, 20:4) that when the nation of Moav wanted to know the power of Klal Yisrael they went to the nation of Midyan, where Moshe lived for many years, before going back to Egypt. The representatives of Moav asked those of Midyan, 'What is Moshe's power?' They responded, 'His power lies in his mouth.' Moshe's power was in his speech, although earlier he was not aware of this power. He considered himself a stutterer, and probably the other *Ivrim* / Hebrews did as well. Due to this limiting self-perception, he was not yet able to manifest his power as the speaker he really was.

Yet, there is another, almost opposite reason why Moshe has a K'vad Peh and is unable to speak. It is not because he does not claim his innate abilities, rather it is because he comes from a place of *Tzurah* / form without *Chomer* / substance, space without sound. This is a place of *Neshamah* / 'soul breath', which is a hidden world beyond speech, beyond revelation. Because Moshe dwells in this realm of 'silence', it is 'hard' for Moshe to reveal words that relate to physical or observable reality (וכאשר משה היה נבדל במעלתו, לא היה נוטה אל הגשמי כי אם אל מעלה הנבדלת, היה חסר גמר פטיש זה: Maharal, *Gevuros Hashem*, 28). Moshe's Ruach is in fact exclusively a channel for the world of Neshamah and profound, hidden meaning.

NEFESH / REVEALED WORLD. RUACH / SPEECH THAT REVEALS. NESHAMAH / BREATH, THE INNER WORLD

Nefesh, the lowest level of soul, resides in the world of *Chitzoniyus* / the externalized, observable world. This 'world of Nefesh' is teeming with life — plants, animals, and even 'inanimate' objects such as stones, which too have a living Nefesh. This נפש חיה is the spirit that animates the creature, the inner 'engine' of its body, as-it-were. The body and spirit of an animal, for example, are created simultaneously, as it says (*Bereishis*, 1:24), ויאמר אלקים תוצא הארץ נפש חיה למינה בהמה ורמש וחיתו־ארץ למינה ויהי־כן / "And Elokim said, 'Let the earth bring forth every kind of living creature: cattle, creeping things, and wild beasts of every kind.' And it was so."

Above the world of Nefesh is the world of Ruach. Here, the human being is created, and this is done in two stages (*Bereishis*, 2:19): וייצר ה' אלקים את־האדם עפר מן־האדמה ויפח באפיו נשמת חיים ויהי האדם לנפש חיה / "Hashem formed the human from the dust of the earth. G-d blew into his nostrils a breath of life, and the human became a living being." First Hashem creates the body of Adam, and only then blows into his nostrils a breath of life. The Targum writes that the breath of life is רוח ממללא / a 'speaking spirit'. Ruach is implicitly connected to speech.

Even higher than the world of Ruach is the world of Neshamah, the inner world, the realm of Penimiyus beyond *Ruach* / wind, movement, speech and breath. This level of Creation is for the most part unrevealed, in sharp contrast to the external world of Nefesh, in which life is revealed and observable.

Neshamah corresponds to the inner, abstract, subtle World of Beriah, while Nefesh corresponds to the outer, physical World of Asiyah. Ruach corresponds to the World of Yetzirah, a dynamic 'place' flowing between Beriah and Asiyah, which can draw energy from, and direct energy to, either Nefesh or Neshamah.

TWO TYPES OF SPEAKING / REVEALING

One form of speech is drawn from the level of Nefesh. This is *Stam* / 'just' words and *Pitput b'Alma* / common chatter — the 'body' of speech, without the dimension of Neshamah breathing in it. Nothing is really being revealed. It is merely a movement of *Ruach* / wind animating the world of Nefesh and creating 'external' sounds, like the rustling of leaves or the chirping of birds. This is the external realm in which Galus becomes possible.

Another kind of speech is revealed from a place of Penimi-yus, from the Neshamah. It is 'harder' to speak such words, as they emanate from a world of 'silence' and stillness beyond all *Tenuah* / movement. Yet, when such speech occurs, there is a Geulah, a *Gal* or revealing of something of substance.

'REVEALING' GALUS

Certain manners of 'revealing' information are intertwined with and expressive of Galus (and slavery: see *Medrash Rabbah*, Bereishis, 36:4. *Gur Aryeh*, Bereishis, 9:23). In fact, the exile in Egypt is basically an exile of Dibbur, as the Zohar teaches. Two 'Galus' modes of *Gal* / revelation and speech referred to by the sages are *Peh-Ra* / bad speech (which is connected with *Pa-Ro* / Pharaoh), and *Peh-Rach* / weak speech (which is connected with *Avodas Pe-Rach* / harsh labor).

וירא משה ויאמר אכן נודע הדבר / "And Moshe was afraid, and he said, 'Indeed it is known.'" Says Rashi, דאג לו על שראה בישראל רשעים דלטורין, אמר מעתה שמא אינם ראויין להגאל / "He was worried because he saw in Israel wicked men (i.e. inform-ers). He said, if this is so, perhaps the Israelites do not deserve to be redeemed" (*Tanchuma*, Shemos, 10).

Moshe thought for a moment that maybe the people do not deserve, or are not able, to be redeemed. Even worse, maybe they even deserve exile (מה חטאו, תמה עליו שהייתי הדבר לי נודע ומדרשו ישראל מכל שבעים אומות להיות נרדים בעבודת פרך, אבל רואה אני שהם ראויים לכך: Rashi, *Shemos*, 2:14. Maharal, *Gur Aryeh*, *Shemos* 2:14).

Here are the words in the Medrash (*Shemos*, 1:30): "He became fearful of Lashon haRa and said, 'Surely the thing is known'... Moshe would wonder to himself and say, 'What was Israel's sin for which they became more enslaved than all other nations?' When he heard his (the Hebrew who struck his fellow) words, he (Moshe) said, 'Such *Lashon haRa* / evil tongue is among them, how would they be worthy of redemption?' And so Moshe said, 'Surely the thing is known'— now I know what the cause of their enslavement is."

In other words, Moshe understood that this type of 'revealing', or expression, was the cause of their Galus. The Ruach of this negative speech and 'informing', and even mere *Pitput* / blabber, is spiritually *Kotzer* / cut, shortened, and thus it 'cuts the Ruach' of Klal Yisrael and in turn created their Galus. Galus is a communal contraction of spirit and vitality. Even when Pitput and nonsense do not literally 'cut down' others, they still cut down one's Ruach; the vitality of the person speaking nonsense becomes depleted of energy, as taught by the Baal Shem Tov.

"Speech is the vitality of the human being, and that vitality comes from Hashem, blessed be He. Thus when a person utters 'good speech', it ascends on high and stirs the 'Supernal speech'. This, in turn, causes further vitality to emanate to him from on high. If, however, a person speaks something that is bad, the vital force has departed from him and will not ascend. Thus it is likely that his total vitality may cease from him altogether. This is indicated by the vernacular expression *Er Hott*

Oys-Geredt / "He has spoken (it) out" ('he let *himself* out; he is spent').*

In other words, negative speech מקצר רוח / cuts down a person's Ruach, spirit and vitality. This is the idea of running out of energy when we speak nonsense, as we are not connected to something deeper and thus run out of steam. When a person speaks negative speech, he becomes depleted.

Think about a time you spoke ill about a person or even just spoke *Avak Lashon haRa* / the 'dust' or derivative of negative speech, into which practically everyone is *Nichshal* / fallen. Recall how you felt at that moment, the surge of excitement, and then how you felt afterwards, perhaps ashamed, disgusted, or depressed. This type of Lashon haRa takes you away from your sense of 'home'; it is a form of exile from who you really are.

The people had פה רע / *Peh Ra* / negative mouth, negative speech. Sometimes the best form of speech is to have control and mastery, and remain silent. The middle letters of the word מצרים / Egypt is יצר / inclination, generally referring to

___

* *Tzava'as haRivash*, 103. See also *Tzava'as haRivash*, 2b. *Likutim Yekarim*, 4b: כשאדם מדבר דיבור טוב, והדיבור הוא החיות של האדם, והחיות הוא ממנו יתברך שמו, אז הדיבור סלקא לעילא ומעורר הדיבור העליון, ומשפיע עליו יותר חיות מלמעלה, אבל כשהוא מדבר דיבור רע, אזי יוצא ממנו החיות, ולעילא גם כן לא סלקא, אז קרוב הדבר להיות נפסק ממנו כל החיות לגמרי, וזהו מה שאומרים העולם, ער האט אויס גירעט / "When a person speaks 'good speech', and (he is aware that) his speech is the life force given to him from HaKadosh Baruch Hu, then this speech is taken up Above and it illuminates the supernal speech, and this bestows upon him even more life force from Above. However, when he is speaking negative speech, then the life force leaves him, and it is not taken up Above...."

our negative inclination. The first letter is an open Mem, מ, representing an open mouth, whereas the final letter is a closed Mem, ם representing a closed mouth, a mouth that is silent. A spiritually, emotionally, mentally healthy *Peh* / mouth (פ is numerically 80) is one that knows the balance of when to open and when to close their mouth (two Mems is also 80). The exile in Egypt represents a separation, a divide, a disunity between these two possibilities of the mouth, speech and silence. It is where Peh Ra, which would be best left unspoken, is expressed, and this leads to a weak mouth, a powerless mouth, an energyless mouth. But even just speaking Pitput can deplete one's energy.

If you are speaking on the level of Ruach as it draws from Nefesh, the revealed world, the external, physical soul, your words are not drawing from the Source of Life. You are drawing from the 'effect', rather than the Cause. Because of this the vitality of your speech can become 'spent' and depleted, leaving you empty or even depressed:

"When you speak, your life-force 'leaves' you. By means of the speech of Torah study and prayer, you receive new vitality from your Supernal Source, as it says: "The living creatures ran (left) and returned (were replenished)" (*Yechzekiel*, 1:14). However, depression does not resonate with holiness, and therefore, speech from a depressed state depletes your life-force, G-d forbid" (*Duda'im baSadeh*, B'ha'aloschah). This speech is the *Gal* of Galus.

And then there is speech in which, like Moshe, your Ruach draws from your Penimiyus, your Neshamah and from the Source of Life, and due to this, your speech is always replenished with new vitality and depth of meaning, inspiring hope and insight. This cycle accelerates toward Geulah. This is why a person giving over Torah never gets tired, but rather, the Torah that he brings down to the world always increases, as described in the Chassidic teachings, that צדיק כתמר יפרח / "A Tzadik is like a flourishing date palm" — the teachings of a Tzadik are continuously יפרח / flourishing, flowering and growing in life-giving power, depth, and reach.

Enduring aliveness is a sign of Kedushah, as what flows from the Eternal draws its vitality from the Eternal, and is continuously replenished with *Koach* / strength and dynamism.

Depleted energy, intelligence and strength is a sign of *Kelipah* / a negative side. Perhaps there are temporary states of excitation, but these are followed by even deeper valleys of depletion. Negative speech, and even Pitput Devarim, come from the level of Nefesh as it is already revealed to Ruach. This type of speech is merely broadcasting, reporting the obvious, adding nothing to the conversation nor to the quality of life, revealing no insight, no 'soul', and no light of redemption.

Hashem tells Moshe, "I will take them out, I will save them, I will redeem them and I will take them...." In other words, I will 'transport' them to a new place. "I will bring them to the Promised Land" — I will bring them to a redemptive state of being, in which their 'movement' will be rooted in their 'Home'. Their speech will flow from the inside-out, with authenticity and true freedom.

MOSHE-NESHAMAH AND AHARON-RUACH

Geulah comes from the *Dibbur* / speech that draws from and reveals the Neshamah. Redemption is synonymous with a higher level of revelation through speech, and thus the word *Pesach* is spelled *Peh Sach* / the mouth that speaks.

Matzah, which is poor man's bread, bread of affliction, is 'short of breath', contracted in Ruach. An afflicted person is focused only on their Nefesh, their immediate surroundings and circumstances — for he cannot afford to dream and focus on his inner world of Neshamah. But through our reciting of the Haggadah, and activating the light of Peh-Sach, we draw down into the "poor man's bread" a new *Ruach* / wind, speech. We infuse our "Matzah," our current state of affliction and depletion, with a redeemed Ruach emanating from our Neshamah.

Moshe comes from a place of Neshamah, 'extended breath', beyond the 'noise' of Ruach fused with Nefesh. Moshe is an archetypal embodiment of Neshamah. The letters of his name, משה, plus the letter Nun / 50, standing for the Fifty Gates of Understanding, spell the word נשמה / *Neshamah*. In fact, Moshe is also called מנשה / Menasheh (*Bava Basra*, 109b), which includes all of the letters in the word נשמה.

Because Moshe is so identified with the level of Neshamah, he has a K'vad Peh, and he therefore cannot easily enter the world of Ruach. And so Hashem tells him, ואהרן אחיך יהיה נביאך / "And Aharon your brother will be the prophet" (*Shemos*, 7:1).

Aharon is a Navi. Asks Rashi, "What is a Navi? A Navi is connected to speech: והוא מגזרת ניב שפתים / 'The term Navi is derived from the root of "I create the ניב / speech of the lips.'"

Similarly, wherever this term of נבואה is mentioned it refers to a man who publicly proclaims and utters to the people words of reproof."

In other words, Aharon is the *Madreigah* / level of Ruach and speech, and thus can draw from the Madreigah of Moshe, Neshamah, breath, and reveal it. Indeed, at the end of Moshe's life, when he *Davens* / prays to Hashem about the next leader of Klal Yisrael, Hashem says, יפקד ה' אלקי הרוחת לכל־בשר איש על־העדה / "Let Hashem, *Elokei haRuchos*, 'Source of the breath of all flesh', appoint someone over the community...." And then Hashem specifies, קח־לך את־יהושע בן־נון איש אשר־רוח בו / "Single out Yehoshua bin Nun, a man who has Ruach within him..." (*Devarim*, 27:18). The leader who is to complete the redemption, by bringing Klal Yisrael into the Promised Land, must have within him a Ruach that is rooted in its Source.[*]

---

[*] There are two steps in Geulah: Moshe takes us out of Egypt, and then Yehoshua brings us into Eretz Yisrael. Moshe is the person who is chosen by HaKadosh Baruch Hu to help facilitate the redemption from Egypt. In Hebrew, the name *Moshe* comes from the word משיתהו / drawn out,

Redemptive speech is that which comes from our inner self and expresses who we truly are. It is a vibration that travels outwards, allowing our inside to be revealed and articulated on the outside. This is the *Gal* of Geulah. May we merit to redeem our power of speech and liberate the Neshamah concealed within ourselves and this world.

extracted (*Shemos*, 2:10). And indeed, it becomes Moshe's mission and life purpose to 'extract' and help redeem Klal Yisrael from Egypt.Moreover, some of the Rishonim write that really, linguistically, Moshe's name should have been *Moshui* (Mem-Shin-Vav-Yud), as he was pulled from the water. But, Hashgacha had it, that she would call him Moshe, which sounds like *Moshia* / redeemer, as Moshe does become the Moshia of Klal Yisrael from Galus (ואע"ת והלא מצריית היתה והיאך קראה בלשון עברי וי"ל שהיא קראה בלשון מצרי שם שמשמעותו משה והתורה קראו משה בלשון עברי: *Da'as Zekeinim, Pirushei haTorah l'Baalei Tosefos*, Shemos, 2:10).

Chapter Seven:
Freedom & Humility:
Living Beyond Enslavement

P ESACH IS THE OPENING OF THE PORTAL THROUGH
WHICH ALL OUR INNER AND OUTER FREEDOM IS
ATTAINED.

If any moment throughout the year we feel truly free, it is
because of the energy we invested and experienced on Pesach.
Whenever we need to be liberated from something, we need to
make contact with our 'Pesach point' within.

Enslavement and freedom can be understood on multiple levels. There is a literal, externally imposed slavery, when someone else is oppressing us, and there are more subtle forms of inner slavery, such as being stuck within ourselves, or tied to the validation or appreciation of others. Yet, essentially, inner and outer slaveries are the same. The basic definition of a slave is someone whose life is a *Murkav* / a composite of external ingredients — dependent upon and completely identified with their master or their surroundings. A free person is independent and autonomous.

'Rich bread' is a composite mixed with other ingredients such as juice, milk, eggs, sugar, nuts, etc. The flour of 'rich bread' is only a vehicle for or servant of the other ingredients, and the flour is dependent upon these other ingredients for its enhanced flavor or image. In contrast, Matzah (the Matzah we eat to perform the Mitzvah of eating Matzah) is *Pashut* / 'simple', having only the most essential ingredients, and thus is 'free' from other influences. It is what it is, rather than existing only in order to serve an extrinsic entity.

Matzah is called 'the bread of affliction' and 'the bread of poverty', as it is flat and humble and was the simple food of the slaves of old. Yet, it is also the bread we ate on the night we were freed from Egypt, and in this way it is the 'bread of freedom'. In truth, it is paradoxically both 'the bread of poverty' and 'the bread of freedom', as 'poor' also means 'simple', not mixed with any other ingredients, free to be itself, and not needing anything else in order to exist. In this sense, 'poverty' actually means 'free'. Let us understand this construct from its more pronounced ideas to its more subtle interpretations.

A common type of subtle 'enslavement' to one's environment and outside world involves the weather. For example: a person wakes up in the morning and the sun is shining, they feel like it will be a nice day, and so they feel happy. Conversely, they wake up and it is raining, so they feel it is going to be a bad day, and they feel down. Thus, they are psychologically enslaved to the external changes in the weather. If phenomena of the external world dictate to you how you are going to feel and act, you are trapped in a *Murkav* / composite of external forces beyond your control. Similarly, but much more devastatingly, a person is a Murkav if they are affected by other people's opinions; when someone praises them, their self-confidence soars, and when someone insults them, their confidence collapses. Their inner temperament is dependent on others as a slave is dependent on their master.

To be enslaved means to live as the effect of life and not as its cause. For example: if your well-being is dependent on someone else's perspective of who you are, your well-being, or lack thereof, is an 'effect' of their perspective. If you choose not to react to their limited perspective and derive your well-being instead from the true Source of well-being, then you are living as the cause of your life.

A free person lives as the cause of life, while an 'enslaved' person lives as the effect of life. How do we transition from a slave mentality to a redeemed mentality? Firstly, we need to develop some form of *Hishtavus* / equanimity, for not reacting to others and to our environment allows us to maintain our individuality and composure in different situations, and yet be open and engaged in them.

Hishtavus is a sense that life is always as it should be, essentially whole and perfect. Whether people adulate or scorn you, and for that matter, whether you are served foods which you relish or foods which you dislike, all is equal to you. This does not mean becoming stoic or indifferent to people. Praise is still welcome, and tasty foods are still enjoyed, but insults and disliked tastes do not throw you off kilter and take you away from the Cause of Life. Nor do praises and tasty foods excite you so much that you lose your balance and become obsessed with them.

On a subtler level, reactivity is enslavement and exile within a specific narrative. Say, for example, you are an artist and someone mocks your work. If this does not fit with a narrative that you are dependent on, such as 'I am an admired artist,' you might be tempted to give them an angry rebuke, at least in your thoughts. It is for this reason that Chazal tell us, "One who becomes angry is as if he served idols" (Rambam, *Hilchos De'os*, 2:3. *Teshuvos haRashbash*, Siman 370. *Zohar* 1, Bereishis, 2:16. See also *Shabbos*, 105b, where it states: "One who 'acts' upon their anger...," which is different from one who simply 'feels' anger: *Maharatz Chayos*, ad loc).

Why is anger like idol worship? It is because underlying every expression of anger there is a hidden sense of heresy, a sense that I know how things should be and how people should respond to my artistic talents, as in the metaphor above. In the act of becoming angry, one is ultimately saying that he rejects the way the Creator's Light has become manifest to him at the present moment. He pushes away the Cause and attempts to find refuge in an 'effect', a created thing. If a person driving on the highway is cut off by another car and he becomes angry, he is essentially rejecting Hashem's plan that, for whatever reason, he needs to experience being cut off while driving. He is asserting that he has a better idea of how things should happen.

When you become angry you are at that moment enslaved to your narrative and self-perception, 'I deserve respect... I must do something to enforce this.' Respect is an external 'effect', not the cause of your feelings or actions.

A deeper level of subtle slavery manifests when we become slaves to our feelings themselves. Feelings come and go just like all other phenomena, but when we react to them and attempt to get rid of them or hold onto them, we solidify them into little 'idols'. Venerating these inner idols can drag us deeper and deeper into dependency, self-pity, and exiled consciousness.

How do we untangle ourselves from reactivity and subtle idolatry and reach some form of freedom? The Torah prescribes a full dose of the one remaining *Mitzvah d'Oraisa / Torah Mitzvah* food on Pesach Night: Matzah. Matzah is the bread of humility, and humility is the code that unlocks our inner freedom.

In every moment of 'enslavement' there are two parts: the core narrative and its simple resonance as sensation. Let's say your narrative of who you are and how life should treat you is disrupted and you experience anger. The raw, uninterpreted sensation of 'anger' in itself does not in fact enslave you; it is just a simple, direct experience of being alive, and the sensation is clearly not mixed into the story of 'you'. This is the uncomplicated bread of affliction, which is paradoxically the bread of freedom. It is *Pashut* / simple, fresh from the Cause of Life.

It is only when the flour of raw sensations is mingled with the mental ingredients of your core narrative, your assumed self, that it becomes a Murkav of effects. It then becomes 'rich bread', a bread of subtle arrogance, of "This is bad; I don't deserve to feel this. I need to eliminate it.' It is ultimately our choice what to eat, whether the bread of simple humility and freedom, or the bread of complex arrogance and exile. We can at any moment eat from the simple 'Tree of Life' or from the complex Tree of 'Good Versus Bad'.

People become enslaved to their assumed selves because they think they *are* their narratives or their emotions. If you feel 'sad' sensations and believe that *you* are sad, then, if a significant person in your life does not acknowledge that self you believe yourself to be, you may get upset and act out. However, the narrative and emotion of sadness is not your real identity. Your actual identity is prior to all narratives and emotions.

Our core identity is not a void; we have a self, but it is in a constant state of flux. The objective of practicing humility is not to eliminate the ego, but to transcend our reactivity, rendering the self transparent to the Cause of Life. Trying to 'eliminate' the self would be just another reactive strategy. Instead we practice humility in order to unveil the eternity of the deeper self, the Neshamah. In the end, after our journey through this life with a body, we do not disappear, rather we live on in this eternal state.

The goal of life is not to lose our unique place within the universe, rather it is to find our deeper self, our particular soul quality, within the universe, and to live fully and expressively from that space. This is a level of 'coming into the Promised Land'. But first, we need to liberate ourselves from the subtle idolatry and exile of our identity. We need to let go of arrogant narratives and reactivities and find our specific soul purpose, aligning ourselves with our spiritual and physical makeup, as the Cause of Life has designed us. Then we can articulate and manifest our individuality from a place of Neshamah.

At the core of who we are, there is no story. We are simple and humble, like Matzah. Any anxiety or anger that is mixed into our lives is there because of our attachments to our narratives and the 'effects' of life. While our natural inclinations, traits and true desires are in themselves inherently consistent with the 'Matzah' of our soul, 'Chametz' can appear when our desires become reactive and mixed with our temporal identity. Desire is represented by the element of water, and when this is mixed into the 'flour' of our ego, in such a way that percolates and ferments, it inflates and grows out of proportion.

Yearnings and desires are meant to fuel our ego to mobilize us to do the right thing, but when the ego absorbs and takes ownership of a natural desire, it becomes Chametz. Then the desire becomes actively egoistic: 'I must get what I want, what I need' — until the person's satiation comes at the expense of someone else's wellbeing. Riddled with egoistic desires, one's experience of the world becomes one of a threatening place, a theater of 'me-against-you', 'us-against-them', and 'consume or be consumed'.

Chametz represents the inflated ego and distorted reality, as when our mental stories are blown up out of proportion. We all carry 'stories' of our past and who we are, but when we do not put them in perspective, 'inflation' builds up until these stories become costly and hurtful to ourselves and others. Eating Matzah with Kavanah deflates these stories, bursting the ego, and letting out the air of our stagnant narratives.

Matzah is humility. Matzah is freedom.

Chapter Eight:
Dreaming, Feeling, and Planning – Miriam, Aharon, and Moshe

THE BEGINNING OF THE GEULAH FOR KLAL YISRAEL IS when they first began to regain their voice in Egypt. "Now it came to pass in those many days that the king of Egypt died, and the children of Israel sighed from the labor, and they cried out, and their cry ascended to Hashem from the labor" (*Shemos*, 2:23). Precisely when they cried out, the process of their redemption began.

Following this redemption of the voice, there needs to be a redemption of the imagination. Once one cries out that things are not good, and even before they can develop a language of what they truly want from life, one needs to dream, plan, and envision what they need.

Knowing that oppression hurts and that it is wrong is the first step toward regaining one's freedom. In the midst of their enslavement, Klal Yisrael suddenly realized they were hurting and cried out in pain. Their cry was not even in the category of *Tefilah* / prayer, rather, as the Ohr haChayim writes, they simply cried out from pain and Hashem Above *heard* their cry as a prayer. Yet, identifying what is wrong in one's life, and what one needs to be released from, is not enough. One also needs to have a yearning for something new. In fact, people cannot move towards true freedom without a vision of what could be — without an inner life of positive desires.

There are actually three steps to freedom: 1) realize how bad the situation is and cry out, 2) dream of a better reality, and then 3) give voice to this vision and articulate it. Once these three steps are secured, the individual or community has the necessary tools to leave their condition of enslavement or oppression and to begin their journey toward freedom and autonomy.

These three elements of freedom are reflected in the three siblings who were instrumental in the redemption from Egypt to become possible: Moshe, Aharon, and Miriam.

It is by no coincidence that these three leaders were integral to the redemption from Egypt. Although Moshe was the messenger of Hashem and had the most prominent role in taking the people out of Egypt, the *Navi* / prophet says, "I brought you up out of Egypt and redeemed you from the land of slavery; I sent Moshe to lead you, *and also Aharon and Miriam* (*Michah*, 6:4).*

Besides being siblings, all three were part of the *Sheivet* / tribe of Levi, who were never actually enslaved to hard labor in Egypt, and in a way, being 'above' the enslavement gave them even more power to help bring about the people's redemption from Egypt, as "a prisoner cannot set himself free from prison" (*Berachos*, 5b).

MOSHE / AHARON / MIRIAM

All three holy siblings played an important part in the Exodus from Egypt, and are in fact hinted to in some of the items of the *Ka'arah* / Seder plate.

The two "cooked foods" (the egg and the bone) (*Pesachim*, 114b) correspond to Moshe and Aharon (*Sefer Rokeach*, Siman 59). The bitter Maror (as its root is *Mar* / bitter) corresponds to Miriam, whose name is also rooted in the word *Mar*, as the Rishonim write (see *Pirushei haTorah l'Baalei Tosefos*, Shemos, 1:14).

---

* The two "cooked foods" for the *Ka'arah* / Seder Plate (*Pesachim*, 114b) correspond to Moshe and Aharon: *Sefer Rokeach*, Seder Leil Pesach, Siman 59. Yet, based on the above Pasuk, there was a custom in the times of Rav Sharira Gaon to place three items on the Ka'arah: one for Moshe, one for Aharon and one for Miriam: *Ma'aseh Rokeach*, ibid.

What is more, the Medrash says (*Pesikta d'Rebbe Kehana*, Piska 5:9), the main apex of the enslavement of Klal Yisrael in Egypt occurred at the time of the birth of Miriam, and this is why her parents named her Miriam from the term *Mar*. Miriam was 86 at the time of the Exodus, and thus the real "bitterness" of Klal Yisrael was experienced during the last 86 years they were there. The number 86 is the numerical value of *Elokim*, the name of harsh *Din* / judgment.

As another Medrash teaches (*Medrash Rabbah*, Shemos, 26:1), וימררו את חייהם: והעמיד לו הקדוש ברוך הוא גואל, זו מרים, על שם המרור / "'And they embittered their lives': and HaKadosh Baruch Hu established from there a redeemer, who is Miriam, who is named for the bitterness." On one hand, we thus see Chazal connect Miriam with bitterness, and on the other hand, Miriam is called a *Goel* / redeemer.

Let us understand a little bit deeper how these three played their unique roles in Yetzias Mitzrayim, beginning with the most prominent person in the Exodus story, Moshe *Rabbeinu* / Our Teacher.

WHAT DOES MOSHE REPRESENT & WHY IS HIS NAME NOT MENTIONED IN THE HAGGADAH?

It is interesting to note that the name 'Moshe' is not mentioned in the story of the Haggadah, except once in passing.*

---

* The Haggadah only mentions 'Moshe' once, and only in passing when Rebbe Yosi the Galilean quotes the Song of the Sea: "…And they believed in Hashem and in Moshe His servant." It is only since the Haggadah is quoting here a Pasuk of the Torah, it needs to quote the entire Pasuk and

What does this mean? He would seem to be the most important character in the entire story, and yet his role is all but omitted — this is clearly intentional.

Later on in the Haggadah, its compilers quote at length P'sukim from *Sefer Yehoshua* (24:2-4) about the going out of Egypt: "Thus said Hashem, the G-d of Israel, 'Your fathers used to live on the other side of the river — Terach, the father of Avraham and the father of Nachor, and they served other gods. And I took your father Avraham from beyond the river, and I led him throughout the whole land of Canaan. I increased his seed and gave him Yitzchak, and to Yitzchak I gave Yaakov and Eisav. To Eisav I gave Mount Seir to inherit, and Yaakov and his sons went down to Egypt.'" The compilers of the Haggadah do not continue with the next Pasuk (24:5), "Then I sent Moshe and Aharon, and I afflicted the Egyptians by what I did there, and I brought you out." Rather, they stop before quoting a mention of how Hashem sent Moshe (and Aharon) as messengers to take them out of Egypt.

Why is Moshe omitted as a character in the Haggadah? Here are three potential solutions:

---

include the name of Moshe. It is interesting to note that the Mechilta, from which this passage of "Rebbe Yosi…" is taken from, omits the end of the Pasuk, and "they believed in Hashem and in Moshe His servant" is not quoted, as only the first part of the Pasuk is needed to prove his point that the Makos at the sea were 'five times' those in Egypt. Yet, the compilers of the Haggadah added the end of the Pasuk, seemingly intentionally.

1) Moshe is omitted in order that when we think about the Redemption, we will focus on HaKadosh Baruch Hu taking us out of Egypt, rather than on Moshe, as Hashem says, "I, I alone took you out of Egypt. Given humanity's pension for idolizing great leaders, mentioning Moshe could be a distraction from the essence of what is really occurring — Hashem liberating us through whatever channels and instruments are necessary.

Here is what the Rambam writes: לפי דעתו של בן אביו מלמדו. כיצד, אם היה קטן או טפש אומר לו בני כלנו היינו עבדים כמו שפחה זו או כמו עבד זה במצרים ובלילה הזה פדה אותנו הקדוש ברוך הוא ויוציאנו לחרות, ואם היה הבן גדול וחכם מודיעו מה שארע לנו במצרים ונסים שנעשו לנו על ידי משה רבנו / "The father should instruct his son according to the child's understanding. For example, he should say to one small or foolish: 'My son, all of us were slaves in Egypt, like this maidservant or like this manservant, and on this night Hashem redeemed and liberated us.' If the son is grown up and intelligent, he should inform him about everything that happened to us in Egypt, and about the miracles that were wrought for us by Our Teacher, Moshe" (*Hilchos Chametz uMatzah*, 7:2).

The obvious distinction between our explanation to a foolish child and to a more intelligent one, is the appropriateness of mentioning "the miracles that were wrought for us by our teacher Moshe." Moshe is not mentioned only to the less developed child because he may focus too much on Moshe as an obvious and tangible source of redemption, and he may overlook the more intangible Source, the Infinite Creator who redeemed us. (Obviously, this does not only apply to children. For the adult who makes an idol out of any human leader, no matter how great, is in the aspect of the 'foolish child'.)

It is also interesting that the miracles are only described to the wiser child. One would think that the younger, less intelligent child should be told about the miracles, while the older, wiser child should be told less about the miracles and more about the meaning of Pesach. However, even miracles could be a distraction to the younger child. It can take away from the essence of the story. For this reason we need to tell the less developed child simply that we were slaves and HaKadosh Baruch Hu took us out of slavery and brought us to freedom.

That is the simple *Peshat* / literal explanation. Here is a more metaphorical explanation.

2) The Mitzvah of telling the story of going out of Egypt is upon Moshe as well as on us. In this sense, Moshe is 'reading the Haggadah'; he is therefore not *in* it, but outside it, looking in. He is the hidden narrator.

3) A more *Penimi* / internal interpretation is as follows. When we recite the Haggadah on Seder Night, we need to speak about the historical Exodus from Egypt from a personal perspective: "In every generation a person has to see himself as if he left Egypt." The Haggadah is not merely speaking about an event in the distant past, but is a means for us to experience

the Geulah of Dibbur right now; we need to take it personally so that the experience should liberate us in the present. Therefore, all of the characters depicted in the historical story of the going out of Egypt should be seen as reflections or representations of different parts of ourselves. For example, Pharaoh represents our negative inclination and stubborn ego, and the slavery of Klal Yisrael represents our enslavement to our passions, emotions and our subjectivity. However, Moshe's name does not appear in the text, because he does not represent a mere *part* of us. As we tell the stories of the Haggadah, it is as if Moshe is telling the stories; the "Moshe within us" (*Tanya*, 42) is the awareness that views and understands the stories. The Moshe within us inspires us to leave our constraints, and becomes the instrument for our liberation.

Moshe, the receiver of Torah, represents the 'free mind', the objective awareness of truth. It is this objective awareness that stands outside the drama of the story, 'outside' the enslavement, witnessing all the interactions of the different characters within ourselves, and ultimately guiding them to spiritual freedom.

Yet, no matter how wise, detached, or objective you are, if inner slavery is your assumed reality, you will not be able to 'think' your way out of it. There still needs to be a strong desire and emotional yearning for freedom in order to reach freedom. We need to enlist the help of 'others': the *emotional self* that can connect to other people and unite them, as well as the *dissatisfied self* that can yearn bitterly for freedom and motivate actual practical steps of action. These two additional 'selves' are represented by the two other main catalysts in our redemption from Egypt (also not mentioned in the Haggadah): Aharon and Miriam.

As Moshe represents the mind or detached intellect, his brother Aharon represents the emotional, the relational, the place of heart — and his sister Miriam represents the raw, physical yearning, the place of longing and dreaming.

MOSHE:

Moshe represents the soul-level of *Neshamah*. The name 'Moshe' is spelled Mem Shin Hei. As mentioned earlier, if we add the letter Nun, we have the four letters of the word NeShaMaH. The letter Nun, which is numerically fifty, corresponds to the fifty gates of Binah, the idea of transcendent intellect. Moshe is the transmitter of the Torah, the Divine blueprint, and he represents the spiritual mind of the Jewish people. Within the greater 'body' of Klal Yisrael, Moshe is the *Bechinah* / level of the detached and objective intellect.

AHARON:

Aharon represents the soul level of *Ruach* / the place of emotions. He embodies the heart space. His name alludes to the words "*Ah-(Avad)-Ron* / O, our greatness has been lost (see *Pirushei haTorah l'Baalei Tosefos*, Shemos, 1:14). The sigh of "Ah" comes from a person who is open about their feelings.

Aharon is the one who reveals and renews love between people. He is a lover of peace. He is the one who continually brings people together as a marriage counselor, outreach worker, and community peacemaker. As the *Cohen Gadol* / High Priest, he wore the Choshen Mishpat upon his heart, which graphically and tangibly unified the twelve tribes of Israel. Within the 'body' of Klal Yisrael, Aharon is their heart space, the facilitator of their emotions and connectivity.

MIRIAM:

Miriam represents the soul level of *Nefesh*. The name 'Miriam', broken into two, means *Mar-Yam* / 'the sea of bitterness', referring to the bitter yearning of the people for redemption. For example, in her own continual yearning and vision for redemption, Miriam motivates her parents to reunite after having separated, and conceive the baby who later becomes the redeemer, Moshe.

Within the 'body' of Klal Yisrael, Miriam is their place of longing, yearning and dreaming.

MIRIAM:
THE FUNDAMENTAL INGREDIENT FOR REDEMPTION

We need all three elements, Moshe, Aharon and Miriam, in order to bring about a personal, inner redemption, whatever it might be.* The role of our inner 'Miriam', however, is primary. She begins the process of redemption by acknowledging the suffering of exile, and responding with a visceral yearning

---

* In the birth of Moshe, Miriam is present, as she is Pu'ah (*Sotah* 11b). In another version, Pu'ah is Elisheva, Aharon's wife. This way, at Moshe's birth both Miriam and Aharon are present.

for freedom. Her bitterness is not like the dullness of depression, but rather like a jolting burn of freshly grated horseradish, Maror. The visceral rawness of this discontent stimulates a *Cheishek* / yearning, longing and eventually a dream, 'What if we could escape this place? What if life could actually be better out there?!' Miriam's dream germinates subconsciously within the experience and imagination of the people, until they realize how confined they really are. For the first time, they "groan," and Hashem hears their groan, opening the way for them. These are the first contractions that eventually birth the redemption.

In order to get un-stuck anywhere in our lives, we first need motivation, Cheishek, yearning, longing, and dreaming of liberation, or at least a better situation.

ותתצב אחתו מרחק לדעה לדעה מה־יעשה לו / "And his sister stationed herself at a distance to learn what would befall him" (*Shemos*, 2:4). After Miriam finally convinces her parents to reunite and have more children, they have a beautiful child who is born circumcised and radiates light and goodness. He is later named Moshe. And then, a mere three months later, Moshe, as a vulnerable infant, is placed in a basket on the Nile, in one last desperate attempt to save his life. As his mother places the little Moshe in the water, his sister, still a young girl, stations herself at a distance and waits to see what will happen. She is dreaming, yearning, desiring that somehow there will be a positive result, perhaps that Moshe will be saved and grow up to be the redeemer of Klal Yisrael.

She is "standing from afar," and looking into the distance; she is metaphorically looking toward an eventual future. She does not give up, looking intently from the distant, glorious past of her People, and yet, anticipating and yearning for a brighter future.

Miriam also awakens this Cheishek within Klal Yisrael. She was a prophetess, one of the very few in all of the Torah narrative, because she dreams and inspires others to dream. She feels acutely the bitterness of the present oppression, and yet envisions and yearns for a positive and healthy outcome.

The second element needed for redemption from any constriction or limitations, is the friendliness and love that shines from our inner 'Aharon'. Aharon builds on Miriam's motivation, dream, and desire, by giving the slaves feelings of hope and inspiration. Bitterness at 'what is' can get us moving, but only sweetness can give us the hope we need to continue. We need supportive people to lift our morale when we feel like giving up. Aharon's inspiration and communal rapport began to awaken the hearts of the slaves, like the warm buzz of wine. Once we have a dream, we need positive emotion to strengthen us for the journey forward.

Aharon was the root of Klal Yisrael, and in our own journey, the emotional space is a foundation of the journey forward.

Aharon also serves as Moshe's mouthpiece. When Moshe complains to Hashem that he is unable to speak and has a "heavy mouth," Hashem says אהרן אחיך הלוי ידעתי כי־דבר ידבר הוא / "There is your brother Aharon, the Levite. He, I know, speaks readily," and הוא יהיה־לך לפה / "He will be your mouth-piece."

In other words, Aharon is the flow of emotion, the soul level of *Ruach* / wind, which is so vital to speech, the ability to move emotions outward into expression.

The third element of redemption is the intellectual clarity of our inner 'Moshe'. From a more detached, objective place, we can see what it will take to reach freedom. Moshe's job is to receive Divine wisdom, issue warnings to Pharaoh, and to direct the people, transmitting to them Torah and Mitzvos according to Hashem's plan. Once we have a dream and positive emotional connections, we need an escape route, a plan of action, so to speak. Moshe transmits Divine knowledge to us and guides us toward what we need to do and where we need to go, in order to get out of Egypt.

To connect deeply to redemption during the Seder, we should aspire to connect with all three redeemer archetypes. We can do this very concretely when we eat the special foods of the Seder. When we eat the *Maror* / bitter herbs, we can acknowledge the pain in our lives and embody the bitter yearning of Miriam for goodness, and for us, the Ultimate and Complete Redemption from exile. When we drink the four cups of wine, we can connect with the quality of Aharon, by arousing our emotional state, and uniting in friendship with our friends and family around the table, to inspire them that they too feel the longing for Geulah, both personal and collective. When we eat the Matzah, we can embody the intellect of Moshe, by thinking of our spiritual intentions, and contemplating some of the profound mystical meanings of Matzah and Geulah.

Person	Faculty	Activity	Sefirah	Level of Soul	Ritual food	Stage of Redemption
Moshe	Detached Intellect	Witnessing, Knowing	Chochmah-Binah-Da'as	Neshamah	Matzah	Stage Three: Plan
Aharon	Emotional Heart	Feeling, Relating to People	Six Emotional Sefiros of Zeir Anpin	Ruach	Wine	Stage Two: Feel / Speak
Miriam	Active Body	Yearning, Motivating	Malchus	Nefesh	Maror	Stage One: Dream

Chapter Nine:
Redemption of Imagination:
MIRIAM AND THE SANCTIFICATION OF THE NEW MOON

L ET US FURTHER UNFOLD THE ARCHETYPE OF THE SISTER of Moshe and Aharon, the great prophetess of the Exodus narrative, Miriam.

Miriam, as just explored, is connected to Maror and a sense of the bitterness of present circumstances. This bitterness is not to be confused with 'depression' or lack of hope — it is quite the opposite. True bitterness arouses strong desire, awakens longing, and creates a platform upon which we can dream of a brighter future. Appropriately, Miriam is the prophetic 'dreamer' in the story of the Going Out of Egypt; she is the one who never gives up and is always aspiring for a better future.

Not only does Miriam have the vision of a future redemption, she even prepares musical instruments to be played *after* the redemption. These instruments are indeed played after the Splitting of the Sea, once we have finally transcended the bitterness of exile.

Miriam lives in a present that is magnetically pulled forward by a future, rather than a present that is merely being pushed along as an effect of the past. She is always leaning forward, instead of looking backwards. She lives in tune with possibility, rather than being stuck within seeming inevitability; she stands at the Cause of life, rather than at its effect.

OWNING TIME

When Klal Yisrael was about to leave Egypt, they received their first *Mitzvah* / instruction from HaKadosh Baruch Hu: to 'sanctify the month': החדש הזה לכם ראש חדשים / "This month shall be to you the first of the months" (*Shemos*, 12:1-2). Through sanctifying the new moon, it "shall be for you"; you will 'own' or 'create' time by determining when a new month begins, and thereby sanctifying it.

A major distinction between a slave and a master is that a slave has 'no time' of his own — his time is owned and shaped by his master — while a free person owns their life and their time. The Seforno comments on "This month shall be to you...": מכאן ואילך יהיו החדשים שלכם, לעשות בהם כרצונכם, אבל בימי השעבוד לא היו ימיכם שלכם, אבל היו לעבודת אחרים ורצונם,

לפיכך ראשון הוא לכם לחדשי השנה, כי בו התחיל מציאותכם הבחיריי / "From now on these months shall be *yours*, to do with as you wish. This is by way of contrast to the years when you were enslaved, when you had no control over your time at all. Your slave owners owned your time and did with it as they pleased. Thus, החודש הזה לכם ראש חדשים — in this month you began your existence as a free people" (*Seforno*, Shemos, 12:2).

At this moment, we are becoming a free people and Hashem is empowering us to leave the paradigm of slavery and enter the world of freedom, in which we are not mastered by anyone, not even by time. We are to stand 'above' time, to master it and 'create' it.

A slave may possess certain objects that belong to him prior to his enslavement, but he can never own his time. Klal Yisrael, too, kept some vestiges of their identity as a People, but their time was 'owned' by Mitzrayim. As such, when HaKadosh Baruch Hu began to set them free, the first Mitzvah was, 'Sanctify the new moon; you can start to count time because time is now yours'.

We must own time — not be owned by time.

We have freedom to choose what we do and what we do not do. Even deeper than owning time, as a free person we have the ability to create and fashion time. This is the secret of the Mitzvah of Sefiras HaOmer, in which we count and shape our days and imbue them with meaning. When we declare, 'Today is day one,' 'Today is day two,' we are exercising a private, individual prerogative to make that day truly our own. For example, if you cross the international date line and people there are counting a day ahead of you or a day earlier, the Halachah (according to the Rebbe's ruling) is to continue to count your sequence and rhythm of time, despite everyone around you counting a different day.

In this way, even your "day one" of the Omer is not defined by the collective counting. Rather, your "day one" is defined by you, individually, as you have harnessed your creative ability, empowered by the Source of the Mitzvah, to count and create that "day one." We thus have the ability to create our time.

MOON - DREAMS - MIRIAM - WOMEN

HaKadosh Baruch Hu gave us the Mitzvah to sanctify the new moon thereby connecting us with time as it is specifically related to the lunar cycle, and not the solar cycle. HaKadosh Baruch Hu wanted us to begin looking at the world through the lens of the fluctuating, vacillating moon; to see life and reality from a different perspective than the Egyptians, who worshiped the 'static' sun.

According to our calendar, months are defined by a lunar cycle, whereas years are defined by a solar cycle. The solar system is rigid and unchanging; the sun rises and sets in the same way each day. As such, the sun represents a world of predictability. The reality of a slave is, as well, rigidly predictable; there is no room for any real change in his life, at least from his own perspective.

Appropriately, as the Shaloh haKadosh points out, the name פרעה / *Pharaoh* is numerically 355, the same value as the word שנה / *Shanah* / year. Pharaoh, the quintessential Egyptian sun worshiper, embodied a world-view of rigidity and predictability, and is therefore connected with the idea of Shanah and of *Yashan* / 'old' (same letters as *Shanah*), routine, and predictability. The sun represents rigid, linear, inevitable structures, as it is always 'full' in the sky, even if it is tucked behind the clouds.

Ein Chadash Tachas haShemesh / "There is no newness under the sun" (*Koheles*, 1:9). Yet, as the Zohar succinctly adds, "While under the 'sun' there is no newness, the moon is new; the moon is in fact a 'newness' that is under the sun" (*Zohar* 1, p. 123b). The word *Chodesh* / month comes from the word *Chidush* / new. The moon waxes and wanes, sometimes it is observable and sometimes not. The moon represents a paradigm of renewal and the potential for novelty that breaks the monotony of linear time. Renewal is possible because of fluctuation and movement.

In a rigid, predictable universe there is no newness as there is no fluctuation, waxing, or waning. But in the constant fluctuation of the moon there is an element of unpredictability. Sometimes it seems that it has disappeared, but soon it will be full once again. Sometimes a people seems to be enslaved, but soon it will be free.

Sunlight is an expression of the empirical, the observable and immediately tangible. Everything can be seen clearly in the light of day. Moonlight, on the other hand, is dim and fleeting. It represents the world of dreams, night, and imagination. The Hebrew word for sun is *Shemesh*, which comes from the Hebrew word *Mash* / tangible (see *Shemos*, 10:21), the world of 'manifest being'. The word *Levanah* / moon comes from the word *Lavan* / white or transparent, connected to elusiveness, intangibility, and a perpetual process of 'becoming'.

Commenting on the Pasuk, "The sun knows its setting" (*Tehilim*, 104:19), our Sages say, "The sun knows its setting and its movement, but the moon does not know" (*Rosh Hashanah*, 25a. Rambam, *Hilchos Kiddush haChodesh*, 17:23). The moon represents a realm beyond set patterns, beyond what is seen, the undefined potential and possibility of imagination and dreaming.

For this reason (among the infinite and inscrutable 'reasons' of HaKadosh Baruch Hu), we received the *Mitzvah* / Divine mandate to sanctify the new moon and view time from a lunar perspective — while we were still enslaved. To attain our freedom, to leave the unchanging ontological status of 'slaves', we needed to break free from the grip of a strictly solar perspective. The sun was, in fact, the chief Egyptian deity ("Ra") and the definition of their consciousness and culture. In Mitzrayim, no slave had ever been freed. If you were born a slave or free, rich or poor, that is what you and your descendants would always be, in life as well as death.

With no room to break out of the order of things, there is no room to become a free person. There is no room for dreams, nor a glimpse of a reality outside the entrenched stagnancy of existential alienation. To break out of such a narrow world, one would first need to 'believe' in the possibility of freedom, to believe that HaKadosh Baruch Hu, the source of every status and perspective, can uplift one into a new reality at any moment. For this belief to be possible, one needs to connect to the paradigm of the moon.

Ever since our miraculous exodus and redemption from the tyranny of the sun, we count time according to the moon, and, we are collectively compared to the moon (*Sukkah*, 29a. More specifically, the full moon: *Zohar* 3, p. 281). As the moon does not have any light of its own, rather it simply reflects the light of the sun, we too recognize that our light, life, and power all come from a source greater than ourselves, the Ultimate Light of Hashem. Our collective and individual history too is like the moon; we go through periods of waxing and waning, both communally and individually. Sometimes up, sometimes down, sometimes full and bright, sometimes empty and dark. We are constantly in flux, perpetually renewed and reborn through our tenacious hopes and seemingly impossible dreams.

Our bitterness drove us to throw off the yoke of the Egyptians. We desperately needed to leave, to let go of the world of the sun and its rigidity, and to enter into the world of the moon, and its vision of hope for the future. Sanctifying the moon was a new Mitzvah, a new gift and empowerment from the Creator of all Life, which we received in Egypt, while we were still living in a world of sun-worshipers, and thus susceptible to the influence of sun-time. As we were living in Goshen, within the land of Egypt (although perhaps it was part of Eretz Yisrael: *Yehoshua*, 11:16. Radak, Shach on *Bereishis*, 47:27), we still had some influence from the moon (*Ahavas Yonasan*, Vayetze). However, the time had come to make a complete break from the *Kelipah* / negative chokehold of the sun with all of its constriction and its limitation of any upward movement or imagination. Sanctifying the new moon gave even the lowly slave the possibility, while still being physically a slave (although Chazal say the Shibud ended in Tishrei: *Rosh Hashanah*, 11a, even though the Makos took place over a twelve month period [*Mishnah*, *Eduyot*, 2:10: משפט המצריים, שנים עשר חדש], still they worked until Tishrei), to stand in the fields with the sun beating down on his back and an overlord with a whip above him, and to imagine and dream of redemption by the light of the moon. Even under such crushing conditions, we were able to envision leaving slavery, becoming free, standing at the foot of Mount Sinai, and eventually entering the Promised Land.

SUN / MASCULINE / PREDICTABILITY / STRICT LOGIC - MOON / FEMININE / POSSIBILITY / IMAGINATION

Everything in this world has a masculine and feminine counterpart ("Everything that the Holy One, Blessed be He, created in His world, He created male and female": *Bava Basra*, 74b). In terms of the two "great lights," the sun represents the steady 'masculine', whereas the moon is the fluid 'feminine'. The sun corresponds to the father, and the moon to the mother (*Zohar*, Vayikra). Our sages tell us that if a person dreams of kissing the moon, it suggests a romantic encounter with a woman (*Berachos*, 56b).

Sun-time is masculine whereas moon-time is feminine. Day, in which things are simply revealed, defined, and seen as objective and predictable, is masculine. The mystery and hiddenness of night is a feminine attribute; one closes their eyes, enters their 'unpredictable' subjective, subconscious mind, and dreams or imagines the future.

Like the moon, the body of a woman constantly fluctuates and changes, even long after the changes of adolescence. In feminine and lunar cycles, there is an apparent diminishment of light, a kind of 'death' or dwindling of potential life, and then there is a renewal of light and the power to create new life. Due to this, the feminine perspective of life and time includes hope, dreams and possibility, even where the masculine perspective does not see any.

Being connected to anticipation, outside of the world of predictability, women are connected to the world of night, of dreams, of imagination, and the hope and yearning for a different and better world.

Zachar / male is connected with the word *Zachor* / memory, suggesting a tendency to dwell on the past. *Nekeivah* / female comes from the world *Nekev* / opening, suggesting the openness necessary to move into the future. Another word for 'woman' is *Ishah*, from the word *Nashah* / forgetting ("*Ki Nashani...*" says Yoseph, when he names Menasheh), alluding to the power of allowing oneself to let go of the past and move on, and to dream and yearn for a brighter dawn.

Having a secure awareness of the bitterness of the present, the women in Egypt — perhaps inspired by Miriam — had a tenacious Emunah that a better life would indeed come. Because of the Emunah of the women, all of Klal Yisrael merited to be redeemed: "In the merit and in the reward of the righteous women we were redeemed from Egypt" (*Sotah*, 11b. *Medrash Rabbah*, Bamidbar, 3:6. Medrash *Yalkut Mechiri*, 78:14). It was the Emunah of the women that inspired the men to soldier on and continue procreating, creating hope and the possibility for future generations.

The Gemara (*Sotah*, 11b) tells us, "At the time when these women would go to the river to draw water, the Holy One, Blessed be He, would materialize for them small fish that would enter into their pitchers, and they would therefore draw pitchers that were half filled with water and half filled with fish. They would then come and place two pots on the fire, one pot of hot water for washing their husbands and one pot of fish with which to feed them. Then they would take what they prepared to their husbands, to the field, and would bathe their husbands, anoint them with oil, feed them the fish and give them water to drink, and bond with them in intimacy (and eventually give birth to children)."

In other words, while the men were slaving away in the fields, reduced to mere statistics, robbed of their humanity, with only the urgency of survival on their minds, wrapped up in their immediate needs, the women came along and gave them a hot meal, bathed them, and made them feel human again. The women revitalized them and gave them energy to become intimate; to love and be loved and feel unity with another human being. The women inspired them to let go of the darkness and death all around them, and to have faith that they could bring life, children, and future into the world. This way, the men began to feel connected to a brighter future, to feel a thread of hope reaching out from the future into the present. They began to feel that better times were coming, and that freedom and safety were just around the corner. This was the power of the feminine worldview.

THE WORLD OF MIRRORS & IMAGINATION

Women are also associated with the world of imagination, and specifically as symbolized by reflections and mirrors. A powerful Medrash, similar to the above Gemara, tells us about the Emunah that the women had while in Egypt: "The Jewish women in Egypt possessed mirrors of copper into which they used to look when they adorned themselves. When the time came to build the Mishkan, the women came with these mirrors and offered them as a contribution toward the Mishkan. Moshe was about to reject them since they were apparently made to pander to their vanity, but HaKadosh Baruch Hu told him, 'Accept them; these are dearer to Me than all the other contributions, because through them the women reared many children in Egypt! For when their husbands were tired through the crushing labor they used to bring them food and drink and induced them to eat. Then they would take the mirrors, and each gazed at herself in her mirror together with her husband, saying endearingly to him, "See, I am handsomer than you!" They awakened their husbands' affection and subsequently became the mothers of many children'" (Rashi, *Shemos*, 38:8. See also *Tanchuma*, Pekudei, 9).

Mirrors create an image, but one that is elusive and fleeting; turn the mirror ever so slightly and the image disappears. This is much like the allusiveness of the moon. Yet, just like the night and the moon open up the world of imagination, so do mirrors open up yearning and possibility. A mirror can reflect something that is behind you or in front of you that would otherwise not be seen. It enhances and expands what the eyes can see, and takes vision beyond what is readily perceivable. Thus, mirrors are intricately bound to the world of dream, arousal of interest and activation of imagination.

Offering these mirrors to be used in the building of the Mishkan was reminiscent of the Mitzvah to sanctify the new moon. In both instances, Hashem favored the feminine perspective of life. Hashem wanted us to connect to the rhythm of lunar time, and it became a Mitzvah upon all of Klal Yisrael (through the High Courts). The semi-*Moed* / holiday of Rosh Chodesh (*Shavuos*, 10a. *Eichah*, 1:15. *Ta'anis*, 17b), celebrating the renewed moon and the beginning of the new month, is therefore especially connected to the feminine and to women (*Yerushalmi, Ta'anis*, 1. הוסיף המקום י"ט לנשים בר"ח בשכר שלא נתרצו על מעשה העגל :שאין הנשים עושות מלאכה בהן... ושמעתי מפי .Tosefos, Rosh Hashanah, 23a מורי הזקן ז"ל שניתנה להם מצוה זו בשביל שלא פירקו נזמיהן בעגל :Rashi, *Megilah*, 22b. נשים אסורות במלאכה לפי' שלא פרקו נזמיהן במעשה העגל :Tosefos, ibid).

In fact, many women celebrate even today by refraining from mundane activities on Rosh Chodesh (e.g., from doing laundry: *Shulchan Aruch*, Orach Chayim, 417. See *Pirkei d'Rebbe Eliezer*, 43). This is because women are intrinsically connected to the renewal of the moon and the world of faith and hope in a brighter day, even when things are seemingly getting darker and darker. Women naturally have a deeper awareness that inevitably the light of life will eventually return.

Women's Emunah, with their mirrors of imagination and holy enticement, inspired their beaten down, despairing spouses to love and dream again. The feminine principle inspired the masculine principle to revive, to unite again, and dive into the future. This power to spark revival and redemption is also the power of the paragon of women in the Egyptian Exile, Miriam.

ALL REDEMPTIONS ARE INSPIRED BY WOMEN

"All redemptions" of Klal Yisrael throughout history, including the future and Ultimate Redemption, "came about through women" (*Eitz Yoseph*, Shir haShirim, 1:37). The beginning of Klal Yisrael's redemption from Egypt was marked by Basyah, the daughter of the Pharaoh, saving the life of three-month-old Moshe in the Nile and raising him in a place free from slavery and oppression.

Moshe's mother, Yocheved, too, was instrumental to the redemption. She was born "between the gates" — between worlds, between the descent from their homeland of Israel and the descent into their place of enslavement, Egypt. Being born 'between' realities, she gives birth to Moshe, a child who is raised 'between' realities. He is Jewish by birth and thus can identify fully with his brethren's pain, suffering and enslavement — but he is raised in the palace of the Pharaoh and in the lap of luxury and freedom. As he knows both 'freedom' and 'exile', he becomes the instrument through which HaKadosh Baruch Hu brings Klal Yisrael out of exile and into freedom.

Centuries later, during the Purim narrative, when the Persian king decreed the death of the Jewish people, Queen Esther arose as the primary figure to bring about the annulment of the decree. Sometime later, with the Greek-Assyrian chokehold on the Land of Israel and the eventual Chanukah miracle, it was Yehudis who put to death an enemy general and turned the tide of the battle. As a result, eventually the Jewish warriors were able to regain the Beis haMikdash and rededicate it, following which the miracle of Chanukah occurred.

These women fully experienced the harsh decrees against the entire Jewish People (as Rashi writes, *Megilah,* 4a: שאף על הנשים גזר), and they suffered as did the men. However, their bitterness did not drive them to despair, rather it drove them toward redemption — and the main miracles in these stories occurred through them (as *Tosefos,* ibid, brings down: פירש רשב״ם שעיקר הנס היה על ידן בפורים על ידי אסתר בחנוכה על ידי יהודית. And as Rashi on *Shabbos,* 23a, writes: ועל יד אשה נעשה הנס. Rashi and Rashbam on *Pesachim,* 108b: דמשום דע״י אסתר נגאלו וכן גבי נר חנוכה).

DEATH OF THE FIRST BORN

As mentioned, Egypt is connected with the world of the sun, the world of inevitability, predictability, and strict, fixed hierarchy. The sun above beats down on the earth below, and it also gives nutrients to the earth. Mirroring this natural hierarchy, Egyptian society had an unimpeachable top-down pyramid of 'order'. There were slaves, free people, masters, priests, first-borns, 'demigods' and finally 'gods incarnate'. Indeed, most early civilizations were founded on hierarchies of power, and believed that in this way their societies were aligned with the natural order of the cosmos and the ranks among the heavenly bodies above. The religious rituals and monuments that were erected in most ancient civilizations were established to mirror these heavenly hierarchies.

Absolute hierarchy is reflected as well in the architectural symbols of the ancient world, from the ziggurats of Mesopotamia to the pyramids of Egypt: they are broad at the base and narrow or peaked at the top. In their societal structure, the monarch sits on top, and beneath him his children, and beneath them his advisors, then the priestly caste, the free men, and finally the slaves at the wide base. Those at the bottom of the pyramid are just there to support and uphold the ones above them. No one was able to change their rank. One was either first-born or not, and either born a master or slave. A slave could never become a free man in Egypt; such an idea could never even enter their consciousness.

The Pharaoh was considered the incarnation of a 'deity', and those born to the Pharaoh were the sons and daughters of the 'god' (This is why when the daughter of Pharaoh converted to monotheism, her name was changed from her Egyptian name denoting her as 'Daughter of the pharaoh-god' to the Hebrew name 'Basyah' / 'Daughter of Hashem'). Within ordinary free Egyptian family units, all firstborn boys were revered, believed to be closer to the 'gods' above and therefore treated with utmost respect. A firstborn was stamped as privileged for life. One could never be as close to the 'gods' as his older sibling, just as a commoner could never rise to become the Pharaoh — it was a 'divine' birthright. Likewise, slavery was ontological and freeing a slave was not a possibility. All of this was rooted in Egyptian cosmology and the worship of the sun, which impregnated their entire worldview and imprinted its limitations upon their society.

The final stage of the Ten Plagues, which allowed for the freedom of Klal Yisrael and also made the Egyptians aware of Hashem's Presence and Unity, was the death of the first-born (the female firstborn also died when the family's firstborn child was female: *Medrash Rabbah*, Shemos, 18:3). For redemption to occur, this rigid hierarchical structure needed to be wiped out.* This breaking

---

* The Torah teaches us to sanctify our firstborns because Hashem saved the firstborn of Klal Yisrael at the plague of the death of the firstborn. Asks the Ran, is it possible to say that a king would tell his subject, 'You belong to me because when I put to death a murderer I did not kill you?' We were not 'saved' from death in Egypt, as we did nothing wrong to deserve death. Says the Ran, when Hashem brought the plague of the death of the firstborn, it was a collective decree upon the entire constitution of the 'first-born', and it affected all people, both the Egyptians and Klal Yisrael — וכשרצה הש״י להכות בכורי מצרים, חידש איזה ענין מפסיד ומתיחס לבכורות. כי הבכורות יש יחס

of the rule of primogeniture loosened the rigid Kelipah of hierarchy as a whole.

YISRAEL, THE FIRSTBORN OF EGYPT

HaKadosh Baruch Hu struck the *Bechorim* / firstborn of *Mitzrayim* / Egypt, and as a counterpoint revealed His essential relationship to Klal Yisrael: *B'ni Bechori Yisrael* / "My firstborn son, Israel." The *Kedushah* / holiness of the Bechorim of Klal Yisrael was also established. What is the difference between the Bechorim of Mitzrayim and the Bechorim of Klal Yisrael?

For Klal Yisrael, a Bechor is only *Mukdash* / sanctified through the Rechem of his mother — *Rechem M'kadeish* / "the womb sanctifies (the child)" (*Bechoros*, 9a). This means that the nature of our Bechorim lies not in their personal honor, rather in honoring their source. For Mitzrayim, the honor was in the birthright itself, without any relationship to its source. This corresponds to their foundational idea, the epitome of Avodah Zarah, 'I created myself', 'I am my own source'. The foundational idea of Klal Yisrael is humbly honoring HaKadosh Baruch Hu, our Creator; we are only a 'moon' reflecting the light of our Source.

Now we can better understand why the 'first' Mitzvah is to sanctify the moon. Becoming connected to the *Hischadshus* / sense of constant renewal and the (seeming) unpredictabil-

---

ביניהם כולל ומשתף אותם. והוא שאין ספק שאין הרחם אשר לא נולד בו עובר מעולם
בו ולדות נוצרו כבר אשר הרחם יהיה אשר התכונה באותה: *Derashos haRan*, 8.

ity of the moon cycle, allowed Klal Yisrael to break free of the constricted, absolute rigid mindset entrapping them, and imagine the possibility of freedom. It allowed Klal Yisrael to transcend the absolute 'order' of Egypt, and enter into a place beyond order, a place of infinity and transcendence.

EVERY MOMENT IS NEW

"In every generation, a person must regard himself as if he had gone out of Egypt" (*Pesachim*, 116b). In every generation, every day and every moment, we need to connect with this power of *Hischadshus* / renewal, of moon-time and the power to dream of the 'impossible'. By counting lunar time, we connect with this sense of radical Hischadshus. It helps us relate to time, to life, and to ourselves with a sense of continuous renewal and ever-unfolding possibility.

Geulah / the redemption of Klal Yisrael began on Rosh Chodesh Nisan, the moment they empowered themselves with the Mitzvah of sanctifying the new moon — the moon embodying Hischadshus. Similarly, our *Geulah Peratis* / individual, personal redemption begins when we let go of the chokehold of the 'Pharaoh' within; the enslaving mentality that holds us within our conditioning, trapping us in the paradigm of 'yesterday'. We become freer when we connect with moon-time and let go of our belief in rigid sun-time, of *Shanah* / year and *Yashan* / oldness that does not allow us to fully connect to 'today' or 'tomorrow'. The *Navi* / Prophet Yechezkel, one of the only prophets to prophesy outside of Eretz Yisrael and within a state of exile, laments and says, "And I am in exile, sitting on the banks of the river כבר / *Kevar*" (*Yechezkel*, 1:1). It is no coincidence that the river where he experiences prophecy in exile is called Kevar. *Kevar* in Hebrew means 'already', 'it was' — past. Exile begins with the notion of 'already'; living in the past, without a sense of any possible future. When a person's 'present' is nothing more than the effects of his past, for better or for worse, the present is stable and predictable.

When we allow our past to limit our present, we become nothing more than mechanical, predictable, and thus susceptible to eventual inertia and despair. When we think that if we were not successful yesterday we cannot be successful today, then our past imprisons our present. In this state of constricted consciousness, change is never a possibility and any real movement is unattainable. Sadly, by living this way, the future is already closed in front of us. This is another reason, perhaps, that the Name that Hashem reveals to Moshe at the Burning Bush is *Eh'yeh* / "I Will Be," a Name that is connected to a wide open future, a Name connected to perpetual 'becoming'.

This is the positive, empowering and holy aspect of being *Chadash* / new. We are enabled to take full responsibility for our past, yet be fully in the moment with an open door to the future. We have the conviction that we can start over and begin anew at any moment. We are never defined by our past, nor pulled into a predetermined future.

There is also a flip side of being Chadash that is deeply negative. Our descent into slavery begins when ‎וַיָּקָם מֶלֶךְ־חָדָשׁ עַל־מִצְרַיִם / "a 'new' king arose over Egypt, one who did not know Yoseph" (*Shemos*, 1:8). This new king (or 'renewed king') did not (or chose not) to remember Yoseph and all the good he did for the Egyptians during the times of famine. He did not 'remember' how, through the innovations of Yoseph, the entire land of Egypt was spared from destruction. He was connected to newness, but a newness that willfully forgets and denies the past, including all responsibility, accountability or gratitude for all the blessings and lessons of the past. This is the Kelipah of newness, the exile of true newness, living *for* the now instead of *in* the now. Yet in a state of healthy, holy newness, one can take full responsibility for his or her past, yet does not become defined by it. One recognizes both the awesomeness of the present as well as the pull towards the undefined, free future.

This is the power of Miriam, through which she inspires her parents to reunite — despite the harsh decree of Pharaoh — enabling them to give birth to the redeemer, Moshe. She similarly inspired all of the women to arouse their husbands with mirrors and thus to build a future generation. Living in the present, feeling the *Merirus* / bitterness of circumstances, yet not being filled with despair, she is aroused with a holy *Teshukah* / desire for the future. She recognizes the newness and potential rebirth in the present that will allow for a brighter future for herself and all of Klal Yisrael. She does not identify with the stale, inevitable effects of the past, nor with the stifling hierarchical reality she was born into, rather everything appears to her as a precursor to a redemptive future, which indeed came to pass.

THE FIVE STEPS OF FREEDOM

Within the Yetzias Mitzrayim narrative we can glean five stages of liberation. And in this, we can also find five steps to freeing ourselves from our own personal enslavements, whether these be physical, mental, emotional or spiritual:

Step One: We need to stop being complacent with our predicament and cry out to HaKadosh Baruch Hu to help us. We need to say 'Enough is enough,' and cry out to Hashem. This step corresponds to the moment when Klal Yisrael cried out, not even as a form of yearning or prayer, rather a simple, raw cry. There was a break in the monotone drudgery of slavery when the 'old king' died, this triggered a shocking recognition of their own demoralization, and they cried out in pain.

Step Two: We need to access Emunah and believe in the possibility of a better future. Miriam and the women inspired Emunah in the miraculous and in the possibility of future freedom.

Step Three is connected with the mirrors, imagination, and not only believing in the possibility of miracles, but envisioning them, along with a brighter future. Like Miriam and the other women, we need to 'see from a distance' and look through the 'mirror' of imagination at the new reality that is beginning to

form. Right now the new reality may not be clearly and directly visible, but the image can be seen nonetheless, in a distant or
indirect way. We can see it inwardly and even outwardly when
we intuitively know what to look for.

Step Four is reflected in the Mitzvah of *Maggid* / telling
the story of exile and redemption, especially on Pesach night.
It is not enough to hope, to have faith, nor even to imagine a
reflective picture of redemption. We need to verbalize it as well,
bringing it more fully into our bodies, minds, and experience.

Klal Yisrael's exile began with a *Galus haDibbur* / exile and
constriction of speech, and their redemption unfolded in the
recovery of their names and their capacity to express themselves from within their experience. At first, this recovery came
in the form of 'complaining'. Moshe, the one who had difficulty speaking, becomes able to 'protest', 'question' and verbally
'debate' with Hashem. Eventually, Klal Yisrael became storytellers, and finally 'singers' at the Sea, at the completion of the
Exodus.

This fourth stage in our own personal liberation is what we
will, with Hashem's help, achieve on the night of Pesach: speaking fluidly and expansively about *Yetzias Mitzrayim* / going out
of Egypt. We will hopefully continue to live with this ability
throughout the year. In order to do so, we need to continue to
speak about going out of our own personal Mitzrayim, and to
articulate our dreams, hopes and aspirations, and affirm them.

Step Five is actually leaving Egypt, and courageously setting off on the journey into the unknown. Klal Yisrael marched into the unknown as they left Egypt and entered the Desert with little to no provisions. On an even deeper level, they followed Nachshon ben Aminadav, and walked after him into the Sea. We too need to start acting upon our dreams, and act as if they have already been manifest and realized.

This is the reason that on this night, as we sit at our Seder, we 'act out' our freedom no matter how harsh our external world is at the moment. We celebrate our future freedom now, as we drink four cups of wine, reclining like royalty, luxuriating in the light of redemption revealed.

Now we will explore a bit more about the significance and symbolism of the four cups of wine that we drink during Seder Night.

Chapter Ten:
Four Cups of Wine &
Four Levels of Freedom

P ESACH NIGHT IS THE NIGHT OF OUR FREEDOM. IT IS
a time in which we can become free of all exiles, both
personally and collectively, emotionally and mentally. Going out of our own 'Mitzrayim' means transcending our
limitations and constrictions, our exiles in alienation, disconnection and displacement. Redemption is a return from these
exiles to our deepest selves.

A mere glance through the Haggadah reveals a pattern of fours, the number four resonating throughout all aspects of the Seder. The multiplicity suggested by the notion of 'four' (2 times 2, a double duality), is actually a concealment of a deeper unity, and the revelation of unity is the *Bechinah* / concept of redemption. In this way, each set of four within the Seder alludes to redemption: the four cups of wine reveal our redemption from the four types of exile, the four questions inform us of the specific Mitzvos of the Seder which activate a redemptive process in us, and the discussion of the Four Sons in the Haggadah illustrates the archetypes of the four levels of consciousness and their relationship to redemption.

Let us look more closely at the four cups of wine which are drunk throughout the night. Why are there four cups in the first place, and why specifically wine? Besides the obvious connection between moderate intoxication and a release of emotional inhibitions and mental constraints, what is the relationship between wine and freedom?

WINE:

The *Yerushalmi* / Jerusalem Talmud (*Pesachim*, 10:1) explains that the four cups of wine represent the four terms or expressions that the Torah employs with regard to Yetzias Mitzrayim: 1) "I will take you out," 2) "I will save you," 3) "I will redeem you," and 4) "I will take you to Me." All four invocations are elements of a single progressive process of redemption.*

* Besides the above four expressions of redemption, the Medrash writes (*Yerushalmi, Pesachim*, 10:31. *Medrash Rabbah*, Bereishis, 8:5) that the four

Wine is a *Davar Chashuv* / 'important drink', and a substance that "brings joy to the hearts of man" — a celebratory drink. This is why we initiate Yom Tov and Shabbos with a recitation of Kiddush over a cup of wine (*Pesachim*, 106a). And since we recite Kiddush, the first of the four cups, over wine, we therefore drink wine for the remaining three cups.*

---

cups are also connected with the four times the word *Kos* / cup appears in the conversation between Yoseph (whose descent into Egypt represents the beginning of the actual exile of Egypt) and the butler and Pharaoh (*Bereishis*, 40:11-13). Alternatively, they correspond to the four cups of retribution that will be offered in the times of Moshiach for those who perpetuated evils, and also the four cups of consolation that Hashem will offer us.

When the Gemara tells us that women are also obligated in the four cups, Rashi on *Pesachim*, 108a, writes that the four cups are related to the four cups in the episode of Pharaoh and the butler (שלשה כנגד ג' כוסות שנאמרו בפסוק זה וכוס זה ופרעה בידי). Yet, Rashi also writes, when the Mishnah and Gemara first introduce the concept of the four cups, that they correspond to the four expressions of redemption (כנגד ארבעה לשוני גאולה האמורים בגלות מצרים).

Perhaps, the *Ikar* / main reason is the four expressions, and women are part of the redemption and they even inspired the redemption (Rashi, 108b: כדאמרינן בשכר נשים צדקניות שבאותו הדור נגאלו). Yet, since women did not experience the same hardship as men — for example, the decree was to throw into the Nile only the male children — thus, if the reason for the four cups is 'only' the four expressions of redemption, maybe women should not be obligated to drink all four cups. Rashi, therefore, offers the reason that the word *Kos* / cup appears four times in the Yoseph, Pharaoh and the Butler narrative.

* With regards to Kiddush, Chazal tell us, תנו רבנן: זכור את יום השבת לקדשו זוכרהו על היין / "'Remember the day of Shabbos to sanctify it;' Remember it over wine": *Pesachim*, 106a. In other words, the Mitzvah of Kiddush is to "remember," to declare and sanctify Shabbos. Also, since wine is a Davar Chashuv, and Tosefos (*ibid*) writes, דזכירה כתיב על היין / "The idea of remembrance is connected to wine," we recite Kiddush over wine in order to "remember" Shabbos in an honorable way. In the words of the Ram-

Wine is also one of the only substances that does not 'spoil', rather it gets better with age. And so on a Yom Tov, when we are celebrating our history and its living presence in the now, it is fitting to drink wine. We show an appreciation for our past in such a way that it brings us joy in the present and hope for the future.

---

bam, היא שצונו לקדש את השבת ולאמר דברים בכניסתו וביציאתו / "The Mitzvah of the Torah is to sanctify Shabbos with words, at its beginning and end: *Sefer haMitzvos*, 155. With regards to the four cups, it seems that Tosefos is of the opinion that they are similar to Kiddush, a blessing that is also connected to wine. In other words, the *Ikar* / main idea of the four cups is (not the wine, rather) to declare a blessing; the first cup for Kiddush, the second cup for the blessing and declaration of redemption, the third cup for the blessings after the meal, and the fourth cup at end of Hallel. These are the words of Tosefos (on *Pesachim*, 99b): מתוך הלשון משמע קצת שאין נותנין לבניו ולבני ביתו כי אם לעצמו והוא מוציא את כולם בשלו וסברא הוא דמאי שנא כולם. Note also the Gemara: ארבע כוסות מקידוש דכל השנה שאחד מוציא את כולם אמר ליה: ארבע כסי תיקנו רבנן דרך חירות, כל חד וחד נעביד ביה מצוה / "The Sages instituted the drinking of four cups in the manner of freedom, and on each and every one of them we will (also) perform a Mitzvah": *Pesachim*, 117b. This seems to suggest that the Four Cups are also connected to a Mitzvah; each cup another Mitzvah. And in the language of the Rambam (although the Rambam clearly does not learn like Tosefos), כל כוס וכוס מארבעה כוסות הללו מברך עליו ברכה בפני עצמה. וכוס ראשון אומר עליו קדוש היום. כוס שני קורא עליו את ההגדה. כוס שלישי מברך עליו ברכת המזון. כוס רביעי גומר עליו את ההלל ומברך עליו ברכת השיר: *Hilchos Chametz uMatzah*, 7:10. This understanding of Tosefos, that the four cups are similar to Kiddush, is a big Chidush, and the Maharal is puzzled by this Tosefos: *Gevuros Hashem*, 48. A more simple reading of the Gemara suggests that part of the Ikar of the Four Cups is the actual wine (unlike regular Kiddush throughout the year), as wine is intricately connected to riches and luxury and is the mark of a free person, and therefore wine is not just as an add-on to the declaration: see Rambam, *Hilchos Chametz uMatzah*, 7:7. *Chidushei haGriz*, ibid, 7:9.

Besides being a Davar Chashuv, a substance that brings joy, a reminder of our past, and that the four cups correspond to the four expressions and progressive stages of redemption, the nature of drinking wine is that the effects palpably increase with each subsequent cup. It is progressive in terms of enjoyment and intoxication. This progressive effect parallels the four phases of redemption which increase one from the next: "take you out," "save," "redeem," and "take you to Me." There were also stages in our liberation from Egypt: first our hard labor was stopped already six months before Yetzias Mitzrayim (*Rosh Hashanah*, 11a), leading to our freedom from actual Egypt, until Matan Torah where Hashem "took us to Him," culminating in our entry into the Promised Land. This is another reason we drink four cups of wine, which is a similarly progressive experience.

On a deep level, it is precisely through wine that we can tap into our personal freedom. The Hebrew word for wine is *Yayin*, and our sages reveal that *Yayin* has a numerical value of 70. This is the same value as the word *Sod* / secret. As such, "When wine goes into us, the secrets come out" (*Eiruvin*, 65a). Freedom is always hidden within us, we need only to call it forth.

Having begun to drink the four cups, we begin to tell the story of going out of Egypt. Using our capacity of speech, we redeem our Penimi, and our real, inner self begins to emerge.

Wine comes from the hidden depths of the grape, and it ferments in a concealed place. When we drink wine, we reveal its latent powers and at the same time reveal the deepest re-cesses of our soul. This is an activation of our *Geulah Peratis* / personal redemption. Similarly, the *Geulah Kelalis* / collective, cosmic level of redemption comes from a hidden inner uni-verse where everything is eternally and forever unified, whole and perfect.

There is an external world / consciousness / level of percep-tion of reality in which everything is separate from everything else: time, space, and people all function from a place of dif-ferent individual wills and forces. And there is an inner world / consciousness / level of perception of reality that is an *Alma d'Yechidah* / world of Unity, where the apparently absolute di-vides of time, space, and soul are known to be unified in an 'inclusive transcendence', a unity that maintains all diversity.

This inner point of Yichud is the 'place' of redemption itself, a state beyond all brokenness and possible exiles (In the words of the Baal Shem Tov, כי בדבר שאין לו שטח אין שייך שבירה: *Me'or Einayim*, Naso. *Baal Shem Tov Al haTorah*, Vayera, 12). In order to reveal redemption within ourselves, we need to experience true Yichud on our own level. Wine is connected with the past through its aging and fermentation. It is also connected to the potential for joy that lies deep within the grape. Therefore, when we drink it at the Seder or as Kiddush, it allows us to go into our past, and beyond. It gives us access to the deepest recesses of self, and reveals our deepest self in the present.

We tap into the world of Yichud through the drinking of the wine with *Kavanah* / intention, and as such, we drink specifically four cups, as four represents the world of multiplicity, as in the four directions, to show that the Oneness of Hashem is perceived and experienced in the world of four.

Conversely, when we break the redemption down into a four-fold process, we can begin to digest freedom and integrate it more deeply.*

---

* On a deeper level, as the 'four' cups are part of one process, the Mechaber (*Orach Chayim*, 474:1) rules that the blessing over the wine, for the first cup, also applies to the second cup and we do not need to recite a separate blessing over the wine (שותה כום שני ואין מברך עליו לא ברכה ראשונה ולא ברכה אחרונה שאין מברכין בורא פרי הגפן כי אם על כום של קידוש ועל כום של ברכת המזון). However, the Rama rules that the Ashkenaz custom is to recite a separate blessing for each cup (והמנהג בין האשכנזים לברך ברכה ראשונה על כל כום וכום).

The question is, however, why is there a need for another blessing over the wine for each cup? Normally the blessing before eating or drinking is a ברכת הנהנין / blessing before enjoyment, as we are to recite a blessing before we enjoy anything of this world. Yet, it is possible to argue that according to the Rama, the blessing over the wine in the Kiddush for example, is not merely a ברכת הנהנין / a blessing for the enjoyment of the wine, but also a ברכת המצוות / blessing over a Mitzvah, the Mitzvah of the four cups, and thus each cup is a Mitzvah in its own right and demands a separate blessing over the Mitzvah. Yet, the Mechaber would argue that since, in this case the Mitzvah (of the four cups) is connected with drink, the blessing over the wine is a ברכת הנהנין / blessing before enjoyment nonetheless, and thus, each cup does not warrant a separate blessing: see *Rosh Hashanah*, 29a-b.

Perhaps the argument in the laws of the four cups is related to another argument between the Mechaber and the Rama, and that is with regards to a Bris on Yom Kippur.

On Yom Kippur we are not allowed to eat or drink. The general custom is to perform a Bris and recite blessings over a cup of wine as well. What do we do on Yom Kippur? The Mechaber rules that on Yom Kippur we should perform the Bris without a cup of wine, since if we recite the blessing over the wine and no one drinks it, it would be a blessing in vain. The Rama, however, rules that we recite a blessing over the wine and give the wine to

As the four cups represent the four stages of our freedom, they also in turn reflect the four principal forms of exile from which we were, and continually need to be, redeemed. The four principal exiles are embodied by the four empires who exiled and persecuted Klal Yisrael (after Egypt): the Babylonians, Persians, Greeks and Romans (*Medrash Rabbah*, Bereishis, 88:5). Each of these four exiles included the quality of the exile that

a child to drink. If the blessing over the wine is a ברכת הנהנין what does it help if a child drinks the wine, since when can an adult recite a blessing for enjoyment for a child or for that matter even an adult if he himself does not enjoy the food or drink כל הברכות כולן אף ע"פ שבירך ויצא ידי חובתו מותר לו לברך לאחרים שלא יצאו ידי חובתן כדי להוציאן, חוץ מברכת ההנייה שאין בה מצוה שאינו מברך לאחרים אלא אם כן נהנה עמהן, אבל ברכת ההנייה שיש בה מצוה כגון אכילת מצה בלילי הפסחים וקידוש היום הרי זה מברך לאחרים ואוכלין ושותים אף על פי שאינו אוכל עמהן: Rambam, *Hilchos Berachos*, 1:10. Wine at a Bris is not a Mitzvah, rather a custom). Thus, perhaps the reason for the Rama's ruling is because he holds that since the cup of wine is connected to a Mitzvah (Bris, as the four cups), it too is a ברכת המצוות / blessing over a Mitzvah, and therefore, even if no one drinks it is not a blessing in vain. See also *Shu'T Tashbatz*, 3:79,3: וא"כ ברכת קדוש היום וברכת אכילת מצה היא ברכות המצות ומי שיצא מוציא אחרים אבל בורא פרי הגפן והמוציא הם ברכת הנהנין אם מי שיצא יכול להוציא כדין ברכת המצות או לא כדין ברכת הנהנין ופסקו בגמרא (ר"ה שם) שאע"פ שיצא מוציא. ועתה שאלתך היא ברכת הכוס שעל המילה אם היא כדין ברכת הכוס שעל הקדוש ולא מצינו בגמרא שנזכר.

Parenthetically, the Rama rules like the Rosh. Wondering why on Pesach night we are not worried to drink in pairs, the Gemara offers three answers, the third answer is, רבינא אמר ארבעה כסי תקינו רבנן דרך חירות כל חד וחד מצוה באפי נפשה הוא / "Ravina said the Sages instituted four separate cups, each of which is consumed in a manner that demonstrates freedom. Therefore, each and every one is a distinct Mitzvah in its own right." In other words, each cup is treated separately and one is not considered to be drinking in pairs. The Rosh, ad loc., writes that therefore each cup needs a separate blessing ואמרי רבוותא הואיל וכל חד וחד מצוה באנפי נפשיה הוא צריכים לברך בפה"ג לכל (כסא וכסא).

preceded it. In this way, our current exile includes all the principles of the previous three.

These four externally imposed exiles correspond to the four levels of our own conscious awareness — physical-bodily, emotional-psychological, philosophical-theological, and ontological-existential. These are otherwise known as the exiles of the *Guf* / body, the *Nefesh* / spirit, the *Seichel* / intellect, and *haCol* / totality. The inner design of the Pesach Seder evokes an experience of liberation on each level of exile and each level of awareness. When we meditate on the four terms of freedom connected to each cup, this experience becomes all the more vivid and visceral.

First Cup: The first cup corresponds to the exile of the *Guf* / body and an exile in the world of *Asiyah* / action. This is reflected in the Persian exile which featured the story of Purim (Even though the Persian exile occurred after the Babylonian exile, still these two kingdoms are deeply linked with each other, and come in close proximity both in time and location with each other). In the tale of Purim, Haman literally wanted to destroy the Jewish people through mass murder. This was a clear danger and threat to the survival of the body of the Jewish People. The oppression and exile was inflicted upon our physical selves. The Divine antidote is, "I will take you out." HaKadosh Baruch Hu says, I will physically move you from your place of constraint and put you in a safe place where you can attain freedom.

On a more internal and personal level, the exile of the body is manifest in one's excuses about the limitations of their body: 'I would love to wake up early every morning to learn Torah or *Daven* / pray...' or, 'I would love to go volunteer to give out food to the needy, but I am so tired in the morning, so exhausted in the evening. I know this is what I should be doing, but I am very lazy, my body aches, I'm just not up to it.' The first cup brings redemption from all exiles of the body and the exaggerated limitations of the body.

We can break the concealment and exile of the body, and even the sense of physical tiredness, by performing an action. This is the simplest way to get out of a physical rut: do something. The act of Kiddush is a 'doing'. Stand up, get yourself to the table, literally and metaphorically. Hold the cup and initiate the process of the Seder.

We fully activate this power of redemption from the exile of the body when we separate from the mundane world and take on a spiritual reorientation by making Kiddush. The word *Kodesh* / holy, translates as detached, transcendent, or separate. We stop all of our preparations for the Seder, we physically move away from these more mundane activities and walk to the table, and then we quiet ourselves and make the blessings over wine. Through this meditative and yet visceral action, we walk out of the mundane world. We leave our personal physical confinements and enter into the sacred world of the Seder. Suddenly everything looks different.

After Kadeish, and as an extension of the Kiddush, we perform *Urchatz* / *"and* wash hands." We cleanse ourselves of any
residue of distraction and physical constrictions and sit down
for the Seder.

Second cup: Having moved away from physical constrictions, and experiencing a measure of redemption on the level
of Guf, we now aspire to attain spiritual and emotional freedom. It is difficult to begin to deal with our emotions when our
bodies are still a distraction, when, for example, our head hurts.
Only once there is a sense of Geulah on the bodily level can
we move upwards and inwards into the world of our emotions.
The second cup speaks of the liberation of our spirit.

Historically, the second cup is connected with the Babylonian exile and redemption. The Babylonian exile began with
the destruction of our spiritual center, the first *Beis haMikdash*
/ Temple. After this devastating and national trauma, we were
exiled from the Land of Israel, our sacred space, and because
of that we also lost the mystical art of prophecy and higher
Ruach haKodesh / holy spirit. This was and is an exile on the
level of *Nefesh* / spirit. The collective spirit of Klal Yisrael experienced exile and then we were redeemed on this level. The
Divine antidote is "I will save you," and this is the inner effect
of the second cup.

On the night of Pesach, we reveal and further unpack the
power of this declaration, "I will save you," when we recite
the Haggadah in a raised voice and awaken our emotions.

נפשי יצאה בדברו / "My Spirit expires through (his) speech," (*Shir haShirim*, 5:6). In Maggid, we tell the story of our people, of our descent and eventual ascent from Egypt, the miracles and wonders that we experienced in the going out of Egypt, over this filled second cup of wine. We become excited and awakened, and our emotions become free-flowing when we, with our children and families, sit and recall the miracles of the past and offer thankfulness and gratitude in the present. The story awakens our emotions, and we experience liberation on an emotional level.

A more internal level of the exile of our spirit is our imbalanced emotions and moodiness. Sometimes we know something to be right — we know intellectually what we need to be doing or not doing — but our emotions get the better part of ourselves. Even when we know we should not be doing something, we nonetheless act to the contrary, simply because we are 'not feeling good'. We refrain from doing something we should do, simply because we are 'not in the mood'. Sadly, some people have experienced a traumatic event that has closed down their emotions and they have stopped feeling. Some, because of a past hurt, have even willingly closed down their ability to love again.

We can begin to break these emotional exiles and heal from them, whether they are felt as a lack of happiness or enthusiasm, or a withdrawal from love or healthy vulnerability — by filling up the second cup and verbally exploring our situation and hardship. In the beginning of the Haggadah, we speak about our collective lowliness; our traumatic enslavement in Egypt, our stuckness in the world of idol worship, and our compulsion to worship outer appearances. Inwardly, we are contemplating our own subtle enslavements, our emotional exile and stuckness. As the story progresses, we begin to speak about how HaKadosh Baruch Hu began to take us out of exile, gradually deconstructing the rigid hierarchy and boundaries of Egypt, and inspiring our ancestors to a higher calling, to establish a *Bris* / covenant with the Infinite. Inwardly, we need to think about what this means in our own lives. The mere act of expressing our exile-experiences, our doubts, our worries and uncertainties, this is already part of the Geulah.

דאגה בלב־איש ישחנה / "If there is anxiety in a man's mind, ישחנה" (*Mishlei*, 12:25). The word ישחנה is read by Chazal to mean, "he should tell his troubles to others" (*Yuma*, 75a. *Sotah*, 42b). When we tell our story to others, others can hold our story, and this in itself can be cathartic. Certainly if the 'other' is HaKadosh Baruch Hu, speaking to Hashem about our troubles, hardships, stuckness, and also aspirations, dreams and hopes, is itself already part of our healing.

Besides just expressing our emotions, which is already an act of liberation, telling the story of exile and redemption to our children invites them to participate in the process of becoming self-aware and liberated. They can get excited about the potential for redemption in their own lives. Then, when we see the awe-filled eyes of our children, we ourselves become even more inspired. We are filled with child-like excitement and our emotions open up more. Children live in radical amazement and wonder, with their eyes and minds wide open. This is a key that unlocks the stuck, hardened spirit of adults. On this night, we need to speak to and engage our children, and to do so even metaphorically if we don't have children. In both cases, we need to inspire our inner child, so that our adult self will similarly come alive.

With the second cup, we have already moved away from the physical constrictions of the body, and we now aspire to attain psychological and emotional freedom. The second cup brings redemption from all exiles of the spirit, and all emotional limitations.

Third cup: Having told the story in great detail, awakening and engaging our emotions and imagination accordingly, we move into a mindful state and begin the process of freeing our *Seichel* / intellect.

Historically, the third cup corresponds to the Greek exile. The Greeks attempted to Hellenize the world, including Israel, by means of intellectualism and the 'worship' of reason and empirical knowledge, culminating in the utter exclusion of any sense of Transcendence or received Divine wisdom. This exile unfolded historically in the Chanukah story. The Divine antidote, "I will Redeem you," corresponds to this third cup and the redemption from mental exiles.

Internally, an exile and *Meitzar* / constriction of *Seichel* / intellect can be manifest in a propensity to be intellectually lazy.

For example, faced with a difficult intellectual task or complicated text of Torah, we give up. The excuse we make is, 'I am a simple person and this is way too complex.' Or, 'I am just not deep enough to understand this.' We resist the toil and discomfort that it takes to successfully internalize a difficult *Sugya* / topic in Torah. So instead of keeping our mind open and staying present with the challenging text, or repeating it until a measure of clarity dawns, we just get up and walk away, or switch to a topic or activity that is mentally more attainable. It is particularly challenging if the type of text is new and unfamiliar to us. One might feel comfortable studying articles on the Parsha, for example, but when asked to learn Gemara, one responds that such is for scholars or advanced students of Torah. If one learns Gemara and is invited to learn the Tosefos, he may recoil. For that matter, even those who learn Gemara with the *Rishonim* / Early Commentators and *Achronim* / Later Commentators, and the fine distinctions brought by Reb Chayim, Reb Baruch Ber, and the Rogatchover, when invited to learn *Sod* / Torah secrets and Chassidus, they retort that this is for the deeper people of the world, and they are only able to study 'rational' Torah, or *Nigleh* / explicitly revealed ideas. This too is all part of the *Meitzarim* / constrictions and assumed limitations of one's Seichel.

Excuses such as, "I am a simple person, and this is beyond me," "I am not smart enough," "I am not 'spiritual' enough," or even, "I don't have the time and patience to begin building the necessary textual skills," are all part of this exile. We begin to break the concealment of intellectual fatigue and hesitancy by pushing ourselves beyond what we think we can do, even if it is as small as focusing for one minute on a challenging topic. The Seder is designed to break through these components of inner exile. For example, before drinking the third cup, we perform the Mitzvos of the night with sharp mental presence and mindful Kavanah.

We reveal the power of this Divine promise, "I will Redeem you," through the third cup and everything that is done in the context of the third cup. After drinking the second cup, we wash our hands and with clear intentionality we perform many of the Mitzvos of Seder night from the Torah and the sages. We are careful to eat certain amounts of Matzah and Maror, and we eat them with a strong mental focus on their meanings and effects. We follow these acts with the Mitzvah of 'blessing Hashem after the meal' while holding the third cup of wine in our hand. When we finally drink this cup, we have reached a redemption of the intellect.

Fourth cup: Having been freed physically, emotionally, and now intellectually, we enter the domain of the fourth cup: liberation of the totality of self and of our deepest self-expression.

This cup corresponds to our exile under the Roman Empire, and this remains the basis of our current historical exile, as well. Beyond being philosophers and ideologues, Roman civilization gathered all available technologies, systems and philosophies, and integrated them into a totality. The Roman civilization, certainly as reflected in modern Western culture, represents secularism and a sense of apathy to anything spiritual. Deeper meaning, purpose, and transcendent faith are at best subjective indulgences in the world view of Western civilization. At worst, they are obstacles to be eliminated. As an expression of this, the Romans destroyed the Second Beis ha-Mikdash, and cemented the fate of Klal Yisrael's journey and dispersion throughout the diaspora for thousands of years. This was, and still is, an 'existential' exile — an exile on every level of our being. Everything of value was and is challenged. In fact, aspects of each of the previous exiles are included within the Roman exile, and for this reason, it is called an exile of *haCol* / everything, the totality of our life and awareness.

Corresponding to this fourth cup, the Divine antidote, "I will take you to Me," corresponds to the dimensions of this complete exile. The Absolute gathers us up into the world of absolute Totality, the world of Unity in which everything of value shines and interconnects.

An internal level of the exile of haCol is a sense of existential depression. People give up on life in a sweeping generality such as, 'Nothing ever works out for me,' or, 'Nothing I do ever amounts to anything.' Someone who is having a hard day, instead of pointing out specific challenges, says, 'I just don't have the strength to go through this day.' It seems like life is 'all or nothing': 'If I don't get this job, my entire past was worthless.' This type of existential exhaustion makes people feel as if they want to get off the wheel of life and go to sleep.

We can begin to break the concealment of this state by honestly recognizing the gifts and blessings that we have in life, even the small things, and expressing gratitude for them. Therefore, before drinking the fourth cup, we wholeheartedly sing Hashem's praises.

Ecstatically articulating our gratitude has such redemptive power because it counters the apathy, despondency, arrogance, and 'atheism' behind the exile of haCol. We reveal the power of "and I will take you" when we gratefully acknowledge that all of life belongs to the Source of All Life. Hallel and Nirtzah are the two final steps in the Seder. In Hallel, we soar with ecstatic praise because all of us — our spirit, body, emotions and intellect — is drunk on the wine of redemption. Nirtzah is the only part of the Seder where there's nothing at all to do except realize our total oneness with our Source, and to overflow with the bliss of freedom consciousness. With the fourth cup, we tap into the level of Nirtzah — total existential acceptance and liberation on all levels of self. There is nowhere left to go, we have arrived.

On this night, not only should we offer praises and thanks to Hashem for all the miracles that Hashem did for us *there*, in the historical Exodus from Egypt (*Chinuch*, Mitzvah, 21), but as the Peleh Yoetz writes (*Erech Dibbur*), "Not only should we speak about the miracles of the going out of Egypt, rather we should speak about all the kindness and miracles Hashem has done for *us*, in our own lives and times, both collectively and individually; and one who does so fulfills a Mitzvah."

When a person learns to be grateful for small, 'mundane' things and blessings that are often unacknowledged, such as an ability to stand vertically and to breathe, the power of appreciation begins to permeate all of life. Also, even small demonstrations of gratitude to others can lift a person out of the stupor of apathy.

As the sequence of the four cups and their blessings and recitals progresses, we open up to deeper stages of freedom from all exile. Yet there is actually one more cup that appears at the Seder. It is the mysterious, hidden 'fifth cup', today connected to Eliyahu, and is called the Cup of Eliyahu. Eliyahu the Prophet will hail and usher in the ultimate redemption and eternal freedom for all creation. Most customs direct us not to actually drink the fifth cup, and this is for a technical Halachic reason. On a deeper level, one does not drink it because it is 'beyond' *Seder* / order or process, beyond actions or recitals, beyond the world of duality and separation. Inwardly, it represents the perfection of our soul that does not labor in the world of opposites, the *Yechidah* / Unique self that is One with the *Yechidah* / Uniqueness or Oneness of the Creator, as will be explored further on. Indeed, the 'revelation' of the Yechidah is synonymous with the ultimate redemption and eternal freedom for all.

THE FOUR QUESTIONS

As the four cups represent four stages, so do the 'four questions of *Mah Nishtanah*'. The first question, concerning the two "dippings" that we perform on Seder Night, reflects the world of Asiyah, the world of action and the *Guf* / body. First we dip the Karpas in salt water, to remind us of the tears of our affliction, and later, we dip the Maror in Charoses to remind us of the sweetness of our physical liberation from Mitzrayim. The second question, concerning the eating of Matzah and the exclusion of Chametz, reflects the world of *Yetzirah* / emotional reality, the world of spirit. Matzah, as juxtaposed to Chametz, reminds us that we must transcend our inflated egos and reach humility before we are able to open to emotional redemption. The third question, regarding eating Maror, reflects the world of Beriah and *Seichel* / intellect. The sharpness of Maror clears our minds, thus elevating our consciousness to a redeemed state of Beriah (Note, Tosefos, *Pesachim*, 114a: פרפרת קרי המרור שאוכל אחר המצה ופרפרת כלומר ממשכת המאכל כמו פרפראות לחכמה). Finally, the fourth question which refers to reclining reminds us that we have arrived, and have reached the inner world of Atzilus, unity and stillness. Reclining is a posture of stillness and a total relaxation of body and mind, compared to standing or sitting. The latter two are temporary conditions, while reclining is a reflection of an unmoving, permanent state of freedom.

Similar to the cups, the 'four sons' of the Haggadah are a map of the four levels of consciousness and redemption. There are many ways to place them in a progressive order.[*]

---

[*] The Arizal reveals that the Chacham is Atzilus. Tam exists in Beriah. She'eino Yodei'a Lishol is Yetzirah, and the Rasha is Asiyah. The order explored above is *b'Derech Efshar* / another possibility suggested for the purpose of l'Hagdil Torah.

While usually we see the Chacham as the highest level, it is possible to arrange the sons differently, for example: a) The *Chacham* / the wise child, reflects the world of Asiyah because his intellect can be seen as cynical, and he introduces a concept of the 'pointlessness' of having a Seder. Because he is passionate about his questions, the *Rasha* / 'wicked one' reflects Yetzirah, the emotional universe. The *Tam* / simpleton, paradoxically reflects Beriah, the world of understanding, because in asking questions which are unassuming in their simplicity, he is dialectically open to receiving higher knowledge. The *She'eino Yodei'a Lishol* / child 'who does not know how to ask', on a deeper level does not ask questions because he has no questions; he has arrived. Thus he personifies the world of Atzilus, simple unity.

The following table is to aid your understanding of how the different variables between each realm correlate and interact with each other. Included in the table is a column with reference to the four letters in the Name of Hashem,* which is a wonderful access point to understand the significance of how the four cups correlate to the four exiles and the four realms of redemption.

---

* The four exiles correspond to the four letters of the Name of Hashem, with the *Kotzo Shel Yud* / the crown or tip of the Yud, corresponding to the root of all exiles, the exile of Egypt: Arizal, *Sefer haLikutim*, Ki Tetze.

The Four Cups Mapped on the Internal Structure of Reality

DIVINE NAME	EXILE	LEVEL	QUESTION /PRACTICE	4 SONS	UNIVERSE	CONSCIOUSNESS
HEI	Persian	Guf (body)	Dipping Twice	Chacham (wise)	Asiyah	Nefesh
VAV	Babylonian	Nefesh (spirit)	Matzah	Rasha (rebel)	Yetzirah	Ruach
HEI	Greek	Seichel (mind)	Maror	Tam (simple)	Beriah	Neshamah
YUD	Roman	haCol (transcendence)	Reclining	She'eino Yodei'a Lishol (the son who does not ask)	Atzilus	Chayah

THE FIFTH CUP: ELIYAHU'S CUP

Divine Name	Consciousness	Level	Universe
Kotzo Shel Yud	Yechidah	Infinity	Keser

Chapter Eleven:
A Tikkun for Da'as:
Redeeming Awareness & Unity

THE MITZVAH OF *KORBAN PESACH* / PASSOVER OFFERING includes providing שה לבית־אבת שה לבית / "a lamb for a family, a lamb to a household" (*Shemos*, 12:3). We are meant to celebrate Pesach with family and community, not alone. At the Seder today we should host a diversity of people — not only the wise child, but the *Rasha* / 'wicked' child as well. All our children and family should be present, feasting with us. All of our inner 'children' and layers of self need to be lovingly gathered and illuminated within the embracing light of Pesach. Redemption comes from including others and unifying with them and HaKadosh Baruch Hu. The higher force that welcomes, binds, and unifies all together is called דעת / Da'as, 'knowing' or conscious awareness.

Our exile in Egypt is the prototype of all subsequent exiles, and it is essentially an exile of Da'as (*Pri Eitz Chayim,* Sha'ar 21:1). It follows that the prototype of all redemptions is redemption on the level of Da'as.

As described in the writings of the Arizal, the exile and redemption of Da'as refers to Da'as on a cosmic, meta-spiritual plane. Yet in the *Nimshal* / interpretation of these teachings by the Baal Shem Tov and the Chassidic teachers, the exile and redemption of Da'as is also a practical, personal and communal matter.*

In general, there are three basic categories of דעת / *Da'as* / knowing or intimacy:

- To know Hashem: בכל־דרכיך דעהו / *B'chol Derachecha Da'eihu* / "In all your ways know Him" (*Mishlei,* 3:6).

- To know another person deeply: והאדם ידע את־חוה / *V'ha-Adam Yada Es Chavah* / "And Adam had known Chavah..." (*Bereishis,* 4:1). Although here, *Da'as* refers to in-

---

* Thus, on a deep level, Da'as is Redemption, Moshiach, Olam haBa. וזהו ענין תחיית המתים ומשיח שהוא סוד הדעת והוא סוד עולם הבא: *Toldos Yaakov Yoseph,* Lech Lecha.

timate spousal relations, we can use the term more broadly as understanding and befriending and drawing closer to another person.

- To know yourself: דעת עצמך / *Da'as Atzmecha* / self-awareness, knowing who you are on all levels.

Sefer haZohar / the Book of the Zohar teaches us that the Egyptian Exile was an exile of speech (*Zohar* 2, 25b), yet, an exile of speech is intricately connected with an exile of Da'as. Whenever there is an exile of Da'as there is an exile of speech (*Likutei Moharan*, 56:7. Da'as is the 'middle' column which is reflected in Malchus, the place of speech, the lowest of the middle column). Da'as is where information of the mind becomes knowledge of the heart and penetrates our actions. Da'as is the place of our decisions, where abstract ideas become real and actionable. We can clearly 'understand' that a certain behavior is good for us or not good for us, but if we lack Da'as, this information remains abstract. Lacking Da'as, we are like children — even if we have a high level of intellectual understanding. We lack the ability to forge a connection between our understanding of 'what is right to do' and our actions.

In an exile of Da'as, our Da'as cannot serve as a medium through which intellectual ideas affect our heart and actions. The ideas remain stuck, as it were, in our 'neck',* and they can-

---

* The Arizal teaches in *Sefer haLikutim*, Bo, that the exiles correspond to parts of the human body: the Egyptian Exile is the neck, the Babylonian Exile is the head, the Persian/Median Exile is the hands, the Greek Exile is the torso, and the Roman and Yishmaelite Exiles are the two legs.

not reach outer expression or speech. In fact, in Hebrew, *Oreph* / neck has the same letters as *Paroh* / Pharaoh — who is the epitome of disconnection between the mind and speech.

Speech is a function of being in a conscious relationship with another; knowing and understanding them. One reason a slave has no voice is that trauma can suppress feeling, knowledge, communication, and relationship. In the deepest level of exile, the loss of *Da'as* can be so complete that a person no longer realizes that they are in exile; they stop noticing that they are disconnected and cannot even relate to themselves. One becomes disconnected from their true self, from life itself and from the Creator of Life.

THE TREE OF KNOWLEDGE AND THE EGYPTIAN EXILE

Cheit, classically transacted as 'sin', really means missing the mark or missing the point. When Adam and Chavah ate from the Tree of 'Knowing', they missed the point of their relationship with Hashem. This caused a separation, so-to-speak, between themselves and HaKadosh Baruch Hu, so much so that they felt they had to 'hide' from the Divine Presence after eating from the Tree of Knowledge. The Cheit had dramatic cosmic and personal effects on them as well, and our sages tell us that after eating from the Tree of Knowledge, they were 'divorced' from each other for 130 years. It also created a rift between them and the outside world. For instance, from then on, when they ate or drank, some of the nutrients were assimilated into the body, integrated within themselves, and some were rejected and became waste. And lastly, the eating from the Tree of Knowledge caused a rift within themselves individually, blocking their Da'as, their self-knowledge and self-communication.

What was the Cheit of eating from the Tree of Da'as? It was not simply that they ate from it; in fact, to the contrary, they were supposed to do so. The only problem was that they ate from it too early; they internalized Da'as immaturely, as the Arizal explains. The Cheit was ingesting Da'as before tasting and experiencing Shabbos, which is the fruit of the Tree of Life. They were supposed to wait until Shabbos and then ingest the Tree of Da'as from within a context of the Tree of Life, of Unity, of Shabbos. As such, the Cheit was just a 'missing of the mark'; it was an off-target experience of Da'as.

When Hashem informs Avraham that his descendants will descend into exile in Egypt, the Torah states, ידע תדע / *Yadoa Teida* / "Know, you shall know" — know with certainty — "that your descendants will be strangers in a foreign land for 400 years" (*Bereishis*, 15:13). Hashem repeats the word *Da*, the root of the word *Da'as*, as if to emphasize that it will be an exile of *Da'as*. However, the repetition also suggests that they will 'know' that they are in exile; although they will lose their 'knowing', they will *know* that they do not *know*. This itself is the seed of their redemption.

The name מצרים / *Mitzrayim* alludes to the word מצר / narrow, or the 'narrowing' of Da'as in particular. In Egypt there

was a diminished state of awareness. Cosmically, the exile below manifested because the Divine Da'as, which is none other
than the revealed Presence of Hashem, was not *Mispashet* /
flowing down and 'spreading out', or being recognized in the
world (*Sha'ar haKavanos*, Derush 9, Pesach). There was a lack of Da'as
below because there was a lack of Divine Da'as being revealed.

The archetype of the disconnected power below, the mighty
ruler Pharaoh declares, "Who is Hashem that I should heed
his voice." What Pharaoh is arguing is that he does *not* sense
Hashem's Presence in this physical world and therefore he
can do as he wishes. Pharaoh was arguing against the Da'as
of Hashem being present, and as such, the words מלך מצרים /
Melech Mitzrayim / king of Egypt are numerically 470. With
the four letters in Pharaoh's name, it is 474, which is the same
value as the word דעת / *Da'as* (Rameh miPano, *Mayan Ganim*, 3, *Seder Shel Pesach*). The antidote in Mitzrayim then, and also today,
in our own space of constriction and narrowness, is to water
the seeds of Da'as in this world. This means becoming more
and more aware of Hashem's Presence and internally increasing our Da'as until we eventually achieve *Mochin d'Gadlus* /
expanded awareness, total clarity and faith in Hashem — and
by extension, faith in our own self.

For this reason, during Seder Night (writes the Rashash, *Nahar
Shalom*, 37a), the night of liberation and revealed Da'as, there is
a Tikkun for the *Penimiyus* / inner aspect of the sin of Adam,
the eating from the Tree of Da'as (Rosh Hashanah is the Tikkun for
the external aspect of the Cheit). And this Tikkun occurs on all three
levels of Da'as and intimacy, as will be now explored.

INCREASING KNOWLEDGE OF ONE ANOTHER

The story of the exile — and of all exiles — begins with the selling of Yoseph by his brothers, as the Megaleh Amukos explains (Parshas Beshalach'). Similarly, *Sefer haZohar* (*Zohar Chadash*, Vayeshev, 44a) teaches that the exile in Egypt was due to the sin of the sale of Yoseph. The Medrash (*Medrash Tehilim*, also known as *Medrash Shocher Tov*, 10:3) says, "Hashem tells the *Shevatim* / Tribes, 'You have sold him to be a slave,' as it says, 'Yoseph

---

* It was the older brothers' jealousy of their younger brother that brought about the descent to Egypt. שבשביל משקל שני סלעים מילת שנתן יעקב ליוסף. יותר משאר בניו, נתקנאו בו אחיו ונתגלגל הדבר וירדו אבותינו למצרים / "Due to the weight of two *sela* of fine wool that Yaakov gave to Yoseph in making him the striped coat, beyond what he gave the rest of his sons, his brothers became jealous of him and the matter unfolded, and our forefathers descended to Egypt": *Shabbos*, 10b. This pattern of brother rivalry goes back to the beginning of time, with Kayin and his younger brother Hevel, where because of jealousy the older brother killed his younger brother. Similarly, the older brother Yishmael does not get along with the younger brother Yitzchak. And the older brother Eisav, because of jealousy, wants to kill his younger brother Yaakov. In the story of the Shevatim / tribes, the older brothers are jealous of Yoseph. The beginning of this Tikkun is with the blessing of Ephrayim, the younger brother, before the blessing of the older brother Menasheh, and we do not find any jealousy on the part of Menasheh. But the ultimate Tikkun is with the going out of Mitzrayim, led by the younger brother Moshe, and his older brother, Aharon, serving as his spokesman. When Hashem tells Moshe, that due to his speech impediment, Aharon will be his spokesman, the Torah says, "ויאמר הלא אהרן אחיך הלוי ידעתי כי־דבר ידבר הוא וגם הנה־הוא יצא לקראתך וראך ושמח בלבו / There is your brother Aharon the Levi. He, I know, speaks readily, and when you go to meet him, he will be happy for you": *Shemos*, 4:14. As Rashi explains, not only will he, the older brother, not be jealous, but he will be happy for you. Such commences the Tikkun of Kayin and Hevel, and the Geulah from Mitzrayim.

was sold as a slave' (*Tehilim*, 105:17), therefore, you too will read every year *Avadim Hayinu...* / "We were slaves to Pharaoh in Egypt...""*

The sale of Yoseph represents a break, a mismatched relationship in the *Da'as* / intimacy of their family unit. For many years thereafter, the family remains in disarray and disconnection. The oldest son, Reuvein, keeps going off on his own to practice Teshuvah and penitence for the sale of Yoseph, and Yehudah, their 'leader', after the sale, is demoted from his position.

When, generations later, a new Pharaoh becomes king over Egypt, then the hardship begins. The Torah says, "A new Pharaoh was established who לֹא־יָדַע / did not *know* Yoseph" (*Shemos*, 1:8). Sadly, this not-knowing is a continuation of the brothers who sold Yoseph and chose to ignore him and act as strangers who did not *know* Yoseph.

---

* Even though Klal Yisrael was destined to be in exile for 400 years without the sale of Yoseph, this exile could have occurred within the boundaries of Eretz Yisrael itself: Abarbanel on *Bereishis*, 15:2. Chida, *Devash l'Phi*, 10:11. As such, Yoseph's going out of prison in Egypt is similar to Klal Yisrael's release from bondage in Egypt. Thus Yoseph is released from prison on Rosh Hashanah, and the bondage and harsh labor in Egypt ceases on Rosh Hashanah, six months before the Exodus in Nisan: *Rosh Hashanah*, 11a. Indeed, a source for the four cups of wine on Pesach night is the mention of "cup" four times in the dream that Yoseph interpreted in prison: *Yerushalmi*, *Pesachim*, 10:1, as Yoseph's release is directly related to the going out of Egypt. See Meiri on *Pesachim*, 99b.

Therefore, on the night of Pesach we create a Tikkun for the breaking apart of Yaakov's family, the first family of Klal Yisrael, and the matrix which produced and shaped the Tribes of Israel. And this is why we need to have our entire family and a diversity of guests present at our Seder — including the so-called Rasha. If the breaking apart of the arch-family of Klal Yisrael is the root of exile, part of its Tikkun is the ingathering and unification of the family unit.

To create a Tikkun for the brothers of Yoseph, we facilitate the unification of our family with the Mitzvah of *veHigadeta l'Vincha* / "Tell your children" about the Exodus from Egypt, engaging them in the Seder, and communicating with them and with our guests in ways that draw everyone together. In addition, the Mitzvah to eat the Pesach offering is שה לבית / *Seh laBayis* / "a lamb for each household" (*Shemos*, 12:3). In fact, the word בית / *Bayis* / home appears in various forms *thirteen* times in the section where the Torah describes the offering of Pesach. Pesach is thus all about restoring the "home," the family unit, and the *Shalom* / peace of the Bayis.

When we dip the Karpas in the bitter water, the first 'dipping' of the night, we should also remember how the brothers of Yoseph dipped his coat in blood, in order to make their father think that he had been killed by a wild animal. We can also bring this bitter story to awareness any time that we have avoided responsibility for creating separation within our own family or community.

Sharing food unites people. This is our intention when we declare at the very beginning of our Seder, "Those who are hungry come and eat." On a deeper level, when at the Seder we discuss the exiles and redemptions in our personal lives, we can satisfy our hunger to know one another more deeply.

PHARAOH OPPOSING THE 'FAMILY' OF KLAL YISRAEL

When Moshe debated with Pharaoh and tried to persuade him to let Klal Yisrael leave Egypt, Pharaoh asked him a strategic question. ויאמר אלהם לכו עבדו את־ה' אלקיכם מי ומי ההלכים / "And Pharaoh said to them, "Go, worship Hashem your G-d — but who are the ones to go?" Moshe responded, בנערינו ובזקנינו נלך בבנינו ובבנותנו / "We will go with our old and young, with our sons and daughters." Pharaoh responded, "Only the adults can go," and then the Pasuk continues: ויגרש אתם מאת פני פרעה / "And they (Moshe and Aharon) were expelled from before Pharaoh" (*Shemos*, 10:8-11).

Pharaoh says, 'Fine, if you want to leave Egypt to serve Hashem, go, but just leave your families here; maintain your dissociation from them, your exile of communal Da'as.' Moshe, speaking as a prophet in the name of HaKadosh Baruch Hu, says, 'No. We must go with our entire families, the old and the young together.' Pharaoh is agitated by Moshe's assertion, and he and Aharon are expelled from the court.

This is the only time during the long duel and dialogue between Moshe and Pharaoh that Moshe is expelled, for Pharaoh realizes that to keep them in exile he would need to destroy what remained of the family unity that still existed among Klal Yisrael. And when Moshe insists that all of Klal Yisrael are one people, with intact families and unified generations, all Pharaoh can do is cut off the dialogue.

Similarly, we find this idea of Pharaoh trying to break apart the family of Klal Yisrael in his decrees. In the story of our enslavement in Egypt, Pharaoh decreed that all the male children should be thrown into the Nile. The idea was that if there were no males, there would be no future children and thus no families. As Pharaoh desired to break apart the family of Klal Yisrael, he and his people were punished *Midah K'neged Midah* / 'measure for measure', and in Mitzrayim "there was no home without death." Every family of the oppressors of Klal Yisrael experienced death; a breaking apart of their family unit.

All of this reveals that the issue of creating family and communal wholeness is at the very essence of redemption and the Tikkun for broken Da'as.

130 YEARS IN EGYPT BEFORE THE BIRTH OF MOSHE

We know that the children of Yaakov lived in Egypt for 130 years before the birth of Moshe, who would become their redeemer, as Yocheved was 130 when she gave birth to Moshe (Rashi, *Shemos*, 2:1, and she was born when Yaakov and the family entered Egypt). These 130 years of continuously deepening enslavement — falling deeper and deeper into the world of separation and absence of Da'as — correspond to the 130 years that Adam and Chavah were separated after eating from the Tree of Knowledge, before they eventually reunited and gave birth to Sheis. It was during these 130 years of Adam being separate from his wife that he omitted *Zera Levatalah* / 'wasted seed' and thus created unfocused, unfinished, and improperly channeled sparks of soul energy.[*]

These souls, energetic projections omitted by Adam while he was in solitude, are the root souls of the Generation of the Flood, which too were destroyed because they wasted their seed by not having proper relationships, and even improper relationships with animals. Later, these souls reincarnated and became reflected in the first 130 years in Egypt; 130 years of slavery corresponding to the 130 years of Adam's lack of Da'as.

After 130 years of Egyptian enslavement and absence of Da'as, when she was 130 years old, Yocheved experienced an *Ibbur* / impregnation from the soul of Chavah and then gave birth to Moshe, who was the *Gilgul* / reincarnation of Sheis, the child that was born to Adam and Chavah after their 130 year separation (Moshe is a Gilgul of Sheis, but also of Hevel, thus his name, Moshe, is an acronym for **M**oshe, **Sh**eis, **H**evel: *Sha'ar haKavanos*, Pesach, Derush 1. *Megaleh Amukos*, Shemos, 2:1). In this way, the Tikkun of Adam and Chava's 130 years of separation, occurs with the birth of Moshe, the individual who reached the highest levels of conscious unity with the Creator that are humanly possible. Moshe brings a great Tikkun of Da'as to Klal Yisrael, and is

---

[*] *Eiruvin*, 18b: כל אותן השנים שהיה אדם הראשון בנידוי הוליד רוחין ושידין ולילין. These are demonic forces, which represent misguided and incomplete creations, as it were.

in fact the embodiment of the Sefirah of Da'as (*Pri Eitz Chayim*, Sha'ar Chag haMatzos, 1. כי ענין גלות מצרים הי' שחסר מהם הדעת שידעו להכריע שיש בורא אחד המחדש בטובו תמיד מעשה בראשית וכו', עד שבא משה בחינת הדעת, ועל ידי הנסים שעשה נתפרסם בעולם שיש בורא אחד המחדש תמיד. *Toldos Yaakov Yoseph*, Vayishlach).

Separating a fruit from a tree, and the act of eating itself — from chewing and breaking the fruit down into a finer substance, and during digestion separating the nutrients from the waste — are both forms of deconstructing and breaking apart. Eating the fruit of the Tree of Knowledge caused a breaking of Da'as and a disconnection and breaking apart of the union between Adam and Chavah. The Tikkun of Da'as thus began with the union of the Ibbur of Chavah (Yocheved) and the eventual birth of the Bechinah of Da'as, Moshe. Like the separated couple Adam and Chavah, Amram and Yocheved reunited, giving birth to the Tikkun for Da'as, and the agent of redemption.

For the first 130 years in Egypt, Klal Yisrael entered and eventually descended into the depths of *Tumah* / impurity and stuckness, entrapped by Pharaoh. *Pharaoh* spelled backwards is *Oreph* / back side, the other side of Da'as. When Yocheved reunited with her husband and became pregnant with Moshe, it marked the subtle beginning of their redemption, as it revealed the proper, unitive quality of Da'as, and created an opening for the revelation of Hashem's Presence.

INCREASING KNOWLEDGE & AWARENESS OF HASHEM

When Moshe comes before Pharaoh and says, "Let my people go," Pharaoh responds, "Who is G-d?" לא ידעתי / "I do not *know* him" (*Shemos*, 5:2). Hashem then sends the Plagues, וידעו מצרים כי־אני ה' / "so that they (the Egyptians) will *know* that I am Hashem" (7:5). And the entire objective of going out of Egypt is so that the People of Israel will וידעתם כי אני ה' / "*know* that I am Hashem…" (6:7).

The two most prominent foods of the Seder are connected with the Cheit of the Tree of Knowledge. According to our sages, the 'fruit' that Adam and Chavah ate was either wheat or grapes.* In order to fix this primordial exile of Da'as, during the Seder we eat wheat Matzah and drink grape wine with spiritual knowledge and intention. This Tikkun triggers the beginning of redemption. The three Matzos are connected with Chochmah, Bina and Da'as. When we eat Matzah at the Seder, our 'knowledge' increases. Additionally, wine increases joy, leading to *Mochin d'Gadlus* / expanded consciousness.

The deeper we move into the Seder, the higher and deeper our Da'as, our conscious awareness, is of HaKadosh Baruch Hu and all the miracles in the past, and all the gifts in the present with which we are showered continuously.

---

* Or it was a fig. In the case of wheat, according to Chazal, the wheat grain *before* the Cheit grew in the form of a tree: *Medrash Rabbah,* Bereishis, 15:7

INCREASING KNOWLEDGE & AWARENESS OF OURSELVES

The internal exile of Da'as, the lack of proper self-awareness, shows up when we are so out of touch with ourselves, that we think we are perfect and flawless and have no room to grow (*Toldos Yaakov Yoseph,* Pekudei, 75a). This is not to say that we need to focus on negativity, but until Klal Yisrael became aware that they were slaves, and that their lives were miserable, and then they cried out, the process of their liberation did not ensue. And until we are able to acknowledge our imperfections and subtle enslavements, and express in speech our sincere yearnings for freedom, we remain unliberated as well.

In the Land of Israel, according to Torah law, there are seven (Biblical) days of the year when we refrain from eating any *Chametz* or leavened products. Therefore, there are 358 days of the solar year when we can eat *Chametz.* The number 358 in Hebrew is indicated by three letters: Shin (300), Nun (50), and Ches (8). When these letters are rearranged, they spell the word נחש / *NaChaSh* or 'snake'.

The Snake represents the 'ego' or *Yesh.* Regarding the *Cheit Eitz haDa'as,* Chavah says, הנחש השיאני ואכל / "The snake convinced me and I ate" (*Bereishis,* 3:13). The letters of the word השיאני spell יש אני / I am a *Yesh,*' a 'thing', or an ego. This is 'snake-consciousness'. The snake strives to convince us to objectify ourselves, to 'know' ourselves as a separate, limited 'thing'. This obscures our knowledge of who and what we really are, for we are not a Yesh. It also separates us from other people and from the world around us, for another person too is not a

Yesh, but what we think *we* are is what we see in others and in the world.

To rectify not knowing ourselves deeply, we must carefully check our 'domain', our self for 'Yesh'. Thus we must check our home and work environments for any Chametz that we may own. When we dispose of, burn, or sell 'our' Chametz, we are getting rid of the stuff that holds us back from knowing ourselves, the opaque ego and sense of separation that obscures true insight into self.

We need to rid ourselves of 'negative' Da'as, the exiled Da'as that tells us *we* are our ego and we need to always fight to protect this false self. This illusion creates a life of frustration, manipulation, self-doubt, and uncertainty, which further obscures our inherent freedom. We need to rid ourselves of the Kelipah Da'as that clouds our true vision of self, as well as covers over our flaws, preventing us from properly assessing where we are holding in life and how we can progress.

THE TIKKUN OF MATZAH

When we are convinced by the Snake — representing the voice of fantasy and externality — that we are a mere ego, we naturally react by puffing ourselves up in arrogance. Matzah, the flat bread of humility, counteracts this by waking us up to our *Ayin*, our no-thing-ness.*

---

* Matzah is also connected with the Tree of Life. Through the Cheit Eitz haDa'as, a rift was created between the outside and the inside, and thus, every form of eating encompasses a death of sorts, as some of the nutrients are assimilated into the body, and some are rejected and become waste. The

The snake says, "Eat from the Tree of Life and you will be 'like G-d'" (*Bereishis*, 3:5). This is contrary to Adam's original humble nature. When he first comes into being, he looks around at Creation and proclaims, "Come let us bow...before Hashem" (*Zohar* 3, 107b). This is Adam's original posture, a posture of humility and gratefulness, but the snake entices him with real or imaginary grandiose visions of himself. Moshe is called the most humble of all people. The Medrash tells us that Pharaoh represents the Snake (*Medrash Rabbah*, Shemos, 3:12), and the Prophet Yechezkel actually calls Pharaoh a snake (*Yechezkel*, 29:3). Pharaoh is the prototype of arrogance, the force that attempts to keep us from recognizing Hashem and recognizing our true self, which is pure, holy and infinite.

During the Seder we uncover the Matzos and affirm, "We were slaves to Pharaoh in Egypt, but Hashem took us out from there...." This awakens our humility, our knowledge of who we really are — vulnerable and grateful. We admit the humble beginnings of our collective and individual journeys, and the utter kindness of Hashem.

Much like Moshe himself, the more humility we internalize, the more true Da'as comes into focus; the Da'as of HaKadosh Baruch Hu, Da'as of ourselves, Da'as of others and Da'as of the world around us.

---

original Matzah that they ate as they came out of Egypt had a Manna-like quality: *Kidushin*, 38a. With regards to the Manna, being from the Tree of Life, there was no waste, no separation between inside and outside, and no 'death' or separation within the body. Matzah, as the Even Ezra and Abarbanel write, takes a long time to digest, suggesting a subtle link between the Matzah and the Manna, even today.

THE TIKKUN OF WINE

Depending on one's intention and context in drinking it, wine can either bring a person to self-indulgence and separation from others, or it can bring them to elevation and closeness to others: "Those who drink together dream together." Wine drinking can bring a person comfort and joy, or hardship and woe; it can lift a person to become like "the head, or cast a person below, and make him poor" (*Sanhedrin*, 70a). It really depends on the spiritual preparation and balanced psychology of the drinker, the intention in the drinking, and the people and atmosphere in one's surroundings.

Not only can wine bring people together, drinking in holiness can also bring together our inner and outer selves, as the sages say, "When wine enters, secrets are revealed." Both *Yayin* / wine and *Sod* / secret numerically equal 70 (*Eiruvin*, 65a). Drinking wine can also bring a person closer to Hashem if the inhibitions of the ego and the left brain are released and the 'heart is gladdened', especially within the context of *Simcha shel Mitzvah* / the joy of a Mitzvah, such as communally reciting holy words and singing praises to Hashem over our cup. This kind of wine drinking can lead one toward a redemptive state of 'expansive mind'.

Says the Ra'avad on *Sefer Yetzirah* (brought down by the *Megaleh Amukos* in Parshas Yisro), when Adam ate from the Tree of Knowledge, he damaged the (letter) Dalet from the Name *Ado-nai* / אדנ-י as well as the Dalet from the Name שד-י / *Shad-ai*. These

Names, when missing their Dalets together spell the words אני
יש / *Ani Yesh*, 'I am a *Yesh*'.

The letter Dalet stands for *Dalus* / 'poor' and a humble receiver (*Shabbos*, 107a). Therefore, to rectify the Cheit Eitz ha-
Da'as and to create Redemption we meditate on humbleness
and drink *Dalet Kosos* or 'four cups' of wine,* these 'Dalet Kosos'
restoring the Dalet of the Divine Names. Through the Dalet of
humility — the opposite of the Cheit — we restore the Names
Ado-nai and Shad-ai.

Adam and Chavah ate from the Tree of Knowledge because
of their arrogance. They were told by the snake, the ego, that
Hashem told them not to eat from the tree because, "Hashem
knows that when you eat from it your eyes will be opened, and
you will be like gods" (*Bereishis*, 3:5). The snake, the personification of the self-worshiping ego, attempts to infuse Chavah
with a pompous and presumptuous vision of herself by telling her that the reason she was told not to eat from the Tree
of Knowledge is that if she did, she would become all-powerful. With this as their Kavanah in eating from the Tree of
Knowledge, Adam and Chavah diminish the Dalet of their
humility, and this brings about an acute and devastating sense
of self-consciousness. They suddenly 'see' a separation within
themselves, they 'realize' they are shamefully naked, giving rise
to a perspective of separation between each other and between
them and their Creator.

* We also eat four Matzos — after Yachatz, when we break the middle
  Matzah in half, there are four pieces.

When we drink the *Dalet* / four cups, with proper intention and mindfulness, losing our sense of self-consciousness in the process, it restores the Dalets to the Divine Names and us to our humility. This restores our authentic selves to a state of proper relationship—with others and with HaKadosh Baruch Hu.

Chapter Twelve
The State of Klal Yisrael at Yetzias Mitzrayim

A S EXPLORED EARLIER, PESACH IS CONNECTED WITH the Tikkun of Da'as, within one's deeper self, in ◆ relation to others, and with HaKadosh Baruch Hu. Now let us go a little deeper into the world of Da'as.

Galus / exile simply means separation from one's homeland, but on a deeper level it means separation from one's root, existential estrangement and alienation from one's true place in the world, from one's soul or deepest self (and that of others), and from Divinity Itself. We have explored the idea that this essentially 'inner disconnect' is based on a lack of proper דעת / *Da'as* / conscious awareness, and all exiles, external or internal, with Egypt being the prototype, are essentially exiles of Da'as (*Pri Eitz Chayim*, Sha'ar 21:1). And as such, all redemptions are liberations of Da'as. A free mind is a free person. A free person is able to reside in his proper space, to be who he really is, and to serve HaKadosh Baruch Hu in joy (אמנם בחינת דעת זה שנתגלה ביציאת מצרים, היה דעת דנוקבא, אך דעת דדכורא יתגלה לעתיד לימות המשיח: *Toldos Yaakov Yoseph*, Vayishlach).

Aveirah / 'sin' comes from the word *Avar* / crossed over. Every exile is rooted in the concept of *Aveirah*, in which a person 'crosses over' a certain fundamental, ethical, moral, or spiritual boundary, and thus becomes estranged from their deepest self. When such a boundary is crossed, it becomes an internal line of separation, dividing and blocking Da'as.

In eating from the 'Tree (or 'reality') of the Da'as of (separation between) Good and Evil', Adam and Chavah crossed a boundary. Once internalized, this 'fruit' colored their Da'as with conflict, separation, and struggle.

Later on, with the exile of Egypt, there was a contracted state of spiritual awareness, and they descended into Egypt precisely because higher Da'as of the revealed presence of Hashem did not at that time penetrate the world and its inhabitants. The occlusion of the Infinite narrows one's perception of the world and oneself. The antidote to exile, as it was in Egypt as well as today in our own constricted and narrow states, is to water the seeds of Da'as by becoming more and more aware of Hashem's Presence and deepening this awareness until we eventually achieve *Mochin d'Gadlus* / expanded awareness, total clarity, and faith in Hashem, and by extension, faith in ourselves.

Pesach and the Seder provide a repairing for three different levels of Da'as — within oneself, with others, and with HaKadosh Baruch Hu. Now let us go a little deeper into the world of Da'as in order to understand the significance of these rectifications.

THE FRENZY OF IDOL WORSHIP & THE FRENZY TO CONSTRUCT THE MISHKAN

In the beginning of the Book of Shemos, the second book of the Torah, Klal Yisrael descends to Egypt and eventually becomes enslaved there. Later, as Klal Yisrael is released from Egypt (and all that it represents), the Torah tells us about the events of Yetzias Mitzrayim and of Klal Yisrael's ensuing journey to Mount Sinai to receive the Torah. Following Sinai and the transmission of many of the ethical laws of the Torah, Moshe is given the laws and details related to erecting the *Mishkan* / the temporary Temple in the Desert. Following this personal transmission and Moshe's return from the mountain, the Torah describes the tragic episode of the people fashioning and eventually serving a Golden Calf, sparing no detail about the devastating consequences of this idol worship. Toward the end of Shemos, Moshe informs Klal Yisrael of the

Mishkan and of the Mitzvah to donate the materials needed to construct the Mishkan. The book then concludes with
the construction of the Mishkan and the resting of the Divine
Presence within it.

As Moshe is about to transmit the Mitzvah of donating
and creating the Mishkan, the Torah narrates, ויקהל משה את־
כל־עדת בני ישראל ויאמר אלהם אלה הדברים אשר־צוה ה' לעשת
אתם / "And Moshe then **gathered** the whole community of
Israel and said to them, 'These are the things that Hashem has
commanded you to do'" (*Shemos*, 35:1).

Rashi (ad loc) notes the word ויקהל / *Vayakhel* does not
literally mean "and he gathered," because "one does not actually 'gather' people with one's hand." It seems as if Klal Yisrael
actually gathered on their own. Why then is the phrase
Vayakhel Moshe used?

The Medrash (*Pesikta*, ibid.) conceptually ties this use of
Vayakhel to an earlier mention of the same term in the episode
of the Golden Calf, when ויקהל העם על־אהרן ויאמרו אליו קום
עשה־לנו אלקים אשר ילכו לפנינו כי־זה משה האיש אשר העלנו מארץ
מצרים לא ידענו מה־היה לו / "*Vayikahel* / 'the People **gathered**'
against Aharon and said to him, 'Come, make us a god who
shall go before us, for that man Moshe, who brought us from
the land of Egypt — we do not know what has happened to
him'" (*Shemos*, 32:1). There, the Torah uses the same word to describe the people as 'gathering' on their own — no one gathered them. Our sages point out that these two gatherings are

apparently spontaneous. The Arizal as well (*Likutei Torah* on this Pasuk) ties the *Vayakhel* of the Mishkan to the *Vayikahel* of the Golden Calf.

Yet, there is a stark difference between these two gatherings: by the Mishkan the Torah says ויקהל כל־עדת בני ישראל / *Vayakhel Col Adas Bnei Yisrael* / "the whole community of Israel gathered," whereas by the Golden Calf the Torah says, ויקהל העם / *Vayikahel haAm* / "The nation gathered...." The difference is symbolized by the contrasting terms *Adas Bnei Yisrael* and *haAm*.

The word ויקהל comes from the word קהל / community, a gathering of people. *Col Adas Bnei Yisrael* can also carry a meaning of "all the 'testimony' of the Children of Israel." עדת / *Adas* comes from the word עד / *Ayd* / witness, and it has the same three letters as the word דעת / *Da'as*. By the Golden Calf, the Torah merely calls Klal Yisrael העם / "the Nation." The question is, why is עדת used in reference to the gathering by the Mishkan, whereas by the Golden Calf it is simply העם?

Following the gathering by the Mishkan, Moshe tells them, אלה הדברים אשר־צוה ה' / "These are the things that Hashem has commanded." What are אלה / "these things"? Before he begins telling Klal Yisrael about the Mishkan, Moshe first tells them about the laws of Shabbos. In this context, Chazal tell us (*Shabbos*, 70a) that the words אלה הדברים are an allusion to the 39 prohibited *Av Melachos* / 'parent' or primary actions not allowed on Shabbos. The word אלה is numerically 36. דברים

/ "things" is plural, alluding to '2', raising the sum to 38, and finally the letter Hei / 'the' in "the things," counts as '1', bringing the total to 39.

This is the technical explanation, yet the question still remains: what is the Torah trying to convey to us? The relationship between the words אלה הדברים and the 39 main prohibited works which we are not allowed to perform on Shabbos seems very tenuous.*

After gathering together and hearing from Moshe "these things Hashem has commanded," Moshe speaks to the people about Shabbos, that "Six days you shall do work and on the seventh day rest." He then continues, לא־תבערו אש בכל משבתיכם ביום השבת / "You shall kindle no fire throughout your settlements on the Shabbos day." Why does he single out the prohibition of kindling fire among all the 39 primary actions that are not allowed to be performed on Shabbos, such as, for example, writing or erasing, constructing or deconstructing?

Chazal deduce two reasons for the singling out of this prohibition. Perhaps it is to tell us that lighting a fire on Shabbos

---

* In fact, there are other sources for the 39 Melachos. For example, corresponding to the 39 times the word *Melachah* / work appears in the Torah: *Shabbos*, 49b. *Yerushalmi, Shabbos*, 7:2. See Rabbeinu Chananel, *Shabbos* 49b. *Tosefos Yom Tov*, Shabbos, 7:2, regarding which (appearances of the word) *Melachah* are counted and which are not. Or corresponding to the 39 curses to Adam, Chavah, and the earth: *Tikkunei Zohar,* Tikkun 48. Corresponding to the harsh labors in Egypt: *Tosefos*, Pesachim, 117b.

is ללאו יצאת / singled out as a prohibition to communicate that one who does it merely violates a prohibition and possibly receives a consequence of lashes, but nothing more. Or perhaps it is to tell us that lighting a fire on Shabbos is לחלק יצאת / singled out as a specific case in order to equate the other prohibited labors to it and to tell you that just as kindling is one of the 39 primary categories of prohibited labor, and one is liable for performing it on its own, so too, with regard to every primary category of prohibited labor, one is liable for each labor on their own (*Shabbos*, ibid). Yet, every word and letter of the Torah is precise and profound, so we need to ask, especially regarding the opinion that it is לחלק יצאת, why the Torah specifically chooses fire as the example to teach this law. Any one of the 39 actions would have taught the same idea.

A little further on, after the Torah describes how the people gathered and brought all the materials required to erect the Mishkan, the Torah tell us, ויבאו כל־החכמים העשים את כל־ מלאכת הקדש איש־איש ממלאכתו אשר־המה עשים / "All the artisans who were engaged in the tasks of the sanctuary came, each from the task upon which he was engaged." In other words, Klal Yisrael was excited about this project, and enthusiastically left what they were previously doing and began giving all the materials required to fashion the Mishkan.

At some point, the artisans came to Moshe. ויאמרו אל־משה לאמר מרבים העם להביא מדי העבדה למלאכה אשר־צוה ה' לעשת אתה / "And they said to Moshe, saying, 'The people are bringing more than is needed for the tasks entailed in the work that Hashem has commanded to be done.'" As such, ויצו משה ויעבירו קול במחנה לאמר איש ואשה אל־יעשו־עוד מלאכה לתרומת הקדש ויכלא העם מהביא / "Moshe thereupon had this proclamation made throughout the camp: 'Let no man or woman make further effort to bring gifts for the sanctuary!' So the people stopped bringing them" (*Shemos*, 36:4-6).

The obvious question is, what is the problem of bringing too much? מרבים העם להביא / "The people are bringing more than is needed." If they brought too many materials, maybe they could have stored them in case they needed them in reserve for when the first ones wore out. Apparently, it was so inappropriate to bring more, that it warranted a grand warning: ויעבירו קול במחנה / "And a proclamation was made throughout the camp." Ringing throughout the encampment was a grave "proclamation"; something terrible was occurring and had to be stopped — people were giving too much charity?

It is interesting that Chazal *Doresh* / tease out from this Pasuk the *Melachah* / prohibition of carrying from one domain to another domain on Shabbos, and this is how we know that carrying is a Melachah.[*]

---

[*] "Where is carrying out itself written?... As the Pasuk says: 'And Moshe commanded, and they passed a proclamation throughout the camp'": *Shabbos*, 96b. From here we (also) learn that carrying is a Melachah: Rambam, *Hilchos Shabbos*, 12:8.

The Mishnah says that a person is also not allowed to throw an object from one domain into another. Regarding this, the Gemara asks, "Consider: throwing is a derivative of carrying an item, and where is carrying itself prohibited?"

אמר רבי יוחנן דאמר קרא ויצו משה ויעבירו קול במחנה משה היכן הוה יתיב במחנה לויה ומחנה לויה רשות הרבים הואי וקאמר להו לישראל לא תפיקו ותיתו מרשות היחיד דידכו לרשות הרבים / "Said Rebbe Yochanan, the Pasuk says, 'And Moshe commanded, and they passed a proclamation throughout the camp: "Let no man or woman do any more work for the offering for the Holy." So the people stopped bringing them.' Where was Moshe stationed? In the camp of the *Levi'im* / Levites, which was a public domain, and he said to them: 'Do not carry and bring objects from the private domain (your camp) to the public domain (the camp of the Levi'im)'" (*Shabbos*, 96b).

This is a very perplexing teaching of the Gemara. The simple reading of the Pasuk is that Moshe tells the people to stop bringing more material for the Mishkan; this has nothing to do with the prohibition of Shabbos, rather, as stated, it is because 'they had enough.' The issue at hand is that מרבים העם להביא / "the people are bringing *too much*," not that they are carrying objects, and therefore, ויעבירו קול במחנה איש ואשה אל־יעשו־עוד מלאכה לתרומת הקדש / "Let no man or woman make *further* effort toward gifts for the sanctuary." What compels Chazal to read into this, and to learn from it that we are not allowed to carry from one domain to another domain on Shabbos? Somehow, on a deeper level, this idea of 'ceasing to bring' —

because they brought too much — is interconnected with the Melachah of carrying from one domain to another. How so?

The Arizal (*Likutei Torah*, Vayakhel) teaches (apparently based on the Medrash, Pesikta above) that since Klal Yisrael 'gathered' to create the Golden Calf, an act of frivolity, Moshe needed to 'gather them' and to reveal to them the light of Kedushah and intentionality, as a Tikkun for that gathering. As such, he gathers *Adas B'nei Yisrael* / עדת בני ישראל. *Adas* comes from the word *Da'as* / awareness, intentionality. And because they sinned, saying, אלה אלקיך ישראל / *Eileh Elokecha Yisrael* / "This (these) are the god(s) of Israel," their Tikkun came about when Moshe said to them and they listened, אלה הדברים / *Eileh haDevarim* / "These are the things…," which, as mentioned, alludes to the 39 Melachos of Shabbos.

Besides the etymological parallels, the Arizal is conveying something much more profound. Let us try to unpack and explain this concise, although complex, teaching.

DRAWING DOWN DA'AS

As is already clear, there are two gatherings: one for the construction of the Mishkan, and one for the fashioning of the Golden Calf. Both of these gatherings seem to 'gather on their own', almost a spontaneous assembling of the masses. Yet, at the Mishkan there is an addition: the idea of *Adas Yisrael*, meaning that Moshe is drawing down *Da'as* / intentionality into this mass of people.

Moshe is the *Bechinah* / paradigm and embodiment of Da'as, the one who brings Torah, Divine wisdom and higher Da'as, to Klal Yisrael. By the creation of the Mishkan, he is drawing down Da'as to the *Adas* of Klal Yisrael. Moshe is bringing healthy, productive, life-affirming awareness of Kedushah to a people who had gathered only a short while before without proper Da'as of themselves nor of their relationship with the Elokim Chayim. He is drawing down stabilizing Da'as to a community who had lost their minds, their Da'as, and in frenzied excitement and rapture followed the *Eirev Rav* / the mixed multitudes and submitted themselves to an idol.

The mixed multitudes, who initiated the Golden Calf, represent the Da'as of *Kelipah* / spiritual blockage, and thus ערב רב / *Eirev Rav* equals *Da'as* numerically. Da'as is the place of connection, and the Torah uses Da'as as a euphemism for intimacy. Yet there is a 'dark' side of Da'as, as it were, a Da'as of Kelipah. Da'as of Kelipah involves an infatuation with and cleaving to objects, becoming obsessed with an idea or object or a person, as an idol. The fact that the people gathered on their own to create the Golden Calf suggests there was a community-wide combustion of fervor. Such is the nature of mass-hysteria, people flocking together in the heat of passion, without any sense of healthy or measured Da'as. Therefore, Moshe must bring to the people who have gathered to build the Mishkan holy Da'as to counteract the Da'as of Kelipah injected into them by the Golden Calf.

How could a nation, a few months after all the miracles of leaving Egypt and receiving the Torah, rush to create an idol with such a fever of enthusiasm? How could they in one moment forget their Da'as and everything that they had come to know as true and meaningful? The entire process of Going Out of Egypt was "so you shall know (*Da'as*) that I am Hashem." Similarly, the Divine revelation at Sinai is summed up: "You have been shown (this day) to know (*Da'as*) that Hashem is Elokim, and there is nothing else." Klal Yisrael apparently had clear Da'as of HaKadosh Baruch Hu, and a Da'as of themselves in relationship with HaKadosh Baruch Hu. And yet, a mere 40 days later they are swept off their feet by idol worship. How is this possible?

Regarding the frenzy of the people as they ran to make the idol, the Pasuk says, ויתפרקו / *VaYisparku*... / "they stripped their gold rings from their ears" (*Shemos*, 32:3). The Zohar (*Zohar* 2, 192a) connects the word *Hisparku* to the word *Perikas Ol* / throwing off the yoke of Heaven. They threw off, stripped themselves, of the 'golden' yoke of Divine responsibility, mindfulness and intentionality. They went from Matan Torah, where they proclaimed with tremendous enthusiasm, "We will do and we will listen," to the manic excitement of idol worship. And a few months later the pendulum swung back, and the people enthusiastically contributed to the building of the Mishkan to the extent that they threw all they had into it, to the point that a proclamation had to be made throughout the camp: 'Let no man or woman make further efforts toward gifts for the sanctuary!'

How can such enthusiasm swing so effortlessly from one extreme to its opposite, and then back again? We need to examine more closely the state of Klal Yisrael during the Exodus which allowed such rapid and radical changes in their spiritual status.

THE STATE OF KLAL YISRAEL AT YETZIAS MITZRAYIM

There seems to be a fundamental argument among many of the great sages and *Mekubalim* / mystics regarding the state of Klal Yisrael when they left Egypt.

On the one hand, the *Zohar Chadash* (Yisro) teaches us that Klal Yisrael had sunk to the 49th level of *Tumah* / impurity in Egypt, the next-to-lowest level, the lowest being the fiftieth. Yet, after a mere 49 days after leaving Egypt, on the fiftieth day they received the Torah and reached a state of *Taharah* / purity, immortality, and freedom from all negativity.

Forty-nine represents the world of opposites, which includes choice-making. The dimensions of this world are connected to the number seven, as in the Seven Days of Creation, and the fullest measurement of this world is 49, seven sublevels within each of the seven dimensions. In fact, the word *Midah* / measurement has a numerical value of 49 (*Sefer Rokeach*, Hilchos Pesach, 294. *Megaleh Amukos*, Parshas Behar). And since "Hashem created the world with opposites, one against the other," there are 49 positive, holy, pure states, paralleled by their opposite: 49 negative, unholy, impure states. The first rung of purity parallels the 49th rung of impurity, and the second rung of purity parallels the 48th rung of impurity, and so forth. Thus the Torah itself is refracted into 49 possible ways of *Isur* / prohibition and 49 possible ways of *Heter* / permission (*Medrash Tehilim*, 12), as well as 49 levels of purity and 49 levels of impurity (*Yerushalmi, Sanhedrin*, 4:2. See also *Eiruvin*, 13b; Ritva, *ad loc*). This is, however, a 'sliding scale'; on every rung of one ladder, there is a potential to skip to the other ladder. On the 49th level of impurity one can choose to jump onto the first rung of the ladder of purity and begin to climb its 49 steps.

At the time of the Exodus story, Klal Yisrael had descended to the 49th level of impurity, the lowest rung of negativity. They were almost swallowed eternally into the 50th, absolute level of darkness and negativity, a place of no return. Once one descends beyond the map of 49 levels, they no longer have the ability to choose; their pattern is irreversibly set. This is similar to what happened to Pharaoh during the 10 plagues. For the first five plagues, the Torah tells us that Pharaoh "hardened his heart," whereas for the final five plagues, it says that Hashem "hardened his heart." Once the arrogant ego has asserted itself so many times, it takes on a life of its own, overriding one's power to make conscious decisions.

Speaking about the condition of Klal Yisrael as they left Egypt, the prophet says, ואת ערם ועריה / "You were still naked and bare" (*Yechezkel*, 16:7). This means that we were "naked of Mitzvos" (*Medrash Rabbah*, Shemos, 1:35). And not only were we not yet on the rungs of purity and the Kedushah of Mitzvos, but the angels on high 'protested' at the time of the splitting of the Sea: "These people (the Egyptians) are idol worshipers, and these people (Klal Yisrael) are idol worshipers" (*Medrash Tehilim*, 1:20. *Zohar* 2, 170b. *Yalkut Reuveini*, Beshalach, 82). In other words, Klal Yisrael was so enmeshed in idol worship, and so deeply stuck in impurity, that they were almost at a point of no return.

"This Matzah that we eat is for what reason? Because the dough of our fathers did not have time to become leavened before the King of the kings of kings, the Holy One, blessed be He, revealed Himself to them and redeemed them." This passage that we recite during the Seder is from the Mishnah. It speaks about the great haste with which Klal Yisrael left Egypt; we left so quickly that even our bread was unable to rise. Many Mekubalim write in the name of the Arizal that the reason they could not be delayed is that they had sunk to the 49th level of *Tumah* / impurity, spiritual sickness and stuckness. If they were to stay for even one more moment they would have sunk to the fiftieth level, and they would not have been able to leave Egypt (The Alshich, *Siddur Rebbe Shabtai*, Haggadah, and *Chayei Adam*, in their respective commentaries on this passage in the Haggadah. See also *Chesed l'Avraham*, 2:56. Ramdu, *Eis laChenina*. *Ohr haChayim*, Shemos, 3:8. *Beis haLevi*, Derush 2).

If Klal Yisrael had delayed their Exodus any longer, we would have fallen off the ladder into such a dark, traumatized state, that we would have not been able to be extricated, freed, and redeemed. Just a few more moments, and we would have fallen into the fiftieth rung, and thus we needed to leave Egypt, the physical, mental, emotional, and spiritual place of our enslavement, in great haste.

Indeed, everything about the Mitzvos of the night of Pesach, the night we left Egypt, is connected to 'haste'. Matzah is baked in great haste, ensuring that it does not rise. Similarly, the other two Torah-based Mitzvos of the night, eating the *Korban* / offering of the Pesach lamb and the Maror (during the times when we offered a Korban Pesach), are also connected to the idea of haste. The Torah instructs us that the offering needs to be roasted, not cooked or boiled. Cooking takes much longer than roasting, not including the time it takes to boil the water and slice the meat. Roasting is a much quicker process; the offering is placed on an open fire and it roasts. The *Maror* / bitter herbs are also connected to haste. The Mishnah (*Pesachim*, 2:6) mentions five types of herbs that are considered Maror. The first is *Chazeres* / lettuce. Today, the most common vegetables used as Maror are romaine lettuce and horseradish. While many vegetables need to be cooked before eating, Maror can be uprooted from the ground and eaten right away. Also, the manner in which the offering of Pesach was eaten in Egypt demonstrated haste: "This is how you shall eat it: your loins girded, your sandals on your feet and your staff in your hand; and you shall eat it hurriedly" (*Shemos*, 12:11). We needed to eat the offering in a posture of urgency, about to flee. Pesach is a night of haste.

As mentioned, 49 is the matrix of opposites. In this world there is a possibility of sliding from one opposite to the other, from purity to impurity, from an ascending trajectory to a descending one, and the choice is always ours. On any of the

98 rungs between the 49 rungs of purity and the 49 rungs of impurity (corresponding to the 98 'curses' in the Torah) there is a binary system at play and we can always choose goodness and life, or their opposites. Wherever we may find ourselves, we can choose to live a higher life, a life of meaning and purpose, or, alternatively, to slide down the other ladder. However, the 50th level of each ladder is absolute, beyond the dichotomy and mobility of duality. The 50th level of Kedushah is absolute goodness, where a person transcends the world of free choice and enters the world of absolute goodness and life. At this level, purity, goodness is a מחוייב המציאות / 'necessary existence'; there is no alternative and there is no falling from this rung. Purity, transcendence, holiness, connectivity, unity, on this level, are boundless and everlasting. Moshe himself only reached this level of total transparency, goodness, and G-dliness, as he ascended Mount Nevo (the word *Nevo* means 'Nun / 50 is *Bo* / in him') to pass-on from corporeal existence. Similarly, there is a 50th level of Tumah, of stuckness, of inward death, alienation, and the impurity of ego-based existence (Note that the Gra writes that there is no actual fiftieth level of Tumah, only 49 of levels. כל פעל ה' למענהו וגם־רשע ליום רע (Mishlei, 16:4). כל / Col / All, writes the Gra, is numerically 50, indicating a place beyond choice, and there in פעל ה', there is no possibility for Ra. Yet, the word וגם / V'gam / and also, which equals 49, indicates a place where there is still the possibility of choice in Ra: וגם... רע).

The fiftieth level of Tumah is a space where one can become so removed from their *Yetzer Tov* / positive inclination, their inner purity and inner perfection, that there is no longer even a possibility of choosing to do good. Here *Ra* / negativity, evil, sin, is absolute and there are no alternatives; a person on this level is so stuck in his negativity that there is no way for them to make a decision to get out of the situation. Sometimes a person can be so stuck in an addictive, negative behavior that they cannot even imagine an alternative; they seem to have 'become' the addiction.

Whatever the case, these Mekubalim are revealing that Klal Yisrael was so low, teetering at the bottom of the 49th level, that had they not immediately fled in haste they would have sunk into the 50th level of absolute darkness. They would have *become* Egypt. This is one version of the story.

On the other hand, Klal Yisrael seems to have been on a very high spiritual level during Yetzias Mitzrayim. The elapsed time between going out of Egypt and the pinnacle experience of receiving the Torah is only 50 days. Having left Egypt, Klal Yisrael actively counted down the time to Matan Torah. They counted 'day one', 'day two', until they arrived at day 49 and a total of seven weeks, all in tremendous anticipation of hearing the Divine Voice at Har Sinai.* And when they finally reached the 50th day they reached the 50th and highest level of purity.

---

* Ran, *Pesachim*, at the end in the name of the Medrash. *Sefer haChinuch*, Mitzvah 306. We too count the days from when the Omer is offered, the second day of Pesach, until Shavuos. Even though, in the year they left Egypt they did not bring the Omer (as the Omer offering was only brought once Klal Yisrael settled in the land of Israel), yet, the *Zohar* (3, 96b) teaches that Klal Yisrael nevertheless counted the Sefirah in anticipation of receiving of the Torah: *Ohr haChayim*, Emor, 23:15.

When they received the Torah, they experienced a freedom from the effects of eating from the Tree of Knowledge Good and Evil (*Shabbos*, 156a), the Tree of Duality and Opposites, and they became free of all *Tumah* / impurity, and *Yetzer haRa* / negative inclination (*Zohar* 3, 97b). Moreover, they experienced total transcendence and freedom from the 'angel of death' itself (*Medrash Rabbah*, Shemos, 41), as death is a derivative of the Tree of Knowledge, of separation, regarding which Adam and Chavah are told, "The day you will eat from it (the Tree of Knowledge), you will die." Klal Yisrael was on the highest level at Matan Torah, and this suggests that if they were able to reach the 50th level of purity a mere 50 days after leaving Egypt, perhaps they were not so utterly stuck in the depths of Tumah when they were redeemed from Egypt.

Furthermore, it could be argued (as does the Leshem: *Sefer ha-Dei'ah*, 2, Derush 5:2, 5), that after the display of all the wonders and miracles in Egypt, Klal Yisrael was on a very high level. The entire intention of the *Makos* / the plagues was that all people shall "know that I am Hashem," and certainly after several months of Makos they achieved their intended goal by the time of the Exodus. The intention of the Makos was for Klal Yisrael, and even the Egyptian oppressors, to come to realize the "existence," the "providence," and the "Unity" of Hashem; certainly this Divine intention attained its result. All this suggests that Klal Yisrael was perhaps on a level close to the fiftieth level of Kedushah already during the Exodus.

Were they, then, on the lowest level or the highest level? Also, why is this even a question? It seems there should be no argument of whether Klal Yisrael was on the lowest level or was on the highest at the most defining moment of their history and destiny.

STATES OF IMMATURITY

Birth is an analogy that our sages use regarding Yetzias Mitzrayim. The Going Out of Egypt is the birth of Klal Yisrael, like a newborn being drawn out of the mother's womb (*Medrash Tehilim*, 114:6). The pre-Exodus Ten *Makos* / Plagues, the Arizal teaches, are the birth pangs that occur during the release of a child — the blood, the croaking frogs, wild animals, the darkness, and so forth all represent the process of giving birth and the passing of the child through the birth canal (*Likutei Torah*, Shemos). The first action the People of Israel, who were still slaves, were asked to perform was to bring the Korban Pesach, the Paschal Lamb, which was then sacrificed immediately preceding their Exodus from Egypt. In order to eat it, the offering needed to be roasted over a spit, "with its head upon its legs" (*Shemos*, 12:9). This posture, writes the Tzemach Tzedek (*Derech Mitzvosecha*, Korban Pesach. See also *Ta'amei haMitzvos*, Arizal, Parshas Bo), is similar to the fetal position of a child in the womb, ready to be born (*Niddah*, 30b). In Egypt we were in a condition of *Ibbur* / gestation (*Sha'ar haKavanos*, Derushei Pesach 1), as a fetus in the womb, and Yetzias Mitzrayim was our collective birth, the birth of Klal Yisrael.

If Yetzias Mitzrayim is our birth, then our journey through the desert parallels the growth of a child into a mature adult. It is a forty year journey from the slavery of Egypt to the responsibility of the Promised Land. Forty is the age of *Binah* / understanding, and at forty one reaches a fuller mental maturity.[*]

By extension, this means that in the Desert we were like young children and adolescents. In one metaphor of Chazal, after Matan Torah, Klal Yisrael ran away quickly from Mount Sinai כתינוק הבורח מבית הספר / "like children running away from school." This image of Klal Yisrael being born as an infant at the Exodus, and then gradually becoming a child slowly maturing throughout the journey in the Desert, helps us understand the spiritual, mental, and emotional condition of Klal Yisrael as they left Egypt.

Both opinions or perspectives are thus correct, and have verifiable textual and Medrashic sources. In truth, they are not contradictory: the people were not spiritually mature, nor did they need to be in order to be present on the fiftieth plane of Kedushah, neither were they so low that they could become stuck on a plane of total Tumah. Rather, their states fluctuated rapidly, from moment to moment. Because there was a lack of maturity, they were like children quickly moving in and out

---

[*] בן ארבעים לבינה: *Avos,* 5:21. אף משה רבינו לא רמזה להן לישראל אלא לאחר ארבעים *Avodah Zarah,* שנה...אמר רבה ש"מ לא קאי איניש אדעתיה דרביה עד ארבעין שנין :שנה 5b. The word נשמה / soul has the letter of מ' שנה / forty years. The highest levels of Neshamah, connected to intelligence, do not enter a person's life until the age of forty.

of higher and lower states. In one moment, a child is crying inconsolably because their toy broke, and in the next moment they are blissfully eating a cookie. In one moment they are speaking irrationally, and in the next they are proclaiming an idea that seems far beyond their level of development.

Klal Yisrael's pendulum swung rapidly from the highest highs to the lowest lows and back again in the blink of an eye. In one moment, they beheld the Presence of Hashem at the splitting of the sea and the Torah could declare, "They believed in Hashem and in Moshe His servant." Yet, in the very next moment, the next episode recorded in the Torah, they complained bitterly that they lacked fresh drinking water.

אמר רבי בא בר אחא, אין את יכול לעמוד על אופי שלאומה הזאת. נתבעין לעגל ונותנין נתבעין למשכן ונותנין / "Rebbe Abba bar Acha said: You cannot discern the true nature of this people, as donations are requested for the Golden Calf and they give; and later, donations are requested for the Mishkan, and they also give" (*Yerushalmi, Shekalim*, 1:1).

If they were like newborns coming out of Egypt and young children at Sinai, then in their journey through the Desert, they were like immature teenagers who are easily swayed by public opinion and open to be swept into a frenzy; to soar very high and fall very low. A person in such a stage of development can scream their head off at a meaningless ballgame or concert, and then, a few minutes later, sing a beautiful Nigun of

Deveikus, of yearning to be closer to HaKadosh Baruch Hu.*

Intense enthusiasm, excitement and passion that has no real, internal permanence is a sign of immaturity. The way many teenagers express themselves is dependent on the external situation at hand. In the narrative of the fashioning of the Golden Calf, and, *l'Havdil*, the contributions to the building of the Mishkan, Klal Yisrael moved very quickly from one state to its opposite. In one moment they were so passionate about the Golden Calf that they stripped their wives of their gold ornaments for the idol worship, threw off the Yoke of Heaven, and danced and reveled around the false idol, submitting to debauchery and a complete eradication of all morality, in-

* Interestingly, this developmental metaphor also helps deepen our understanding of another important facet of the Exodus story: the overwhelming presence of miracles. Throughout Jewish history, all other redemptions were 'natural' events. For instance, our return from Babylonian Exile after 70 years occurred when the first Persian King Cyrus had the wisdom to allow the Jewish people to return to Israel and rebuild the Beis haMikdash. So, why was the first redemption from Egypt miraculous, why all the miracles?

The forty year journey of Klal Yisrael through the desert, from birth to mature adulthood, was a journey toward *Mochin* / mindfulness and independence of awareness. To arrive at the point of true maturity, in order to enter the land and make a life for themselves, Klal Yisrael first needed to pass through the stages of childhood and adolescence, as it were.

This explains the need for miracles and wonders as Klal Yisrael was extricated from Egypt. It was, in a spiritual sense, 'age appropriate.' We were children, we needed the excitement. Hashem took us out of Egypt in the way that we teach children, by giving them prizes and making the learning exciting. Then, with Moshe's guidance, we were weaned from this need for such 'treats', as we grew into mature, motivated, and experienced adults, capable of choosing to do the right thing without spiritual coercion.

cluding the prohibition of murder, as evidenced in the killing of Chur. A short time later, they were passionately inspired by Moshe and in a frenzy began throwing everything they owned into the Mishkan, until a proclamation had to be made: "Enough!"

GIVING WITHOUT DA'AS

At the end of Moshe's life, when he recounts and rebukes Klal Yisrael for the events that transpired in the Desert, he specifically mentions a place called ודי זהב / *v'Di Zahav* (*Devarim*, 1:1). Say Chazal (Sifrei, *Devarim*, 1:18. *Berachos*, 32a. Rashi, *ad loc*), the name of the location literally means "Enough Gold." In singling out this location by name, Moshe reproved them on account of the Golden Calf, which they had made from their abundance of gold possessions.

Just as the gold they tried to contribute to the Mishkan was more than enough, the amount of gold they attempted to give to the idol was more than enough. How could they throw their gold into building an idol and then a mere few months later throw all their gold into building the Mishkan? The sages of the Medrash offer the following metaphor:

משל לבחור שנכנס למדינה ראה אותם גובין צדקה ואמרו לו תן, והיה נותן, עד שאמרו לו דייך, הלך מעט וראה אותם גובין לתיטרון, אמרו לו תן, והיה נותן עד שאמרו לו דייך, כך ישראל נתנו זהב לעגל עד שאמר להם די, ונדבו זהב למשכן עד שאמר להם די / "This is similar to a young man who enters a city and sees that they are collecting charity, and they ask him to give, and he gives until they tell him 'enough!'

Then he travels a bit and sees that others are collecting money for a theater. They ask him to give, and he gives, until they tell him 'enough!' Similarly, Klal Yisrael gave gold for the Golden Calf until they were told 'enough! and later on they gave to the Mishkan until they were told 'enough!'" (*Shemos Rabbah*, 51:8).

In the days of the Mishnah and Gemara, a 'theater' implied some form of idol worship and perhaps brutality, such as in gladiator games. In both moments of giving, the young man does not discriminate; he does not give mindfully, rather he just loves to feel inspired, no matter the cause, and throws money at anything which gives him that thrill. There is no Da'as that goes into his decision making, and therefore tending to the poor is equal in his eyes to people beating each other up in the ring.

Maturity is a state of *Da'as* / conscious awareness, mindful sensitivity, discernment, and proper boundaries. Immaturity, a lack of Da'as, does not recognize or respect boundaries or consequences. In this state, 'yes' and 'no' have no meaning, and there is no sense of 'enough'. A child can stuff his mouth with ice cream until he feels nauseous. He can overindulge to an extreme because he has not yet developed the Da'as to recognize and respond to limits in a moment of passion. His enthusiasm for the ice cream throws him completely off balance. This was the state of Klal Yisrael as they took their first steps into the Desert, brimming with enthusiasm and ready to commit to any seemingly inspiring project without taking the time to discern the quality or nature of the project.

Their spontaneous gatherings pulsated with a mob mentality and 'ecstatic' generosity, without conscious choice or any sense of proportion. And so, as they gathered, Moshe infused Da'as into Klal Yisrael by calling them *A-das* Yisrael. He tried to ensure that they were growing up and becoming a *Bar Da'as* / knowledgeable son — even though their Da'as would only be fully assimilated at the end of the forty year journey (ולא-נתן ה' לכם לב לדעת ועינים לראות ואזנים לשמע עד היום הזה :*Devarim*, 29:3. לא קאי איניש אדעתיה דרביה עד ארבעין שנין: *Avodah Zarah*, 5b).

Da'as creates the ability to discern, to not get swept off one's feet by intense emotions or ideas. "Without Da'as there is no *Havdalah* / separation" (*Yerushalmi, Berachos* 5). Da'as establishes boundaries, accountability, and order, on all levels of our being. It allows us to separate ourselves from acting in ways that are not in our deepest integrity; it allows us to say, when necessary, 'no', or 'enough'.

Klal Yisrael's journey from Egypt to the Land of Israel mirrors the process of human development from birth, to childhood, to mindful maturity. And both of these processes mirror the macrocosmic development of Creation as a whole. Much like a child or a young nation brims with passionate reactivity, yearning, and enthusiasm, with little Da'as or sense of borders and guidelines, the new universe, soon after the creation event, was in a state of immaturity, filled with "chaos and void."

A WORLD WITHOUT DA'AS EXPANDS INFINITELY

Originally, the universe was without Da'as, as it were. It kept expanding, enlarging, and rapidly unfolding with great 'enthusiasm', until the Creator said, 'Enough!' This is connected with the World of *Tohu* / Chaos. The Creator then set limits and gave the universe the definitions of finite existence. This limitation still allows the universe to expand, but within certain bounds and guidelines. This is the world we now exist within, the World of Tikkun, order and balance.

Chazal tell us, "At the time that the Holy One, blessed be He, created the world, it went on expanding like two balls of yarn (which lengthen as they unravel), until the Holy One, blessed be He, rebuked it and brought it to a standstill... And that, too, is what Reish Lakish said: 'What is the meaning of the Pasuk, I am G-d Sha-dai? (It means), I am He that said to the world: Enough'" (*Chagigah*, 12a).

In the first phase of the creation of the world, it was unstoppably unfolding, like the unraveling of two balls of yarn that are rolling away so fast in different directions there is no way to catch and stop them. The world kept on מתפשט ומרחיב / expanding and intensifying, without brakes. But then, the Creator declared, 'Enough!' and the boundaries of Da'as were set and the infantile universe began to mature. Similarly, when the proclamation was made throughout the camp, "Let no man or woman make further effort toward gifts for the sanctuary" and they stopped, they understood, at least for that moment, the idea of 'enough'. Moshe's effort to establish Da'as and civility was heeded and Klal Yisrael was able to stop.

This is the deeper reason that Chazal read the laws of 'carrying' from one domain to another on Shabbos from the Pasuk, "Let no man or woman do any more work." At the gathering of *Adas* Yisrael, Moshe was transmitting Da'as, an awareness of boundaries and balance, the internal ability to not 'trespass' or overstep established borders, even in a state of great enthusiasm. Yes, we can and should be enthusiastic, passionate, filled with desire and yearning, but this needs to be supported by and grounded within emotionally and spiritually healthy borders. And so, from this unique gathering of Klal Yisrael to build the holy Mishkan, Chazal learn the laws of spiritual trespassing, of moving objects from the domain where they rest and 'belong' during the present Shabbos to another domain.

In this transmission, Moshe also tells Klal Yisrael the prohibition of kindling fire on Shabbos: לא־תבערו אש בכל משבתיכם / "Do not kindle fire in all your dwellings" (*Shemos*, 35:3). Besides telling them about the prohibition of literally lighting fires on Shabbos, in the context of the gathering, Moshe is also hinting to them — yes, you can and should have the "fire" of passion and desire, yet, passion needs borders and limitations; you need to know how to stop, let go, be still, and experience life as already 'enough'. By imparting a sense of order, rest and maturity within the chaos of their exuberance, Moshe creates a Tikkun for Klal Yisrael.

THE YOUNG ARCHITECT OF THE MISHKAN: UNITING PASSION WITH MINDFULNESS

For the fashioning of the Mishkan, the chief architect was Betzalel. Why was Betzalel chosen for this role?

Speaking about the delicate dexterity required for building the Mishkan, the Ramban (*Shemos*, 31:2) writes that the entire Klal Yisrael was crushed under the burdens of mortar and brick labor, and thus no one had acquired the refined art of manipulating gold and silver. Indeed, it was a *Peleh* / wonder that there was a person like Betzalel who was able to craft such materials.* The Ramban is telling us that it was a miracle of sorts that Hashem had invested within him the wisdom of how to craft the materials of the Mishkan. This is one answer to the question; Betzalel was the only one who had the skill.

On the other hand, Chazal tell us (*Sanhedrin*, 69b) that Betzalel was only 13 years old when he was chosen as the chief architect of the Mishkan. If the whole issue is immaturity and lack of Da'as, as described above, why have a young child who had just become a *Bar Da'as*, or Bar Mitzvah, be the chief architect of the Mishkan?

---

* כי ישראל במצרים פרוכים בעבודת חומר ולבנים, לא למדו מלאכת כסף וזהב וחרושת אבנים טובות ולא ראו אותם כלל. והנה הוא פלא שימצא בהם אדם חכם גדול בכסף ובזהב ובחרושת אבן ועץ וחושב ורוקם ואורג, כי אף בלומדים לפני חכמים לא ימצא בקי בכל האומניות כלם, והיודעים ורגילים בהם בבא בא ידיהם תמיד בטיט ורפש לא יוכלו לעשות בהן אומנות דקה ויפה. ועוד, שהוא חכם גדול בחכמה בתבונה ובדעת להבין סוד המשכן וכל כליו למה צוו ואל מה ירמוזו.

In contemporary terms, most people would hesitate to allow a 13 year old to drive the family for a trip in their new car — how much more so to construct the dwelling place of the Creator within this world?

The answer is that he was chosen specifically because he had just become Bar Mitzvah, and just entered the world of Da'as. His inner maturity was new, but it was vivid and undiluted.

HEAVEN IS 'BEING', EARTH IS 'BECOMING'

Regarding Betzalel, it is said that "he knew how to לצרף / l'Tztaref / to combine the letters through which שמים וארץ / Shamayim vaAretz / Heaven and Earth were created" (*Berachos*, 55a).

Shamayim and Aretz are opposites. שמים / Heaven comes from the words שם מים / there is water there (*Chagigah*, 12a). Heaven is a 'place' of "there is," of already being present — it is a 'being' state. *Aretz* is connected with the word *Ratz* / running, as the Medrash (*Bereishis Rabbah*, 5:8) says, למה נקרא שמה ארץ שרצתה לעשות רצון קונה / "Why is the earth called *Aretz*? Because it 'runs' to perform the will of her Creator." Earth is in a constant state of becoming. We live our journey on earth, and eventually we get to Heaven. Heaven is a goal, an end, a destination; it is fixed and unmoving being. Earth is a place of desire and journeying; becoming.

In terms of our discussion, Aretz represents the immature state, never being satisfied, wanting more and more, a place of infinite yearning, longing, aspiring, and wanting — running in search of water. Shamayim is a place where "there is," the place of maturity and restfulness, the place where we can say, *Dai /* enough, or *Dayeinu /* we have enough. Here one sees there is already sufficient water, and there's no need to run after anything. *Shamayim* can be called a 'mind space', consciousness at rest, or Shabbos, whereas *Aretz* can be referred to as a heart space, representing the restlessness, lack or yearning of the six days of the week.

Betzalel is someone that stands in the liminal space between the two, in the crossroads between Shamayim and Aretz, immaturity and maturity, heart and mind, desire and 'enough'. And thus he knows how to לְצָרֵף / *l'Tzaref /* to combine Heaven and Earth, and unify the construct of what they each represent.

Betzalel had just left his childhood and immaturity, the place where nothing ever seems enough, and one is always moving and becoming, 'carrying' things from one domain to another and constantly lighting fires. He has now entered into a mature, settled mind space, he has a more expansive sense of proportion and is able to just be. He knows when to continue building and when to stop building.

Hashem wants us to dedicate ourselves to living inspired lives, with overflowing enthusiasm and youthful excitement, abundant zeal, alacrity and a fiery heart. It is, in fact, good for us to be so inspired that we *want* to give everything away, and to ride the power and newness of the world of *Tohu* / chaos, and to break through into redemption. However, Hashem also wants for us to restrain ourselves at times, and to maintain this unbridled power of Tohu within the *Kelim* / vessels of Tikkun, of Da'as, of presence of mind.*

---

* A similar idea is expressed by the life of Sarah. The Pasuk says, ויהיו חיי שרה מאה שנה ועשרים שנה ושבע שנים / "This is the life of Sarah, one hundred years, and twenty years, and seven years..." (*Bereishis*, 23:1). Why is each unit of time specified? Says the Medrash (*Bereishis Rabbah*, 58:1 as Rashi quotes), לכך נכתב שנה בכל כלל וכלל לומר לך שכל אחד נדרש לעצמו בת מאה כבת עשרים לחטא ובת עשרים כבת שבע ליופי / "The reason the word שנה is written with each category is to tell you that each term must be explained by itself as a complete number: at the age of 100 she was as a woman of 20 with regard to sin — for just as at the age of 20 one may regard her as having never sinned, since she had not then reached the age when she was subject to punishment, so, too, when she was 100 years old she was sinless — and when she was 20 she was as beautiful as when she was 7."

An alternative Medrash writes, אלא בת מאה שנה היתה כבת עשרים לנוי ובת עשרים כבת ז' לחטא / "At one hundred years she was like a twenty year old in beauty, and at twenty she was like seven, with no sin" (*Medrash Lekach Tov*, 23:1-2). Clearly, whether twenty or seven is beauty depends on the type of beauty. The beauty of seven is a type of innocence, whereas twenty is more of external beauty.

There are three periods or ages in our lives: the age of innocence, the age of ambition, and the age of maturity. Normally, we think of time as progressing linearly; we leave the age of innocence and enter the world of drive, ambition, desire, the age of *Shir haShirim* and passionate love — and then we enter midlife and beyond, becoming wiser and more settled, in our maturity. Sadly, however, as we get older, we may become less innocent and less ambitious. Often, people give up on their dreams, their youthful desires, and as they become more level headed and 'realistic', they lose their innocence and their trust in the inherent goodness of humanity and Hashem's Creation. Yet, this Medrash is teaching us that at every stage of life we need to be able to include the beneficial aspects of the other stages. Being wise and mature should not come at the expense of our ambition and our innate innocence.

We need to learn how to be like Betzalel and to unify the Light of Tohu, of youthful dynamism, with the vessels of Tikkun, maturity and Da'as.

The ultimate objective is to combine Aretz with Shamayim, to bind Earth to Heaven and draw Heaven down to Earth. This requires combining the movement and fire of passion with the stillness of the waters of pure being.

ויקהל / *Vayakhel* / gathering occurred at both the casting of the idol and the building of the Mishkan. And that is indeed the Divine desire, that Klal Yisrael gathered with intense excitement to build the Mishkan, and that they yearned to give everything away and reach for Infinity. And Hashem also wanted for Moshe to instill Da'as into Klal Yisrael and show them that they were always already more than enough.

This is the *Chidush* / novelty of the project of the Mishkan, and in fact, of all of life: harnessing the unrestrained, wild, child-like 'heart' of Tohu by circulating it within the vessels of Tikkun, the orderly, clear space of 'mind'. We should be, in this way, like a young person on the border between adulthood and childhood; we should have mature Da'as and also the enthusiasm of a child. This is why the chief architect of the Mishkan is a 13 year old boy.

This idea can also help us better understand some deeper teachings on the foundation of the Mishkan.

THE AMUDIM / PLANKS OF THE MISHKAN STAND FOREVER

We are told that the Mishkan is an eternal edifice and was never destroyed. The Mishkan that was erected by Moshe is eternal, and when the Beis haMikdash was built, the Mishkan was buried (*Sotah*, 13a).

An eternal aspect of the Mishkan is the *Amudim* / pillars or planks supporting the walls and overall structure of the Mishkan. The Torah tells us that the Amudim need to be עֲצֵי שִׁטִּים עֹמְדִים / "Upright acacia wooden planks" (*Shemos*, 26:15). The word עֹמְדִים / upright, says Chazal, means שֶׁעוֹמְדִין לְעוֹלָם וּלְעוֹלָמִים / "they stand upright forever and ever" (*Yuma*, 72a). The planks of the Mishkan seem to lend eternality to the structure of the Mishkan.

Acacia wood in Hebrew is called שִׁטִּים / *Shittim*. Why is Shittim used above all other woods? Says the Medrash, it is to create a Tikkun and bring a healing for an earlier experience with שִׁטִּים. As the Pasuk says, וַיֵּשֶׁב יִשְׂרָאֵל בַּשִּׁטִּים וַיָּחֶל הָעָם לִזְנוֹת אֶל־בְּנוֹת מוֹאָב / "While Israel was staying at Shittim, the people profaned themselves by whoring with the Moabite women" (*Bamidbar*, 25:1). In a geographical location called Shittim, Klal Yisrael sinned with licentiousness and sensual debauchery, i.e., *Tohu* / untamed, unfocused self-expression. Their Tikkun then needed to come through holy Shittim — bringing Shittim to create the Mishkan (*Tanchuma*, Terumah, 9. עצי שטים עומדים כמה מיני ארזים הן ומכלם לא בחר אלא בזה ששמו שטים לפי שישראל חטאו בשטים לקו בשטים ונתרפאו בשטים: Rabbeinu Bachya, *Shemos*, 26:15).

As a location, the name *Shittim* comes from the word *Sotah* / going astray (*Bamidbar*, 5:12), and from the word *Sh'tus* / foolishness, nonsense, as in שֶׁנִּתְעַסְּקוּ בְּדִבְרֵי שְׁטוּת / "They were engaged in matters of nonsense" (*Sanhedrin*, 106a. *Medrash Rabbah*, Bamidbar, 2:22). This is related to a general principle: "A person sins only if a spirit of *Sh'tus* / folly first enters him" (*Sotah*, 3a).

To replace the negative, destructive type of foolishness (Sh'tus, Shittim), Klal Yisrael is asked to construct the Mishkan with a positive, constructive kind of Shittim. This is referred to as שטות דקדושה / *Sh'tus d'Kedushah* / holy silliness or craziness.

'Sh'tus of Kelipah', of negativity, involves descending to a place below the mind, as it were, opening oneself to indulge desires of the flesh, for example, despite knowing intellectually that one should not. Allowing temptations for instant gratification to rule over one's better judgment is negative Sh'tus. Positive, holy Sh'tus is to transcend the mind, to have faith in positive outcomes, despite not seeing a logical way out. It means to go beyond the letter of the law in Mitzvos and acts of kindness, beyond what you normally think is your capacity. Whereas Sh'tus of Kelipah is sub-rational, letting go of your mind and free choice, submitting to animal instincts, Sh'tus of Kedushah is super-rational, beyond mind.

Where did Klal Yisrael find Shittim wood in the desert? Says the Medrash (*Tanchuma*, Terumah, 9), Yaakov planted these trees hundreds of years earlier when he first descended into Egypt, telling his children, 'Eventually you will leave Egypt and you will need these planks to build a Mishkan.' Hundreds of years prior to their redemption from Egypt, and even before they were actually even enslaved, Yaakov prepared the wood that they would only need after they had been redeemed. Therefore, for hundreds of years, in their most harsh moments of enslavement, Klal Yisrael were able to look at those majestic trees growing and attain some hope.

Faith is what sustained Klal Yisrael in Egypt: faith in a brighter future, faith that one day, despite being oppressed and broken by the supreme power of the ancient world, they (certainly the women) had faith that despite all odds, redemption would come. This supra-rational faith is the Sh'tus of Kedushah, which is mystically the Shittim, the very walls and supports of the Mishkan.

Our Sh'tus of Kedushah counters our Sh'tus of Kelipah. Holy 'foolishness' defies all logic, transcends all predictions, and thus also literally becomes eternal, transcending the ravages of time, thereby becoming the essential foundation of the Mishkan, the eternal dwelling place of HaKadosh Baruch Hu in this world.

FROM DA'AS TO BEYOND DA'AS: THE NIGHT OF THE SEDER

On one hand, the entire process of Seder Night, this sublime celebration, reenacting and reliving our redemption, is all about assimilating Da'as into our consciousness. The inner constriction of Egypt was a constriction of Da'as and redemption occurs when all of Klal Yisrael, and even the Egyptian oppressors, finally "know that I am Hashem." The medium through which Hashem's Presence is revealed is Moshe, the Bechinah / aspect of Da'as.

On Seder Night, we drink wine together as a Mitzvah, and as we do so we create a Tikkun for the original drinking of wine, which was the eating of the grapes of the Tree of Knowledge that caused death and separation. And we also eat Matzah, which is also connected to the rectification of the Tree of Knowledge (according to another opinion that the Tree was actually stalks of grain). The grain of the Matzah is also connected to Da'as, as our sages tell us, "A child does not יודע / know how to call out 'father,' or 'mother,' until he tastes grain" (*Sanhedrin*, 70b). This implies that the consumption of wheat is associated, in some way, with our intellectual development, specifically, Da'as. Matzah brings Tikkun and maturity into our spiritual constitution. Yet, on the other hand, at the end of the Seder, we reach a point of *Atik* / Cosmic Transcendence (such as the level Klal Yisrael reached at the Splitting of the Sea), an aspect of the Sefirah of *Keser* / Crown, a place higher than all knowing, beyond Da'as.*

Da'as is the world of order, Tikkun, definition; where everything is distinct and marked and orderly. Indeed, the whole structure of Pesach night is called the *Seder* / Order, and everything is set up on the Seder plate in a very orderly fashion. As we move through the Seder, drinking more and more wine, slowly the orderly quality unravels and we attain a level *beyond* Seder.

---

* Keser is *Ratzon* and *Ta'avah*, beyond Mochin. And within Keser itself there is the level of *Radla / Reisha d'Lo Isyada*, beyond knowing, even knowing itself, as it were. Radla is the level of *Reisha d'lo Isyada* / 'the Unknowable Head' or 'the head that does not know'. This is the highest of the three levels within Keser. 'Below' Radla there is a level called *Galgalta* / skull, which is the meta-source of all defined masculine qualities. Below that, there is *Mochin Stima* / hidden 'brains' or mind, which is the meta-source of all defined feminine qualities. The level of Radla is so transcendent, it cannot be known by any living being or angel, nor even by itself, so-to-speak. Radla is beyond all Da'as.

We end the night singing praises to HaKadosh Baruch Hu, almost in the manner of a 'drunken' lover, singing love songs to his Beloved One at the end of the night.

Indeed, ultimately we are seeking a total Yichud of love, a Yichud between Da'as and the Crown beyond Da'as, between mind and heart, between maturity and child-like passion, the unbridled desire of Tohu and the vessels of Tikkun. This Yichud allows us to harness the *Ohr* / Light of Tohu within the *Kelim* / vessels, context and container of Tikkun.

Chapter Thirteen
The Meta-Structure of the Night of Redemption

THERE ARE VARIOUS DIFFERENT WAYS TO THINK ABOUT the structure of Pesach Night in particular and the Yom Tov of Pesach in general. The Arizal revealed a deep, inner structure that helps explain all the various different aspects of Pesach and Seder Night. The language of the Arizal can be very terse and abstruse to those not familiar with his terminology or the language of Kabbalah in general. Let us explore the actual words of the Arizal and then unpack one meaning from these words. But first, a couple points regarding the Ten *Sefiros* / Divine Attributes (as it were):

"Just as the Divine Self can express Itself (so to speak) as Infinity, It can also express Itself as finitude; otherwise It would not be complete."* *Ohr Ein Sof* / Light of the Infinite is juxtaposed here with the Ten Sefiros. The Ten Sefiros are like ten screens through which the Infinite Light of the Ein Sof penetrates our finite reality. The distinct forms, shapes, and colors of the Sefiros filter the infinite, colorless, formless, unified Light as it enters our world of form. Passing through the Sefiros causes the Light to appear differentiated and colored.

The first Sefirah to appear is *Keser* / Crown. The quality of Keser is the deep desire and primordial will of the Infinite One to create finite existence. One level of Keser is also called *Arich Anpin* / Large Face.

After the will and desire to create, the Sefiros of the Divine Mind manifest: *Chochmah* / wisdom (intuition), *Binah* / understanding (reason), and *Da'as* / (practical) knowledge. Collectively, these three Sefiros are called *Mochin* / Mind. Chochmah is called *Abba* / Father. Binah is also *Ima* / Mother. The proper Unity of Chochmah and Binah gives 'birth' to 'ZA' — *Zeir Anpin* / Small Face, the Six Emotional Sefiros:

---

* Rebbe Azriel of Gerona, *Bi'ur Eser Sefiros*: כשם שיש לו כח בבלתי בעל גבול כך יש לו כח בגבול. שאם תאמר שיש לו כח בבלתי בעל גבול ואין לו כח בגבול, אתה מחסר שלימותו. ואין סוף הוא שלימותא דכולא: *Avodas haKodesh*, 1:8.

Chesed: Loving-Kindness, giving, momentum

Gevurah: Strength, withholding, restriction, discipline

Tiferes: Beauty, balance, compassion

Netzach: Victory, ambition, courage

Hod: Humility, gratitude, ability to compromise

Yesod: Foundation, relationship

The Six Emotional Sefiros are 'masculine', like the 'son' that is born to Ima and Abba. And also in its relationship with what is 'below' it, Zeir Anpin ('ZA') serves as a masculine, impregnating quality.

Then comes the final Sefirah, Malchus: Kingship, nobility, receptivity, and Divine Immanence. Malchus is the vessel that receives from the preceding Sefiros.

In comparison to Malchus, ZA is Transcendence, whereas ZA in comparison to his 'parents' is 'immanence' and the vessel that receives their light.

During the exile in Egypt, the level of ZA / the Divine Six Emotional Attributes, which is also a code word for *Keneses Yisrael* / the People of Israel* and for the Name of Hashem**

---

* Adam is Tiferes, the essential Sefirah of ZA.
** The Yud-Hei-Vav-Hei, as the Name of Hashem is also Tiferes.

return, ascend (upwards) into a pre-birth state and fetus position within the Higher Divine Mother, the Sefirah of Binah. This is the 'root cause' of the apparent exile and this is why Pharaoh is able to say, "Who is Hashem... I do not know Him." He does not say Hashem does not exist, rather says, "I don't know Him," meaning, he is saying that the level of Hashem (ZA, "Him," the masculine) has been hidden from Pharaoh and cannot be revealed. Pharaoh is like a fetus covered in his mother's womb, and thus he claims he is not afraid of Hashem.

When the Light of ZA is hidden, not shining into Malchus, then our world of Malchus itself is in a condition of concealment and thus exile, estranged and alienated from its Root.

On the night of the Geulah from Egypt and on the Seder Night, there is a 'rebirth' or re-revealing of the Light of ZA, which becomes unified with Malchus. ZA becomes 'active' again and can unify with Malchus when the *Mochin* / Mind of the higher Sefiros are activated and drawn down into ZA.

On the night of the Geulah, and ever since on Seder Night, redemption occurs when there is a drawing down of *Mochin* / intelligence and clarity from Chochmah (Abba) and Binah (Ima) into ZA, awakening and arousing ZA so that it can unify with Malchus.

By eating Matzah, we draw Divine *Chochmah* / wisdom down into ZA and into our 'higher self'. In our consciousness, Chochmah is the kernel of intellectual 'right-brain' intuition, inspiration and clarity. It is like the seed given over from the

Abba to the Ima to create a child. The four cups draw Binah / understanding down into ZA and into us. Binah, is the fuller 'left brain' understanding and articulation of the kernel of Chochmah, much like the developing of the fetus in the womb of the Ima into a full child (*Pri Eitz Chayim*, Sha'ar Chag haMatzos, 1 & 7. *Sha'ar haKavanos*, Pesach, Derush 1).

Wine brings joy and *Binah* / Ima is connected with the joy of fully understanding and absorbing what we did not know. This understanding reveals the 'fullness' of an idea, like the fullness of wine which looks and tastes and feels good.

With the first cup of wine we draw down the Chochmah of Ima into ZA and ourselves.

With the second cup we draw down the Binah of Ima.

With the third and fourth cup we draw Da'as of Ima.

In Da'as itself there are two levels: Da'as of Chesed (the third cup) and Da'as of Gevurah (the fourth cup). Both cups are part of the drawing down of Da'as and this is the deeper reason why we should not drink other drinks between the third and fourth cup.*

---

* The Gra writes that the third and fourth cup are both *v'Ga'alti*, and in that itself, there are two aspects, "out-stretched hand" and "great judgments" and thus, the third and fourth cup are two dimensions of one idea, and thus, we cannot drink anything in between. Note the word לחפשי / to freedom (*Shemos*, 21:2) is numerically is 428. As are the words Chochmah (73) Binah (67) Chesed (72) Gevurah (216) = 428: Rebbe Levi Yitzchak Schneerson, the illustrious Mekubal and father of the Rebbe, *Yalkut Levi Yitzchak*, Vol. 5, 100.

This is the overall structure in the writing of the Arizal. While it may still seem a little abstract, a gorgeous tapestry is being revealed by the Holy Arizal, so let us delve deeper and unpack this idea further.

FREEDOM FROM WITHIN

ZA is an inner realm within the 'devolution' of Creation, as well as a *Mashal* / metaphor and code word for *Hashem*, the Transcendent Name of the Creator, especially in relation to how Hashem interacts with the world. There is a *Bechinah* / paradigm of ZA as well within our own life and consciousness.

ZA is our emotional state, essentially, our most dominant self. Our autopilot responses to life come from physical instincts and reactive emotions. We recoil from touching hot coals, we have a flight-or-fight response when our ego seems threatened, and we draw closer to someone when we perceive their warmth. The trouble with this way of living is that we dangle on our fickle impressions of others, and our behavior is dictated by external conditions. This is an outside-in flow of causality.

A redemptive mode of life emphasizes an inside-out flow of causality — when our behaviors flow from our *Keser* / innermost desire and will, to our Mochin / intelligence and perception of reality, into our 'ZA' / emotions and finally into actions and interactions in the physical world. *Geulah Peratis* / individual redemption requires that our innermost desire to fulfill our purpose and mission is 'understood' in our Mochin, including the 'what' and the 'how'. This understanding must also affect our emotions and practical focus in ways that ensure that the original inner desire is expressed in speech and action.

Freedom comes from such a perfect flow of clarity; knowing our innermost dream, understanding how it needs to be actualized, arousing our emotions — whether 'bitter' or positively enthusiastic — and acting on it. When we know what we need to be doing and how we need to do it, and trust ourselves to do it, our life becomes filled with clarity, certainty, and practical self-knowledge.

A lack of freedom, a personal 'exile', comes from one's actions and their 'ZA' not being aligned with their Mochin and inner level of Keser. When one's emotions and actions are not guided by their intellect and innermost desires, they feel off kilter, out of place. When there is an absence of Mochin and Keser, there is a lack of purpose and means to reach one's purpose. One cannot find their 'place' in the world. They end up weighed down by nagging uncertainty and crippling doubt. Their emotions become reactive and automatic. Authentic, deeper emotions go dormant, and one's 'ZA' ascends or conceals itself, returning to a fetal position, receding into the womb of Mochin. One's redemptive actions are no longer revealed in the world.

EXILE OF DA'AS / AWARENESS

ZA is the 'child' of *Mochin* / Active Intelligence (again, Mochin is composed of *Abba* / Chochmah, and *Ima* / Binah, which together give birth to the *Midos* / the six primary emotions). For Mochin to conceive healthy, focused, intended, and aligned children, Da'as as well needs to be activated, as in אין קישוי אלא לדעת / "There is no male arousal without Da'as" (*Yevamos*, 53b). On a personal, inward level, when our ZA, emotions are in exile — whether they are aggressive and overbearing, or displaced and unfocused, unexpressive or unresponsive — this means that one's Da'as is lacking, misaligned, or misguided.

Our emotions follow our Da'as. Galus is a condition of improperly expressed emotions, and the deeper root of this negative phenomenon is misaligned Da'as.

Egypt represents a place of constriction of one's Midos; the epitome of Egypt is מלך מצרים / *Melech Mitzrayim* / king of Egypt. Melech Mitzrayim, as mentioned, in numerical value is 470, with the 4 letters in Pharaoh's name added it is 474, which is the same as the word *Da'as* (Rameh miPano, *Mayan Ganim*, 3. Seder shel Pesach). He is the embodiment of negative Da'as. Indeed, ערב רב / *Eirev Rav* / the Mixed Multitudes, those who became attached to Klal Yisrael as they left Egypt and caused Klal Yisrael to continuously stumble and continuously be apprehensive about leaving Egypt, is also numerically *Da'as*.

Within negative Da'as there are two possibilities: a *lack* of Da'as and a Da'as of *Kelipah* / negative concealment. Da'as of Kelipah can manifest as attachment to negative ideas or being stuck on an idea in a way that creates blindness or limitation. People can get stuck in what they think they 'know' and thus cannot see what is really going on and therefore cannot move forward. This is the Da'as of the ego, which tells the individual, 'You are nothing but your ego and therefore you need to fight for yourself, be aggressive, manipulative, whatever it takes to come out ahead.' When a person listens to this 'advice', he eventually feels uncertain, incapable, not smart or charming or confident enough to act as a free person. This negative Da'as guarantees a life of frustration and eventual depression.

A deeper level of this personal exile is when a person is not even aware that he is stuck in smallness, ego and the Kelipah of Da'as. He is so busy trying to fight and fend for himself that he cannot see how petty, mean, despondent, or reactive he has become.

An inner redemption begins when there is a re-revealing of proper Mochin into our ZA, our Midos, our emotional attributes. When our higher, inner Da'as, our inner 'Moshe Rabbeinu' becomes revealed, we begin to understand our lives and see our ideas, emotions, words and behaviors for what they are. When we start living with this clarity of vision, our purpose and reason for being, and what we need to be expressing in life, become obvious. When this higher Da'as is revealed, our emotions, actions and speech feel 'right', aligned, Divinely guided and effective.

When Da'as is in exile, there is a trickle-down effect through all the Sefiros below it.
Liberation (like 'Libra') comes from balance.
When Da'as is redeemed and all the channels of the Midos are balanced and rectified, the flow moves from Da'as through the Midos to Dibbur / speech.
The Seder activates the process of redemption through all the Sefiros:

When Da'as was in exile in Egypt, we received Da'as from Moshe. Today, we get higher Mochin and a redemption of Da'as through the eating of Matzah and Drinking of the Wine.

When Tiferes, composed of the five Sefiros or 'Midos' of ZA, was in exile, it manifested as unredeemed emotions.
In the Redemption from Egypt, there was a revelation of healthy Midos. Today through reciting Maggid, we arouse the heart and redeem our emotions.

In Egypt, Malchus, which is Dibbur, was in exile, manifesting as Peh-Ra / negative speech. Peh-Sach means 'a liberation of speech', and as we recite the Haggadah, we too experience a redemption of speech.

MOCHIN OF CHOCHMAH AND MOCHIN OF BINAH

With the eating of 'pure' Matzah, we create a vessel to draw down the Mochin of Chochmah. With the drinking of the 'tasty' four cups of wine, we are making a vessel to draw down the Mochin of Binah.

In fact, even if we were to swallow the Matzah without tasting it, we would still be drawing down the Mochin of Chochmah. Matzah is "poor man's bread" representing simple, wholehearted faith, and as such, through eating it we are lifted higher into intuitive clarity and faith, even beyond our *Keilim* / vessels — our 'taste'. This clarity catapults us to a place of freedom and openness, a state of *Gadlus* / expanded spirituality and awareness.

Wine, in contrast to empty, bland, 'white' Matzah, is brimming with taste and color. This 'fullness' represents the reality of *Binah* / experiential understanding reached through deeply assimilating ideas into our consciousness. When drinking the wine, we are gifted the Mochin of Binah.

Mochin of Binah is different from Mochin of Chochmah. Mochin of Binah is a deep knowing and *feeling* of rightness — for example, sensing what you are supposed to be doing in life. Mochin of Chochmah is more of an *intuitive clarity* of what you are supposed to be doing, but this knowing is even clearer than Mochin of Binah.

In Mochin of Binah, you 'taste' that everything is exactly the way it is supposed to be. For instance, when you are about to recite Kiddush and drink the first cup, you can 'taste' that your life makes sense. There is a felt sensation, a *Yesh* / tangible, physical feeling, that everything is clear. Chochmah is a subtler, but higher sense. It is not *b'Murgash* / felt as a sensation in the body. It is a clear intellectual intuition that all is perfect and exactly as Hashem wants it to be. One even sees that *Maves* / death and the 'Maror' of life, are ultimately sweet and exactly how they should be.

Parallel terms for these two levels of Mochin and clarity are: 1) *Gadlus Rishon* / first (lower) level greatness or expansiveness, which is Mochin of Binah, and 2) *Gadlus Sheini* / second (higher) level of greatness or expansiveness, which is the Mochin of Chochmah.

We start the Seder with the first cup of wine, immediately rising into Gadlus Rishon.*

---

* Although Gadlus Rishon and Sheini are attained during the Ma'ariv service, they 'leave' the person after Davening and are returned during the Seder, beginning with Gadlus Rishon: *Sefer haKavanos* (Yashan), Kitzur Derush Pesach. *Mishnas Chassidim*, Seder Leil Pesach, 1:2. Yet, the Rashash understands that during Ma'ariv we receive Gadlus of *Mochin* / intelligence in a *Penimiyus* / internal level, through speech and words of Tefilah, whereas during the Seder there is Gadlus of Mochin also on the *Chitzoniyus* / external level, and thus the actions, the Mitzvos we 'do' during the Seder: *Nahar Shalom*, p. 34d. The Leshem writes that during Davening, in Shul, the Mochin is drawn down into the higher worlds, and during the Seder into the 'lower' worlds.

Normally, night/questions/bitterness/immaturity comes *before* day/answers/sweetness/maturity, but on this night we begin with Gadlus, we are gifted Gadlus from Above right away. We do not begin the Seder by asking questions, nor speaking about our enslavement, rather, we begin with Kiddush over wine and stimulate Mochin of Binah.

As we recite Kiddush, a lightning-bolt of Gadlus Rishon is revealed to us. It is like you are walking at night in a dark, thick forest, when lightning suddenly lights up the sky, the forest becomes revealed, and you see the path out. Everything is clear for one moment. Your whole life 'makes sense' — everything that has ever happened to you, where you are in your life now, who your parents, siblings or children are, the job you have, the place you live — everything 'makes sense' in a single flash.

FROM GADLUS INTO KATNUS – WHILE REMEMBERING GADLUS

After drinking the first cup, we descend directly into the *Katnus Sheini* / second smallness, the contracted place of questions, the story of being slaves, and admitting that we were originally idol worshipers. Plummeting from Gadlus into Katnus is bitter; we re-enter our state of exile, we ask questions, and we eat the Karpas, a vegetable from the ground, representing our lowliness, after dipping it in salty, bitter water. We break the Matzah and feel our brokenness and confusion. Following Maggid, we finally move to the Gadlus Sheini, Mochin of Chochmah, upon eating the Matzah.

Perhaps the Katnus experienced between the first cup and the eating of Matzah is the reason why some people experience frustration during this part of the Seder. A person with less understanding may lack enthusiasm or even feel bored during the Maggid section of the Seder. Indeed, we are, at this point in the process, put in contact with our state of Katnus. But this is for a reason. Right after Kiddush, the flash of light is over and we fall back into the darkness — yet we have already experienced and felt that there is light, meaning, and clarity. Since we already experienced Gadlus, even when we are in Katnus we know that Gadlus is who we really are and where we really belong.

Truthfully, most of our life is not lived in Gadlus. But when we have 'tasted' Gadlus and experienced a deep understanding of the light of life, then, when we descend into Katnus, we know that we can always get back to Gadlus — because that is who we ultimately are.

So, yes, we are still in Galus, practically, and yes, there are poor people that are hungry, physically and spiritually. There is still death and mourning in the world (in fact, Matzah, the bread of freedom, is also the bread of 'mourning': *Lechem Oni*, with an Ayin, as in 'poor', but similar to *Oni*, with an Aleph, meaning, bread of acute mourning. The Mitzvah must be fulfilled with a Matzah that can be eaten during a period of acute mourning: *Pesachim*, 36a). There is bitter Maror, immaturity, questions and doubt — yet, we still celebrate *Cheirus* / freedom, because we know that Gadlus is where we are rooted, and at any time we can get back to Gadlus. And at any time

Hashem can, and will, redeem us.

We were once idol worshipers. We were once slaves in Egypt. But, we know that we are *b'Etzem* / essentially people of Cheirus and Gadlus. No matter the circumstance, we always have the possibility to be free. This is why we celebrate Pesach on this night, even while we are living in an apparent Galus. The world has not yet been redeemed; there are still wars and strife, destitution, illusion, and most of us are still living mostly in a personal state of exile. Yet as we recognize that we come from Gadlus and will return to Gadlus, we realize that we essentially are Gadlus.

FROM GADLUS TO KATNUS, TO GREATER GADLUS

After Kiddush, the first cup of wine, we move from Gadlus into the world of Katnus, but this is only in order to rise into a higher *Bechinah* / level of Gadlus which has the power to elevate all Katnus.

As the phase of Maggid progresses, we slowly build our vessels, asking the right questions, acknowledging the place of our uncertainties, and recognizing that we are still functioning in a level of Katnus, yet stimulating a desire to connect to redemption and yearn for extended periods of Gadlus. When we finally arrive at the eating of the Matzah, we experience a higher form of Gadlus, higher than the one we experienced at Kiddush. We attain and internalize a higher or deeper level of Mochin — the Mochin of Chochmah.

Through eating Matzah we are each given a deeper sense of intuitive awareness, in which even the more challenging aspects of life make sense. Once we attain this higher Mochin, we can even eat the Maror and 'internalize' the bitterness in our lives. We effect a *Hamtakah* / sweetening even in the areas in our lives that are as painful as death (*Maror* is numerically related to the word *Maves* / death). The 'deaths' in our lives include dramatic endings, falls, and failings. The Matzah has given us such a deep awareness that everything is exactly the way it is meant to be, that we can say, "Ah, now I know why I needed to go through that devastating experience!"

Overall, on the night of Pesach we move from Gadlus (*Rishon* / First), to Katnus, and then to higher Gadlus (*Sheini* / Second). Yet, beyond Gadlus of Chochmah is Gadlus *Shelishi* / third-level expansiveness, which is the Mochin of Keser. Gadlus Shelishi is the way the world and ZA (the human being) existed prior to the eating from the Tree of Knowledge, Separation and Duality. Experientially, this level is perfect clarity regarding our place in the world, our mission and purpose, an absolute knowing from a place of 'beyond knowing'. G-d willing, 50 days after Seder Night, having reached Shavuos, the day of *Matan Torah* / the Giving of the Torah, we receive Gadlus Shelishi, as we receive the Keser of Torah (as explored in great detail in the book "The Month of Sivan: The Art of Receiving").*

---

* Following the initial states of Gadlus that are gifted to us on the night of Pesach, the gifts of Gadlus Rishon and Sheini disappear and we descend into a deeper Katnus of constriction and ambiguity. The Katnus that

This is the way this dynamic is played out in the world of Nefesh, within our own lives and consciousness; drawing down Mochin into ZA is reflected in our personal lives. Yet, this cosmic, supernal dynamic of ZA (*Tiferes* / Hashem) and Malchus unifying through the revealing and drawing down of higher Mochin of Binah and Chochmah, is reflected and refracted in the more impersonal world of historical time, as well.

GADLUS WITHIN TIME / HISTORY:

Everything that the Arizal speaks about is true on multiple levels, from higher cosmic levels to more subtle levels, from the level of *Nefesh* / the soul of the person, to the level of Divine Rulership, in which Hashem is *Manhig* / guiding the world and revealing Himself through history.

Gadlus Rishon, the Mochin of Binah, is revealed (Ramchal, *Sefer haKelalim*, printed in back of *Da'as Tevunos*, p. 272) through the mysteries, miracles and great wonders that Hashem performs in this world — especially the revelations of Divine Presence during the period of the First *Beis haMikdash* / Holy Temple, "a time of miracles" (*Yuma*, 21b. Note, *Avos*, 5:5). During that

---

is manifested during the counting of the Omer is so influential that even in the world of finance it appears in the form of financial difficulties: *Imrei Pinchas*, Shabbos uMoadim, 301-302. We reside in this state of Katnus until Shavuos, when we receive Gadlus Shelishi in a more transformative, integrated and compassionate way. The Arizal calls this Gadlus Shelishi, as Tiferes is then unified and received from Keser. Throughout the Omer period we are building the 'vessels', the desire to receive Gadlus Shelishi, so that when it finally does descend upon us, that Gadlus is truly appreciated and assimilated, and not merely 'gifted' to us.

period, Divine prophecy was being regularly revealed, and as a result there was a world-wide explosion of worldly and ethical wisdom. Still, direct revelation was accessed only by prophets, and those meriting to be in or near the Beis haMikdash.

Gadlus Sheini (Chochmah) within the dimensions of time will be revealed in the Era of Moshiach, when the entire world will be filled with "the knowledge of Hashem" (*Yeshayahu*, 11:15). We will no longer need 'miracles' to point us to the Presence of HaKadosh Baruch Hu, because in all places and in all moments "all flesh together will see the *Kevod* / glory of Hashem" (*Ibid*, 55:8).

Gadlus Shelishi, the clarity and expansiveness of Keser, will be collectively experienced in the time of *Techiyas haMeisim* / Resurrection of the Dead. This will be a revelation of the world of immortality, the eternal revelation of the absolute Oneness of Hashem. On the night of Shavuos we are connected with this level of Gadlus, and thus Shavuos is connected to immortality: "Know, that anyone that banishes sleep the entire night of Shavuos, and studies Torah the entire night is guaranteed to live through the year, and no harm will befall them the entire year" (*Sha'ar haKavanos*, Derushei Chag haShavuos, 1). And indeed, when we received the Torah at Mount Sinai, we experienced Techiyas haMeisim, as the Gemara says, our soul left our body and it was returned with the *Tal Techiyah* / the dew of revival (*Shabbos*, 88b). Yet, because of the sin of the Golden Calf, the first Luchos, the Luchos of freedom from the angel of death (*Medrash Rabbah*, Shemos, 41), were shattered and we entered again the world of duality. This encompassing sense of duality lasted until the time of the First Beis haMikdash when we witnessed Gadlus Rishon being revealed.

THE DAY AFTER THE SEDER

On Seder Night, sitting in our finest attire before our table adorned with our finest dishes, reclining as the royalty of old and drinking wine, we are made acutely aware that Gadlus is who we are. When Hashem took us out of Egypt, it created and solidified our state of existential freedom. We are a 'free people' b'Etzem, in our essence. We are a *Goy Kadosh* / a holy people, and *Bnei Malachim* / children of kings. On the night that we are birthed as a people, we own this and behave accordingly. We receive a Divine *Shefa* / flow that arouses and inspires this essential Gadlus. Yet, sadly, in parallel to the high can be the low, and many people wake up the next morning after the Seder not only physically, mentally and emotionally fatigued, but they feel spiritually fallen.

Chazal teach us a concept of להזהיר הגדולים על הקטנים / "to warn adults regarding minors." This means, for example, that an adult may not feed a minor non-Kosher foods with his hands (*Yevamos*, 114a). Metaphorically, it can mean 'to draw זוהר / illumination from a *Gadol* / 'great one' (adult) upon the *Katan* / 'small one' (a minor)'. We need to ensure that our states of 'greatness' or Gadlus illuminate our states of Katnus. We need to taste what it means to live in our Gadlus, to feel it during the Seder, and to interact with ourselves and others with that clarity, openness and expansiveness. We need to internalize and know that this Gadlus is our birthright to the extent that any time we react to life from a place of Katnus we will recognize that we are robbing ourselves of our true potential. In this way, our expansive states need to illuminate our constricted states.

Imagine as an example, you are dancing at the wedding of your daughter — or experiencing some other moment of elated celebration, and in walks in a person who deeply irritates and offends you. Imagine that, because of your great joy, their presence does not bother you at all. You're in such a good space that your narrative about the person seems completely trivial. Now consider the fact that if something seems trivial when you are in an expanded state, then it is actually *always* trivial.

Now imagine you are not feeling any Gadlus. You feel frustrated, exhausted, constricted, or even angry — but you have previously tasted Gadlus. You remember how it felt, how the tone of your thoughts registered, and how you spoke and acted in that state. You know what it means to live in the light of higher Mochin, so now it is your choice whether or not you assimilate the Gadlus of Pesach into the rest of the day, and even into the rest of the year. Imagine you can call forth a glimmer of that Gadlus and let it shine upon your sense of smallness. Let yourself resonate with the sounds of Gadlus, and feel the experience of Katnus softening and being slowly dissolved into the soothing light of inner expansion.

Our descent into Katnus is only for the sake of a greater ascent into Gadlus.

Chapter Fourteen
Four Levels of Slavery
& the Four Mitzvos of Freedom

HERE ARE MANY TERMS THE TORAH USES TO DESCRIBE the form of exile in Egypt: *Inui* / affliction, *Avodas Perach* / hard labor, *Merirus* / bitterness, *Shi'bud* / subjugation to servitude, and *Lachatz* / stress. "So they put slave masters over them למען ענתו בסבלתם / to afflict them with forced labor" (*Shemos*, 1:11). "And the Egyptians made the children of Israel serve בפרך / with *Perach* / harsh labor (1:13). וימררו / "and they embittered their lives" (1:14). "Now the cry of the Israelites has reached Me; moreover, I have seen את־הלחץ / the stress" (3:9)....

These are all different forms of hardship, for example, לחץ /
Lachatz is external financial burden, whereas דוחק / *Dochak* is
internal stress caused by each other (*Malbim*, Shoftim 2:18), and
Perach, which could refer to the disorientation of not being
able to fill your essential role or destiny. All in all, these are all
forms of hardship.

What exactly creates the hardship of exile, whether external
or internal, and what tools do we have that can ensure that
we, today, do not become entrapped in a slave-like condition
of constriction or ego-based reactivity? What does it mean
'to be in Egypt'? The answers lie in how the Torah tells us to
celebrate Pesach

There are four Torah-based Mitzvos of Pesach:

1. *Korban Pesach* / The Pesach Offering: This is the Mitzvah to bring an animal offering to the *Beis haMikdash*
   / Temple in Yerushalayim / Jerusalem when the Beis
   haMikdash was still standing, or at least when we are able
   to ascend to the Temple Mount and do so. This offering
   can only be eaten by the members of one's household,
   שה לבית / *Seh laBayis* / "a sheep for each household, and
   those nominated to be a part of the offering." Thus, this is
   a Mitzvah connected to the 'home'.*

* A home is only really called a home in Eretz Yisrael (דבחוץ לארץ לא מיקרי
ביתך אלא בארץ: Tosefos, *Avodah Zara* 21a), and within Eretz Yisrael, the
Ultimate בית / 'Home' for all of Klal Yisrael is the בית המקדש / Beis (House)
HaMikdash. The Mitzvah to offer the Korban Pesach is only if one is close
to the Beis HaMikdash. The Torah says that someone who is בדרך רחקה /

2. Maggid is the Mitzvah of telling over the story of Yetzias Mitzrayim, utilizing the power of speech. The Mitzvah to talk expansively about our Exodus is a Mitzvah of speech.

3. Matzah is the Mitzvah of eating unleavened bread, which is a simple, pure food (note, *Gittin*, 22a), transcendent of any 'outside', external ingredients. Bread of Freedom. This Mitzvah is connected with freedom from all influences.

4. Eating *Maror* / bitter herbs is a Mitzvah on Pesach night.*

---

a long journey away (*Bamidbar*, 9:10) is exempt from bringing the Korban Pesach, see *Pesachim*, 93b. The question among the Poskim is whether one needs to try to be close to Yerushalayim in order to be able to bring the Korban Pesach or not? (This is an argument between the *Tz'lach* and the *Minchas Chinuch*, see, *Minchas Chinuch*, Mitzvah 5). In other words, we could say that the argument is whether being in a distant location is an exemption from the *Chiyuv* / obligation or there is no Chiyuv to begin with. So, we see the Korban Pesach is deeply connected to the idea of "Home."

* In the Torah, the eating of Maror is connected with the offering of the Pesach, the Mitzvah is to eat the Maror with the Korban: *Pesachim*, 120. מרור בלא פסח אינו מצוה שנאמר (במדבר ט, יא) על מצות ומררים יאכלהו :Rambam, *Hilchos Korban Pesach*, 8:2. So much so, that according to the Rambam (and most other Halachic authorities, besides Rav Sa'adia Gaon and others) Maror is not an independent Mitzvah, rather, a Mitzvah only connected with the Korban Pesach exists, it is like the relish for the meat, and thus, when eaten with the Pesach does not even need a *Shiur* / measurement of Kezayis (Reb Chayim Brisker). Today, it is a Mitzvah of our sages (not a Torah-based Mitzvah) and thus does need a Kezayis (proof is that we recite an independent *Berachah* / blessing: Rosh, *Pesachim*, 10:20. משום דמברך על אכילת מרור צריך שיאכל כזית, דאין אכילה בפחות מכזית, although see *Sha'agas Aryeh*, 100) as it is an independent Mitzvah: Avnei Nezer.

The reason we eat Maror today is to remind us of the "bitterness" in Egypt. In this way, it is a Mitzvah of 'remembering'.

Through these four Mitzvos, and their connection to home, speech, freedom, and memory, we can unearth the root of any collective or individual form of exile and existential alienation.

Essentially, home, speech, freedom, and remembrance are forces that help us out of exile and internal alienation. Conversely, the descent into personal or communal exile can be described as a gradual dive into a sense of homelessness, silence, codependency, and deep forgetfulness. These are four regressive stages in the descent into exile and inward enslavement:

1. Homelessness: In step one, people do not feel comfortable where they are; they are 'out of place'. The first thing the Torah tells us in *Sefer Shemos* is that the people descended into Egypt. This is the first step into exile; literal displacement. Not being home, not being rooted in our *Makom* / space, creates a vulnerability to the next stages of descent.

2. Silence: Because they felt out of place they silenced their voices; they no longer expressed themselves clearly and openly. Losing one's voice means ceasing to express who one truly is, the most deafening silence of all.

3. Codependency: Without self-expression, they lost their equilibrium and started acting like others in order to fit in; they became enslaved to external influences.

4. Deep forgetfulness: In acting like others, they completely lost their sense of self and 'forgot' who they were. They had no identity related to the past or future, no dignity or dreams. Sadly, most people do not know who they really are, making redemption seem irrelevant.

These four descending stages can be observed in a simple social setting. You go to a social event where you do not feel comfortable. Feeling a little out of place, you cautiously quiet your voice. To fill the void of self-expression, you become open to the influences of others to the point that you start to speak and act like another person, just to fit in. Acting like someone else, eventually you forget your true identity and your personal dignity. You may not even 'remember your name'; 'you' are in exile.

THE FOUR REGRESSIVE STAGES IN GREATER DETAIL

Exile is not merely a national event, but also a deeply personal one, and not just a physical displacement, such as being uprooted from one's homeland or environment, but an existential one as well. To live within a paradigm of exile means to be inauthentic to who you truly are.

1. *Being Displaced:* The first step in exile is being uprooted and displaced beyond one's ability to re-orient oneself. This

may be the most damaging step, as it is a slippery slope toward the subsequent steps. Going down into 'Mitzrayim', one becomes estranged and then disconnected from one's source, from one's past, one's journey, and one's vision of the future.

The first 'homelessness' described in the Torah is the restless sojourner, Kayin, after he has killed Hevel.*

After Kayin killed his brother, he was punished that נע ונד תהיה בארץ / "You shall become a ceaseless wanderer on earth" (*Bereishis*, 4:12); he was punished, as a direct result of his actions, with homelessness. Just as he 'stole' the מקום / *Makom* / space in the world that his brother inhabited, his own space in the world was taken from him, and he forever felt homeless and cursed with a sense of restlessness. He carried an inner split within himself that caused him to feel that he could not find his true Makom. He always sensed that the current place was no good, and that he needed to travel elsewhere.

Sadly, this is not only the condition of a person who has G-d forbid, robbed someone of their life. Even a person who has robbed himself of his own authentic self, begins to feel a gnawing restlessness and cannot carve out a space for himself. A person who lives out of touch with his deeper self loses his Makom in the world and seeks false 'spaces' to create for

---

* Although Adam and Chavah leaving their home in Gan Eden could be considered the first 'homelessness', the Torah itself does not describe their state of wandering.

himself. In a stark Medrash, our sages tell us that an adulterer, as he is about to perform a sin, pleads with the Master of the Universe and says, סלק את עצמך, ותן לי מקום לשעה, הדבר קשה עד מאוד / "Remove Yourself and give me a Makom for a few moments, as my life is unbearable" (*Tanchuma*, Naso, 4). He is asking the מקומו של עולם / *Mekomo shel Olam* / the Essential Space of all space, to leave him alone so that he can carve out a space within the world to perform his sin. He asks for a temporary space to be created — a place that is so-to-speak devoid of HaMakom, the Presence of Hashem — so he can feel 'present' for a few fleeting minutes. As a result, he begins to feel out-of-place, as if homeless in the world.

2. Silencing: Once a person feels displaced, without a Makom in this world, he tends to 'mute' himself, stuffing down the cognitive dissonance that would arise would he express who he really is and what he truly believes.

If one believes in righteousness, goodness, and spirituality, yet in practice he is grossly misaligned with those beliefs, he tends to stop speaking about them. However, silence does not just mean 'not speaking'; it also means silencing one's inner voice, freedom, and life. As a result, his speech is just filling the air with sound. It is readily observable that people who are deeply uncomfortable about themselves either close down in social settings, or speak very loudly, in an attempt to drown out their inner sense of not belonging, lacking a true Makom.

Before the first signs that their redemption was dawning, Klal Yisrael could not even complain. Someone who has silenced their authentic voice cannot even admit an honest, heartfelt complaint about their condition of exile. His voice rattles on with artificial cheerfulness, mockery, or scorn, parroting the pre-fabricated sentences which he has filled his mind with in an attempt to escape the growing sense of emptiness.

3. Being Influenced: Once an individual's sense of place and voice are lost, they become highly vulnerable to being influenced by outside forces and voices. Other people's opinions, assessments and worldview become the defining barometer of their life.

Literal slavery is defined by one person acting in subservience to another. Subtler forms of slavery include being persuaded and influenced by external stimuli to act in ways that are not consistent with one's inherent self and values. The life of a slave is *Murkav* / mixed with and dependent upon his master. When a person's actions are dictated by outside voices, he is living as a slave. One can be enslaved to nearly anything; certainly to advertisements, billboards, media, social pressure, substances, cultural expectations, and improper 'spiritual teachers'.

As a result, "Most people are other people." In a habit of living inauthentically, people end up conforming to the influences of other people around them, pathetically squeezing their soul into someone else's ideas, ideals, aspirations, and projects. One's life becomes a hodgepodge of other people's thoughts, feelings, impressions, choices, and reactions. This secondary, externally-generated sense of agency supplants a person's ability to make their own decisions, have their own dreams and to act from their own conscience.

4. Forgetfulness: Without a place and a voice, and having relinquished one's capacity for independent thinking and action, one completely forgets who he truly is. The Arizal speaks of Egypt and Pharaoh in particular as the Kelipah of *Shich'chah /* forgetfulness, leading to a total lack of *Da'as /* self-awareness and knowledge of who we truly are. One also forgets who he *was*, and what his aspirations and hopes were.

In the beginning of the *Sefer Shemos /* 'the Book of Names', the Torah elaborates how Yaakov and his entire household descended into Egypt. The Pasuk says: "These are the names of the Children of Israel who came down with Yaakov...Reuvein, Shimon, Levi, and Yehudah. Yissachar, Zevulun, and Binyamin. Dan and Naftali, Gad and Asher...and Yoseph was (already) in Egypt." Each son and tribe is named and clearly identified. However, as explored earlier, as they descend into the Egyptian exile, the Torah begins to refer to them not with names, but with pronouns: "*They* multiplied; *they* increased; the land was full of *them*..." (*Shemos*, 1:7). They have no more names, no identity.

Earlier, Yoseph is languishing in jail when Pharaoh's butler and baker are also imprisoned. They both have dreams and Yoseph interprets them correctly, and says to the butler, "But 'remember' me when it shall be well with you" (*Bereishis*, 40:14). Yet the Torah says, ולא־זכר שר־המשקים את־יוסף וישכחהו / "Nevertheless the chief butler did not remember Yoseph, but forgot him" (*Ibid*, 23). Asks the Zohar, if it says, "the chief butler did not remember," why then add the seemingly repetitive phrase, "...but forgot him"? Says the Zohar, "forgot him" indicates a world of *complete* forgetfulness. In other words, the reason the butler "forgets" Yoseph, is that he enters into the domain of Pharaoh, the pinnacle of forgetfulness, denial, ambiguity, and obscurity.

Such forgetfulness puts a lock on exile and throws away the key. With no past or future, and no self-identity, there is not even a concept of redemption. "No slave ever escaped Mitzrayim."

THE FOUR ANTIDOTES

To break these four descending levels of exile we were taken out of Egypt and then given four powerful Mitzvos, tools to make sure we never return to a state of exile, whether collectively or personally.

1) TO COUNTER DISPLACEMENT, BECOME ROOTED

The Korban Pesach is connected to family and being rooted in the Holy Land. The Mitzvah is to be performed on the Har haBayis, our spiritual center, our essential home, and the essence of all מקום / Makom in Creation (*Yuma*, 54b. *Yalkut Shimoni*, Koheles, 2:967. ויפגע במקום. לפי שהוא מקומו של עולם הן מצד ששם אבן *moni*, Koheles, 2:967. שתיה ומשם הושתת העולם, הן מצד שעדיין כל העולם מיוסד עליו *Kli Yakar*, Bereishis,

28:11). It is then to be eaten in our homes and with our families. Today, as we are displaced and without safe access to the Har haBayis, the Mitzvah is to celebrate the Seder in our home or with our family and friends. Unlike how we would with the Korban Pesach, we can spontaneously invite guests to participate with us, so we should also invite others to join and become rooted with us in the spiritual 'place' of the Seder.

2) TO COUNTER SILENCE. SPEAK UP

The Mitzvah of *Maggid* / 'telling the story' of Yetzias Mitzrayim, is the means through which we redeem our exiled voice. When we speak about our freedom, our national, global, but also individual and personal hopes, dreams and visions, we are reversing the negative effect of silencing our voice. As we vocally thank Hashem for the past and express our hope for the future, we trigger the process of redeeming our speech.

3) TO COUNTER BEING INFLUENCED. BE THE INFLUENCER

The Mitzvah of eating Matzah, the bread of freedom, empowers us to become free of outside influences. Matzah is simple, having only the most essential ingredients, and thus is free from dependency on 'others'. Outside elements such as sugar and salt are not used to make it. For that matter, time is not an 'ingredient'; Matzah is made in the least time possible.* Matzah is what it is, without deferring to extrinsic embellishment or validation.

---

* Once water touches the flour and we begin to work with the dough, it is better if we never stop working the dough; it should never sit idle: *Orach Chayim*, 459:2.

A slave's life is intermingled and mixed up with their master. On an inward level, when the state of your mind or heart is heavily influenced by past predicaments or reactive patterns of behavior, you are subject to a 'master'. A free person is independent, not 'mixed' with others, nor determined by their past. This is the paradigm of 'poor person's bread', a bread that is not mixed with juices, flavorings or other non-essential ingredients. And it is also 'free person's bread', expressing our independence and freedom from our past and other external influences.

A slave is an effect of an exterior cause; if someone insults him, that is the 'cause' of his reactive behavior. Only when we choose not to 'react' can we become the 'cause' of our life, and act as an influencer. This does not mean that we shouldn't 'react' by crying out to Hashem or pouring our heart out to the Compassionate One in Tefilah. This kind of reaction, rather, binds us more deeply to the Cause of Causes. The reaction of an enslaved person is taking things into his own hands and fighting back, or suppressing his fight instinct and becoming inwardly resentful or depressed. He then feels he must 'release stress' by indulging addictions and soul-demeaning activities. A slave is at the mercy of a myriad of outside influences.

Simple, pure, humble, and present, a 'Matzah-like' person has only his own ingredients: his Divine soul and the ever-new 'now', and he is thus free from being dictated by outside or past influences. Just as Matzah takes a very short time to make, as we had to leave Egypt quickly, a free person lives in a space that is above the flow of time.

Time gives rise to a confluence of many forces; past, present, and future complicate each other, as the past impregnates the present and the present informs the future. Exile is time-bound and always surrounded by 'walls' of complication and confusion. But beyond this world of struggle, movement, and tangled influences, is the world of spontaneous unity, and simplicity, the spiritual space from which Matzah emerges. Matzah is rooted in a realm 'beyond time', kneaded and baked with an almost 'miraculous' speed — free from hesitative calculation and resistance. It is the bread of *Emunah Peshutah* / simple faith, and *Zerizus* / swift action. It embodies and inspires the quality of decisive and instant liberation from exile.

On the other hand, since Matzah does not digest quickly, it keeps a person satiated for an extended period of time, longer than other forms of bread. This too indicates its freedom from natural influences, as the eater becomes less dependent on 'external' foods for satisfaction and energy. All of this reveals that Matzah is not from the world of 'effects', rather the world of the 'cause.' When we eat Matzah we are lifted out of our exile of 'effect', time and complication, into a world of pure freedom.

Experientially, Seder Night gives us the *Koach* / power to live in a redemptive state, to 'come home' and become rooted in the place where we truly belong, to speak up and use our truest voice, to never forget who we are as individuals, as part of Klal Yisrael and as a Divine soul, and to always live as the cause of our life, not as the effect.

4) TO COUNTER FORGETFULNESS, REMEMBER

The Mitzvah of eating Maror is connected with the sharpening of the mind and memory. Through eating the bitter Maror we remember who we are and how far astray we have gone. We remember what happens when we do not live in emotional, mental and spiritual freedom — how bitter our lives become. The sting of Maror stimulates our longing for a better, more authentic life. Maror is a visceral 'mnemonic', similar to how one might tie a string on his hand to remember something vitally important (כאדם המזהיר לחבירו על ענין אחד שקושר קשר באזורו כדי שיזכרנו. *Tur*, Orach Chayim, 24). Eating something abnormally sharp triggers our memory and alerts us to the fact that we must put our freedom into practice, or lose it. The act of eating Maror each year makes sure we never forget where we are going.

To break patterns of reactive, programmed negative behaviors and exiled consciousness, we need to remember these four basic truths:

1) We always belong; we are always essentially at home. Wherever we find ourselves, that is exactly where Hashem wants us to be. Wherever we go we can always orient toward an unconditional sense of belonging. This is our choice; we are its cause.

2) Whatever happens, we should never allow ourselves to feel compelled to quiet our real voice, the voice of Torah, and

words of truth, righteousness and justice. Sometimes it is a wise and beneficial choice to be quiet, however this too can be chosen from a place of freedom and empowerment. The ability to speak or to remain silent when one is so moved is a sign of freedom.

3) If you find yourself in a negative environment, remain conscious of any ways that you are being influenced by it or becoming dependent on it. Whenever possible, do not become dragged down by external conditions and complexities, rather stand firmly in your independence and become the influencer.

4) The one thing no one can ever take away from you is yourself, your identity. Never forget who you are and what you believe and stand for. Remember your roots and also your ultimate destination — complete Redemption.

Chapter Fifteen:
Chametz vs. Matzah

A BASIC DIFFERENCE BETWEEN LEAVENED BREAD AND Matzah is that leavened bread rises and inflates, while Matzah remains flat and deflated. A state of *Chametz* / 'leavened', comes into being when there is a fermentation of a particular enzyme found in grain. When water is mixed with any of the "five grains" mentioned in the Mishnah (wheat, barley, spelt, rye, and oats), fermentation begins, and these flours mixed with water are considered leavened after only eighteen minutes of lying dormant.* After a period of about 18 minutes from when the water is mixed into the flour, if not constantly kneaded, the dough will begin to rise slightly.** Chametz dough rises due to bubbles of oxygen and carbon dioxide that are released in the process of fermentation.

Both the words חמץ / Chametz and מצה / Matzah contain three Hebrew letters, and they share two of these letters, Mem and Tzadik (מ, צ). The differing letters are the Ches in Chametz and the Hei in Matzah. There is only a small difference, graphically speaking, between the letter Hei and the letter Ches. Whereas the left leg of the Hei is suspended in mid-air (ה), the left leg of the Ches rises up to the top of the letter (ח).

The empty gap in the Hei represents humility and an openness to receive, a sense of malleability, softness, and less rigidity

_____

* שיעור מיל / the Shiur of walking a *Mil*, which is 18 minutes, as the Mechaber posits (ושיעור מיל הוי רביעית שעה וחלק מעשרים מן השעה), is the standard accepted standard time in which flour mixed with water becomes Chametz. See also Alter Rebbe, *Orach Chayim*, 459. *Magen Avraham* and *Bi'ur haGra* hold the Shiur is 24 minutes. The Rambam rules that so long as one is kneading or rolling the dough, it does not become Chametz even after many hours. The Mechaber rules this way: *Orach Chayim*, 459:2 — וכ"ז שמתעסקים בו אפילו כל היום אינו מחמיץ. Others argue that once the flour and water are mixed, it will become Chametz after a Shiur of 4 Mil, even if one is kneading or rolling the dough: *Shiltei haGiborim*. Regarding this, the Bach, in *Bayis Chadash*, Siman 459:4, writes: ולפיכך אין ראוי להורות איסור לאחרים בדיעבד אלא להזהיר לכתחלה לחוש לדברי הגדול באחרונים והמחמיר לעצמו אף בדיעבד תע"ב.

** As in the note above, other opinions assert that even if the dough is kneaded, over a certain longer period of time it will still become Chametz.

of ego. The closed gap in the letter Ches represents arrogance, a 'rising up' that closes the space of humility and forgiveness. Chametz represents egocentrism, a sense of self that has become inflated, appearing to be more than what it really is. Indeed, even just a tiny bit of arrogance can make a big difference, and creates a closure within and without, leaving no room for any flexibility or humility.

Spiritually, 'Chametz' forms when our desires, represented by the element of water* is absorbed by flour, represented by our ego, and allowed to fester, so that our desires percolate and ferment, expand, and inflate.

While desires and yearnings are not negative in themselves, they can fuel our ego, our basic crude sense of self. The ego, in itself, is not negative; it is what drives us to get up in the morning, to go to work, to eat and sustain ourselves, and to look after ourselves and our loved ones' survival and success. Desire, too, is necessary; it is the engine of life. Yet, when our ego absorbs our desires and takes rulership over them, and especially when this mixture stagnates for a time, our desires become Chametz, as it were. Then life is all about the ego; grabbing what I want and need, until the condition arises in which my wants come first, even at the expense of someone else. If I am thirsty, and I am ruled by my ego, then if I see a child walking down the street with a drink in his hands, and my ego is not worried that I will be caught, I may grab the drink from the child.

---

* Water is the element connected to desire: *Tanya*, Chap. 1.

Whenever the ego becomes a person's center, their world becomes a threatening place, whether in their imagination or in reality. They invest themselves in a paradigm of me versus you, or us against everyone else. There is constant conflict with virtually everything in Creation.

BREAD OF IDOLATRY

The Torah guides us to carefully eliminate every particle of Chametz in our possession before Pesach, and to maintain a Chametz-free environment throughout the duration of the Yom Tov. The absolute prohibition of Chametz is very unusual among prohibitions, because normally a very small amount of a prohibited substance, such as an unkosher food, might be considered neutralized and nullified under certain conditions. For example, if a prohibited food is mixed beyond recognition into a permissible food, and it does not offer any perceptible taste to the permissible food, that mixture may be considered neutralized and it may be eaten. This is not so for a mixture of Chametz and permissible food. Chametz is such a serious prohibition that we are not even allowed to see Chametz if it belongs to us, let alone eat even one particle of Chametz.

The reason that Chametz is such a stringent prohibition is that leavening symbolizes the *Yetzer haRa*, the human egoistic inclination that leans toward negativity. Chazal refer to the Yetzer haRa as שאור שבעיסה / the yeast of the dough (*Berachos*, 17a. שאור שבעיסה – יצר הרע שבלבבנו המחמיצנו :Rashi, *ad loc*), and for this reason, the Rishonim write that physical Chametz is symbolic of the Yetzer haRa.[*]

In truth, the Yetzer haRa is not a *negative* inclination per se, rather it is just an "inclination" of the ego. In fact, "If not for our Yetzer, nothing would compel us to build a home, enter a relationship, have children, or do business" (*Medrash Rabba*, Bereishis, 9:7). Again, the ego gives the human being certain essential drives necessary for survival and self-preservation. The trouble arises when these drives are not properly balanced. When people are one-dimensionally self-centered, their relationships with others become vampiric and abusive, and their business dealings become exploitative.

---

[*] Rav Yoseph Gigataliya, *Haggadah*, printed in *Haggadah Torah Sheleimah*, p. 113. Rabbeinu Bachya, *Kad haKemach*, p. 313. See also Rabbeinu Bachya, regarding the prohibition of adding yeast to offerings, *Vayikra*, 2:11. The Radbaz explains that the only 'reason' why Chametz is so stringent, is because it represents the Yetzer haRa. See *Radbaz*, 3:977: ועל כן אני סומך על מה שאמרו רז"ל במדרשות כי חמץ בפסח רמז ליצה"ר והוא שאור שבעיסה ולכן כלה גרש יגרש אותו האדם מעליו ויחפש עליו בכל מחבואותיו ואפילו כל שהוא לא בטיל. והרי זה אמת ונכון. See also *Berachos*, 17a, Rashi, s.v. *Seor she-b'Isa*, where yeast is connected with the Yetzer haRa. The Rogatchover explores whether the איסור / Issur / prohibition of Chametz is an איסור עצמותי an Issur in essence (if the object of Chametz is transformed, when Pesach arrives, into a *Cheftza* / prohibited object), or an איסור זמני / time bound Issur. Similarly, there is a debate whether the Issur of Chametz is an איסור גברא / prohibition on the *Gavra* / person or an איסור חפצא / an Issur on the *Cheftza* / object itself (although, in general, all Torah Mitzvos are on the Cheftza, and Mitzvos from the sages are on the Gavra). Understanding that Chametz represents the Yetzer haRa within man is more aligned with the Issur Gavra, and understanding that Chametz represents Avodah Zarah is more aligned with the Issur Cheftza.

What has begun as a neutral, natural drive can end up as a source of destructive behavior. As such, it is man himself who exaggerates these egoistic inclinations, passions and necessities, and employs them for 'evil.' In this framework, the term *Yetzer haRa* does not imply an 'evil' inclination, for it is not intrinsically evil, nor is it even its nature to gravitate towards negativity. Rather, it is an inclination that can be easily transformed, when left unchecked, into an evil force (*Tanchuma*, Bereishis, 7:רע אותו עושה אתה, הוא ברוך הקדוש אמר). Only when the ego inflates and dominates one's personality does it truly become Chametz. Only then does the Yetzer become *Ra* / evil and utterly harmful. This is what must be completely expunged from every corner of our lives.

A step deeper, according to the Zohar, Chametz is equated with *Avodah Zarah* / idolatry — and so much so that "Whoever eats Chametz on Pesach is as if he prayed to an idol" (*Zohar* 2, 41a. 184a).

When Yeravam ben Nevat wanted to convince Klal Yisrael to serve idols, he said (*Yerushalmi, Avodah Zarah*, 1:5), "Look, people, at the contrast between the Torah and (*l'havdil*) idol worship. The Torah say,s 'Do not offer the blood of your offerings while you have Chametz,' whereas worshipers of Avodah Zarah say, תודה מחמץ וקטר / "...And offer up a thanksgiving offering of leaven" (*Amos,* 4:5). The custom of idolaters, when bringing meal offerings to their deities, was specifically adding leavening agents to them (as *Moreh Nevuchim* explains and is quoted in *Rabbeinu Bachya*, Vayikra 2:11).

SUBTLE FORMS OF IDOLATRY

While perhaps people no longer worship literal idols, the basic notion of idolatry is still practiced. Essentially, idolatry is the belief that a force or idea other than HaKadosh Baruch Hu can help us. Sadly, often money, possessions, power, fame, and even 'safety' are worshiped. When people make an offering of themselves to these 'objects', they ascribe to them the power to make them feel happy, successful and 'worthy' of self-esteem. The venerated object seems to become the 'cause' of their sense of righteousness and wellbeing, as if they had been blessed by a false god. If one merely regards a temporary phenomenon, such as money, to be substantially real, one can easily become enslaved to it. Without venerating them, gold and silver are recognized as nothing in themselves. At most, they are just tools to serve the one true Source of Life.

In numeric value, the words *Zahav* / gold and *Kesef* / silver together equal 174. This number is the amount of hours that we are not allowed to eat Chametz during the festival of Pesach. In the Torah (and in practice in the Land of Israel), there are seven days of Pesach. If you multiply seven days by 24 hours, the product is 168. If you add six for the six hours on Erev Pesach during which we are not allowed to eat Chametz, you reach a total of 174. These 174 hours of Chametz-free living empower us to be free from subtle idolatry, such as the worship of 'gold and silver', throughout the entire year. This underlines the importance of letting go of all ownership and addiction to Chametz, cleaning our homes and space from its presence and rulership, and expunging from our lives the false-hoods that Chametz represents.

In the world of *Halachah* / law, this relationship between Chametz and Avodah Zarah appears quite strikingly. Fascinatingly, the laws of Chametz mirror the laws of Avodah Zarah:

- Regarding both Avodah Zarah and Chametz on Pesach, there is 'no *Shiur*' / no permissible measurement; one must be completely rid of them, and even the tiniest speck cannot be considered nullified if mixed with something else. The prohibitions of possessing or eating Chametz on Pesach are like the prohibitions of owning an idolatrous image, even the smallest amount is prohibited.

- It is also prohibited to derive any kind of *Hana'ah* / benefit from Chametz on Pesach, whether monetary gain or enjoyment. Similar is the prohibition to derive benefit from idolatry at any time.

- On the Eve of Pesach, we should burn, crumble and destroy all Chametz in our possession. This is similar to the commandment to destroy all idolatrous images.

YEAST AND EGYPTIAN CULTURE

Egypt was a place of profound *Tumah* / impurity and idol worship, and during their stay, Klal Yisrael became demoralized and mired in that state and those practices. HaKadosh

Baruch Hu therefore thrust them out of Egypt, extricating them from their place of Tumah, and brought them to Mount Sinai and Matan Torah. While celebrating this miraculous experience, the physical and spiritual Exodus from Egypt, we are asked to refrain from all forms and amounts of Chametz. This is because not only is Chametz associated with idol worship, but it is specifically connected with the paradigm of Egyptian culture.

The ancient Egyptians were actually the ones who invented yeasted bread — as well as beer, which is also made with yeast and grain — and these were the foods of the idolatrous slave-owners. By contrast, according to the Even Ezra and Abarbanel, Matzah was the food of slaves, since it takes much longer to digest than other foods and thus staves off hunger for longer periods of time. During Pesach, when we celebrate our physical and spiritual freedom from Egypt, we withdraw from all forms of Chametz, even the smallest amount, and thereby withdraw from any trace of Egyptian culture, and Egyptian idolatry.*

---

* While the prohibition to eat Chametz is for all seven (and in the Diaspora, eight) days, the positive Mitzvah to eat Matzah only applies to the first night: תניא כוותיה דרבא: "ששת ימים תאכל מצות וביום השביעי עצרת לה' אלקיך". מה שביעי רשות, אף ששת ימים רשות...יכול אף לילה הראשון רשות, תלמוד לומר: על מצות ומרורים יאכלוהו: *Pesachim*, 120a. In other words, there is a Mitzvah to eat Matzah on the first night of Pesach, but on the other six days it is only a רשות / an optional Mitzvah. Such is the ruling of the Rambam (*Hilchos Chametz uMatzah*, 6:1), and the *Tur* and *Shulchan Aruch*, Orach Chayim, 475:7. However, the simple reading of the Pasuk, ששת ימים תאכל מצות / "Six days you shall eat Matzah" (*Devarim*, 16:8), means that there is a Mitzvah to eat Matzah all six days following the first day, although it is not a 'full' Mitzvah, not a חובה / obligation, and in comparison to the first night it

can be called a רשות, but if you do eat Matzah during the six days you are fulfilling a Mitzvah — *Chiz-*: וכל הששה ימים הנשארים משם ואילך תאכל מצות *kuni*, ad loc. שבעת ימים מצות תאכלו (*Shemos*, 12:15), and as the Even Ezra writes, שבעת ימים צוה לאכול מצות להיות זכר לאשר קרה לכם בצאתכם ממצרים. As the Chizkuni (*Ibid*, 12:18) writes, שבעת ימים מצות תאכלו כתיב כלומר אם אכל מצה כל שבעת הימים קיים הפסוק זה של שבעת ימים מצות תאכלו. This seems to be the source of the Gra's opinion in *Ma'aseh Rav*, 185. This seems to also be the opinion of the Alter Rebbe and Tzemach Tzedek: *Otzar Minhagei Chabad*, Nisan, p. 33-37. See also *Mishnah Berurah*, 475:25 and 639:24 in the context of Sukkos. *Aruch HaShulchan* 475:18. The Baal *haMaor* (end of Pesachim) asks why do we not recite a Berachah any time we eat Matzah all seven days of Pesach, as we recite a Berachah every time we sit in a Sukkah? He answers, because theoretically one can survive Pesach without eating Matzah, by eating others foods, but it is impossible to go three days without sleep, so you have to use the Sukkah. From his question it is clear that he is of the opinion that eating Matzah all days of Pesach is a Mitzvah, albeit not an obligation. Indeed, the simple reason we do not recite the Berachah "...*Asher Kid'shanu...Al Achilas Matzah*," except on the first night, is because (according to the Shulchan Aruch) there is no Mitzvah "to eat Matzah" on the other days — מה שאין מברכין על מצה כל ז' היינו משום שאין מצוה באכילתו אלא שאין אוכל חמץ: *Magen Avraham*, Orach Chayim, 639:17. Thus, perhaps, according to the *Baal haMaor*, Even Ezra, Chizkuni, the Alter Rebbe and the Gra, maybe a Berachah does need to be recited: see *S'dei Chemed* 8, Chametz uMatzah, 14, 10. *Teshuvas Maharsham* 1, 209. *Teshuvos Meishiv Davar* 1, 77. See also *Chasam Sofer*, Yoreh Deah, 191, where he brings the opinion of the Chizkuni. Rebbe Tzadok haCohen writes in *Pri Tzadik* that since the simple reading of the Pasuk is that there is a Mitzvah to eat Matzah on all seven days, thus, הואיל ונפיק מפומיה / "Since this statement emerged from the mouth of (the Holy Torah)," we should certainly accustom ourselves to eat Matzah on all seven days.

Alternatively, the simple Peshat / literal interpretation of the often quoted statement in the Torah, "seven days you shall eat Matzah," is as follows: The Torah is telling us that any bread that we wish to eat for these seven days shall be Matzah. Not that we are obligated to eat Matzah for seven days, rather, anytime during these seven days that we wish to eat bread it should be Matzah. As such, by eating Matzah on the first night of Pesach, which is obligatory, we establish this pattern, and what's more, it is as if we have eaten Matzah all seven days (as all seven days are a שטיינ"א — in old French

Matzah, as opposed to Chametz, is our food during these days when we celebrate the going out of Egypt, and out of all that Egypt represents.

LEAVENED BREAD, INFLATED STORIES

Chametz, as explained, is associated with Egyptian culture and idol worship. There is a classic definition of idol worship, and then there is a more subtle definition relating to self-worship, placing one's 'I', one's ego, above all else, always thinking how 'I' can gain and what 'I' can get out of a given situation. The flour and yeast are the Yetzer, yet the grain, the egoic sense of 'I' itself, is impartial and morally neutral. However, when our sense of 'I' is mixed with the 'water' of desire, and this mixture is allowed to stagnate or 'ferment', it can quickly rise and become egocentrism and arrogance. When the 'ego' becomes '-centric', it fills our picture of who we are, eclipsing our deeper, truer self, and everything in life is then seen through the prism of the ego.

Fermented ego means an inflated reality in which one's narratives fester and inflate, and no longer reflect the truth.

— one group of seven days, as Rashi, *Shemos*, 12:15, writes. In other words, all seven days are as if one 'long day'). Much like when the Torah says that Rosh Hashanah needs to be a "day of Teruah/Shofar," this does not mean that we need to blow the Shofar the entire day, rather, we blow in the morning, the beginning of the day, and thus the entire day becomes a day of Shofar. Similarly, we eat Matzah on the first night, and all the following days are 'potentially' days of only Matzah.

We all carry around 'stories' about our life, some good, some less good. Maybe someone hurt us physically or emotionally, or maybe someone ignored us at a social gathering. If we do not confront the person or the issue and our perceptions right away, our narrative festers, ferments, and eventually inflates to such a degree that it overwhelms our life. The 'story' goes like this: someone seemed to ignore us, and then we started thinking, 'Why is this person being nasty to me? Probably, because I did this or that, or said this or that. But the truth is, I was right to do or say that, he is just being unreasonable!' And then, as we start thinking about how unreasonable the person is, we start reviewing other instances in which the person seemed to ignore us. We extend their unkindness to other traits that we do not like in them, and over time we build a castle in the air of dislike for them and all the terrible things they have done to us.

This 'inflation' filled our consciousness because we did not deal with the issue right away, and it grew until it was out of proportion. Perhaps, all along, the person never actually ignored us, but simply did not see us. Or perhaps he was having a hard day and was not up to engaging other people. But because our narcissistic ego clouded our vision, all we saw was a person "ignoring" us. Our self-absorption, together with our desire for honor, created this 'Chametz'. But not everything is about *us*.

A Chassid once came to the Rebbe, the Tzemach Tzedek, and complained to him: "Rebbe, whenever I am in Shul, people are always stepping all over me." "Who asked you to spread yourself across the entire floor?" the Rebbe responded. In other words, if everything is "always" about you, you will "always" feel people are stepping on you wherever you go, when in fact, it has nothing to do with you.

Most people are not ego-maniacs, nor pathetically self-absorbed. Stories and life experiences with others may nevertheless be left unresolved, and they can fester, ferment, and inflate. Over time, if the issue is not resolved, resentment can set in until they can no longer speak to, or even look at, that other person. Sadly, one sees 'best friends' and even close relatives, who have not spoken to each other in years, because they have let a small argument go unresolved.

We need to rid ourselves of these inflated, narcissistically-fueled stories; they are real inner Chametz. The impact of Pesach is meant to be felt throughout the entire year. The Matzah that we eat is 'humble', open and honest. Even though the dough of Kosher Matzah never had time to rise, we punch hundreds of tiny holes into the thinly rolled piece of dough before it is placed in the hot oven to bake, in order to demonstrate that no inflation *could* have occurred. A deflated ego has 'holes' which let the 'air' and *Chayus* / vitality of foolish narratives dissipate.

A full day before eating the Matzah, we perform Bedikas Chametz, checking for literal Chametz throughout our homes. At the same time, we need to check ourselves for 'inner Chametz'. The word Bedikah, besides meaning 'checking', comes from the same root as the word *Boka* / to pierce, to puncture. When we do Bedikas Chametz, the idea is to pierce the Chametz of our life so that it will deflate. Only then will we be ready to eat Matzah, and internalize its qualities and meanings.

Matzah brings us humility, and thus freedom. We have identified, 'pierced' and resolved all our old, fermenting narratives, letting go of our inflations that hold us back and create resentment and shame. We burn away this inner Chametz with the fire of higher consciousness. When there is no detectable Shiur or measure of egocentric negativity left, we can be simple again, uncomplicated, humble and independent, like Matzah. The letter Ches (ח) of Chametz has been pierced, and is now open, like the letter Hei (ה) of Matzah. We ourselves are now open to receive the miracle of inner freedom from our *Galus haPerati* / individual exile. When we are free as individuals, we contribute significantly to freedom from our *Galus haKelali* / general communal exile, hastening the revelation of Moshiach, speedily, in our days.

Part Two
Seder Night

Chapter One:
The Seder of Pesach:
Order Beyond Order

S*EDER* MEANS 'ORDER'. THE EARLIEST ORIGIN OF THE word *Seder* in relation to Pesach Night seems to be in the writings of the Rambam, when he mentions "the Seder of the night," suggesting that there is a format and order of what to do.

To really understand any process, we need to uncover its order: what comes first, what follows, and how it concludes. Let's say you want to understand the process of building a house. You must understand the order of steps, such as first digging and forming the foundation, then erecting beams, walls and a roof, and finally installing items such as windows and doors.

To understand the mechanics of freedom, we need to understand the Seder, the order of the night. However, a glaring question arises when we contemplate the idea of Seder. 'Order' suggests the world of the ordinary, routine, of predictability and linear progression; even rigid hierarchy. Yet this is a night of miracles which defy the natural 'order'; a night when a broken, enslaved nation was suddenly released from the rigid hierarchy of the most powerful empire of the ancient world, triumphantly and confidently. This is a night of the supernatural, beyond all predictability, beyond all processes, beyond all 'Seder'. In fact, we need to ask, what is the use of focusing intently on 'Seder' while we are celebrating spontaneous, extraordinary miracles? Why in fact do we follow a Seder at all?

Strictly speaking, in the realm of 'order', there is no room for freedom. There are fixed inflexible rules; the past inevitably affects the present, and the present impregnates the future, and there is no way to escape this progression of causality. In the world of 'order' there is no room for *Teshuvah* / returning in the present to what is real and changing our lives for the future. What has been done is done, and there is no way of undoing or changing course. Such is the world of linear order.

Egypt was such a place of immutable order and hierarchy. If a person was born into slavery, this was his inevitable reality and ontological condition forever, with no possibility of freedom. We were supposed to be stuck in physical and spiritual enslavement of Egypt for all time. Our liberation was a complete miracle, beyond all time, causality and order. Why, then, on our night of liberation from Egypt, do we observe so many fixed rules, time-bound processes and limitations? It seems to be a direct contradiction to the spirit of freedom that we are meant to experience.

BEYOND ORDER

Although the Seder does indeed include numerous sequences and complex limitations, such as eating prescribed measurements of ritual foods within defined time periods — and this does seem to be the opposite of a meditation on freedom — the objective of the Seder is to move from order to a place beyond order, beyond the Seder. When we give ourselves over to the structure of the night, we can actually bring about an implosion of 'order', and even a meltdown and transcendence of intellect, the 'source' of all perception of order. Through the Seder we can 'pass over' the paradigm of Seder altogether, and arrive in a realm of freedom and miracles beyond all Seder.

As the end of Seder Night nears, what seemed previously to be so orderly, now looks like a holy chaos. The Seder plate is usually a terrible mess. Even the person themself who is careful to follow the laws with great precision, after four cups of wine and a lot of Matzah and horseradish, looks a bit disheveled.

Chazal tell us, "One cup (of wine) is good... two is a disgrace (as one begins to become drunk). With three cups (one has) no verbal control…, and with four, one totally…(loses all self-respect)."* Once a person drinks four cups of wine, he seems to lose his sense of 'order' and control. Coupling this drinking, with a tremendous amount of Matzah and Maror eaten at a late hour of the night, perhaps close to midnight, after a very long and busy Erev Yom Tov, one certainly loses some sense of order and control.

At the end of the order of the night we arrive at the final step of Nirtzah, and a profound silence can be sensed. We are overwhelmed with tiredness and with wine, but we are also overcome with the timelessness of Nirtzah. There is no longer anything to do or say. The elaborate order of prescribed words and procedures is over. Those who sing the songs after the conclusion of the Seder notice how — though very deep — they appear almost like 'drinking songs'. They seem simple and light hearted, with much repetition, easy-to-follow lyrics, fixed rhythms, and almost childlike melodies. Even in this little 'Seder' of songs there is a sense of imploded order, or a reaching beyond order. The truth is, this is part of their depth.

'BEYOND ORDER' WITHIN 'ORDER'

Still, the question remains: why do we need an elaborate Seder to reach a point that is 'beyond Seder'? This idea itself indicates a type of order — first we have to traverse 'order', and then later reach 'beyond order'. The truth is that we cannot

---

* *Kesuvos*, 65a, regarding a woman drinking wine, yet on Pesach night, women are equally obligated to drink four cups of wine.

escape order. After the peak of Nirtzah, there is still cleanup to do, and the next day will soon arrive, with its own observances. But even in a life devoid of ritual and delineated observances, life is full of structure and order. The secret of freedom is to be free from order *within* order. From this vantage point, the closer we look at the structure of the Seder, the more permeable and 'anti-order' it appears.

Within the Seder itself, we do things that seem to be the opposite of a normal order. We eat Karpas, customarily a vegetable dipped in salt water, before we begin reciting the story of Maggid, how we were enslaved — although the reason we eat Karpas is that it symbolizes part of the story of slavery. We eat Matzah, the bread of freedom, before Maror which represents the bitterness of exile. There are other abnormal proceedings which seem to be solely for the sake of stimulating the children to ask questions. The order of the Seder may not be as rigid or 'limited' as it appears.

On the night of Pesach, writes the Chinuch, there is a Mitzvah to tell about the going out of Egypt and "to sing praise and to offer thanks to Hashem for all the miracles that Hashem did for us *there*" (Mitzvah 21). That is, we thank Hashem for all the miracles that Hashem did for us *in* Egypt. Even within the ultra-hierarchical society of Egypt, the epitome of order, there were miracles that broke the fixed natural order.

Not only were there 'extraordinary' miracles within the 'ordinary' world of Egypt, the very first Seder, the original celebration of freedom, happened *within* Egypt, while we were still technically exiled and enslaved. We observed a 'Seder' beyond order — proclaiming liberation within the confines of the ultimate domain of order.

In the present time, as well, as we celebrate our Redemption, we nonetheless admit and openly declare that we are in exile: "This year we are slaves; next year, may we be free people." We ask, "Why is this night different from all other nights?" As 'night' alludes to exile, we are also asking why this exile is so different from all other exiles. All past exiles had an order, a sequence of stages that led to implosion and redemption within a defined period of time. In comparison, the current exile seems endless. And yet, Redemption has never been so vivid. If we look closely, there is actually 'redemption' within the 'exile', and there is 'beyond Seder' within the 'Seder'.

THE 'ORDER' OF MIRACLES

If there is freedom from structure within structure, we have another question: why do we not simply reveal what we want — freedom — and then discard the structure of the Seder? The answer is that there is inherent value in Seder itself.

Rosh Chodesh Nisan is called the 'Rosh Hashanah of (Jewish) Kings' (*Mishnah, Rosh Hashanah,* 1:1). The inner meaning of this is that it is the Rosh Hashanah of Nisim, 'miracles', since the Divine King who created the laws of nature has the right to bend them at any juncture.

Pesach, being the full moon of Nisan, is the fullest expression of this *Rosh* / 'head' of miracles. *Nisan is named after the

---

* Although on some level, all judgments on Rosh Hashanah — even the more spiritual, mental, and internal forms, are mostly related to our physical well-being: *Hagahos Maimoniyos*, Hilchos Teshuvah 3, in the name of the Ramban, *Sha'ar Gemul* — although see *Tosefos* on *Rosh Hashanah*, 16b. Tishrei is connected with Adam whereas Nisan is connected with Klal Yisrael. In Tishrei, the world is pregnant, *Haras Olam*, only to be birthed in Nisan: *Pri Eitz Chayim*, Sha'ar haShofar, 5. See also *Elye Rabbah*, Orach Chayim, 592:6 — ולעניות דעתי לתרץ על פי מה שהקשה תוס' בראש השנה דף כ"ז על ר' אלעזר הקליר ומסקי דבתשרי עלה במחשבה לבראות ולא נברא העולם עד ניסן אם כן שפיר נקט הריון שהוא על מחשבה אבל לידה נקרא מעשה. See also *Ben Yehoyada*, Rosh Hashanah, 10b. Winter is a time of pregnancy, as the world is more 'concealed', and this is the metaphysical reason that there is less flourishing of vegetation and less sunlight. Spring is the birth of the world. In Tishrei, the Chitzoni worlds were actually created. This is the first month of the solar year, the sun being connected with the 'revealed', the external world, whereas in Nisan, the Penimi world of souls was created: *Sha'ar haKavanos*, Derush 1, Rosh Hashanah. Nisan is the first month of the year, the beginning of the lunar year. The moon represents the hidden, the mystery, the internal world. In other words, the 'birth of Klal Yisrael' is in Nisan, as Chazal tell us, "The going out of Egypt was like a fetus being removed from her mother's belly." In this way, Rosh Chodesh Nisan, and Pesach specifically, is the Rosh Hashanah on the Penimi level. The solar year flows from Tishrei to Nisan, following the 'evolutionary' order of Creation: first the Chitzoni of the world was created and only on the Sixth Day were Adam and Chavah created, beings with Neshamos, and only then was Shabbos (*vaYi-Nafash* / Nefesh) brought into the world. Even with Adam, first his body was created and only later did Hashem blow into his nostrils a breath of life: *Sanhedrin*, 38b. What this means is that with regards to the *Penimiyus* of the world, the perspective of the soul, Tishrei is only the pregnancy and Nisan is the real birth. But with regards to the Chitzoniyus of the world, Tishrei is the 'birth' of the world, and Nisan is a further maturation. All opinions agree that Sarah was *Nifkad* / Divinely 'remembered' on Rosh Hashanah (*Rosh Hashanah*, 11a), when she became pregnant with Yitzchak, the first person to be 'born Jewish'. While Avraham *entered into* the covenant — in a sense born as a body and only later manifesting a spiritual soul, as all of Creation — Yitzchak was born into the covenant,

Nisim / miracles which were revealed during that month (*Pesikta Zutresa*, Bo, 12:2. *Medrash Lekach Tov*, Shemos 12:2). In the words of Rashi (*Berachos*, 56a), שע"י נסים נקרא ניסן / "Nisan is called *Nisan* because of the miracles." There is also a well-known statement: "One who sees (the word) *Nisan* in a dream (a word with two Nuns, ניסן), Nisim will happen to him" (The Rebbe coined this phrase based on the Gemara, *Berachos*, 57a and Rashi, *ad loc*, regarding seeing the name חנינא in a dream: *Sefer haSichos*, Tav / Shin / Nun / Aleph, 1, p. 383. *Haggadah, Likutei Ta'amim uMinhagim*, 2. p. 689).

The head is the source of intelligence that communicates messages to all the limbs and cells of the body. The Tur brings down how Pesach communicates the energy of miracles and freedom throughout the limbs of the year, which are the various Yom Tovs of the year (*Orach Chayim*, Siman 428:1). In the alternative sequence of the Aleph-Beis called *At-Bash*, the first letter of the Aleph-Beis is connected with the last letter, and the second letter is connected with the second-to-last (e.g., Aleph=Tav, Beis=Shin, Gimel=Reish, Dalet=Kuf, Hei=Tzadik, Vav=Pei). The Tur shows us an 'At-Bash of Pesach':

---

born with a Neshamah, and he was born in Nisan, the month of the birth of Klal Yisrael. The Din on Tishrei is primarily with regards to the external reality, the physical world whereas the judgment on Nisan is primarily with regards to the Penimiyus of the world. In this way, Rosh Chodesh Nisan, and specifically Pesach is the Rosh Hashanah on the Penimi level. Once on Pesach, a disciple told the grandson of the Tzemach Tzedek, Reb Shmaryahu Noach of Bobruisk (whose Sefer, *Shemen l'Moar*, the Rebbe asked to reprint), לשנה טובה תכתב ותחתם, the traditional greetings for Rosh Hashanah. Reb Shmaryahu was happy with this greeting, as indeed, Pesach is the Rosh Hashanah of the Penimiyus of the year.

- The first day of Pesach (Aleph) always falls on the same day of the week as the upcoming **T**ishah b'Av (Tav).

- The second day of Pesach (Beis) falls on the same day of the week as the upcoming **Sh**avuos (Shin).

- The third day of Pesach (Gimel) falls on the same day of the week as the upcoming **R**osh Hashanah (Reish).

- The fourth day of Pesach (Dalet) falls on the same day of the week as the upcoming Simchas Torah, which is the day of *Kinyan Torah*, 'acquiring the Torah' (Kuf).

- The fifth day of Pesach (Hei) falls on the same day of the week as the upcoming Yom Kippur, the great **Tz**om, or 'fast' (Tzadik).

- The sixth day of Pesach (Vav) falls on the same day of the week as the previous **P**urim (Pei) (and additionally, the upcoming day of Lag baOmer).

- The seventh day (and in the Diaspora, both the seventh and eighth day) are connected with the future Redemption and the Era of Moshiach.

Without the order of head-to-limbs — without Seder — there would be no communication. Without communication, the consciousness of miracles and freedom could not be revealed through the other holidays of the year, and through the holidays into every day and every moment in time.

The Maharal explains that there is an element of Seder even in miracles that transcend the natural 'order'. As Rebbe Aharon Karlin would say, "On Pesach Night there is a Seder within *beyond Seder*." When our lives are open to miracles and infinite possibility, then this paradigm of 'beyond order' becomes *our* 'order'. Our liberation from limiting, conventional structures can become the very structure and 'convention' of our lives. The miraculous, the extraordinary, becomes our norm. Miracles become natural.

Chapter Two
The Simanei /Signs of the Seder:
Fifteen Steps to Liberation

1) Kadeish	*1) Sanctify*
2) Urchatz	*2) Cleanse*
3) Karpas	*3) Appetize*
4) Yachatz	*4) Break*
5) Maggid	*5) Tell*
6) Rachtzah	*6) Wash*
7) Motzi	*7) Bread*
8) Matzah	*8) Matzah*
9) Maror	*9) Bitter Herbs*
10) Korech	*10) Wrap*
11) Shulchan Orech	*11) Set the Table*
12) Tzafun	*12) Hidden*
13) Beirach	*13) Bless*
14) Hallel	*14) Praise*
15) Nirtzah	*15) Accepted*

Pesach, and specifically Seder Night, is not merely a celebration of past events, a commemoration of a physical and spiritual, mental, and emotional liberation from the ancient Land Egypt; it is also a time of the opening of cosmic and ever-present gates of liberation. Pesach is an open portal to all levels of *Geulah* / redemption, including historical, generational, and personal, on both inner and outer levels of being. This powerful day beckons us to release our personal enslavements in every moment — any attachment to narrow passions, emotions, instincts, or negative beliefs. It may seem difficult or even impossible to become lastingly free of habitual states such as depression or anger. How can we pass through the gate of Pesach into a persistent state of greater freedom?

Psycho-spiritual liberation, as revealed by the Baal Shem Tov, unfolds through three necessary stages: *Hachna'ah* / submission, *Havdalah* / separation, and finally *Hamtakah* / sweetening. In order to integrate the gift of freedom, we need to aspire to transverse these three rungs.

For us to sense inner freedom, and for that matter a freedom from external impositions, we must first become aware of our enslavement and taste its 'bitterness'. This unpleasant sensation allows us to reach Hachna'ah, submission to the call of liberation. This is step one, recognizing the issue and humbling oneself in relation to it. The second stage is to 'separate' and detach ourselves from whatever it is that is entrapping us, attaining inward Havdalah. I may be struggling with anger, for example, but *I am not my anger*; I am not entrapped or defined by any emotion. The third stage is Hamtakah, reconnecting to our past and those parts of self that we separated from, and integrating them in a rectified and sweetened way. We feel the bitterness and challenge of our condition, we separate the good from the bad, and finally we extract the good and redirect it into a holy and positive purpose.

These three stages play out on Erev Pesach and Seder Night.

SEARCHING FOR CHAMETZ

The stage of Hachna'ah actually begins before the Seder when we perform the Bedikas Chametz, searching for, and then getting rid of and burning, our Chametz. As explored earlier, Chametz represents the ego and the fermentation of unresolved narratives that inflate and overwhelm us. As such, even before the Seder and the night of cosmic and microcosmic liberation, we have to submit to our story; we need to own our Chametz, take possession of it, and then discard and burn it. In doing so, we humble our egotistical narratives, our pettiness and smallness. Finally we declare, 'Enough! All my Chametz is *k'Afra d'Ara* / dust of the earth!' and we throw the last crumbs into a fire where they are turned to ashes. This is the beginning of the stage of *Havdalah* / existential separation from Chametz.

Before we can attain a level of 'Matzah', we have to find, own, and then renounce and destroy our Chametz. We cannot move forward until we completely let go. And we cannot let go of what we don't own. Therefore, we first have to admit to the fact that our lives are riddled with Chametz, and we must search for it and set it aside where we can recognize it and contain it. Only then can we sincerely throw away, disown, nullify, and destroy it, separating from ourselves every last trace of Chametz.

After we have concluded the stage of Hachna'ah and initiated the state of Havdalah, we are spiritually prepared to begin the Seder. The Seder itself begins within the stage of Havdalah and moves us step by step into the stage of *Hamtakah* / sweetening.

FIFTEEN STAGES OF THE SEDER

There are fifteen well-known *Simanim* / signs or sections of the Seder. While these Simanim are not found in the Gemara,* they date back to the early period of the Rishonim. According to most sources, the Simanim are attributed to Rashi or his

---

* The reason the Simanim are not mentioned in the Gemara and only appear later on is, perhaps, because in the times of the Mishnah, the order of Pesach night was very different than today. This is the way the sequence of the night of Pesach is recorded in the Mishnah, in the final chapter of the tractate Pesachim. First: מזגו לו כוס ראשון, בית שמאי אומרים, מברך על היום, ואחר כך מברך על היין. ובית הלל אומרים, מברך על היין ואחר כך מברך על היום / "they poured the wine of the first cup...." On the first cup one recites Kiddush. Then the next Mishnah states: הביאו לפניו, מטבל בחזרת, עד שמגיע לפרפרת הפת. הביאו לפניו מצה וחזרת וחרסת ושני תבשילין, אף על פי שאין חרסת מצוה. רבי אליעזר ברבי צדוק אומר, מצוה. ובמקדש היו מביאים לפניו גופו של פסח / "The (attendants) brought vegetables before the leader of the Seder prior to the meal. He dipped the Chazeres into water or vinegar, to taste some food before he reached the dessert. They brought before him Matzah and Chazeres and Charoses, and at least two cooked dishes (in honor of the Festival), although eating Charoses is not a Mitzvah (but merely a custom). Rebbe Eliezer ben Tzadok says: 'Actually, it is a Mitzvah (to eat Charoses).'

And in the period when the Mikdash stood, they brought before him the body of the Korban Pesach." This seems to suggest that right after the first cup they would eat the meal: two cooked dishes and the Matzah, Chazeres and Charoses, and then the Korban Pesach. Then, after the meal, as the next Mishnah continues, מזגו לו כוס שני, וכאן הבן שואל אביו / "(The attendants) poured the second cup for the leader of the seder, and here the son asked his father." מתחיל בגנות ומסים בשבח, ודורש מארמי אובד אבי עד שיגמר כל הפרשה כלה / "He begins with disgrace and concludes with their glory. And he expounds from the passage: 'An Aramean tried to destroy my father'… until he concludes explaining the entire section." So they would fill up a second cup, and then say the Haggadah on the second cup (after the meal). Then would fill up a third cup and Bentch: מזגו לו כוס שלישי, מברך על מזונו. רביעי, גומר עליו את ההלל / "They poured the third cup of wine, and he recited the blessing over his food, Grace After Meals. Next, they poured him the fourth cup and he completed Hallel over it." They first ate the meal, and the Matzah, Maror, and Korban Pesach, and then said Maggid; this is a very different order than what we follow today. However, it helps us understand our present Seder. It helps us understand how the young child already knows about everything in the Seder and knows to ask the four questions even before the Seder. He knows that they are going to "eat only Matzah," and "dip twice," etc. He knows this because originally the four questions were asked after the meal, and he asked from his observation. Later the order was reversed, maintaining the questions. It appears that only during the time of the Gemara was the practice established of *Okrin haShulchan* / taking away or pushing aside the table, i.e., eating the meal and the Matzah and Maror, after reciting Maggid. Perhaps, the reason for this newer custom was so that children can be awake to ask the four questions, as it is still early in the night, and one of the first things done at the Seder, as opposed to Maggid being at the end of the meal.

Here is a Talmudic story that shows that Abaye, as a young child, was not yet familiar with this custom:

למה עוקרין את השולחן אמרי דבי רבי ינאי כדי שיכירו תינוקות וישאלו אביי הוה יתיב קמיה דרבה חזא דקא מדלי תכא מקמיה אמר להו לא קא אכלינן אתו קא מעקרי תכא מיקמן אמר ליה רבה פטרתן מלומר מה נשתנה / "Why does one remove the table? The school of Rebbe Yannai say: So that the children will notice that

school (*Machzor Vitri*, 65. Others attribute the Simanim to Rav Shmuel m'Pleiza, one of the authors of Tosefos, or to Rav Yoseph Tov Elem. See *Siddur Rashi*, Siman 435. Rav Yoseph Tov is the composer of the famous Piyut with which many conclude the Seder, חסל סדור פסח כהלכתו. He was also one of Rashi's Rebbes).

These fifteen Simanim are guideposts in the flow of the Seder; they tell us what we are presently accomplishing, and where we are heading. For example, the first Siman is *Kadeish*, telling us to recite the Kiddush, and the second Siman is *Urchatz*, telling us that it's now time to wash our hands. The fact that there are fifteen not fourteen or sixteen or any other number is not mere coincidence (truly, nothing is coincidence, certainly not issues related to Torah and Mitzvos). The number 15 is represented by the letters Yud and Hei, which spell a Name of Hashem. Just as Hashem brought us out of Egypt in ancient times, so will Hashem bring us through the fifteen stages of the Seder into a new level of freedom.

There were fifteen steps of ascent to enter the Beis haMikdash, and there are fifteen progressive stages for us to enter our inner Beis haMikdash. These fifteen stages are progressive and

---

something is unusual and they will ask: 'Why is this night different from all other nights?'" The Gemara relates: "Abaye was sitting before Rabba when he was still a child. He saw that they were removing the table from before him, and he said to those removing it: 'We have not yet eaten, and you are taking the table away from us?' Rabba said to him: 'You have exempted us from reciting the questions of why is this night different (*Mah Nishtanah*), as you have already asked what is special about Seder Night'": *Pesachim*, 115b.

accumulative. With each step we ascend and reach a higher or deeper rung, until we reach the final Siman, the place of *Nirtzah* / acceptance and arrival.

THE SIMANIM OF THE SEDER & THEIR CONNECTION TO THE NIGHT OF THE SEDER

Before we delve into the spiritual processes paralleling these fifteen steps, let us first properly understand how the fifteen Simanim are all unique to the night of the Seder. Each of them are either one of the Mitzvos of the night or events which are designed to cause children to wonder and ask why this night is different, as well as to stimulate discussion about Yetzias Mitzrayim.

Although some of the Simanim are actions that we perform on every Yom Tov or Shabbos, such as reciting Kiddush and eating a festive meal, all of the Simanim are nonetheless unique within the context of the Seder. On Seder Night there is something unique even about the Kiddush, and it reflects the theme of the night. In the same way, the meal of Seder Night, the Siman of *Shulchan Orech*, is different from all other meals and is unique to Seder Night, reflecting the theme of the night.

1. KADEISH / Recitation of Kiddush

THE FIRST SIMAN IS KADEISH, WHICH IS TO RECITE KIDDUSH
as we initiate the Seder. Of course, we recite Kiddush on every
Shabbos and Yom Tov. On Shabbos it is a Torah law to sanctify
the day of Shabbos through 'remembering' (זכור את יום השבת
לקדשו), while regarding Kiddush on Yom Tov, there is a debate
whether it is a Torah law or a Rabbinic law. Either way, the
recital of Kiddush on Shabbos and each Yom Tov includes a
remembrance of the going out of Egypt. Yet the Kiddush of
the Seder is unique among all others. For example, on Shabbos and every other Yom Tov, if a person skipped the sentence
about going out of Egypt, he has still fulfilled his obligation
of reciting Kiddush, but this is not so on Seder Night. On this
night one must remember the going out of Egypt, and if it was
omitted from the recital, one did not fulfill the obligation of
Kiddush.*

---

* *Magen Avraham*, Orach Chayim, 271:1, rules that one fulfills his Torah
obligation to recite Kiddush by reciting the passages of Kiddush during
Ma'ariv: ונראה לי דמדאורייתא בקידוש שאומר בתפילה סגי, דקרא כתיב זכור את יום
השבת דהא דקידוש היום. See also *Pnei Yehoshua*, Berachos, 51b: והרי זכר אותו
דאורייתא לאו בסדר קידוש על השלחן דוקא יוצא ידי חובה, אלא דאפילו בקידוש בתוך
וי"ל דכבר יצא ידי זכירה בתפילת ערבית, 437: *Shu'T Radbaz*, 3. התפילה נמי יוצא
ולפיכך אם אפשר לקיים המצוה דרבנן על היין או על הפת - יקיים, ואם לאו - כבר
נפטר. Although the Gemara, *Pesachim*, 117b, says that we need to remember
the going out of Egypt during Kiddush — אמר רב אחא וצריך שיזכיר יציאת
מצרים בקידוש היום, כתיב הכא (דברים טז, ג) למען תזכור יום צאתך מארץ מצרים,

In fact, in distinguishing Kadeish from other recitals of Kiddush, Rav Saadiah Gaon brings down in his Siddur (one of the earliest Siddurim we have) that there are communities that have an extended Kiddush which speaks more at length about the Exodus and the miracles and wonders that occurred. This extended Kiddush is still the prevalent custom of many Jews from Yemen and Tunis.

Another distinction is that while on every Shabbos and Yom Tov we are allowed to recite Kiddush on bread, if we do not have wine or if wine is difficult for us to drink, on this night we must recite the Kiddush on wine, even if drinking wine can cause us discomfort. This is because this Kiddush is also one of the four cups of wine (*Nedarim*, 49b. כתב הרשב"א (בשו"ת

ח"א סי' רל"ח), "שאלת, מי שאינו שותה יין כל השנה כולה מפני שמזיקו או שונאו, מהו
שיעשה כל הסדר על הפת. תשובה, מסתברא שכל שיש לו יין, צריך לדחוק עצמו ולעשות
כרבי יהודה ב"ר אלעאי (נדרים מ"ט ע"ב), דלא הוה שתי חמרא, ושתי ארבע כוסות ואומר,
חוגרני צידעי מפסחא ועד עצרתא, וכרבי יונה, דגרסינן בירושלמי (פ"י ה"א), רבי יונה
שתי ארבע כסי בלילה דפיסחא, וחזיק רישיה עד עצרתא". וכ"פ בש"ע (סי' תע"ב סעי' י'),

---

וכתיב התם (שמות כ, ח) זכור את יום השבת לקדשו — and during Ma'ariv we do not mention the going out of Egypt, as the Minchas Chinuch points out (Mitzvah 31, 5. See also *Bi'ur Halachah*, Orach Chayim, 271:2), this is nonetheless the ruling of the Magen Avraham. Perhaps this is so because a) neither the Rambam nor the Shulchan Aruch cite this teaching, or b) maybe this teaching is only telling us that according to the sages we need to remember the going out of Egypt during Kiddush (*Bi'ur Halachah*, ibid), or c) because perhaps remembering the going out of Egypt in Kiddush is a *Din* / law in the general Mitzvah of remembering the going out of Egypt, but not a Din in Kiddush. Either way, according to the Magen Avraham, one fulfills his obligation on Shabbos, but all will agree that he does not fulfill his obligation on the night of Pesach, as the Chida writes.

מי שאינו שותה יין מפני שמזיקו, או שונאו, צריך לדחוק עצמו ולשתות, לקיים מצות
ארבע כוסות. There is even an opinion that if one does not have wine, one
should not recite Kiddush over bread (or Matzah) at all: Rav Yoseph and Rav
Hai Gaon — ורב יוסף בר רב ורב האי גאון כתבו מי שאין לו יין מקדש על הפת בלילי
שבתות ויו״ט חוץ מלילי פסח שהרי אמרו ולא יפחתו לו מד׳ כוסות. *Tur*, Siman 483,
Beis Yoseph, ad loc).

Additionally, on Seder Night it is best for *everyone* to recite the Kiddush (Alter Rebbe, *Shulchan Aruch*, Orach Chayim, 472:22),
whereas on every Shabbos on Yom Tov we can fulfill our obligation by listening to another person reciting Kiddush.

Another distinction: if normally drinking from the Kiddush
cup wine an amount of a mouthful (a little over two ounces) it
is sufficient (Alter Rebbe, *Orach Chayim*, 271:24), for each cup of the
Seder, we need to drink the entire cup or at least the majority
of it, even if its a larger cup (*ibid*, 472:19. This is the opinion of the
Ramban, and also seemingly the opinion of the Rambam, ואם שתה מכל כוס
מהן רובו יצא: *Hilchos Chametz uMatzah*, 7:9. However, with regards to Kiddush on Shabbos the Rambam rules מקדש ושותה מלא לגמיו: *Hilchos Shabbos*,
29:7).

Another distinguishing feature of Kadeish is in regards to
the sequence of the night. The prevailing custom on Shabbos
and Yom Tov is to first recite Kiddush then go wash for Ha-
Motzi, the bread, whereas some have a custom to first wash
their hands for bread, and then, after washing, recite Kiddush.
On Seder Night, however, everyone begins the Seder with the
recitation of Kiddush.*

* ולענין הלכה כתב בהגהת ש״ע בהלכות פסח דאין ליטול ידיו כלל קודם קידוש והיינו
כמ״ש במרדכי וכן כתב הרא״ש בתשובה וכן כתב ה״ר ירוחם: *Bach*, Orach Chayim,

Another custom that the Rama brings down in Shulchan Aruch is that another person fills our cup of Kadeish to
demonstrate our freedom. On this night we are like royalty,
whose cup is filled by another person.*

2. URCHATZ / and Wash (the Hands)

THERE IS A PRINCIPLE THAT כל שטיבולו במשקה צריך נטילת ידים
/ anything that has been immersed (or soaked) in liquid (of the
seven types of liquids: dew, water, wine, oil, blood, milk, or bee's
honey) requires washing the hands before eating it (*Pesachim*,
115a). The Halachah follows the opinion of Rashi (ad loc, and
the Rambam, *Hilchos Berachos*, 6:1) and we need to always wash our
hands when we eat a pickle, for example (*Shulchan Aruch*, Orach
Chayim, 158:4, Mechaber and the Rama: אם אוכל דבר שטיבולו באחד משבעה
משקין שסימנם י"ד שה"ט ד"מ [דהיינו יין דבש שמן חלב טל דם מים] ולא נתנגב ואפי' אין
ידיו נוגעות במקום המשקה צריך נטילה בלא ברכה [ואפילו אינו מטבל רק ראש הירק או
הפרי אפ"ה יטול בלא ברכה]).

473:16. This is the ruling of the Rosh, *Shu'T haRosh*, Kelal 14:5. See also
Alter Rebbe, *Shulchan Aruch*, ibid, 4. *Aruch haShulchan*, ibid, 6. As the Rama
(Orach Chayim, 271:12) writes clearly, when he brings down this custom
regarding Kiddush on Shabbos: וי"א דלכתחל' יש ליטול ידיו קודם הקידוש ולקדש
על היין (הרא"ש והמרדכי פ' ע"פ ורשב"א והגהות מיי' פכ"ט וטור) וכן המנהג פשוט
במדינות אלו ואין לשנות רק בליל פסח כמו שיתבאר סי' תע"ג.

* Rama, *Orach Chayim*, 473:1. Indeed, the terminology of the Mishnah is
מזגו לו, although the Mishnah is speaking about the leader of the Seder. The
Alter Rebbe rules the same (*ibid*), although it is not the actual *Minhag* /
custom of Chabad.

Yet, for some reason, many people are not so careful with this Halachah. This is perhaps because they eat a pickle, for example, with a fork, and do not touch the pickle itself with their hands. The Chayei Adam rules that in such cases one does not need to wash. Or they rely on the opinion of Tosefos, who rules that the issue of washing hands is applicable with regards to the laws of purity and impurity, and today, since everyone is anyway impure and does not eat their food in ritual purity, there is no reason to wash the hands (כ"ש אנן שאין אנו נזהרין מלטמאות עצמנו ומלאכול אוכלין טמאין ואין אנו צריכין לאותה נטילה והמברך הרי זה מברך ברכה לבטלה: *Tosefos*, Pesachim, 115a. Today, since everyone is anyway impure, this washing has no relevance: *Aruch haShulchan*, 158:4).

So why do we wash our hands before dipping vegetables in salt water on this night? (As the Taz, *Shulchan Aruch*, Orach Chayim, 473:6, asks). On this night we all wash our hands, and we do so to arouse the wonder and prompt the questions of the children (והא דנוטלין בליל זה הוא כא' מן שאר דברים שעושין בליל זה כדי שישאלו) *Chok Yaakov*, Orach Chayim, 463:28. See also *Aruch haShulchan*, 473:18). Perhaps, to fulfill the earlier opinion, we should also endeavor to eat the vegetable dipped in salt water with our hands and not with a fork. In any case, washing our hands without a blessing before we eat a vegetable that will be dipped in salt water (or Charoses, as the opinion of the Rambam) is unique to Seder Night, and it is intended to arouse wonder.

All opinions agree that in the times of the Beis haMikdash we washed our hands before eating a vegetable, for example, that had been soaked in liquid. So this is another reason to wash our hands on this night — as a remembrance of the era of the Beis haMikdash, when we always washed in this manner. In fact, on this night we do almost everything in the same way we would have done it in the times of the Beis haMikdash, when we brought the Pesach offerings (Netziv, *Imrei Shefer*, Pesichah). On a deeper level, acting as if the Beis haMikdash is already rebuilt is a way of 'rebuilding' the miniature inner Beis haMikdash. On this night we live with *Geulah* / redemption, and we act, think, and practice as if the entire world is already redeemed.

Washing our hands before eating is also a sign of luxury, since washing requires ample running water and some extra time. A slave would not have such luxuries. This is a night of Geulah and freedom. On this night, we experience spiritual, mental, emotional and physical liberation. Thus we wash our hands at the beginning of the Seder to demonstrate the behavior of a free person, of spiritual royalty, of a person living in the times of the Beis haMikdash. As royalty, we have the freedom to be meticulously clean.*

---

* Another reason to wash, writes the Rama, is to prepare for prayer: הדרכי משה (סי' תע"ג ס"ק י"ב): אפשר דסיפור ההגדה הוי כמו תפילה, שאנו מספרים כבוד הא־ל ושבחיו יתעלה, לכן צריך כאן נטילה.

3. KARPAS /
Dip Vegetable into Saltwater

THE PURPOSE OF THIS DIPPING IS AS RASHI WRITES
(*Pesachim*, 114a), כדי שיכיר תינוק וישאל לפי שאין רגילין בני אדם לאכול
ירק קודם סעודה / "so the child should notice and ask why are
we dipping this vegetable in liquid, as the (year-round) custom is to eat vegetables during a meal, not before a meal."
Karpas is unique to the Seder,* and is observed specifically so

---

* Tur, *Orach* :ולוקח ירקות ויברך בופה"א ומטבל כדי לעשות שינוי בשביל התינוקות שישאלו
Chayim, Siman 473. The Tur writes the same as Rashi, and adds that it is better not
to eat a Kezayis of the Karpas, as the purpose is just to arouse the wonder of the
child. However, the Rambam (*Hilchos Chametz uMatzah*, 8:2. See also *Siddur Rav
Saadia Gaon*, p. 136. Mordechai, *Seder Leil Pesach. Sefer haChinuch*, as explained in
Minchas Chinuch, Mitzvah 21:8) writes, מתחיל ומברך בורא פרי האדמה, ולוקח ירק מטבל
specifying ,אותו בחרוסת ואוכל כזית הוא וכל המסובין עמו כל אחד ואחד אין אוכל פחות מכזית,
that one needs to eat a full Kezayis. The question is why? Perhaps unlike Rashi,
the Rosh, and the Tur (who understand that the child asks the question because
he sees that we are eating vegetables before the meal and not during the meal, and
that is why he asks), the Rambam understands that the child asks later on, when he
sees a repeat of this same procedure, when we dip Maror in Charoses. This is more
aligned with how the Maharal explains Karpas (quoted in the *Bach*, 473:19). The
Maharal explains that the question we are trying to arouse is at the second dipping,
the Maror, not the first dipping, the Karpas. So, perhaps the Rambam reasons that
we dip the first time exactly how we will dip the second time — with a full Kezayis.
However, here the child does not yet ask a question, because it is normal to dip a
vegetable once during a meal. Only when the child sees us dipping a second time,
they will ask, have we not done this already? And then we have an open opportunity
to explain the Mitzvah of Maror: מהר"ל מפראג האריך לפלפל בזה וכתב שלדעתו הטבול
הראשון הוא בא כדי שיהא ניכר כשעושין הטבול השני שהוא לשם מצות מרור שאם לא היה

that the children should ask questions.

הטבול הראשון לא היה ניכר באכילת מרור שהוא לשם מצוה שהרי כל ימות השנה דרך לטבול
בפרט בחזרת אבל עכשיו שואלין על טבול שני שבתוך הסעודה למה לי עוד טיבול אחר וישיבו
להם שצריכים טבול משום מצות מרור וטבול ראשון כדרכן כל ימות השנה.

Perhaps this is also the reason that the Rambam holds we need to dip the Karpas in
Charoses ולוקח ירק ומטבל אותו בחרסת, and not in salt water — since according to the
Rambam we need to dip the Karpas in the exact same way we would dip the Maror,
including dipping it in Charoses and eating a full Kezayis of it.

Indeed, washing our hands prior to Karpas would not in itself arouse the questions
of the child, because in the past we would always wash our hands before eating a
vegetable or any other food dipped or soaked in one of the seven liquids (listed
above, *Urchatz*).

Yet, is also possible that the washing of the hands, is not intended for the eating of
the dipped vegetable, rather, for the meal in general, in the words of the Rambam:
בתחלה מוזגין כום לכל אחד ואחד ומברך בורא פרי הגפן ואומר עליו קדוש היום וזמן ושותה. ואחר
כך מברך על נטילת ידים ונוטל ידיו. ומביאין שלחן ערוך ועליו מרור וירק אחר ומצה וחרסת. מתחיל
ומברך בורא פרי האדמה ולוקח ירק.

4. YĀCHAṬZ /
Break the Middle Matzah

WHY IS THE MIDDLE MATZAH BROKEN? MATZAH IS CALLED
לחם עוני / *Lechem Oni*. The Gemara says that it is called לחם
עוני for a few reasons. Two of these reasons are אמר שמואל לחם
עוני כתיב לחם שעונין עליו דברים...דבר אחר לחם עוני עני כתיב מה עני
שדרכו בפרוסה / Shmuel said that the phrase "bread of affliction"
means bread over which one עונין / answers matters — i.e., one
recites the Haggadah over the Matzah. Alternatively, in the
Pasuk, the phrase *Lechem Oni* is actually written without a Vav
(עני), which means 'a poor person', and we eat the Matzah in
the manner of a poor person who eats just a piece of his bread,
for lack of a whole loaf" (*Pesachim*, 115b).

We break the middle Matzah before we recite the Haggadah and "answer matters" over it, and we break it also in order
to have a broken piece, poor man's bread, and in this way we
fulfill both interpretations of the Gemara, as the Alter Rebbe
explains.*

---

* *Shulchan Aruch*, Orach Chayim, 473:36. There is no Yachatz in the Rambam's Haggadah, and one breaks the Matzah right before eating the Matzah
(although the Rashba in Berachos writes that if you break a piece of bread
and then right away eat it, it is not really considered a broken piece of bread;
perhaps the Rambam disagrees with this). From the Rambam's perspective,
the Haggadah is recited on the (full, unbroken) Matzah, simply because we
"answer matters" over it: לחם עוני כתיב לחם שעונין עליו דברים.

Breaking bread *before* we recite a blessing over it is something we do not do throughout the year. It is an unusual observance, unique to Pesach Night.

5. MAGGID / Recite the Haggadah

Maggid is one of the main Mitzvos of the night — reciting the Haggadah and speaking expansively about going out of Egypt. Maggid is performed in a question and answer format, with an audible voice and in an elaborate manner, envisioning yourself as if on this night you left Egypt. Maggid is a unique Mitzvah of Pesach night.

6. RACHTZAH / Wash Hands for Bread

Washing our hands before we eat bread is one of the Mitzvos of our sages, and was initiated by King Shelomo. Rachtzah is the second time we wash our hands during the Seder, and this time we recite a blessing.*

---

* On this night we should wash our hands twice, and not intend that the first washing for the wet vegetable should also cover the eating of Matzah, as the Beis Yoseph writes, וכתב המרדכי ג"ל שאם נתכוון בנטילה ראשונה לגמור בה כל סעודתו בלא היסח הדעת אין צריך לחזור וליטול שניה ע"כ ונ"ל דאין לכוין בכך שלא לבטל תקנת חכמים שתקנו ליטול פעמיים בליל פסח: *Beis Yoseph*, Orach Chayim, 475:1. In other words, according to the Mordechai, the reason we need to wash again is because of *Hesech haDa'as* / discontinuity of intention due to a significant time lapse, as the Gemara, *Pesachim*, 115b says, איתמר נטילת ידים תרי זימני למה לי הא משא ליה ידיה חדא זימנא אמרי כיון דבעי למימר אגדתא והלילא

When we do something twice, it arouses the suspicion of the children. The Maharal explains (see above, regarding Karpas) regarding "dipping twice" — dipping the Karpas and then dipping the Maror — that the children only ask about the difference of this night when they see the second dipping. The same can be said with the washing of the hands. When we wash our hands for the second time, the child is stimulated to ask why we are washing our hands again.

7. MOTZI / Blessing Over Bread

BEFORE WE EAT BREAD, WE ALWAYS RECITE THE BLESSING HaMotzi. Normally on Shabbos or Yom Tov, we recite HaMotzi on *Lechem Mishnah* / two whole loaves. However, on this night, we hold a broken 'loaf' of Matzah together with two whole Matzos (*Orach Chayim*, 475:1, whereas the Rif and Rambam rule that we only hold one and a half Matzos on this night), and recite HaMotzi.

After we recite the blessing of HaMotzi, we recite an additional Berachah, אכילת מצה / *Achilas Matzah* / eating Matzah. The leader of the Seder has three Matzos: the top and bottom are whole Matzos and the middle is the broken poor man's

---

דילמא אסוחי אסחיה לדעתיה ונגע. As such, if we washed our hands and had intention throughout, we would seemingly not need to wash again. Yet, as the Beis Yoseph argues, and this is the Halachah, we need to wash twice as this is the תקנת חכמים.

bread. The question is, upon which Matzah or Matzos do we recite the blessing of HaMotzi, and upon which do we recite the blessing of Achilas Matzah?

There is an argument among the *Rishonim* / Early Commentators regarding the sequence. Simple logic would dictate that HaMotzi is recited over the whole Matzos, as we do throughout the year, and the unique blessing of the evening, Achilas Matzah, is recited over the special Matzah, the broken one.* In lieu of the argument, the prevailing practice today, as ruled in the Shulchan Aruch, is that we recite both blessings, HaMotzi and Achilas Matzah, on the top Matzah and on the broken Matzah (יטול ידיו ויברך על נטילת ידים ויקח המצות כסדר שהניחן הפרוסה בין שתי השלימות ויאחזם בידו ויברך המוציא ועל אכילת מצה: *Orach Chayim*, 475). It seems from the Shulchan Aruch that we should hold all three Matzos for these two blessings (See *Berachos*, 39b, and as Tosefos (*ad loc*) explains, that we can recite two blessings on the broken Matzah, and there is no issue of Mitzvos חבילות, since דהא הוי ברכה

---

* This is the opinion of the Rosh, and the Bach explains the logic: ומ"ש ומברך על השלימה המוציא וכו' כ"כ הרא"ש דמברך על השלימה המוציא דלא גרע י"ט של פסח משאר שבתות וימים טובים שמברכים המוציא על השלימה והא דאמרינן בברכות דהכל מודים בפסח שמניח פרוסה בתוך השלימה ובוצע מ"ט לחם עוני כתיב היינו אותו לחם שיוצא בו על ידי אכילת מצה אבל המוציא פשיטא דעל שלימים בעינן כשאר י"ט (...). Yet, others argue the opposite: HaMotzi is recited on the broken Matzah, and Achilas Matzah is recited on the whole Matzah (*Tur*, Orach Chayim, 475: שיש מי שאומר שמברך על הפרוסה המוציא ועל השלימה על אכילת מצה. Perhaps the reason for this is שלמה שמניח פרוסה בתוך שלמה אמר רב פפא: הכל מודים בפסח, שמניח פרוסה בפסח: *Berachos*, 39b. As such, on Pesach night we recite the blessing which we recite the entire year over a broken — and whole — Matzah.

של נהנין ואינם נקראים חבילות חבילות דהא אקידוש דהא מברכים קידוש וברכת היין, as HaMotzi is a Birchas haNehenin, and *Al Achilas Matzah* is a Birchas haM-itzvos). Nevertheless, the prevailing custom is to recite HaMotzi on all three Matzos, and then to let go of the bottom Matzah before we recite Achilas Matzah.

As such, on this night we recite the blessing HaMotzi like every other Yom Tov, yet, uncharacteristically, we recite HaMotzi on a broken 'loaf' of bread, the broken Matzah.

8) MAṬZAḤ / Eat the Matzah

EATING MATZAH IS OBVIOUSLY ONE OF THE MAIN MITZVOS of the night, and a Mitzvah that is unique to Pesach.

Besides the fact that this night is the only night of the year when there is a Mitzvah to eat Matzah (the other days of Pesach, eating Matzah is only a רשות / optional Mitzvah: *Pesachim*, 120a. Rambam, *Hilchos Chametz uMatzah*, 6:1. *Tur* and *Shulchan Aruch*, Orach Chayim, 475:7. However, see Chizkuni on *Shemos*, 12:18. *Ma'aseh Rav*, 185. See also *Mishnah Berurah*, 475:25 and 639:24 in the context of Sukkos: *Aruch haShulchan* 475:18), it seems that the more we eat Matzah on this night, the more times we are fulfilling a Mitzvah. "Rava would drink wine the entire day of Erev Pesach, so as to whet his appetite to enable him to eat *more Matzah* at night" (*Pesachim*, 107b). This suggests eating more than the *Shiur* / minimum vol-ume of Matzah is also a Mitzvah (*Shu'T Avnei Nezer*, Orach Chayim, Siman 448:7).

9) MAROR / Eat Bitter Herbs

FOLLOWING THE EATING OF THE MATZAH WE EAT MAROR
(*Pesachim*, 114a, Rashbam and Tosefos, ad loc: שהוא אוכל אחר מצה שהוא מברך
על אכילת מרור כדכתיב על מצות ומרורים (במדבר ט, יא) בתחלה מצה ואח"כ מרור.
פרפרת קרי המרור שאוכל אחר המצה), as alluded to in the Pasuk על מצות
ומרורים / "upon Matzos and Marorim" — first Matzah, then
Maror.

During the times when we offered the Korban Pesach, the
eating of Maror was a Mitzvah of the Torah, as the Mitzvah to
eat Maror is intricately bound with the Korban Pesach. Today,
in exile, it is a *Mitzvah d'Rabbanan* / 'Mitzvah of our sages' to
eat Maror, but not a *Mitzvah d'Oraisa* / Torah Mitzvah.

The Rosh writes that since we recite a blessing over the Maror, we need to eat a full *Kezayis* / 'volume of an olive' of Maror.*

---

* We need to eat a Kezayis of Maror. Why a Kezayis? Writes the *Sefer Yere'im*, Siman
94:3, וצריך שיאכל מן המרור כזית דאכילה כתיב ביה ואכילה בכזית. In other words, the
Pasuk speaking about the Mitzvah of eating the Korban Pesach with Matzah and
Maror says, על מצות ומרורים יאכלוהו; the word *Achilah* / eating appears with the word
Maror, and since every Achilah is at least a Kezayis, thus we need to eat a Kezayis
of Maror. The Hagahos Maimoniyos writes the same: Rambam, *Hilchos Chametz
uMatzah*, 8:2. The Rosh writes (*Pesachim*, 10:25), that we need to eat a Kezayis of
Maror, and the reason is that since the Nusach of the Berachah is Achilas Maror, the
idea of *Achilah* / eating, and every Achilah is a Kezayis. The *Sha'agas Aryeh*, Siman
100, asks many questions on this Rosh. For example, since the Pasuk says, על מצות
ומרורים יאכלוהו, Chazal draw a *Hekesh* / similarity between Matzah and Maror and
derive, for instance, that Maror is not a fish, rather something that grows, much
like the wheat of Matzah (*Pesachim*, 39a). Perhaps, then, the reason we need to eat
a Kezayis of Maror is because of the Hekesh to Matzah. Besides, the Rosh brings

"proof" from the Berachah, that we use the word *Achilah*, and thus he rules we need to eat a Kezayis Maror, but this is circular reasoning, for if our sages would have fashioned another form of Berachah, then would we not need to eat a Kezayis?

The *Sevara* / logic of the Rosh, is as *Terumas haDeshen*, Siman, 245, explains, since the word *Achilah* does not appear with the eating of Maror in the Torah, it only appears within the context of the Korban Pesach, על מצות ומרורים יאכלוהו, meaning, the Achilah of the Korban Pesach needs to be with Maror, thus Achilah only refers to the Korban Pesach (and not the Maror, as we will shortly explain). Thus, if not for the Berachah of Chazal in which we say the term *Achilah*, we would not need to eat a Kezayis of Maror. But the fact that Chazal write the term *Achilah* regarding Maror means we need to eat the Shiur of Achilah, which is a Kezayis.

Reb Chayim Brisker (Reb Chayim Stentzil, a.k.a. Stencil), asks on this Rosh (42): even without the word *Achilah* in the Torah or in the Nusach of the Berachah, we would think that one must eat a *Shiur Achilah*, which is a Kezayis, when eating Maror. Why? Because in the Torah or Chazal, anything that is connected to eating, and the Mitzvah or the *Aveirah* / sin is with eating, even when it does not say clearly in the Torah the word Achilah, the Shiur of the Mitzvah or Aveira is a Kezayis. For example, the Torah does not say the language of Achilah by meat and milk, rather it says we are not allowed to cook them together, and yet, what is the Shiur of the prohibition of eating milk and meat together is a Kezayis. Says Reb Chayim, even without the term *Achilah,* wouldn't it make sense that the Mitzvah of Maror (from the Torah, during the times of the Korban Pesach, or today, from our sages) is a Kezayis? Answers Reb Chayim, when the Rambam writes about the Mitzvah of Maror, he writes אכילת מרור אינה מצוה מן התורה בפני עצמה אלא תלויה היא באכילת הפסח / "The eating of Maror is not a commandment from the Torah on its own, but is rather dependent upon the eating of the Korban Pesach" (*Hilchos Chametz uMatzah*, 7:12). In other words, from the simple reading of the Torah, there was never a Mitzvah to eat Maror on its own, rather, it is included within the Mitzvah of eating the Korban Pesach, and as such, there is no *Din* / law of Achilah regarding the Maror, rather the Din of Achilah is only on the Korban, and the Korban has to be eaten with Maror. In other words, just as the meat of the Korban needs to be roasted, and roasting adds a certain 'taste' to the meat, similarly, the Torah says this meat also needs Maror, something sharp, a spice, as it were. And just as the 'taste' of a roast has no Shiur of Achilah, there is no Shiur of Achilah for Maror. And yet, the Rosh is *Mechadesh* / innovating that since in the terminology of the Berachah it says *Achilah*, thus we need to eat a Shiur of Maror which is a Kezayis.

10. KORECH /
Eating the Matzah & Maror Sandwich

ACCORDING TO HILLEL, MAROR WAS NEVER EATEN ALONE, rather it was eaten together with the Korban Pesach and with Matzah (It seems that according to the Rambam, only Matzah and Maror were in the sandwich; ואחר...ואחר כך כורך מצה ומרור כאחת ומטבל בחרסת כך מברך ברוך אתה...ואוכל מבשר חגיגת ארבעה עשר תחלה ומברך ברוך אתה...על אכילת הפסח ואוכל מגופו של פסח: *Hilchos Chametz uMatzah*, 8:6-7. Although see *Lechem Mishnah*, ad loc). Thus, as a remembrance, and according to Hillel's understanding, in order to fulfill the obligation of eating Maror, we do so within a sandwich of Matzah (today we simply omit the Korban Pesach).

One question remains: Yes, Chazal established this Berachah for Maror and since it says Achilah we need a Kezayis, but why did Chazal establish this liturgy if Maror (according to Torah law) is merely a taste and is dependent on the Korban Pesach? The Chasam Sofer (*Shu'T Orach Chayim*, 140) writes (although he did not see the *Sha'agas Aryeh*: כי אין דרכי לחפש בספרים אם לא יוורני אדם עליו), really, we know we need to eat a Kezayis Maror from the Hekesh to Matzah (although see *Shu'T Avnei Nezer*, Orach Chayim 383, 4, that the Hekesh is not for issues of Achilah). Yet, since it does not clearly say so in Chazal, we cannot draw our own conclusions from a Hekesh, and thus the Rosh showed proof that we need a Kezayis from the Nusach of the Berachah: אע"ג דלא כ' אכילה בהדי' במרור לא בראשון ולא בשני מ"מ ודאי דבעי כזית דאיתקש למצה ופסח אלא שאין אנו יכולין להמציא זה מלבינו לכן הוכיח הרא"ש מדאמרינן בפ"ע דמברך על אכילת מרור ש"מ פשיטא לרבנן מהקישא הנ"ל דשיעורו בכזית.

At this point we have already fulfilled the higher, more stringent, Torah obligation to eat Matzah and the less stringent Rabbinic obligation to eat Maror, and thus, when creating a sandwich, there is no issue of ואתי מרור דרבנן ומבטיל ליה למצה דאורייתא / "the Maror which is a Rabbinic obligation will come and nullify the Torah Mitzvah of eating Matzah" (*Pesachim*, 115a), as now both eating Matzah and Maror are merely done as a reminder of "Hillel's sandwich," recalling the time when the Korban Pesach was offered and eaten near the Beis haMikdash.

11. SHULCHAN ORECH / The Yom Tov Meal

ON EVERY YOM TOV WE EAT A FESTIVE MEAL, BUT SEDER Night's meal is distinctive. There are various customs connected to the meal that we find only on Pesach night, for example, the custom to begin the meal by eating an egg, a mourner's food, reminding us of the destruction of the Beis haMikdash (additionally, because Tishah b'Av falls out the same night of the week as the first night of Pesach) and that we no longer are able to offer the actual offering of the Chagigah, which the egg represents. This is an unusual custom for a Yom Tov meal.

Although the Gemara says מיני בשר / "some type of meat" is to be used as a reminder for the Chagigah, which would mean that one should have a piece of meat for the reminder of the Chagigah — and indeed this is how the Rambam rules (ובזמן הזה מביאין על השלחן שני מיני בשר אחד זכר לפסח ואחד זכר לחגיגה: Rambam, *Hilchos Chametz uMatzah*, 8:1) — yet, the prevailing custom is to take an egg, which is also somewhat related to meat. The reason we use an egg, says the Kotzker Rebbe, is that there is an advantage of an egg over a piece of meat. Besides being an animal product (connected to meat), an egg contains the potential of new life (although this is not true of the industrial farmed eggs that we eat today). It serves therefore a double purpose: as a reminder of the Chagigah of the past, and also an inspiration filling us with hope for the future and the Chagigah that will be again offered with the building of the third and final Beis haMikdash. In this way, the egg has a dual connotation: nostalgia for the past and hope for the future.

Another custom of this meal is not to dip any foods into liquid throughout Shulchan Orech, even, for example, dipping solids into soup (נוהגים בקצת מקומות לאכול בסעודה ביצים זכר לאבילות ונראה לי הטעם משום שליל תשעה באב נקבע בליל פסח ועוד זכר לחורבן שהיו מקריבים קרבן פסח ויש נוהגים שלא לאכול שום טיבול בלילה רק ב׳ טבולים שעושים בסדר: Rama on *Shulchan Aruch*, Orach Chayim, 476:2).

Today we eat the meal after eating the Mitzvah-foods, the Matzah and Maror. However, in the time of the Beis haMikdash and when we ate the Korban Pesach, the custom was to begin with the festive Yom Tov meal by reciting HaMotzi over 'rich Matzah', meaning Matzah with eggs or other tasteful ingredients, and only after the meal to eat the Matzah, Maror and Korban Pesach (As the opinion of most Rishonim, Mordechai on *Pesachim*, 119b, although, the Rambam writes (*Hilchos Chametz uMatzah*, 8) that they ate the Matzah and Maror and then the meal, just as we do today).

In any case, sitting down to eat a full meal after having eaten large quantities of Matzah and Maror is an unusual way to eat a meal, and is unique to Pesach night.

12. TZAFUN / Hidden

WITH THE STEP OF TZAFUN, WE EAT THE BROKEN PIECE OF the middle Matzah, which we had put aside as the Afikoman. Tzafun is clearly unique to the Seder. Tzafun means 'hidden', but why is this Siman called *Tzafun*? And why do we 'hide' the Matzah?

The simple reason, writes the Ya'avetz (in his *Siddur*. See the Rebbe's Haggadah, Yachatz), that the Afikoman is put aside and hidden, is so that we will not come to eat it by mistake during the meal. In this way, we hide it from ourselves, as it were.*

---

* In fact, the Shulchan Aruch rules that the broken piece for the Afikoman should be given to another person, to watch and protect it for a later eating. ויתן חציה לאחד מהמסובין לשומרה לאפיקומן: *Orach Chayim*, 473:6.

Also, hiding the Afikoman is a way to arouse children's curiosity and keep them awake. If they steal it, 'find it', or merely 'grab it', and then have to return it towards the end of the Seder, they will more likely remain alert and awake until then.

Today we no longer eat the Korban Pesach, as we no longer offer the sacrifices. According to many Rishonim, the Afikoman is now eaten as a remembrance of the actual Korban Pesach which we offered and ate in times past (As the Rosh explains, *Pesachim*, 119b. Although Rashi and the Rashbam maintain that we eat the Afikoman as a memory of the Matzah that was eaten with the Korban Pesach. As Rashi writes, אין מפטירין אחר מצה אפיקומן – שצריך לאכול מצה בגמר הסעודה זכר למצה הנאכלת עם הפסח). It is said in the name of Reb Chayim Brisker that the hiding of the Afikoman is related and in commemoration of a special Mitzvah that was done as part of the Pesach offering: *Shemirah* / protecting the offering, watching over it so it would not become impure. For this reason, people would 'hide' the Korban Pesach, to protect its purity.

We eat the Afikoman at the end of the meal, similar to the Korban Pesach, which was eaten at the end of the meal (as the Mordechai, quoted above, writes). The Korban Pesach needed to be consumed *Al haSova* / upon satiation, when one's stomach was filled, and as the last food of the night, so the taste of the Mitzvah would last in the mouth.

13. BEIRACH / Grace after the Meal

In the Siman of Beirach we *Bentch*, we recite the *Birchas haMazon* / blessings following a meal. Throughout the year, as we recite these same blessings whenever we eat bread, many follow the injunction of our sages to recite them over a cup of wine if there are three or ten people Bentching together. On Seder Night, we Bentch over a cup of wine even if we are performing the Seder alone. This is unique to this night.*

---

* *Shulchan Aruch*, Orach Chayim, 479, *Mishnah Berurah*, 2. In the words of the *Kaf haChayim,* ‏אפי׳ ביחיד דארבעה כוסית תיקנו אפי׳ ליחיד. תו׳ פסחים ק״ה ע״ב.‏ ‏וכ״כ הרא״ש פ׳ ע״פ סי׳ י״ד. ואפי׳ למ״ד בעלמא בחמ״ז אין טעונה כוס כמ״ש לעיל רסי׳‏ ‏קפ״ב הכא ד׳ כוסות תיקנו רבנן דרך חירות כל חד וחד נעביד ביה מצוה. פסחים קי״ז ע״ב‏. And although ‏מצוה לחזור אחר זימון‏ / *Mechaber*, ibid., a) this is only *L'chatchilah* / the 'a priori' or ideal way to perform it, and b) the reason is not so much for the purpose of *Zimun* / invitation, rather for Hallel, so that Hallel should be said in a groups, as the Poskim explain: ‏משמע בטור דוקא להלל מצוה‏ ‏כדי שיהיו ג׳ גם בשעת קריאת הלל. לבוש. וכ״כ מט״מ סי׳‏ :‏לחזור אבל ב״ה דינו כשאר ימות השנה‏ *Magen Avraham*, 479:2. *Levush, Chok Yaakov.* See *Kaf haChayim:* ‏תרנ״ד דמצוה לחזור אחר זימון וכן להודו. והטעם כתב הדרישה או׳ א׳ אגב שמצריכין ג׳‏ ‏משום הודו מצריכין נמי שיהיו הג׳ ג״כ בשעת הזימון דבזימון נמי אומר אחד לשנים נברך‏ ‏וכו׳ כמו בהודו יעו״ש. אבל הט״ז סק״ג כתב דמ״ש הטור מצוה לחזור אחר זימון לא נתכוון‏ ‏כלל לבהמ״ז אלא משום הודו לחוד אמר כן יעו״ש. וכ״כ מ״א סק״ב. ח״י או׳ ה׳ חק יוסף או׳‏ ‏ה׳ ר״ז או׳ ו׳ ומ״מ טוב ליר״ש שיהיה לו זימון משעת אכילה אם אפשר כדי לצאת מצוה‏ ‏מן המובחר אליבא דכ״ע‏.

14. HALLEL / Chanting the Hallel

Hallel is composed of chapters 113 through 118 of *Tehilim* / Psalms. Our sages call this *Hallel haMitzri* / the Egyptian Hallel, as it speaks about the going out of Egypt (There is also a *Hallel haGadol* / Great Hallel, which is Chapter 136 of *Tehilim*).

Normally, when we recite Hallel we do so without interruption. On this night, our Hallel is divided in two. We recite the first part of Hallel in the first part of the Haggadah before we eat (according to Beis Shamai the first chapter, 113, and according to Beis Hillel the first two chapters, 113-114), and we recite the second part of Hallel after the meal, at the conclusion of the Haggadah.

Each of the cups of wine in the Seder demands its own form of declaring *Shevach* / thanksgiving to HaKadosh Baruch Hu. Upon the first cup we recite Kiddush, and upon the third cup we recite Birchas haMazon. This way, we can recite the first part of Hallel on the second cup, and the second part of Hallel on the fourth cup, expressing Shevach on each of the four cups.*

---

* In the Gemara, there is an argument about which two cups need reclining: the first two cups, or the last two cups. The sage who argues for the first two cups says, "...because it is now that freedom begins." Since reclining is a sign of freedom, while discussing the Exodus from Egypt it is appropriate to drink while reclining. By contrast, the last two cups do not require reclining, because what happened already happened. In other words, by this point one has completed the discussion of the Exodus and has reached the latter stages of the Seder. The sage who argues for the second two cups says, "...because at that time (the last part of the Seder) there is

Before the meal, we recite chapters 113 and 114, the first

freedom — however the first two cups do not require reclining, as one is still saying, 'We were slaves....'" Today we recline with all four cups. יין, איתמר משמיה דרב נחמן: צריך הסיבה. ואיתמר משמיה דרב נחמן: אין צריך הסיבה. ולא פליגי: הא בתרתי כסי קמאי, הא בתרתי כסי בתראי. אמרי לה להאי גיסא ואמרי לה להאי גיסא. אמרי לה להאי גיסא: תרי כסי קמאי — בעו הסיבה, דהשתא הוא דקא מתחלא לה חירות. תרי כסי בתראי — לא בעו הסיבה, מאי דהוה הוה. ואמרי לה להאי גיסא: אדרבה, תרי כסי בתראי — בעו הסיבה, ההיא שעתא דקא הויא חירות. תרי כסי קמאי — לא בעו הסיבה, דאכתי "עבדים היינו" קאמר. השתא דאיתמר הכי ואיתמר הכי, אידי ואידי בעו הסיבה: Pesachim, 108a. The Ran asks, the four cups is a Mitzvah of the sages, and the rule is ספק דרבנן לקולא / where there is doubt regarding the laws of our sages we are lenient, so why do we recline with all four cups? He offers two reasons, a) since it is not difficult to recline with all four. B) If we will be lenient, we will end up not reclining at all, and then נמצאת תקנת חכמים נעקרת / "The established rule of the sages would be totally nullified" (Ran on the Rif, 23). This Ran seems to contradict another Ran, where he writes, regarding a doubt on which day to read the Megilah, ולענין עיירות המסופקות אם הן מוקפין חומה מימות יהושע בן נון או לא, הורו הגאונים ז"ל שהולכין בהן אחר רוב עיירות שרובן אינן מוקפות חומה מימות יהושע וקורין בהן בי"ד ועוד שאפילו תאמר שהוא ספק שקול ה"ל ספק של דבריהם ולקולא ונמצא פטורות בשניהם ומבטל ממנו בודאי מקרא מגילה לפיכך קורא בראשון ופטור בשני: Ran, Megilah, 2a. But according to the first Ran (in Pesachim) we should need to read the Megilah on both days, as the Rambam (and Shulchan Aruch) indeed rules: Hilchos Megilah, 1:11. See, Mishneh laMelech, ad loc. See also Shu'T Eretz haTzvi, 1, 54. Perhaps the difference is that if we only recline, for example, by the first two cups (and not the second two), this shows that we are following the opinion that we recline on the first two cups, and pushing aside the opinion that it is the second two cups. (A similar ruling is found in Shulchan Aruch, Yoreh De'ah, 111:5. היו כאן שתי קדרות של היתר ולפניהם שתי חתיכות אחת של היתר .ואחת של איסור ונפלה אחת לתוך זו ואחת לתוך זו אסורות שתיהן אפילו כאן ששתיהן של היתר אם אתה. This is because, as the Shach, ad loc, writes, באיסור דרבנן תולה האיסור בא' ומתיר השני הרי אתה אוסר א' מהן מהיתירו וא"כ כיון שאתה אוסר עכ"פ אחד מהן מאי חזית דאסרת להאי דלמא איפכא וע"כ שתיהן אסורות). Whereas regarding reading the Megilah, even if we read it only on the 14th, this in itself does not *exclude* the 15th, since it is a location issue, and those who read on the 14th do so not do so to the exclusion of the 15th, rather, it is because in their location the Mitzvah is to read on the 14th. Another way of saying this is if someone read on the 14th and then relocated on the 15th to a place where the Megilah is read on the 15th, he too will need to read the Megilah again on the 15th, even though he already read it on the 14th. וראיה מדאמרינן בירושלמי שם בן עיר שעקר דירתו ליל ט"ו נתחייב כאן וכאן: Bi'ur HaGra, Orach Chayim, 688:5. See also Bi'ur Halachah, ad loc.

part of Hallel, which speak about how we were slaves in Egypt and Hashem took us out, freed us from bondage and split the sea for us. This section refers to our liberations in the past and the present. After the meal we recite the second part of Hallel, which speaks of our future and the coming redemption. As such, before we eat the Matzah, the Maror and the meal, we need to give thanks for our past and present. Once we have eaten the Matzah, Maror and the meal, we have already internalized our freedom. At this point, we are inspired to envision a future freedom, to hope and dream of a world that is fully and eternally redeemed.

This is a night of singing praises to HaKadosh Baruch Hu for everything He has done for us, collectively and historically.[*]

---

[*] In the words of the Rambam (*Sefer haMitzvos*, Mitzvah 157), וכל מי שיוסיף במאמר ויאריך הדברים בהגדלת מה שעשה לנו השם ומה שעשו לנו המצרים מעול וחמס ואיך לקח השם נקמתנו מהם ולהודות לו יתעלה על כל טוב שגמלנו יהיה יותר טוב / "And it is better for one to add upon the telling and stretch out the words by magnifying that which Hashem did for us, what the Egyptians did to us in terms of injustice and oppression, and how Hashem avenged us upon them — and to thank Him, may He be exalted, for all of the good with which He benefited us."

On this night, Hallel is not as a *Din* / principle law of *K'riah* / reading of Hallel, rather it is a *Shirah* / singing of Hallel.

The Ran (*Pesachim*, 118a) writes, in the name of Rav Hai Gaon and other Gaonim, ואין אנו אומרים אותו בתורת קורין אלא בתורת אומר שירה. Or as the Ritva writes (*Sukkah*, 39a), אלא ודאי הלל דבההגדה אינו נאמר בדרך חיוב הלל אלא בדרך זמר. Or in the words of the Maharal (*Gevuros Hashem*, 62), ורב האי גאון אמר שאין לברך על הלל בליל פסחים, שאינו מצוה, כמו שאמר לפיכך אנחנו חייבים להודות להלל לשבח וכו'. ואשמועינן כי אנחנו חייבים מעצמנו להלל לשבח לפאר. And as the Brisker Rav explains in great detail, on every day of Pesach we recite Hallel as the Mitzvah of K'riah of Hallel, but on Seder Night we do so as Shirah: *Chidushei haGriz*, Hilchos Chanukah, 3:7. Since Hallel during the Seder is a Shirah, we do not recite a blessing, as we normally do when reciting Hallel as a Mitzvah. And although the Mishnah (*Megilah*, 20b) says that Hallel is

When we turn the Seder 'inwards' towards our own lives, we also sing praises for what Hashem is doing for us, personally

one of the Mitzvos performed only by day, we recite Hallel by night, as this Hallel is a Shirah.

For this reason as well, we may sit during this Hallel. Generally, the Shulchan Aruch (*Orach Chayim*, 422:4) rules that we should stand when reciting Hallel, yet on this night we sit, as Hallel on this night is a Shirah. For this reason as well, the Rama (*Orach Chayim*, 477) rules like the Ran (ר"ן פרק ע"פ וס"ב דמגילה), that we should endeavor to say Hallel before midnight as well (ויקדים עצמו שגם ההלל יקרא קודם חצות), as Hallel is part of the Seder, the Shirah to Hashem.

During the times when we offered the Korban Pesach, the *Shechitah* / slaughter of the Korban occurred during the day, and the *Achilah* / eating of the Korban was in the evening — at both these events Hallel was sung.

Regarding the Shechitah, the Mishnah says, קראו את ההלל (*Pesachim*, 64a); says Rashi, אבל כיתות קאי, which seems to mean that all those who are offering the Korban Pesach are to recite Hallel while the Korban is being slaughtered. It seems that this is a *Din* / law or element within the offering. The Rebbe learns this Rashi not to mean that all people need to say the Hallel (not just the Levi'im), for how can Rashi argue with a clear Tosefta (see *Tosefos*, Sukkah, 54a), that says that only the Levi'im recite Hallel. Rather, Rashi is merely saying that Hallel needs to be recited with all three groups. Indeed, see Rashi on *Erchin*, 10a, והיו הלויים משוררים בפה את ההלל באותן י"ב ימים, where Rashi says clearly that it was the Levi'im who said Hallel (And we do not need to be *Mechadesh* / innovate that there are two *Dinim* / principle laws in Hallel and Korban Pesach; one Rashi is talking about one Din, the Shirah, and the other Rashi about another Din, the Hallel of the Korban, unrelated to the Shirah: *Chidushei haGriz*, Hilchos Korban Pesach).

Tosefos clearly writes that it was the לוים / the Levi'im who normally sing the Shirah during the Avodah (of *Nisuch haYayin* / wine libation) would also sing during the Shechitah of the Korban Pesach (this is also the opinion of the Rambam, *Hilchos Korban Pesach*, 1:11), and as the Rebbe explains, everyone agrees, even Rashi, and Tosefos learns that Hallel during the Shechitah has a *Geder* / definition of 'Shirah'.

This is with regards to the Shechitah. Regarding Achilah, the Mishnah (*Pesachim*, 95a) says טעון הלל באכילתו / we need to say Hallel while eating the Korban Pesach (the *Korban Pesach Rishon* / the first Korban Pesach).

Today, without the actual Korban Pesach, we sing Hallel as a Shirah.

and presently. In fact, the word *Haggadah*, writes the Avudraham, means 'thanks-giving'. As such, within the Haggadah we recite the very *P'sukim* / verses that the Torah asks us to recite while presenting the *Bikurim* / offering of first fruits: ואמרת אליו הגדתי היום לה׳ אלקיך כי־באתי אל־הארץ אשר נשבע ה׳ לאבתינו לתת לנו / "(You shall go to the priest in charge at that time) and say to him, 'I acknowledge this day before Hashem your G-d that I have entered the land that Hashem swore to our fathers to assign us.'" The Targum Yerushalmi translates the word הגדתי as אודינן ושבחינן / "I am thankful and I offer praise." This is a night of thanks-giving and praise, for our past, present and future.

15. NIRTZAH / Accepted

THE FINAL 'STEP' OF THE SEDER IS NIRTZAH, THE TANGIBLE sensation that our Seder has been received and accepted on High.

Many have a tradition of singing all types of hymns and riddles as an extension of Nirtzah, expressing thanks for the past and awakening longing for the future. Others recite the book of *Shir haShirim* / Song of Songs. All and all, there is a sensation of having arrived and that our Seder and our lives are accepted on High.

The above are the 15 Simanim and how they relate specifically to Seder Night. Now, let us learn a little more inwardly and uncover the 15 Simanim and 15 steps towards personal liberation and inner freedom.

The Simanim of the Seder as a Progression Towards Freedom

1) KADEISH / RECITATION OF KIDDUSH

Kadeish means 'holy, transcendent, or separate'. The act of walking to the table, standing erect and reciting Kiddush marks a visceral, tangible separation between the mundane consciousness of weekdays and a more transcendent consciousness of Yom Tov. We initiate our journey by decisively moving away from our place of comfortable spiritual stagnancy and declare, 'I am separate from that space, and desire to enter a more transcendent space.'

Kadeish is the movement out of the space where we were up until this very moment, separating from it, and choosing to move into a vital state of holiness and presence, unrelated to and unimpeded by the trivialities and anxieties of the past.

To be in this new space means to be utterly present, limited neither by the past or the future; to be totally present without any distractions — this is freedom. If you are about to sit down for the Seder and you start thinking, 'This is going to be a long night,' or even, 'How can I make this interesting for my children,' then you are not truly present. Being present means I have *no* worries or anxieties, and I am not pulling my past into this space: 'Right now I am here, open to experience the holiness and transformational power of the Seder. *I am choosing to be present, right here and right now.*'

As we open ourselves to the awesomeness of the moment, fully present, alert, curious, and ready to receive, we are given from Above a gift of *Gadlus* / 'greatness' or expansiveness, clarity, and a sense of inner knowing why we exist and what is our purpose.

Presence is the first step to progress and any genuine growth.

2) URCHATZ / AND WASH (THE HANDS)

Once we have tasted a sense of "greatness," of transcendence and purity which is called *Gadlus Rishon* / first greatness or initial expansive consciousness, we can settle back into our past. This allows us to cleanse ourselves in the present, without becoming entangled and enmeshed in any negativity or drama from our past. Without first experiencing Gadlus and opening ourselves up to who we truly are, a person involved in the world of negativity, such as lying or any other destructive addiction, might not be able to free themselves. If one would attempt to mend their ways without first discovering their authentic, holy, pure identity, the mere thought of their destructive behaviors could pull them down even deeper into the abyss of negativity, doubt, and hopelessness. That is why, in this case, 'cleansing' comes after 'sanctification'. Urchatz comes precisely after Kadeish.

At this point, when we ritually wash our hands, we do so without a *Berachah* / blessing. The Halachic reason for this was offered above. On a more inward level, washing without reciting a blessing represents a washing away of negativity, rather than a washing for the sake of a positive purpose or experience. It is the negation of negativity, as opposed to a preparation for something positive, and thus there is no sense of 'blessing' in it.

At this point, we are still ridding ourselves of subtle traces of negativity. We cannot make a blessing because it is still a painful experience, and our bitterness has not yet been sweetened. ורחץ / *Urchatz* has the same letters as רוצח / *Rotzeach*, 'murderer'. As we wash, we are 'murdering' any negativity that still clings to our hands, and rinsing away all the negative thinking that mired us in our collective and personal Egypt, in constriction and smallness, in the first place.

3) KARPAS / DIP A VEGETABLE INTO SALT WATER

For Karpas, many take a slice of onion, others a piece of potato, and dip it into salt water. As we eat this 'small' piece of bitter vegetable, it is a sudden plunge back into *Katnus* / 'smallness' and constricted consciousness. Inwardly, the vegetable represents the part of our self that is covered in the ground, the more hidden, lower part of the self which is the undercurrent of much of our instinctive behaviors and limited consciousness.

Dipping a small piece of a bitter vegetable into bitter salt-water brings our attention to our own inner bitterness, and to any smallness which may have become, sadly, the baseline of our functioning. We are still in the process of getting rid of or 'murdering', our pettiness, negative lowliness, and inner enslavement to habitual negative behaviors. The saltwater is like the tears we shed as we continue to regret and release ourselves from any action, speech, thought, or state that has confined our spirit. We do not say a special blessing over this Mitzvah (although we do recite a blessing on the vegetable itself), for we are not yet able to see this stage as a 'blessing', rather as something we must do in order to enter into a healthier, more expansive place. We are still embracing and acknowledging our wrong choices, and are filled with bitter regret. This is an important stage in the process of liberation: to feel the bitterness of life. We cannot move forward, and be gifted *Gadlus Sheini* / second level expansiveness, if we do not first acknowledge the bitterness and Katnus of our paradoxical attachment to exile, and all our apparent problems, dramas and issues.*

4) YACHATZ / BREAK THE MIDDLE MATZAH

Publicly breaking the Matzah demonstrates that we are making ourselves vulnerable, opening up to those around us about our brokenness, so that true healing can begin. The fragile egoic sense of 'wholeness' (not to be confused with the inner soul-sense of genuine wholeness), the sense that I am perfect with no room to grow, is a fundamental obstacle for real growth. As we are about to begin the process of liberation, of redemption, of Maggid, we break the Matzah as if to say, 'I am not perfectly whole.' Only then do we begin to recite Maggid over this broken Matzah.

Once we have realized how fragmented and broken we have become, we set this brokenness aside. We take the larger of the broken pieces and hide it for later, to be internalized as the Afikoman at the end of the meal. For now, we need to put aside the fragmented parts of ourselves, the brokenness, the Katnus,

* The word *Karpas* in numerical value is 360, as the Arizal points out. This is the numerical value of the letter Shin spelled out: Shin (300), Yud (10), Nun (50) = 360. Shin itself is 300. 300 is the five letter Name Elokim spelled out: *Aleph* is spelled Aleph (1), Lamed (30), Pei (80) = 111. *Lamed* is spelled Lamed (30), Mem (40), Dalet (4) = 74. *Hei* is spelled Hei (5), Yud (10) = 15. *Yud* is spelled Yud (10), Vav (6), Dalet (4) = 20. *Mem* is spelled Mem (40), Mem (40) = 80. 111+74+15+20+80=300. The Name Elokim is connected with *Din* / strict judgment, the Divine Power which sets limitations, boundaries and constrictions. In this way, says the Arizal, Karpas is all about Din and the world of Katnus.

and guard them until we can finally elevate and reintegrate them into our personality and sense of self.

It is the middle Matzah that we break. The middle Matzah corresponds to the world of *Gevurah* / severity and strength. When we become aware of the parts of us that are underdeveloped and broken, and yet we do not react towards them but rather save them for a later reintegration, this itself is an act of Gevurah. Only later on in the Seder, when the self feels more complete and whole, can we integrate the broken parts of self in a healthy and holistic manner. Waiting for this state of consciousness to emerge shows deep strength, courage, and self-mastery. Some things need more time to assimilate, and rushing such a process when we are not yet fully equipped can cause more harm than good.

5) MAGGID / RECITE THE HAGGADAH

In Maggid we recite the Haggadah. The word *Maggid* can also mean *Megged* / "sweet." The word מגד, says Rashi, refers to dainties and sweet foods (*Devarim*, 33:13). The beginning of our inner redemption, the *Hamtakah* / sweetening of all the *Dinim* / judgments, constrictions, inner limitations and exiles, thus begins with Maggid.

As explored earlier, the construct of the exile in Egypt is represented by Klal Yisrael's exile of *Dibbur* / speech. Their capacity to speak and to express their experience and true identity was compromised and in peril. They were externally and internally enslaved by Pharaoh, whose name can be split into two words, *Peh Ra* / bad mouth. On the night of Pesach (*Peh Sach* / the mouth that speaks) we sit down to the Seder and recount, debate and elaborate on the Exodus story. We are thus freeing ourselves by freeing our speech. True freedom of speech is not merely a freedom to express 'anything'; it is not a freedom to speak nonsense or empty, harmful words. Rather it is a freedom to express oneself from within one's rich inner life, sharing this dimension of our being with the outside world. To move meaningful sound outward, the Ruach emerging from our inner Neshamah, as explored, is genuine inner redemption.

Slaves do not have a voice. A person who is literally a slave is physically and mentally uprooted from their ability to express their desires and longing — so much so that eventually, through their deep trauma, they lose their connection to the root of their inner life. Finally, they have nothing to talk about; nothing from the inside needs to come out, because the inside has collapsed or atrophied. At first, they were forced to remain quiet, but over time, their muteness became ontological. Similarly, an individual who is in an inner exile — experiencing 'enslavement' to their addictions or whims, shallowness or narrow-mindedness — becomes unable to imagine, let alone speak about, another possibility.

On this night, we are given freedom from both outer and inner forms of enslavement. HaKadosh Baruch Hu schleps us out from our exile and gives us the Mitzvah of Maggid. This Mitzvah brings forth our ability to express our collective disentanglement from the bondage of Egypt, and our personal extrication from our exile in ego. It allows us to give voice to our yearnings and dreams, and to put words to our aspirations and hopes.

By the end of this process, we reach the level of freedom in which we are able to speak, and now we have what to speak about. When we can articulate our dreams of freedom which have been buried deep inside, we can begin to understand them, and begin to manifest them in the world of speech.

True freedom of speech is also connected to possessing the inner freedom to express the goodness of life. During this stage of Maggid, we declare the truth of our inner freedom, and the stage of 'sweetening' begins.

6) RACHTZAH / WASH HANDS FOR BREAD

At this point, we have risen and been extricated from our inner exiles to the point that we are now capable of washing our hands with a blessing. We are no longer merely 'washing away the negative', as we did in the second Siman, rather we are experiencing our own inner purity and the blessing of being alive and of moving forward.

Rachtzah comes from the Talmudic Aramaic word *Rachitz* / 'trust', as in *Bei Ana Rachitz* / 'In Him do I trust.' Now that we have articulated our dreams and hopes of true physical, emotional, mental and spiritual freedom, we can experience true faith. We have the freedom to once again believe. Sadly, sometimes a person is so stuck in *Katnus* / smallness, narrow vision, or inner enslavement, that they no longer even dream or have hope that something different, let alone wonderful, is possible. In Maggid we broke open the floodgates of our inner (and collective) psyche, the inner, truer self became revealed again, and now we can begin to live with hope and optimism again. We are hopeful for our own lives, and hopeful for the world. We are open again to trust that there is an ever unfolding historical and cosmic process towards redemption. We have a deeper certainty that while our life, and the world at large, may seem chaotic and in disarray, unfocused and aimless, or even regressive and getting ever harder, there is a grand plan. לא ידח ממנו נידח / "No one banished from Him by his sins will remain banished" (*Shmuel* 2, 14:14), and, וכבר הבטיחה תורה שסוף ישראל לעשות תשובה / "Indeed, the Torah already assured us that in the end, at the close of the period of exile, Israel will turn in repentance (Rambam, *Hilchos Teshuvah*, 7:5. *Sanhedrin*, 97b). In the end, all souls will be redeemed,* and eventually the physical world itself will follow,

---

* *Torah Ohr*, Yisro, 73d. All souls will reach their Tikkun, as the Alter Rebbe writes שבודאי סופו לעשות תשובה, בגלגול זה או בגלגול אחר, כי לא ידח ממנו נדח / "It is certain that he will ultimately repent, whether in this incarnation or another, since 'No one banished from Him by his sins will remain banished'": *Tanya*, Chap. 39. In the words of the Emek haMelech (*Tikkunei Teshuvah*, 3): ועתה בנים שמעו לי יראת ד' אלמדכם ואהבתו הק' עמנו בני א-ל חי, למה לו כולי האי לטרוח עצמו ברשעים האלו המכעיסים אותו בכל עת ובכל רגע, ב' תשובות בדבר התשובה הא' כו' אע"פ שהם רשעים גמורים כו' ניצוצי קדושה בהם כו' שהם נצר

at the *G'mar haYichud* / the final and complete revelation of the Unity of Hashem.

'Water' is a metaphor for wisdom, and especially Torah, Divine wisdom: אין מים אלא תורה / "(in certain contexts) 'water' refers only to Torah" (*Bava Kama*, 82a). In the times of Moshiach and redemption, the world will be filled and awash with Divine wisdom, as water covers the sea, as the Rambam concludes his masterpiece, ולא יהיה עסק כל העולם אלא לדעת את ה' בלבד. ולפיכך יהיו ישראל חכמים גדולים ויודעים דברים הסתומים וישיגו דעת בוראם כפי כח האדם. שנאמר כי מלאה הארץ דעה את ה' כמים לים מכסים / "The world will only be engaged in knowing Hashem. Then there will be very wise people who will understand the deep, sealed matters. They will achieve knowledge of the Creator to as high a degree as humanly possible, as it says, 'For the Earth shall be filled with knowledge of Hashem, as the waters cover the sea'" (*Hilchos Melachim*, 12:5).

מטעי כו' והיא חלק אלקה היא נצחי כו' והנשמות הם רושם אור עצמותו וכל הנופח מעצמותו הוא נופח כו' ועוד טעם שני מעשה ידי להתפאר כו' הק' הוא ומעשה ידיו חיים וקיימים לעד ולעולמי עולמים ואי אפשר שתתבטל כו'.

כל ישראל יש להם חלק לעוה"ב כו' רק In the words of the Alshich haKodesh, שזה יתקן עצמו בזמן מועט וזה בזמן מרובה אבל סופם הוא להמנות עם הצדיקים ומשום זה שהקב"ה כביכול מטריח את עצמו עם רשעים כאלו לתקנם כו' ולמה כן בשביל שהם נצר מטעי שהוא נצחיי והם רושם אור עצמותו וכל הנופח מעצמו הוא נופח / "All of Israel have a share in the World to Come.... Whether he rectifies himself in a short time or a long time, in the end, one is nevertheless counted among the Tzadikim. And because of this, HaKadosh Baruch Hu, so to speak, troubles Himself with (even) those immersed in deliberate evil, in order to rectify them. And why is this so? Because they, too, are 'My planting in which I take pride,' which is an eternal fact. And they, too, are a residue of the Light of Hashem's Essence, and all who are 'inflated' with ego are (originally) 'inflated' from (within the state of) His Divine Essence." See also *Igros Kodesh*, the Rebbe, 1:85.

This is another deeper reason why we wash our hands at this point. Hands represent the world of action, this physical world. Washing our hands (or immersing our hands in a Mikvah) reflects the state of the world in the times of Moshiach, in which our *Emunah* / faith and *Bitachon* / trust in positivity and in redemption will finally be realized and actualized.

7) MOTZI / BLESSING OVER BREAD

We now recite the blessing over bread: "You are the Source of Blessings… *HaMotzi Lechem Min haAretz* / Who Extracts Bread from the Earth."

Not only do we have trust that there is an unfolding redemptive process, and that we and the entire world will eventually reach a Messianic state, we believe this so deeply that we are ready to recite a blessing, the HaMotzi blessing, over a broken piece of bread (as explained earlier, the blessing of HaMotzi applies also to the broken Matzah). We are at a level where we can now declare a blessing on brokenness, a blessing on being only a "half." In this blessing there is an acknowledgment of our brokenness, and yet a realization that "There is nothing more complete than a broken heart." In fact, we recognize that it is precisely our brokenness, our spiritual frustration, that compelled us to grow into who we are at this moment and who we are becoming. In a mysterious way, there is completeness in brokenness, light hidden within darkness.

Once we can acknowledge and truly assimilate this profound awareness — that even deep within 'concealment' HaKadosh Baruch Hu can be found — this itself causes the darkness and concealment to fade, and one moves "from slavery to freedom, from sorrow to joy, and from mourning to festivity, and from deep darkness to great light and from bondage to redemption," as we have just declared at the end of Maggid. When our brokenness becomes wholeness, it is a great cause for praise and blessing.

Motzi / 'extracted' is technically a past tense verb, yet in the blessing we use it as if it is present tense. Because of this, the term *HaMotzi* is debated in the Gemara, whether it means past or present (future) tense (*Berachos*, 38b). Yet, *HaMotzi* is the *Nusach* / liturgy of the blessing (*Tosefos*, the Rashba, and Rosh ad loc, all bring from the Yerushalmi, that the reason the law follows *HaMotzi* (although all agree that *Motzi* is past tense), is so that the Mem of *Olam* should not be connected to the Mem of *Motzi* and avoid a slip of the tongue. The Ben Yehoyada writes that we say the word *HaMotzi* with an emphasis on the letter Hei, consistent with the Kavanos of the Arizal on the letter Hei of *HaMotzi*). We are thanking Hashem for "extracting bread from the earth." The obvious question is, is that true? Does bread grow like vegetables from the earth, and wait to simply be 'extracted' and eaten? Wheat does grow from the earth, but not as ready-made *Lechem* / bread.

The Medrash (*Bereishis Rabbah*, 15:7) brings a debate between our sages: is HaMotzi past tense, 'extracted,' referring to the pre-sin state of Gan Eden, in which no bread-making process was needed and bread indeed grew out of the earth — or is *HaMotzi* in the future tense, "will extract," referring to the Messianic era when bread will again grow from the ground, just as ready-to-wear clothes will grow from trees?

In our present state of exile, we exist in a paradigm of division; present vs. future, process vs. result, action vs. reaction. There is always a distinction between potential and actual, effort and result, process and goal, means and end. We learn, and then we know; we harvest wheat and then we make bread. This is the world of *Pirud* / separation. In the paradigm of *Yichud* / unity, there is no separation between the 'tree' and the 'fruit'; the process and the result. In the primordial reality of Eden, 'bread grew from the earth' and in the ultimate Messianic era of Yichud, 'bread will grow from the earth', since in the state of Yichud, fruition of all kinds is effortless and spontaneous. Thus, in the Messianic era, no one will have to teach anyone else: "You will all know Me." Just as there will be no need to process food, there will be no lengthy process of teaching and learning.

On every night of the year (except fast days), we may recite *HaMotzi Lechem* / "Who extracts (actual) bread from the earth," even though the bread in our hands did need to go through a lengthy process of refinement until it became nourishing and satisfying. On Seder Night, we hold a broken piece of bread, a broken poor man's bread, bread of slavery — and yet we can honestly declare that we believe that the process of cosmic refinement will immediately reach completion and fruition, exile will end, darkness will dissipate, death will be overcome, tears will be wiped away, and 'bread will grow from the earth'. On this night we truly know it and believe it, even (or especially) from amidst our brokenness.

This is the Emunah and Bitachon of Pesach. Completion and redemption have happened in the past, and will surely happen in the future. The present is merely a holding station between past and future which contains a *Nekudah* / point of both the past and of the future, right now. The past and future redemptions are therefore felt as immediately present at this moment in the Seder.

Inwardly, on this night, we know that we too are vested with the Divine gift of Yichud, and we too can "extract" *Lechem* / bread, substance, or life, light, meaning, and purpose, from the "earth." No matter how low we fall, how disconnected we feel, even if we are so depressed that we feel like everybody is walking all over us, as if we are the "earth" below their feet, we are empowered to "extract" *Chayus* / life and *Ohr* / light from the depths of this darkness. We know that the darkness will end and eventually everything will be only light, and our job right now is to find HaKadosh Baruch Hu, the *Nekudah* / point of Light within all the concealments of cosmic and personal exile.

Regarding exile, the Pasuk says, ובקשתם משם את ה' אלקיך ומצאת / "And you shall seek Hashem your G-d *from there*, and you will find Him" (*Devarim*, 4:29). "From there" means 'from that very place of darkness,' for *Davka* / specifically from that place we will find the Divine Presence.

Such is our Emunah on this night of cosmic and personal redemption.

8) MATZAH / EAT THE MATZAH

At this point, we are ready to literally and figuratively eat the "bread of faith," to internalize and make Emunah a visceral part of our bodies and our physical constitution, as it were.

As the Zohar teaches, Matzah is the "bread of faith" and the "bread of healing" (*Zohar* 2, 41a. 2, 183b). Indeed, the very 'faith' that is revealed on Seder Night brings 'healing', wholeness, and wholesomeness.

We left Egypt in great haste, without our bread having time to rise, and thus we ate Matzah; we left in such haste, and with such faith that HaKadosh Baruch Hu would provide, that we did not take any provisions for our journey through the Desert. This is why Matzah embodied, and embodies ever since then, our complete Emunah.

When we eat Matzah on this night, the simple and unassuming unification of flour and water, we are acting out our faith in HaKadosh Baruch Hu and drawing more and more Emunah into our body, heart, mind, and soul. Eating Matzah is an expression of our Emunah manifest in the world of action.

Matzah in small numerical value is 18 (Mem/4, Tzadik/9, Hei/5 = 18), which is the same value as the word *Chai* / life. Matzah is nurturing and life-affirming. Faith in HaKadosh Baruch Hu, and by extension, faith in the goodness of life itself, restores vitality and brings about all forms of mental, emotional and even physical healing. Ingesting Matzah draws this faith into our bones and essence, along with all forms of healing.

Matzah is numerically 136, which is the same value as the word *Mamon* / money. By eating Matzah, internalizing the bread of faith, we bring down blessings into our lives until they are reflected in the most physical phenomena, including monetary wealth.

בלע מצה יצא / *Bala Matzah Yatza* / "One who swallows Matzah (without tasting it still) fulfills the obligation," as Matzah symbolically represents pure faith that is Transcendent, beyond *Ta'am* / 'reason' and 'taste', as it were. As such, in full numerical value, *Matzah* is 136 (Mem/40, Tzadik/90, Hei/5, with the word itself = 136), the same as the word צום / *Tzom* / fasting. Matzah is 'beyond' the world of taste and food, beyond the reasoning and understanding which satisfy the mind.

Yet, much like faith itself, while transcendent in nature, Matzah permeates our consciousness. Matzah comes from a world beyond Ta'am and intellect, yet it infuses the mind as well, and it is still connected with *Da'as* / mind and awareness. שאין התינוק יודע לקרות "אבא" ו"אמא" עד שיטעום טעם דגן / "A child does not know how to call out *Abba* / "Father!" or *Ima* /

"Mother!" (hinting to the 'intellect' of Abba and Ima) until he tastes grain" (*Berachos*, 40a). Thus, Matzah is specifically connected to the Da'as that gives one the ability to call to and connect with our Divine Parent (and also the ability to synthesize and internalize the intellect of Abba and Ima, Chochmah and Binah).

So, on the one hand Matzah is beyond taste, beyond 'reason', yet it suffuses our Da'as and conscious awareness with both of these qualities. In fact, Matzah is the *Tikkun Cheit Eitz ha-Da'as* / Rectification of the Tree of Knowledge, in which human consciousness lost its simple connection with HaKadosh Baruch Hu. It is the healing of our splintered awareness.

Matzah and Wine are both connected with the rectification of the Tree of Knowledge. Among the "fruits" suggested by Chazal eaten by Adam and Eve in the Garden of Eden were grapes and wheat. During the Seder we therefore eat wheat, Matzah, and drink grape Wine, fixing our primal mistake and creating a repair for human Da'as.

Ever since we damaged our Da'as by eating from the Tree of Knowledge, our faculty of awareness has been distorted and incomplete. The beginning of the exile started when Hashem told Avraham, "Know, you shall know, that your descendants will be strangers in a foreign land for 400 years" (*Bereishis*, 15:13). The root word repeated in the phrase, "Know, you shall know," is *Da*. Regarding the exile in Egypt, the Arizal teaches it was an exile of Da'as, of awareness. An exile of Da'as is the root of the Egyptian Exile, and the Egyptian Exile is the root of all subsequent exiles. This is not only true ontologically but also epistemologically; whenever Da'as is lacking or obscured, the result is a descent into internal and eventually external exile (*Me'or Einayim*, Va'era).

When Moshe comes before Pharaoh and says, "Let my people go," Pharaoh replies, "Who is G-d? I *know* him not" (*Shemos*, 5:2). Thus, the whole objective of the plagues was so that the Egyptians would "*know* that I am Hashem" (7:5), and also that the People of Israel would "*know* that I am Hashem..." (*Shemos*, 6:7). We do our part in the Tikkun for Da'as by internalizing the Matzah and wine of the Seder. Yet, eating Matzah is a Torah law and drinking the wine is only a Rabbinic law, thus Matzah creates a much greater Tikkun.

Matzah is the only remaining 'Mitzvah of eating' of the entire year that is a Torah law. In the times of the Beis ha-Mikdash, there were many other eating related Torah-based Mitzvos, such as eating the *Korbanos* / offerings from the Beis haMikdash. Today, the only remaining Mitzvah of eating (as the Chasom Sofer points out: *Choshen Mishpat*, Hashmatos, Siman 196), is the Mitzvah of eating Matzah. In this way, eating the Matzah has the ability to create a Tikkun for all our eating throughout the entire year. On this night we have the power to elevate all of our consumption through eating Matzah.

At this point in the Seder, we have internalized our faith and integrated our Emunah so deeply that we are now even ready to 'eat' our *bitterness*.

9) MAROR / EAT BITTER HERBS

Earlier we awakened the *Emunah* / true faith and *Bitachon* / trust that eventually we will emerge, individually and collectively from exile to redemption, from darkness to light, from oppression to freedom, and essentially from bitterness to sweetness. Now we are ready to go ahead and directly transform bitterness into sweetness through the eating of Maror.

Maror represents the world of 'death', alienation, estrangement and bitterness (*Maves* / death and *Maror* have the same numerical value). Today, when we no longer have the Beis ha-Mikdash and still live in an existential state of exile, eating Maror is only a Rabbinic law (as discussed previously). On an inward level, in exile, we live in an ontological state of bitterness. For this reason, there is no real need ('Torah law') for internalizing an extra measure of bitterness; we already have enough. There does not need to be a 'command', a Mitzvah, to go out of our way to sense or encounter bitterness; we have it in spades just from life itself.

In any case, Maror is eaten specifically after we have eaten the 'bread of faith' of the middle, broken Matzah and the top, full Matzah. The top complete, unified Matzah represents the letter Yud, singularity, unity, Chochmah. The middle, broken Matzah represents the "bread of affliction" and the "bread of freedom," the world of Binah. Now that we have drawn down this higher, deeper *Mochin* / intelligence, clarity and faith, and internalized it, we are ready to internalize the Maror.

In other words, after we have eaten the 'bread of faith', we can go back and sweeten the bitterness of the past. We do this by taking a piece of Maror, a bitter herb, and dipping it into the sweet Charoses. Our bitterness has a slightly sweet taste now, as we realize that the negativity of the past is precisely what has stimulated us to move forward in life. The bitterness of our situation is what created the longing for something different and better. We now understand the positive value of our bitter experiences, and we are able to even 'make a blessing' over them.

As explained, we sweeten the bitterness of Maror by dipping it into the sweet Charoses. Yet, there is an even higher, deeper, more profound form of transformation, in which the bitterness is healed and sweetened by the bitterness itself. In the Torah, when the people, soon after leaving Egypt, were complaining that they had nothing to drink, as the waters were bitter, Hashem tells Moshe to throw a piece of wood into the water (*Shemos*, 15:25). Chazal tell us that this was a 'bitter' piece of wood. And Rabban Shimon Ben Gamliel said, בא וראה כמה מופרשין דרכי הקדוש ברוך הוא מדרכי בשר ודם, בשר ודם במתוק מרפא את המר אבל הקדוש ברוך הוא מרפא את המר במר / "Come and see how transcendent the ways of HaKadosh Baruch Hu are in comparison to the ways of man; in our world, bitter is healed with sweet, but HaKadosh Baruch Hu heals the bitter with the bitter" (*Mechilta d'Rebbe Yishmael*, Beshalach, 15:25). Eating the Maror, the bitterness itself (even without dipping into Charoses), has the power to transform the bitterness of exile into sweetness.

Bitterness has therefore been transformed on a meta and inward level, and also symbolically on a literal level. The nature of horseradish, one of the items most prevalently used as Maror, is that the more one chews it the sweeter it becomes — bite into it and it is initially very sharp, yet, the more you chew on it the sweeter it tastes. The sharpness of this root vegetable comes from a natural chemical, allyl isothiocyanate, as well as other volatile oils. When the root is cut or grated, the horseradish's natural chemicals are acted on by enzymes, thus developing its characteristic pungent odor and flavor. These complex flavors — heat, intensity, and biting sharpness — are sweetened by saliva, for most people's mouths have an enzyme, amylase, which breaks down certain foods into simple sugars. In any case, the more you chew on Maror, the sweeter it becomes.

The Mishnah (*Pesachim*, 39a) mentions five types of vegetables that a person can eat to fulfill his obligation to eat bitter herbs on Pesach. What is the sign or indication to know if a vegetable you have is one of these five? Says the Gemara, רבי יהודה אומר: כל שיש לו שרף. רבי יוחנן בן ברוקה אומר כל שפניו מכסיפין. / אחרים אומרים: [כל] ירק מר יש לו שרף ופניו מכסיפין / "Rebbe Yehudah says: any plant that has sap (when it is cut, may be used as Maror). Rebbe Yochanan ben Beroka says: anything whose surface is light (green may be used as Maror). Others say: any bitter herb that has sap and whose surface is light (green is fit for this Mitzvah)." Upon this Gemara, Rashi teaches that sap refers to a white that emanates from the vegetable when cut. On a metaphoric level, bitter 'Maror' is something that has a 'whiteness' hidden within it, an element of Chesed (even though at this time it is bitter).*

Chazal tell us that **בלע מרור לא יצא** / *Bala Maror Lo Yatza* / "If you swallow Maror [without chewing] you did not fulfill the obligation" (*Pesachim*, 115b). Unlike the Matzah, we need to taste the Maror and 'experience' it, as it were. Part of tasting is chewing the food to release its deeper flavors. The Arizal teaches (*Sha'ar haKavanos*, Pesach Derush 6) that to eat Maror we need to chew it with our teeth, and by doing so we are *Mamtik* / sweetening *Din* / judgment and concealment.

There are 32 teeth in a grown human being, connected with the '32 paths of Chochmah' through which we can break down all Dinim and elevate them (Arizal, *Likutei Torah*, Ekev). And so, we need to use our teeth and the slow process of breaking down the Maror, and not just swallow it directly (See also Rameh miPano, *Mayan Ganim* 3, Seder Pesach). Swallowing would skip over

---

* These five types of Maror vegetables are connected to the five impure colors of blood that a woman can experience (during the 'bitterness', or hardships, of menstruation and childbirth) — חמשה דמים טמאים באשה האדום והשחור והקרן כרכום וכמימי אדמה וכמזוג: *Niddah*, 19a. Yet, just like with the Maror, there is a sweetening, a transformation of these 'red bloods', the world of *Din* / harshness, and after birth, because of the birth, there is no 'red' blood (איבריה מתפרקין הימנה ואין נפשה חוזרת עליה עד עשרים וארבעה חדש), rather on a deeper, alternative level, דם נעכר ונעשה חלב / the blood is transformed into milk: *Bechoros*, 6b. The red blood becomes the white milk of Chesed that nurtures and nourishes the young infant, and then is ultimately transformed into the infant's pure, life-giving blood. See *Sha'ar haKavanos*, Derushei Pesach, 9.

the conscious process of breaking down the Maror and releasing its deeper, hidden sweetness. We need such processes so we can truly digest the 'Maror' experiences of our lives and reveal the hidden sweetness, the light of redemption and elevation, in them.

מרור / *Maror* has a numerical value of 446, the same as the word מות *Maves*, 'death' (*Sha'ar haKavanos*, Ibid). Living through the traumas of life, one cannot honestly deny life's darkness and various forms of 'death'. Yet, when we come through difficult experiences we are often grateful for the deeper clarity and redemption that they bring us. This is because with processing our experiences, there is a *Hamtakah* / sweetening of the aspect of 'death' in them. When we can look back on our past and retroactively behold the Divine light that was always there, shining within the darkness, then we are also filled with Emunah and Bitachon for the future.

Once we have internalized the "bread of freedom," tasting and feeling the 'death' of challenging experiences helps us move through them and get beyond them. By chewing long enough on these pieces of 'Maror' we get to the Nekudah of sweetness hidden within all of life.

10) KORECH /
EATING THE MATZAH AND MAROR SANDWICH

In this stage, not only are we able to chew through the difficult parts of life and get to the Nekudah of sweetness within, at this juncture we are also able to place the 'bitterness of exile', the apparent hardships of life, into a 'sandwich' with (the offering of Pesach, and) the 'bread of faith', 'healing' and 'freedom'. Interincluding Maror and Matzah in this way means unifying and elevating affliction to the paradigm of liberation.

Maror represents the *Yetzer haRa*, negative inclination, but more appropriately ego, the place of human drive and desire. Now we take the Maror and place it within the context of the humble, selfless *Yetzer Tov* — Matzah, representing our ability to serve and come to life from a place of *beChol Levavcha* / "with all your hearts" — with both our 'hearts' or inclinations. This refers to a state of consciousness in which both our defined creative and limitless destructive impulses are enlisted in the spiritual efforts of a fully realized individual. Both one's selfish survival instinct as well as one's selfless spiritual intuition are united. In this way, we are elevating even the destructive inclination, integrating it, and allowing it to serve transcendence. Death, ego, and slavery are now sweetened, absorbed and transformed into a context of holiness.

Our inner liberation comes about when we are able to sandwich all the components of life, the bitter and the sweet, the difficult and the easy, within a greater context of faith and liberation.

II) SHULCHAN ORECH / THE YOM TOV MEAL

Our 'table' is set and we are now spiritually prepared to eat our meal. We are able to partake of physical pleasures, not only spiritual ones, for now everything is illuminated. On this level, we are bringing *Gadlus* / expansive consciousness into the most external, base reality, the world of food and physical enjoyment.

All creatures eat, including even plants. Eating for survival is one of the most natural things we do, and yet, at this stage of the Seder, in which all of life is included, sweetened and elevated, eating becomes a sacred, transcendent and transformational act.

12) TZAFUN: HIDDEN

All of our life has now been reclaimed, sweetened, and elevated, even our mundane activities such as eating. Now we are ready to go back into the past to retrieve and 'eat', or internalize, the Afikoman — the fragmented, broken parts of self that we needed to *Tzafun* / 'hide away' earlier in the Seder, so that we could move forward into liberation. These parts include old hurts as well as deeper insights that we weren't yet ready to internalize and understand. Rather than leave them swept under the rug or in perpetual storage, we must now reclaim, integrate, and elevate them.

Customarily, the children are the ones who find and bring us the Afikoman (Meiri, *Pesachim*, 109a). Children can stimulate our incomplete areas of self-actualization, and they also bring back our innocent inner child so we can see the world with joyful purity and wonder.

The word *Tikkun* / rectification, wholeness, can be rearranged to spell the word *Tinok* / child. This is because our full Tikkun is to reconnect with our 'inner child' and live with a sense of pure wonder and radical amazement. The child within us brings us that healing. He or she allows us to sweeten even our pre-verbal pain and traumas; everything can now be rectified and sweetened.

Tzafun is the 'dessert' of the meal, and desserts are normally sweet, as the Gemara (*Megilah*, 7b), says: רווחא לבסימא שכיח / "Room in the stomach for sweets can always be found (even if one ate already)." In this way, the Afikoman creates a grand sweetening of our entire lives.

13) BEIRACH / GRACE AFTER THE MEAL

Having created a *Yichud* / 'unification' within every dimension of our past, as all is sweetened, we can now see everything in our lives as a *Berachah* / blessing. We are able to bless and thank Hashem for everything — every single detail of our lives, every single moment, and every last experience, even what previously seemed trivial or painful. We 'bless' as we see blessings, and we ask Hashem that we too become sources of blessing.

14) HALLEL / CHANTING THE HALLEL

At this stage, not only can we see all of life as a blessing — thanking Hashem even for the hardships and challenges from which we have learned and grown — but now looking back and owning all of our life, we can even 'sing praise' to Hashem for those very challenges.

Indeed, the prophet speaks of a time when we can all look back at our entire history and say, 'Thank You': ואמרת ביום ההוא אודך ה' כי אנפת בי / "On that day you shall say: 'I give thanks to You, Hashem, although (or 'because') You were angry with me'" (*Yeshayahu*, 12:1).

The word Hallel means both 'to praise' and 'to shine'. As we sing these ecstatic praises, we shine, revealing the light that was hidden deep within the darkness of our lives and history.

15) NIRTZAH / ACCEPTED

At last, everything is Nirtzah, 'accepted'; we have arrived. There is nothing more to do or say. This is a state of pure being, but it is paradoxically the 'action' we need to take at the end of the Seder. Nirtzah is thus an expression of our faith that if we have performed the Seder as prescribed, then we are certain that its effects are accepted on High. The *Avodah* / spiritual and intellectual 'work' of Nirtzah is to banish all skepticism and doubt regarding whether the Seder really achieved what it is meant to achieve. If there is still somehow an inner voice that asserts, 'After all is said and done, we are still the exact same people as the ones who entered the Seder,' this negative voice needs to be quieted. We need to linger in this spaciousness and state of repose and accept the fact that the transformative power of the Seder is real. All of our efforts are accepted. HaKadosh Baruch Hu loves us and delights in our

Avodah. Our deepest level of soul is now revealed, and we are one with the One.

The truth is, in this moment of acceptance, we have truly attained a state of pure and wordless stillness, an inner world of perfect unity, and a level of spiritual, mental, emotional and physical liberation.

The following forty-nine days of "counting the Omer" will be a period in which we assimilate and aspire to embody this liberation, the freedom of Nirtzah, the great sweetening of all reality.

The 15 Simanim in Short Practical Steps:

1) The first step is to be willing to move forward and let go of the past. First we step out of our smallness and choose to move into a more expansive state. Then, as a result, we are given the gift of *Gadlus* / greatness.

2) Having activated and accessed our inherent greatness, we can now re-enter the place of our 'smallness'. We begin by acknowledging it and then washing it away, thereby disassociating and detaching from it.

3) ...As we do so, we sensitize ourselves to feel the bitterness of our smallness, as we are not yet able to see the hidden bless-

ings in it.

4) We thus perform symbolic actions that demonstrate we are humble and vulnerable, ready to be a vessel to receive genuine greatness from Above.

5) Now begins the process of redemption, unleashing the power of our hopes, dreams, and aspirations.

6) At this point we have regained our ability to trust.

7) Because of our trust, we are able to say a blessing over all our individual and collective brokenness.

8) ...For this reason, we are now able to integrate, assimilate, and truly live our faith in real time.

9) At this point, our *Emunah* / faith is no longer an abstract, philosophical idea. Rather, it is a concrete, living truth through which we can sense the sweetness and blessing in all of life, the ups and the downs, the highs and the lows.

10) We are then able to unify our highs and lows, and all the extremes of life, in one holy, wholesome context.

11) Now even mundane activities which we share with all life forms, such as eating, are revealed as holy, noble, and meaningful acts.

12) Our highs and lows are sweetened, and so are any hid-

den darker energies or memories. What has been hidden is now reclaimed with a childlike innocence and sense of wonder and delight...

13) ...And now we can recite and declare a blessing on all of life, for we have been redeemed and fulfilled...

14) ...From this state of mature expansiveness, we are moved to praise and thank Hashem for everything and everyone, allowing every breath we breathe to offer praise.

15) And finally, we have arrived. There is nothing more to do. We are home; we now sense that our entire life is accepted and loved, and brilliant as a clear day.

Chapter Three:
A Night of Clarity & Haste

O N THE NIGHT OF PESACH, WE PERFORM A SEDER — an 'order', but not simply a natural, causal order, rather an 'order of miracles', an 'order' that is paradoxically and essentially beyond order.

Miracles are the theme of the night, and in fact, the entire month of Nisan is a *Chodesh haGeulah* / Month of redemption and a month of *Nisim* / miracles (*Pesikta Zutresa,* Bo, 12:2). On this night, the night we left Egypt — the fifteenth day of the month, the night of the full moon — the full expression of the miraculous nature of Nisan is revealed.

Tonight is called ליל שמורים / a night of vigil, or a night that is guarded (*Shemos*, 12:42). It is watched, protected, and reserved, as it is the perfect night for redemption (ליל המשומר ובא מששת ימי בראשית לגאולה: *Rosh Hashanah*, 11b. *HaAmek Davar*, ad loc). It is, as Chazal tell us, ליל המשומר ובא מן המזיקין / a night that remains guarded from demons and harmful spirits of all kinds (*Pesachim*, 109b).

It is a night of protection, as no external or internal negative force has any sway over us. As such, on this night we keep our doors open or unlocked, or at least we open our doors for a few moments of the night (ולפתוח הפתח כדי לזכור שהוא ליל שמורים: Rama, *Orach Chayim*, 480). We are not afraid of the darkness, nor what may lie hidden in the night or lurking 'outside'. We are free from all physical and spiritual, external and internal fears.

On this night, we do away with all opacity and darkness, mental or emotional, real or imagined. This is a night of light, clarity and transparency; it is "the night that shines brighter than day."

GADLUS HAMOCHIN / EXPANDED MIND

On this night, we exist in a place beyond all darkness. Darkness can mean mental, moral or ethical confusion; a blurring of what is right and wrong, good and bad.

On this night, as explored earlier, *Gadlus* / expansiveness is granted to us as a gift from Above. Expansive mind is a world of perfect *Emunah* / faith and *Deveikus* / unity with Hashem.*

In the words of the Chassidic Rebbes, Gadlus is *Klarkeit* / clarity. A place beyond dichotomy or ambiguity. Reality is no longer mixed up, *Tov v'Ra* / good and evil, as it was following the eating from the Tree of Knowledge. The Tree, or 'Reality', of Good and Evil is a blurring of goodness, morality, religiosity, and spirituality; everything in life becomes an admixture of good and evil. When you try to do something good, there is a little bad in it. It is unclear what aspects of the deed are right and wrong, and its truth is tangled in an element of falsehood. On this night, the entire entanglement is nullified in the light of Klarkeit. A Tikkun for the eating of the Tree of Knowledge is the gift of Gadlus, the Tree of Life reality, a reality of perfect clarity.

ALACRITY ARISES FROM CLARITY

One of the reasons why the Matzah is baked "in haste," before it has time to rise, is that alacrity is a result of clarity. The other two Torah-based Mitzvos of the night, eating the Korban Pesach and the Maror (during the times when we made the offering), are to be eaten in haste. The Torah tells us that the offering needs to be roasted and not cooked. 'Cooking'

---

* In fact, Emunah is Deveikus. נודע שהאמונה היא דבקות הנשמה בהקדוש ברוך הוא / "It is known that Emunah is Deveikus of the Neshamah with HaKadosh Baruch Hu": *Toldos Yaakov Yoseph*, Ki Savo. Emunah means joined, unified. האגוזים שאמנן / Nuts that had been strung together: *Uktzin*, 2:5.

takes a longer time — including boiling the water, cutting up the meat, and so forth. Roasting is a quicker process: the entire offering is simply placed over an open fire (הצלי יורה על החפזון / "...roasted indicates haste": *Sefer haChinuch,* Mitzvah 7. *Moreh Nevuchim,* 3:46).

Similarly, Maror is also connected to haste. The Mishnah (*Pesachim,* 2:6) mentions five types of herbs that are considered Maror. The first one mentioned is Chazeres, which is lettuce (and being listed first, it is the preferred vegetable for the performance of the Mitzvah: Rashi, חזרת תנא ברישא אלמא היא קדמי לכולהו: *Pesachim,* 39a (*Shulchan Aruch,* Orach Chayim, 473:5 — ועיקר המצוה בחזרת) besides the phonetic reasons connected to Chazeres). Today, the most common vegetables used for Maror are romaine lettuce and horseradish. Some vegetables, especially root vegetables, need to be cooked before they become edible, but the vegetables that qualify for use as Maror can be uprooted from the ground and eaten right away, alluding to the idea of 'haste'.

Matzah is made from wheat, one of the candidates for the "fruit" that Adam and Chavah ate from the Tree of Knowledge. That wheat was, so-to-speak, Chametz, enflaming their Yetzer haRa. Now we create a Tikkun for the Tree of Knowledge by baking our wheat Matzah in great haste, and not letting it become Chametz. Also, in order to fulfill the Mitzvah of eating Matzah, we need to eat it quickly. Similarly, Maror needs to be eaten quickly and not leisurely. Our sages debate the time span within which we need to eat the given *Shiur* / volume of Matzah, and that of the Maror.

The shortest opinion is two minutes, while the longest is nine minutes.[*] Even the latter can require efficiency and alacrity. The same is true with the drinking of the wine. Wine and

---

[*] Even though if one swallows Matzah without tasting it, he is *Yotzei* / fulfilling his obligation: *Pesachim*, 115b. Yet, while we need to eat quickly, we should not stuff our mouth, because that is not דרך אכילה / the normal way of eating, and the Mitzvah is to "eat" Matzah; one would not be Yotzei on the Mitzvah of Matzah if their act was דילמא אתי למיכל אכילה גסה — ואינה אכילה...אכילה גסה אכילה אחת שנפשו קצה מלאכול ועל אותה פטור ביוה"כ: *Tosefos*, Pesachim, 107b. For example, if one grinds the Matzah in water he is not Yotzei, as it is not *poor man's bread* any longer (*Chulin*, 120a), and it is not דרך אכילה, as Tosefos writes, הוה מצי למימר נמי אכילה כתיב ביה. More pointedly, the Gemara says כל איסורין שבתורה אין לוקין עליהן אלא דרך אכילתן...כל איסורין שבתורה אין לוקין עליהן אלא דרך הנאתן / "All prohibitions against eating in the Torah, one may be flogged for violating them only if he eats the prohibited item in its usual manner of consumption...all prohibitions against deriving benefit in the Torah, one is flogged for violating them only if he derives benefit from the prohibited item in the usual manner": *Pesachim*, 24b. This is with regards to transgression, the question is whether the same principle applies to positive Mitzvos. *Mishneh laMelech* debates whether it is a prohibition of eating or a Mitzvah to eat — the type of eating that constitutes a transgression or Mitzvah is an eating of דרך הנאה / way of normal enjoyment: יש לחקור בהא דק"ל דכל איסורין שבתורה אין לוקין עליהם שלא כדרך הנאתן אם נאמר ג"כ במ"ע דרדחמנא אמר תאכל כגון מצה וקרבן פסח אם אכלן שלא כדרך הנאתן אם יצא י"ח. ונראה דלא שנא דכי היכי דבמצות ל"ת דרחמנא אמר לא תאכל אמרינן דאם אכלו שלא כדרך הנאתו דפטור משום דלא מיקרי אכילה ה"נ במ"ע דרחמנא אמר תאכל אם אכלו שלא כדרך הנאתו לא יצא י"ח משום דלא שמיה אכילה אלא שלא ראיתי כעת דין זה בפירוש: *Mishneh laMelech*, Rambam, Hilchos Yesodei haTorah, 5:8. See also *Minchas Chinuch*, Mitzvah 6. *Sha'ar haMelech*, ad loc. Rav Elchanan writes that it is a *Klal Gadol* / great principle of the Torah that one fulfills his obligation only when the act is performed *k'Darko* / in its proper form: *Kovetz Shiurim*, Pesachim, 24b. *Kesuvos*, Os 202 (besides when there is a special teaching that teaches us otherwise: *Sanhedrin*, 54a). See also *Eglei Tal*, Pesichah.

grapes are also, according to one opinion, the foods Adam and Chavah ate from the Tree of Knowledge. On Pesach night there is a custom to try to drink the entire cup (or most of it) in a single gulp. Again, this is the idea of quickness in eating and in drinking. Although throughout the year the principle is לא ישתה אדם כוסו בבת אחת ואם שתה ה"ז גרגרן / "A person should not drink his cup of wine all at once, and if he did drink in this manner, he is (to be considered) a greedy drinker" (*Beitza*, 25b. *Shulchan Aruch*, Orach Chayim, 170:8), however, on the night of Pesach the custom is to attempt to drink the entire cup (*Bach*, Orach Chayim, 472), or most of it, and to do so in one quick gulp (ולכתחלה ישתה רוב רביעית בבת אחת: *Magen Avraham*, Ibid, 11).

CLARITY OF MIND

Internally, the idea of haste as it is related to a mindset, is the notion of making quick decisions. With *Klarkeit* / deep clarity, a person has the ability to make the right choices instantaneously. When something is clear, you do not need to procrastinate, ruminate, and chew it over. For example, if you ask a parent if they love their child, the immediate response is 'yes'; there is no hesitation or lingering on the question. Ask someone who just began dating another if they like the other person and the response time may be longer; even a slight uncertainty creates trepidation.

When we know something deeply, it does not take time to think about it. When we get stuck in the 'Tree of Knowledge' perspective, everything is good *and* bad, and there is no clarity.

Then, thinking about it takes time.

On Pesach night, we are gifted with clarity in our mission and purpose, clarity regarding what is holding us back or allowing us to soar. Clarity is sensing Hashem's presence in our lives and being able to easily recognize anything that is obscuring this presence. Clarity is knowing what is truly important and what is nonsense or trivial. Clarity is knowing our loved ones and seeing them for who they truly are. A general spiritual, mental, emotional, and visceral clarity is knowing why we are here, what our purpose is, and what we need to do in this world. This is the gift of the night: *Mochin d'Gadlus* / expansive clarity in all aspects of our life.

Alacrity is an expression of clarity and freedom from confusion and dichotomy. This 'haste' should not be confused with hurriedness, rushing, or impatience. Such modes of behavior only lead to more confusion, compulsion, and mindlessly slipping into unintentional thoughts, words, and actions. Haste comes from total clarity. It is so clear to you, what needs to be done or said, that you can do so right away, immediately.

Matzah is called "poor man's bread." True 'poverty' is a state of mind, a lack of proper awareness and understanding. As our sages tell us, "We have a tradition that no one is poor except one who lacks *Da'as* / awareness and knowledge" (*Nedarim*, 41a).

In this way, eating "poor man's bread" means eating without needing to generate Da'as. On Purim, a month before Pesach, we eat festively in a state of *Lo Yada* / no Da'as, but on Pesach we have mindful intention and Da'as in our eating. 'Poor man's Da'as' would translate as 'quick understanding'. There is no overthinking as we are eating the "bread of faith." Everything is clear and simple to us and our contemplations are simultaneous with our epiphanies, much like the immediate response of a parent regarding loving their child. On Seder night, we have utter, all-encompassing faith and Klarkeit.

INSTANT GADLUS

Haste is a result of Klarkeit, an awesome sense of clarity of purpose and mission, with no need to mull over and process. This form of instantaneous clarity is due to the fact that on the night of Pesach there is a cosmic "skipping over" of process. (Indeed, the חפזון דישראל / haste of Klal Yisrael, (*Berachos*, 9a) mirrored the חפזון שכינה / haste of the Shechinah. *Mechilta*: Bo, 7.)

This night, the night of Yetzias Mitzrayim, is a night of instantaneous transformation, skipping over the rungs of gradual development, straight to the top of a ladder in one jump.

MEMUTZA / INTERMEDIARY - A FULCRUM FOR
INSTANTANEOUS CHANGE

Parenthetically, for instantaneous redemption to occur, for someone to flip directly from slavery into an opposite state of freedom, there needs to be a fulcrum or interface, a *Memutza* / intermediary point between those opposites. For instance, Moshe was born a Jew but lived as an Egyptian prince, allowing him to confront Pharaoh in ways that no other Jew could, and open the way for liberation. He could speak to Pharaoh in his language and understand the slave-owner mentality — yet, being born a Jew, he could also identify with the suffering of Klal Yisrael as slaves. Moshe was also called *Ish Elokim* / 'a G-dly man', meaning that in a certain sense he was a 'man', yet also, so deeply identified with Hashem that he was beyond any conventional human identity. This is a Memutza on the level of *Nefesh* / personal soul.

There is also a Memutza of *Makom* / space. Klal Yisrael lived in Egypt, yet specifically in Goshen, which was a *Nachalah* / inheritance of Sarah (*Pirkei d'Rebbe Eliezer,* 26. *Yalkut Shimoni,* Lech Lecha, 68), and part of greater Eretz Yisrael (Radak, *Yehoshua,* 11:16. *Da'as Zekeinim,* Tosefos, Bereishis, 46:29). The inwardly redemptive Makom of Goshen thus empowered Klal Yisrael to leave Egypt and eventually journey into Eretz Yisrael. Furthermore, Yocheved was born "between the gates," meaning the 'intermediary space' that is both connected to Eretz Yisrael and descending into Egypt. Because she was rooted in this Makom of transition, she was able to give birth to Moshe, who would take them out of Egypt and lead them back toward Eretz Yisrael.

There is also a Memutza of *Zeman* / time. Up until the going out of Egypt, time was basically defined by '*Erev va-Boker*' / evening and morning. A new dimension of time was revealed in the event of Yetzias Mitzrayim: *Chatzos* / midnight. This was not merely *kaChatzos* / 'like midnight' or approximately midnight, but a pinpointing of the precise moment of midnight

(*Berachos*, 3b-4a. Which is a point of time that does not have a Hemshech / flow of time. In the words of the Avnei Nezer, regarding the Berachah for eating Matzah and Maror; דאי אפשר לאכול בחצות ממש, שאין בו המשך זמן כלל. *Shu'T Avnei Nezer*, Orach Chayim, Siman 381:3).

Moshe had at first told the Egyptians that *Makas haBechoros* / the Plague of the Firstborn would happen *ka*Chatzos, but when this plague started, the Torah says, ויהי בחצי הלילה / "And it was (exactly) midnight...." Midnight is a Memutza that connects the hours when it was getting darker to the hours when it is getting lighter. It is thus the *Nosei Hafachim* / 'bearer of opposites', a moment when the opposites of past and future are contained in one moment. 'Midnight' thus refers to the Eternal Present within every moment, which transcends and includes all time. It is the intermediary that allows for radical, instantaneous change — even someone who knows only slavery and degradation and 'has no future' can in one moment become a free person with honor and a bright future.

FROM SLAVES TO ROYAL PRIESTS

Normally, one would think that just like physical wealth is accumulative and gathered gradually, the same would be true of spiritual wealth — that we have to work a lifetime, progressing step by step and rung by rung until we get anywhere. Yet, on the night of *Pesach* / 'skipping over', we simply walk over to the table to begin the Seder and we are instantaneously likened to the *Cohen Gadol* / the High Priest and to a *Melech* / royal sovereign.

Many have a custom to wear a white over-garment (*Kittel*) at the Seder. Besides the reason of inducing humility (המג"א (סי') תע"ב ס"ק ה') והט"ז (שם ס"ק ג') כתבו שנוהגים ללבוש קיטל בעת הסדר שלא תזוח דעתו עליו מפני השמחה, על כן ילבש בגד מתים), the tradition in the name of the Maharal is that donning white garments is to mimic the white garments of the Cohen Gadol, who wore white when he entered into the Holy of Holies in the Beis haMikdash (Recorded in a Haggadah attributed to the Maharal, see also *Gevuros Hashem*, 51: בהגדת המהר"ל (דברי נגידים) כתב: נוהגים ללבוש בגד לבן בליל פסח לעבודת הסדר...וכדמיון זה היה הכהן הגדול משמש ביום הכפורים לפני ולפנים בבגדי לבן, בשביל שהיה קונה (מדרגה העליונה, וליל שמורים הוא כיום הכפורים בזה העניו.

On this night we bring out our finest dishes, and sit totally reclining* "in a manner fit for a king" (Rambam, Pesachim, *Pirush l'Mishnayos*, 10:1: וחייבנו לאכול בהסבה כדי שיאכל כדרך שהמלכים והגדולים אוכלים).* In the times when we offered the Korban Pesach, we ate the meat of the Pesach roasted, and did not leave over any

---

* There are two ways to think about הסיבה / the idea of reclining. Either the purpose of reclining is for *Pirsumei Nisa* / "to reveal the miracle," meaning that our reclining tonight is a demonstration that on this night the going out of Egypt occurred and we became a free people, as Rashi seems to suggest, שיסב כדרך בני חורין זכר לחירות / "all need to recline (even the poor) as the custom of free men, as this is a remembrance of our freedom": Rashi, *Pesachim*, 99b. In the language of the Yerushalmi, לפי שדרך אמר רבי לוי. עבדים להיות אוכלין מעומד. וכאן להיות אוכלין מסובין. להודיע שיצאו מעבדות לחירות: *Pesachim*, 10:1. Or, the purpose of reclining is to show that we are now a free people, today, as implied by the Rambam, וחייבנו לאכול בהסבה כדי שיאכל כדרך שהמלכים והגדולים אוכלים. Or as the Rambam writes in the Yad, בכל דור ודור חיב אדם להראות את עצמו כאלו הוא בעצמו יצא עתה משעבוד מצרים...לפיכך כשסועד אדם בלילה הזה צריך לאכל ולשתות והוא מסב דרך חרות: *Hilchos Chametz U'Matzah*, 7:6-7.

for the morning, much likes kings or wealthy people who eat roasted meat and are not worried about leaving any for the next day, as they trust they will have plenty tomorrow (*Sefer haChinuch*, Mitzvah 6-7. Royalty eats meat roasted: מתנות כהונה אין נאכלות אלא צלי. Why? למשחה לגדולה כדרך שהמלכים אוכלים: *Chulin*, 132b. Even if the Cohen likes all forms of meat preparation, he should eat it roasted, as *Tosefos*, ibid, explains: אבל אדם שטוב לו צלי כשלוק ומבושל יאכל צלי שהוא דרך (גדולה יותר).

On this night, we are infused with Gadlus, all-encompassing greatness, including both the physical greatness of royalty — and the spiritual greatness of the Cohen Gadol when he enters the holiest place on earth, the Holy of Holies. At our Seder we sit like the High Priest and like kings and queens, attaining the highest possible physical, emotional, intellectual, and spiritual heights.[*]

---

[*] According to Halachah, the eating of קדשים קלים / *Kodashim Kalim* / lightly sanctified items, which include the Korban Pesach, is considered eating משלחן גבוה / from the Table of the Most High. As Rashi writes, כי זכו בין כהנים בחזה ושוק בין בעלים בשאר הבשר משלחן גבוה זכו: Rashi, *Bava Kama*, 12b. This is also the opinion of the Rambam. And when we eat "from the Table of the Most High," we should wear special clothes: Netziv, *Imrei Shefer*, Pesichah. Moreover, generally, a Korban Shelamim (which is also eaten by the person offering the Korban) is considered an offering where the King comes to eat by his servant. In the language of the Gemara, עבד שרבו מצפה לאכול על שלחנו / "a servant whose master expects to eat at his table": *Chagigah*, 4b, which could imply that the Master comes to eat at the table of the servant. Whereas the Korban Pesach is the opposite, the servant is eating at the table of the Master, משל למלך שעשה משתה לאוהביו / "simi lar to a King who makes a meal for his beloved ones": *Medrash Rabbah*, Shemos, 19:5. In this way, the Korban Pesach is 'more' than a Shelamim, as it were, and has traces of being like an Olah. Certainly, this eating is the highest form of eating.

Not only are we, the person, the Gavra, the Cohen Gadol and the Melech, but the *Bayis* / home, the *Cheftza* / object of our homes are transformed as well. Chazal tell us, "In the future, the synagogues and the study halls in Babylonia will be transported and reestablished in Eretz Yisrael" (*Megilah*, 29a). This is true of every *Shul* / synagogue and every Yeshivah, house of study, and this is also true of every home that performs a Seder (Chasam Sofer, *Derashos* 2, p. 236). Every Bayis that experiences a Seder will be transplanted and transported, in the times of Moshiach, into Eretz Yisrael.

When it says that in the future the Beis haMikdash will expand to the size of the city of Yerushalayim, says the Maharsha (*Megilah*, ibid), this is because the future Beis haMikdash will include all the Shuls and Yeshivos from exile, all of them will become part of the larger Beis haMikdash, as it were. As such, says the Maharsha, ונמצא עתה בגלות שאני עומד בבית הכנסת הרי הוא מקום המקדש גופי' דלעתיד / "Therefore, today, when you stand in a Shul in exile, know, that space itself is the place of the Beis haMikdash of the future." When you are in a Shul or Yeshivah, wherever you may be, you are in the Beis haMikdash of the future. Since when we are celebrating the Seder in our home, our home is included in the category of Shuls and Yeshivos, this means that at our Seder we are sitting in the Beis haMikdash; we are the Cohen Gadol, the King of Israel, eating from the "table of the most High."

This highest, deepest level is not necessarily something we earned, or even aspired to, yet this is the gift of Pesach night.

BLESSED BEYOND OUR VESSELS

On this night, we are gifted with a glimpse of
    our deepest potential —
        revealing who we can truly be.

    Hashem lifts us up and takes us out from our exiles,
showing us what life looks like from the
        perspective of freedom.

This is the real freedom —
      not merely freedom to do what you want, but
to be who you are, and to live from that place.

    You are equal to the Cohen Gadol,
      blessed with inherent Gadlus and Klarkeit.

Always remember that Gadlus is who you truly are.

      We are all free in our essence.

Through leaving Egypt we became like kings and noble people (*Sefer haChinuch*, Mitzvos 7-8; 15-16). On this night we have the ability to live this truth outwardly and tap into who we really are. We are all, in fact, בני מלכים / children of kings (*Bava Metziya*, 113b) — this is who we always truly are, but on this night we lay claim to that reality.

Similarly, whether we sit at the Seder in white garments, or not, we are likened to the Cohen Gadol serving in the Holy of Holies, as when we left Egypt, Hashem told us, "You will be to me ממלכת כהנים / a kingdom of priests" (*Shemos*, 19:16). What does it mean to be a kingdom of "priests"? Says the Baal ha-Turim, אלו זכו ישראל היו כולם כהנים גדולים ולע"ל תחזור להם / "If we were meritorious, we would have all been *high* priests. Yet, in the future this spiritual status will return to all of us." Since this status will "return" to us, it means it is who we already essentially are; it is where we came from, and what we will eventually manifest again, because it is who we always actually are. On this night we tap into, and reveal, this eternal truth.

As our homes, or wherever we are making the Seder, are part of the Third Beis haMikdash of the future — so too in this infinite moment of the eternal present, which is unified with the 'future', we are, in fact serving in the Third Beis haMikdash, as the High Priest.

On this night we attain and reclaim our G-d given *Gadlus* / greatness, both *Gashmi* / physical, and *Ruchni* / spiritual; this is who we really are and what we really deserve. On this night we lay claim — by the grace of a gift from Above — to who we truly are.

NIGHT AS DAY

This is a night of 'haste' and *Klarkeit* / immediate clarity into who we truly are and what we are meant to be doing. There is no opaqueness, blurriness, uncertainty or darkness. There is only light; even 'night' is essentially 'day'.

"And it was evening, and it was morning, day one." Days are counted from the evening to the next evening; first comes the evening, and the morning and daylight naturally follows. From one perspective, all of history, too, is a process of elapsed progression, moving gradually from 'evening' to 'morning'. Yet in the world of haste and clarity, which is the world of Unity, 'night' is already 'day'. In the world of Unity, the potential is already actual; there is no separation between cause and effect, evening and day, exile and redemption.

Normally, we move from question to answer, from darkness to light, in a process that gradually and even effortfully clarifies and reveals truth. On this night there is no darkness, only clarity, thus there is no 'night'. On Seder night, the 'night' shines like the day.

When the Torah speaks of the Mitzvah of telling your child about the going out of Egypt, the Torah says "And you shall tell your child on that *day*" (*Shemos*, 13:8). In this context, 'day' does not simply mean a 24 hour unit which includes the night, as in "It was evening, it was morning, day one." Rather "on that day" suggests literally 'day', when the sun is shining (אי ביום ההוא יכול מבעוד יום). Now, although the Mitzvah is to tell your child during the "night" of the Fifteenth of Nisan (אי ביום ההוא יכול מבעוד יום, ת"ל בעבור זה), the Torah calls that night "that day." On Seder night, night and day are unified.

This is the night of the Four Questions which begin with מה נשתנה הלילה הזה / "What (about) this night is different from all other nights?" (Mishnah, *Pesachim*, 116a). הלילה הזה / *haLailah haZeh*, translated as "this night" is a peculiar phrase. Generally, the consensus is that לילה / night is a feminine word. As the Maharal writes (*Gevuros Hashem*, 12), the construct of night and the moon are feminine qualities, whereas day and the sun are masculine. זה / *Zeh* / "this" is a masculine term, and the feminine term for "this" is זאת / *Zos*. As such, the 'correct' phrase would be הלילה הזאת not הלילה הזה, as the Shaloh points out (*Meseches Pesachim*, Ma'aseh Gra, Pirush Haggadah). Thus, the question is why refer to the feminine לילה with the masculine זה? Although we do not find in the Torah the phrase הלילה הזאת, yet, the question is still valid; why is a masculine pronoun used in reference to a feminine word?

Why on this night is the word 'night', in the feminine, equated with or unified with the masculine Zeh? In the world of Halachah, this unity of night and day is manifest in that on this night women (the embodiment of the feminine principle) are as equally obligated in the Mitzvos as the men, even though these Mitzvos are time-bound, and normally women are exempt from obligation toward time-bound Mitzvos.

Additionally, throughout the year, most Mitzvos are performed during the 'day'. Certainly this is true with Mitzvos of the *Yamim Tovim* / holy days. Every Yom Tov has a unique *Mitzvas haYom* / Mitzvah of the day, and this Mitzvah is virtually always done *baYom* / in the daytime, not at night. For example, the Mitzvah of Rosh Hashanah is to blow the Shofar. When do you blow it? During the *Yom* / day. Similarly, the blessing over the Lulav on Sukkos is done during the day, and all of the Rabbinic Mitzvos of Purim, such as delivering gifts and holding a *Seudah* / drinking feast, are done on the day of Purim (*Megilah*, 7b. The main reading of the Megilah is by day, והעיקר הוי ביממא: *Tosefos*, Megilah, 4a). If you do any of these Mitzvos while it is still night, you are not *Yotzei* / discharged from your obligation; you have not yet done the Mitzvah. Yet on Leil haSeder, the Mitzvos are performed at night. The Mitzvos to eat the Matzah and Maror are specifically performed at night (Chanukah is also unique in this regard; see *The Month of Kislev: Rekindling Dreams, Hope & Trust* for a deeper exploration regarding Chanukah and night).

'Day' is both literal and figurative — it also means a time of redemption and clarity. Most Mitzvos we perform today are done during the day. Furthermore, most of the Mitzvos that we do not currently perform are connected to the Land of Israel when the Beis haMikdash is standing — a paradigm of 'day'. Yet, on Pesach we perform all of the Mitzvos at night, and we celebrate the brilliant light of the Seder even in our exile, our collective night.

The reason is, this night is not only a remembrance of the past redemption from Egypt, or even a present redemption from our own limitations, but this night is the precursor to the ultimate *Geulah* / redemption. The gates of the final and ultimate Geulah are palpable for us even now. Of the time of Redemption, the master prophet prophesied that there will come a time when והיה אור - הלבנה כאור החמה / *Ohr haLevanah k'Ohr haChamah* / "the light of the moon will be like the light of the sun" (*Yeshayah* 30:26). The feminine light of the 'night' will shine as brightly as the masculine light of the 'day'. It will truly be לילה הזה, a brilliant unification of darkness and light. A glimmer of that reality was experienced at our redemption from Egypt, as we left Egypt in the middle of the night and yet experienced ולילה כיום יאיר / "night shone like day" (*Tehilim*, 139:12. *Zohar* 2, 131a. In fact, the *Ohr HaChayim* (Shemos, 13:8), writes that part of the Mitzvah of the night is speaking about this very miracle, כי גם נם זה בכלל מצות ההגדה.* As the night was like the day, they were allowed to perform a *Milah* / circumcision even at night — a Mitzvah normally done only by day. Although it could be argued that the Mitzvah to perform the Milah only by day (*Megilah*, 20a) is post Matan Torah).

We experience a glimmer of this truth even today. On one level, we are catapulted from our past and pulled into our future — yet also within the eternal present moment of Pesach 'night' we encounter the 'day', the Klarkeit of an eternal redemption. All our 'nights', darknesses, uncertainties, ambiguities, and any lack of clarity in our mission or purpose, are lit up and illuminated in this ever-present Klarkeit of Gadlus.

This night is a night of miracles, of Gadlus, of fearlessness and expansive clarity. This is a night of embodying the holiness of the Cohen Gadol, the spiritual king, serving in the Holy of Holies — the deepest level of soul which is unified with HaKadosh Baruch Hu.

On this night we have the Gadlus of living in the times of Moshiach, the future within the timeless present. Our life, mission and purpose are absolutely clear to us. The moon, the night, our individual self, is shining like the "sun," the Source of Light.

ROUND MATZAH: EVERY MOMENT IS A NEW BEGINNING

In linear time and progression, 1 comes before 2, and 2 before 3. Spring comes before summer, and summer before fall. Time has a cyclical nature and thus everything progresses in a cycle or spiral. Yet, a circle is a unified entity; all points are equidistant from center and lying upon a single continuum. There is no real beginning or end, up or down in a circle; all is one. In this way, all points on the circle, or spiral of time, are simultaneous. There is no real separation between night and day, body and soul, exile and redemption.

Today, the main item at the Seder, and the one remaining Torah-Based Mitzvah, is Matzah. Matzah is naturally baked in a round shape, as when you hand-roll dough it becomes rounded. Although this is the natural state of such 'bread', it is not a mere coincidence. Making the Matzah round is intentional,* as it represents the state of unity.

---

* *Teshuvas Mahari* (also known as *Teshuvas Yehudah Ya'aleh*), Orach Chayim, 157. Parenthetically, the Gemara tells us a sign to know if the Matzah has been baked fully. כל שפורסה ואין חוטין נמשכין הימנה / "Any Matzah that when it is broken, no strands of dough emerge from its sides": *Pesachim*, 37a. A properly baked Matzah has no חוטין / strands, lines emerging, and even when later broken, no strands emerge. On a deeper level this means that Matzah is connected with the world of circles, not the world of lines. The Pasuk says, "They baked the dough that they had taken out of Egypt as unleavened *Ugos* / cakes": *Shemos*, 12:39. Uga generally means 'round', as in, עג עוגה / 'draw a circle': *Ta'anis*, 19a. Avraham gave the angels עגות (*Bereishis*, 18:6), and the story of the angels and Avraham occurred on Pesach, the 15th of Nisan: *Medrash Rabbah*, Bereishis, 48:12. Thus we know that Avraham gave them 'round cakes' of Matzah. The angels came to Avraham on the third day from his *Bris* / circumcision, as Chazal tells us, יום שלישי של מילה של אברהם היה ובא הקב"ה לשאול באברהם: *Bava Metziya*, 86b. This would mean that Avraham performed his Bris on the 13th of Nisan. Accordingly, the *Chasam Sofer* answers a question on the Magen Avraham. The Magen Avraham writes that the custom is not to say Tachanun the entire month of Nisan. Why? Since the first 12 days of Nisan are the time of the dedication of the Mishkan, and the 14th is Erev Pesach, and then the next seven / eight days are of the Festival of Pesach; on all these days we do not recite Tachanun. And since these are more than 20 days, and the 'full majority' of the month (two thirds) has already passed without reciting Tachanun, we continue through the last eight or nine days of the month to omit Tachanun. The Shulchan Aruch rules, אין נופלים על פניהם בכל חדש ניסן: *Orach Chayim*, 429. Upon this statement the Magen Avraham writes, מפני שי"ב נשיאים הקריבו י"ב ימים וכל יום הקרבן הי' י"ט שלו ואח"כ ע"פ ופסח ואסרו חג א"כ יצא רוב החדש בקדושה לפיכך עושין כלו קדש. The obvious question is then, why do we not recite Tachanun on the 13th of Nisan? Once we reach the 22nd or 23rd of Nisan, and we did not say Tachanun on the majority of days of the month, this argument stands. So, why do we not recite Tachanun on the 13th, which

From one perspective, a round shape represents unity; there are no definite points, measurements or separations on the circumference of a circle. Since Matzah is a manifestation of *Emunah Peshutah* / simple faith, as explored earlier, there are no 'corners', complications, hidden folds or crevasses in it, as it were. Matzah is a manifestation of the recognition that everything is part of Hashem's plan and unity.* Similarly, roundness suggests that any point within the circumference is equally 'the beginning'. Pesach night teaches us that at any moment and in one instant, one can be at the highest levels. Indeed, at the Seder, we are; this is a night of 'skipping over', transcending all processes and gradual forms of transformation. In one 'hasty' instant, we are stationed at highest spiritual and physical elevation, and the pure, open beginning of our lives.

---

is not included in the first 12, nor part of the majority of days? The Chasam Sofer answers that the 13th of Nisan is the day of Avraham's Bris. Avraham's Bris essentially represents the birth of Klal Yisrael, who would eventually be born as a nation at Yetzias Mitzrayim and dedicated to HaKadosh Baruch Hu through the Mitzvah of Bris Milah.

---

* Indeed, there is nothing that is by its nature square — "There is no square in Creation," asserts Rabban Shimon ben Gamliel: *Yerushalmi*, end of Ma'asros, *Nedarim*, 3:2. *Shavuos* 3:8. Whether this is also the opinion of the sages, and whether 'square' literally means a 'perfect square', and whether it only refers to the realm of human experience, and so forth, are points that are greatly debated: the Rebbe, *Igros Kodesh*, Vol. 2, p. 360.

Chapter Four:
The Progression of the Night

THERE SEEM TO BE TWO OPPOSITE SPIRITUAL MOVEMENTS throughout the course of the Seder. On the one hand, it appears that we are moving 'up', higher or more internal, while on the other hand, it seems that we are moving 'down', lower and more external.

In general, moving from higher to lower represents a המשכה / drawing down from Above to Below, so the start is from Above moving into the Below. Whereas moving from the lower to the higher represents a העלאה / elevation from Below to Above, and thus starts with the Below.

A simple reading of the Arizal, as explored earlier (see Chapter 13 for definitions of the Kabbalistic terms here), is that on Pesach, we are moving from a higher level to a lower level. For example, with the first cup of wine we draw down the Chochmah of *Ima* / Mother into *ZA* / Zeir Anpin. With the second cup we draw down the Binah of Ima. With the third and fourth cups we draw down the Da'as of Ima. In Da'as there are two levels: the Da'as of Chesed corresponds to the third cup and the Da'as of Gevurah corresponds to the fourth cup. In this way, we move from a *Penimi* / inner world down into a world that includes physicality, the *Chitzoni* / external world, and this is why we eat the physical meal towards the end of the night.

From this meta-structure of the Arizal, it appears that everything in the Seder flows from the higher Chochmah into the lower levels of Da'as, and from the Penimi realm in which we speak about Geulah, down to the ingestion of the Mitzvos of the night and finally to the actual Seudah, the Chitzoni world of soup and meat and physical satisfaction. And this seems to be the predominant understanding of all the sages who follow the teachings of the holy Arizal.

And yet, the Arizal also teaches that we begin the night on the level of Gadlus Rishon (Binah), and at the end of the night we reach the level of Gadlus Sheini (Chochmah).

In this way, even according to the Arizal, we are paradoxically also moving 'upward' through the Seder.*

Experientially and viscerally, the movement of the Seder seems to be more from a lower level of consciousness to a higher one, from immediacy and physicality toward spiritual transcendence, from bitterness to sweetness, from describing the shame of slavery to the blessings of thankfulness, elation and a sense of perfection and having arrived.

---

* Similarly, these two opposite views of movement, from Below to Above or from Above to Below, are found with regards to the *Makos* / Plagues in Egypt, with their ultimate purpose being the revelation of Hashem's presence within this world. So the question is: are the Makos impacting first the lower levels and then progressing to the higher, or, is their movement from the higher penetrating the lower? The general pattern in the writings of the Arizal is that the Makos are from Below to Above, from Malchus to Keser. *Pri Eitz Chayim,* Chag haMatzos, 7. דם. עולה אהי"ה ברבוע...ומכה זו יצאת ממלכות שבמלכות דקדושה...צפרדע – גימ' תמ"ד...ומכה זו יצא מיסוד שבמלכות... כנים – הם ג"י ק"ך...וויוצא מכה זו, מהוד שבמלכות, and so forth. See also *Mishnas Chassidim,* Seder Leil Pesach, 11. Yet, Rebbe Yoseph Caro teaches that the order of the Makos are from higher to lower. ובאיתערותא דחכמה אתא צפרדע... ובאיתערותא דבינה הוו כנים... ובאיתערותא דחסד הוה ערוב... ובאיתערותא דגבורה הוה דבר, and so forth. *Maggid Meisharim,* 13:4. The Ten Makos correspond to the Ten Ma'amaros that created the world. But here, the order of the Makos is from Below to Above. As the Maharal, *Gevuras Hashem,* 57, explains: ואף על גב שלא היו המכות באות עליהם כסדר מאמרות שבהם ברא הקב"ה את עולמו, מפני שכל אחד ואחד סדר מיוחד. וזה כי לענין הכאת המכה, תמיד המכה שהיא מלמעלה יותר קשה, ואין להביא מכה קשה, ואחר כך שאינה קשה כל כך. ולפיכך היו עולים מלמטה למעלה. Yet, the Medrash ties the Ten Makos to the Ten Dibros, and states that the order of the Makos is from Above to below. נאמרו עשרת הדברות כנגד עשר מכות שהביא הקדוש ברוך הוא על המצרים במצרים אנכי כנגד מכת דם ויהפך לדם יאוריהם... לא יהיה לך כנגד [מכת] צפרדעים... לא תשא כנגד מכת כינים: *Pesikta Rabbasi,* 21:1.

ORDER OF THE MATZOS - UPWARD OR DOWNWARD?

While the order of the cups can be described as following a downward progression, the three Matzos can represent a different trajectory.

We place three Matzos in front of us, one on top of the other, with some form of partition between them. According to the Arizal, the three Matzos correspond to the three types of Jews, the Cohen, the Levi, and the *Yisrael* / general Israelite. The Cohen, priest, is someone who descends from Aharon, Moshe's brother. The Levi is one who comes from the tribe of Levi. Everyone else is simply called Yisrael. When we meditatively stack the Matzah before the Seder, one tradition is to have in mind while putting the bottom Matzah in its place, that it signifies the Cohen. Above the Cohen you place the Levi Matzah, and above them both, the Yisrael.

The acronym of these three roles is *Kli* / vessel (**K**ohen, **L**evi, **I**sraelite), and the order moves from a higher to a 'lower' and more external level. The Cohen, who served in the Beis haMikdash and is dedicated to sacred activity, comes first. He is followed by the Levi, who also served in the Beis haMikdash but more in the external areas, and with more 'external' service. Finally, there is the Yisrael, who stood in the most external areas of the Beis haMikdash, and was usually the kind of person who went out into the world for business or who owned land (in contrast to the Cohen and Levi). Their mission in life included 'descending' to the depths of the external mundane world to make it into a Kli for the Divine Presence.

Others have the opposite custom: one first places the Yisrael Matzah on the bottom, on top of that the Levi, and above that the Cohen, progressing higher and more inward. Here the acronym is *YeiLeCh* / movement (Yisrael, Levi, Cohen), alluding to this upward movement. Similarly, the overarching theme of the Fifteen Steps of the Haggadah is a movement from a lowly state to a higher state of consciousness, from a place of questions to a place of answers, from an inability to express, to fluent expressions of blessing, gratefulness and thanksgiving; from a place of *Havdalah* / separation to a place of *Hamtakah* / sweetening.

According to this view of 'climbing' through the Fifteen Steps, we begin by physically preparing everything needed for the Seder, 'doing' things in the world of *Asiyah* / action. We then ascend to recite Kiddush with Dibbur, the more subtle world of 'speech', and continue in this mode, reciting the bulk of the Haggadah. Here our words arouse our emotions, and we complete our passage through the world of Yetzirah, speech and emotions. When we wash our hands and eat the Matzah and Maror with Kavanah, we enter the world of thought, the inner world of Beriah. When concluding the main part of the Haggadah, we begin singing praises and offering thanks, which is a higher, more subtle and refined state of being. As we sing Hallel and other praises that are normally recited only during the day, we can have an intuitive sense of the dawning of Redemption and of transcending the darkness of all exiles. This occurs in the spiritual world of *Atzilus* / Nearness, which transcends thought, speech and action.

THE FOUR CUPS - UPWARD OR DOWNWARD?

If we momentarily put aside the descending pattern of the four cups which the Arizal revealed, we can also perceive an ascending movement in the progression of the four cups.

Kiddush is recited on the first cup. *Kiddush* or *Kadeish* means 'separation', alluding to the physical world of Asiyah, in which separation from the Source is the most vivid experience of life. Asiyah is connected with the sense of 'touch', the most physical of the senses.

We recite Maggid over the second cup. Speech corresponds to the emotional world of Yetzirah, and the sense of sight. For example, Maggid is recited "when the Matzah and Maror are *Munachim Lefanecha* / set before you (visibly)." We fill the third cup at Beirach, the culmination of the meal. The meal began with Matzah and Maror, which were eaten with thoughtful intention. This is the cup of the intellectual world of Beriah and the sense of taste — we drink it when we still have the taste of the feast in our mouth. We sing Hallel over the fourth cup and reach transcendent levels of consciousness corresponding to the world of Atzilus, and the mystical sense of hearing, communing with realms far beyond what is physically observable.

In this way, the first cup corresponds to the final letter Hei of the Divine Name, or the Sefirah of Malchus, world of Asiyah. The second cup corresponds to the Vav of Hashem's name, the Six Emotive Sefiros, the world of emotions, Yetzirah. The third cup corresponds to the upper Hei of Hashem's name, the Sefirah of Binah, or higher understanding, the world of Beriah. The fourth cup corresponds to the Yud of Hashem's Name, the Sefirah of Chochmah, Divine 'wisdom' or intuition, the world of Atzilus.

The first cup brings redemption from the exiles of the Guf, or body. The second cup brings psychological and emotional freedom, the Nefesh. With the third cup, we move into a more mindful state and begin the process of freeing our *Seichel* / intellect. With the fourth cup, we tap into the level of total existential freedom, haCol or everything, as will be shortly explored. In this way we are attaining higher and higher levels with each of the four cups.

As is well known, the four cups of wine represent the four expressions the Torah employs with regard to Yetzias Mitzrayim: "I will take you out," "I will save you," "I will redeem you," and "I will take you to Me." Clearly, these are four ascending levels of redemption.* "I will take you out" refers to when the harsh slave labor in Egypt ended, which was six months before the actual Exodus (*Rosh Hashanah*, 11a). The promise "I will take you to Me," only occurred seven weeks after Yetzias Mitzrayim, at *Matan Torah* / the Giving of the Torah. Thus, according to the *Peshat* / literal interpretation, the movement of the cups is progressively 'higher'.

---

* The four terms of redemption are four deeper stages of freedom, from slavery to being chosen and being given the Torah: *Col-Bo*, Arvei Pesachim, 50.

The four cups and the four expressions of redemption can also be seen as four stages in personal development: birth, adolescence, engagement, and marriage. In this map, the final, fourth phrase *V'lakachti* / "I will take you," alludes to the mature stage in which one can actually join with another in marriage. *L'kuchin* is from the word *Yikach* (as in *Ki Yikach Ish Ishah* / כי יקח איש אשה: *Devarim*, 24:1) which refers to taking a marriage partner.

There is also a meta-historical way of viewing the four cups, moving from *Olam haZeh* / this world, to *Olam haBa* / the World to Come. The Gra writes that the four cups move in a progressive order, moving from lower to higher. The first cup corresponds to Olam haZeh, as a person needs to 'sanctify' himself in this world. The second cup is connected with *Yemos haMoshiach* / world of Moshiach, as the wonders of the times of Moshiach will be like the wonders of the going out of Egypt (and even greater); "As the days you came out of Egypt, I will show you my wonders" (*Michah*, 7:15).

The third cup is connected with *Techiyas haMeisim* / the resurrection of the dead. On this cup, we recite the blessings after eating, reminding ourselves of the great feast of the Future. The fourth cup corresponds to *Olam haBa* / the future perfect world, thus we recite the "great Hallel" over it, which celebrates the ultimate perfection of all Creation.*

---

* The Tzemach Tzedek, in *Ohr haTorah*, Vayeshev (and Va'era, p. 128), connects the four cups with the four forms of love between Hashem and us: אחתי רעיתי יונתי תמתי / "my sister, my beloved, my dove, my perfect one" (*Shir haShirim*, 5:2). These too are listed in an ascending order, and as the

The Abarbanel writes that the four cups correspond to the four consecutive redemptions: the first with the promise of redemption made to Avraham, the second with Yetzias Mitzrayim, the third with our being sustained throughout the current lengthy exile, and the fourth with the coming of Moshiach. In this way, the cups progress through history, moving closer and closer to the Yemos haMoshiach.

This upward movement is also reflected in the Gemara. The *Yerushalmi* teaches that someone who eats Matzah on Erev Pesach is similar to someone who has relations with his future wife before the wedding night (*Pesachim*, 10:1. *Tosefos*, Pesachim, 99b: כל האוכל מצה בערב הפסח כאילו בועל ארוסתו בבית חמיו). And just like in marriage we first recite the Seven Blessings, and only then can the marriage be consummated, the same is true with Matzah. First we recite seven blessings in the Seder, and then we are ready to eat the Matzah.* What this suggests is that eating the Matzah is like the *Yichud* / unity between a husband and wife, or in the meta-narrative, between HaKadosh Baruch Hu and us. This means that we begin the Seder prior to Yichud, and as the Seder progresses we begin to experience more and more

---

Tzemach Tzedek explains, these four levels are connected with an elevation from Malchus to Keser, and from Olam haZeh to Olam haBa.

* *Zohar*, Raya Mehemna, 3, p. 251b. *Ohr Zarua*, Siman 256. *Shibolei haLeket*, Siman 208:600. *Ra'avyah*, Siman 525. *Rokeach*, Siman 32. Rashbatz, *Maamar Chametz*, 103. *Avudraham*, Haggadah. Maharil, *Seder Haggadah*, 3. The similarity of Matzah to a bride is drawn because Matzah is (one of) the first Mitzvos that Klal Yisrael received: Ritva, *Pesachim*, 50a.

Yichud and intimacy with HaKadosh Baruch Hu, as it were.*

As a movement from below to Above, moving out of estrangement and getting closer to Hashem, the Seder also moves from a paradigm of 'doing' and order, to a place of non-doing, *Nirtzah* / acceptance and being 'beyond order'.

DOWNWARD MOVEMENT:

As mentioned, the Arizal writes that the first cup is Chochmah of Ima, the Chochmah within Binah, as we begin the night with a taste of Gadlus. The second cup is the lower level of Binah, the third cup is Chesed, and the fourth is Gevurah within the lower level of Da'as (*Pri Eitz Chayim*, Sha'ar haMitzvos, Chap. 2. See also *Shaloh*, Maseches Pesachim, p. 188).

An earlier source for this 'downward' movement, although the Holy Arizal is validly his own source, is also found in the Rishonim. Rabbeinu Bachya writes that the four cups correspond to the Name of Hashem, Yud-Hei-Vav-Hei. The first cup is the Yud, the 'highest' letter, and the fourth cup is the 'lower' Hei (*Rabbeinu Bachya*, Shemos, 12:23).**

---

* The seven blessings are counted up until the blessings on the actual Matzah, when we 'reveal' the Matzah, the 'bride'.

** וכן עוד ד' כוסות של פסח כנגדם כוס ראשון של קדוש כנגד אות יו"ד שהוא קדש וכן הוא אומר שאו ידיכם קדש, כוס ב' שאומר עליו ההגדה והוא ספור הנסים כנגד אות ה"א שמשם נמשכים הנסים והמכות, כוס ג' של ברכת המזון כנגד אות וי"ו שנקרא שמים ממה שכתוב ואתה תשמע השמים, ומשם בא המזון ממה שכתוב הנני ממטיר לכם לחם מן השמים, כוס ד' שאומר עליו שפוך חמתך כנגד ה"א אחרונה שהיא מדת הדין

HIGHER IS BROADER

While there appears to be two opposite processes at play, moving higher and more inward, or lower and more outward, there is really no conflict, and this is simply a linguistic and conceptual polarity. The truth is, 'higher' also means 'more inclusive'. Just as the higher one ascends in an airplane the more of the surface of the earth one can see, the higher we climb spiritually the more of the physical world we can embrace within our 'spirituality'. The more *Penimi* / inward we become, the more we can include the world of *Chitzoni* / externality within our concept of 'holiness', without becoming lost and subsumed by it.

When the Arizal explains the Seder as a movement from higher to lower levels — from the transcendence of Kadeish, down to a reality where we are eating a luxurious physical meal — he too is describing a progression of greater and greater inclusivity. As we go lower we simultaneously go higher, and when we eat the meal, we are revealing that the physical world of Asiyah is also holy. Shulchan Oreich, the Arizal writes, is the Yichud of ZA with Malchus in Asiyah, the unification of the Holy Transcendent One with the physical world.

So in truth, these two perspectives — moving from higher to lower and moving lower to higher — are different descriptions of the same phenomenon. Both perspectives express the fact that the Seder guides us toward greater and greater inclusivity and integration. Whether we say it is the 'highest point' or the 'lowest point', the Seder guides to the point where even actions such as eating a delicious feast are included within the world of pure light, the world of Atzilus, of Unity.

Another way to explain how the two perspectives are one, is to distinguish between the dynamics of *Orech* / length and *Rochav* / width. Orech is like a vertical line upon which we can be said to be traveling 'higher' as the Seder progresses, becoming more and more intimate with the Transcendent One, moving from Olam haZeh to Olam haBa, from the Redemption from Egypt to the redemption of the future, from Gadlus Rishon to Gadlus Sheini, and from Mochin of Binah, to Mochin of Chochmah. Rochav is like a horizontal line; the 'higher' we travel or the more supernal light that we draw 'down', the more width and breadth we are able to consciously include within the Infinite Light, as a result, more of the Chitzoni physical world is embraced and 'uplifted'.

This latter point can be illustrated if a person is looking vertically (Orech) from below, the higher the vector of sight ascends, the wider and more inclusive (horizontally) the range of vision. Similarly, as Light is drawn vertically downward from above, the flow at first moves into the extremely 'wide' world of Atzilus, and this is funneled through Beriah and Yetzirah, and finally, at the culmination of the Seder, the most inclusive Light reaches even the physical world of Asiyah. In this way, the Seder in fact brings us deeper, higher, and wider, all at once. The fact that the Light is moving down into Asiyah, which seems lower, in actuality means we are being elevated, as now even Asiyah is included in the radiance of Atzilus.

Chapter Five:
The Unusual Order of the Seder:

R AV MEIR LEIBUSH WISSER, KNOWN AS THE 'MALBIM', writes (*Haggadah*, Ma'amar Yesod Mussar), "The beginning of all knowledge and the source of all wisdom is to have an understanding of the Seder," meaning to understand the order and structure of the idea. He writes how, within the Haggadah for example, some commentaries focus on explaining each passage and delving deeper into the individual passages, yet to really understand the Haggadah, one must find its Seder, its order, its inner structure.

Let us try to understand the inner Seder of the Seder.

FROM NEGATIVE TO POSITIVE

Regarding the overarching theme of the Maggid section of the Seder, the principle is that we should מתחיל בגנות ומסיים בשבח / "begin by recounting our disgrace and conclude with our glory" (*Mishnah, Pesachim*, 116a). What exactly is "our disgrace" is a point that the sages Rav and Shmuel debate. Rav says it means we should begin by saying, "At first our forefathers were idol worshipers…." And Shmuel says, it means we should begin by saying "We were slaves." In other words, Rav is looking at the spiritual disgrace of idol worship, while Shmuel is focusing on the physical dishonor we suffered as we began our journey as a people (This is consistent with Rav and Shmuel's opinions throughout the Gemara; Rav focuses on the spiritual aspect of the issue, between man and G-d, and Shmuel on the more interpersonal, between man and man: *Likutei Sichos*, 16, Shemos 1, p. 9. In general, Rav was more involved and scrupulous with ritual law, and Shmuel with civil issues: ששמואל היה רגיל תמיד לפסוק דינין ולכך היה מדקדק בהן ויורד לעומקן ומשכיל על כל דבר אמת. וכן רב היה רגיל לדקדק בהוראת איסור והיתר לכך סמכו על הוראותיו לעניני איסור והיתר: Rosh, *Bava Kama*, 4:4. Thus, the Halachah follows Rav in 'ritual' debates and Shmuel in 'money' issues, הלכתא כרב באיסורי וכשמואל בדיני: *Bechoros*, 49b).

The general structure of the Maggid part of the Seder begins with the negative, our "disgrace," and concludes with the positive, our "glory." This is consistent with the entire movement of Pesach — from slavery to redemption, from constriction and hardship to freedom.

Clearly, the opposite of idol worship is to serve Hashem, and it would seem that the opposite of slavery is simple freedom, yet the Rambam adds an important subtle addition: "We begin by saying how originally our ancestors were idol worshipers, and we conclude with, שקרבנו המקום לו והבדילנו מהאומות וקרבנו ליחודו / 'Hashem has drawn us close, separated us from the nations of the world, and drawn us closer to His Unity.' And similarly, we begin by stating that we were slaves to Pharaoh in Egypt, and all the evil done to us, ומסיים בנסים ובנפלאות שנעשו לנו ובחירותנו / 'and conclude with the miracles and wonders that were wrought upon us, and our freedom' (*Hilchos Chametz uMatzah*, 7:4). For the Rambam, the opposite of being slaves in Egypt is not being 'free', rather the opposite of slavery is 'closeness'; Hashem performed miracles for us as He took us out of Egypt and chose to bring us close.

Either way, the point is the movement from the negative to the positive, from disgrace to glory, from hardship to redemption, from slavery to freedom, and being chosen. While this is the 'order' of the Maggid part of the Seder, this order is not followed in the overall structure of the Seder.

FREEDOM BEFORE ENSLAVEMENT

So far, this all makes sense; there is a movement from slavery to freedom, from being idol worshipers to being close servants of Hashem. Yet, this is not actually the sequence of the Haggadah and the Seder as a whole. In fact, there is something very peculiar about the entire 'order' of Seder Night. It is true, we are celebrating our going out of Egypt, both the historical going out of Egypt and our being empowered to go out of our own personal "Egypt." We drink four cups of wine, corresponding to the four levels of freedom that we experienced going out of Egypt, we eat our foods, especially the Matzah and wine, reclining, as kings and free men of old. We adorn our tables in the finest silverware and wear our finest garments. Coupled with this free, king-like sensation, we also eat Maror, bitter herbs, and eat *Karpas* / cut up onion (or the like) in salt water, in order to feel the contrast with our state in exile and inner slavery. We can only feel as free as we have felt enslaved in the past.

While we do all this, it does make perfect sense that the 'order' should be first disgrace, hardship, and slavery, and then afterward, glory, redemption, and freedom. It makes sense to eat the Maror before we eat the Matzah, as historically our bitterness came before our redemption. It makes perfect sense to grind the Maror with our teeth and feel its physical sting and meditate on the bitterness of our exile — and then to eat Matzah, the bread of freedom, and drink wine, which induces sensations of the joy and pleasure of redemption.

If we wanted to contrast these two states most vividly in order to gain a greater sense of freedom, it would make more sense to begin the Seder with Maror and Karpas. Then we would begin by tasting the pain of having been beaten down; we could speak about our exile and hardship in Egypt, and begin to understand the bitterness and feel it falling away. Only after that would we lift a beautiful cup filled with fine wine and recite *Kiddush* / the sanctification of the joyful Yom Tov, recline luxuriously and drink like a king or queen. Then, we could continue with recounting the triumphant Exodus from Egypt, sing the praises of Hashem our Redeemer, and sense and envision our complete freedom and closeness to HaKadosh Baruch Hu.

However, in the actual Seder, this is not how it is done. We begin with a royal Kiddush and then begin to contemplate how we were slaves and idol worshipers. Once we begin to feel the sweetness of freedom and praises begin to well up within us and we even internalize the 'bread of freedom' — we seemingly change direction and taste the bitterness of Maror and feel the pain of exile.

A simple reason that we eat Matzah before Maror is as follows. Today, eating Matzah is the night's main Mitzvah from the Torah, whereas Maror, without the *Korban Pesach* / offering of the Pesach lamb is, according to most opinions (although perhaps not the opinion of the *Yerushalmi*), a Mitzvah from our sages. Thus the most essential Mitzvah is performed first. But the question can also be contemplated philosophically: what does it mean that Matzah precedes Maror? And why do we start with the pleasure of a royal Kiddush? Technically, we cannot eat before Kiddush, so it needs to precede the ritual foods, but the question remains: why not have the children first ask questions, and then start telling the story of our exile, slavery, and idol worship, and then make Kiddush, a climactic consecration?

During Maggid, where we speak about and explain the Mitzvos of the night — Pesach (in times when we brought offerings), Matzah and Maror — the Noda b'Yehudah asks, why this order? One would think that first we should explain why we eat Maror, symbolic of the bitterness in Egypt, then the Pesach offering and the Matzah, which are part of the freedom; first we should mention Maror then mention Matzah then mention the Pesach offering.*

Indeed, in the order the Rambam uses to describe the Seder, Maror does in fact come before Matzah: ומגביה המרור בידו ואומר מרור זה שאנו אוכלין על שם שמררו המצריים את חיי אבותינו במצרים שנאמר וימררו את חייהם ומגביה המצה בידו ואומר מצה זו שאנו אוכלין על שם שלא הספיק בצקם של אבותינו להחמיץ עד שנגלה עליהם הקדוש ברוך הוא וגאלם / "And (then) he lifts the bitter herbs in his hand and says, 'These bitter herbs that we are eating are (to commemorate) that the Egyptians embittered the lives of our ancestors in Egypt; as it is stated "And they embittered their lives."' And (then) he lifts the Matzah in his hand and says, 'This Matzah that we are eating is (to commemorate) that the dough of our ancestors did not have enough time to become leavened before the Holy One, blessed be He, revealed Himself and redeemed them immediately'" (Rambam, *Hilchos Chametz uMatzah*, 8:4).

---

* *Tz'lach*, Pesachim, 116b. Only after redemption did they understand that their hardship allowed them to leave Egypt earlier, and refined them to receive the Torah: *Bnei Yissachar*, Nisan, Maamar 9:1.

This is simply because bitterness, Maror, comes before the redemption, the Matzah we ate as we left Egypt.*

Wouldn't it make sense to start the Seder with the experience of *Katnus* / smallness, the questions, the bitter taste of Maror, discussing our slavery — and then turn to the experiences of *Gadlus* / expansive greatness, answers, eating foods of freedom in the manner of free people, and speaking expansively about our redemption?

Even more puzzling regarding the 'order' of the Seder, is that according to the Arizal, the four cups are in descending order, as explored earlier; the first cup represents higher cosmic levels and the fourth cup represents the lower, physical world. Why would we start the Seder on a high level and then descend? How is it possible to experience *Gadlus* / greatness and spiritual expansiveness, drinking a cup of wine evoking liberation and maturity, before experiencing *Katnus* / smallness, spiritual contraction and immaturity? Instead, we stand proudly in our best attire, with the finest cup we can afford, before our table set for kings and queens, some even donning a beautiful white garment symbolizing that of the *Cohen Gadol*

---

* See *Kesef Mishneh*, ad loc.: שתחלה מררו חייהם ואח"כ נגאלו. Although, in the actual Nusach of the Haggadah, the Rambam places Matzah before Maror. This is because today Matzah is a law of the Torah and Maror is only from the sages, whereas in the Mishnah (and in the Rambam's, Rif's and Rosh's version) — the Mishnah being from the times of the Beis HaMikdash when Maror was also a Torah law (and this Torah law is the source of the Rambam's ruling) — *Maror* / the bitterness of exile comes before *Matzah* / redemption: *Mirkeves haMishneh*, Hilchos Chametz uMatzah, 8:4.

/ the High Priest when he would serve in the Holy of Holies with white garments, and we declare, "For You have sanctified us…desired us…chosen us." We begin the Seder as a noble prince and priest, not as an oppressed and silenced slave.

GADLUS IS WHO WE ARE & WHERE WE COME FROM

Starting the Seder on the level of Gadlus and in a state of elevation is the very meaning of *Pesach* / passing over. Pesach means skipping over all levels and stages, and directly encountering our Gadlus, our physical and spiritual greatness. Kiddush is an expression of freedom and restfulness that skips over exile and strain. It is a confident answer that comes before we even consider our nagging questions. Yet this is perhaps an external manifestation of what the Arizal calls *Gadlus Rishon* / first level greatness, a type of *Mochin* / higher awareness that perhaps paradoxically comes before *Katnus Rishon* / first level smallness.

We borrow the word *Pesach* from verses such as *Pasach Hashem al Pesach* / "Hashem skipped over the door" (*Shemos*, 12:23). Generally we need to 'open the door at least as a pinhead' so that Hashem will open to us wide doors.*

---

* The saying quoted is פתחו לי פתח כחודה של מחט ואני אפתח לכם כפתחו של אולם / "Open up for me the door the size of a pinhead and I will open for you an opening like the doorway of the *Ulam* / Temple hall." The closest source for this quote is in the Zohar — פתחי לי פתחא כחדודא דמחטא, ואנא אפתח לך תרעין עלאין: *Zohar* 1, Emor, 95a. In the Medrash there is a similar quote — אמר הקדוש ברוך הוא לישראל, בני, פתחו לי פתח אחד של תשובה כחדה של מחט, ואני פותח לכם פתחים שיהיו עגלות וקרוניות נכנסות בו / "HaKadosh Baruch Hu says to Israel, 'My child! Open up for me the door the size of a pinhead and I will open for you an opening through which wagons can enter": *Medrash Rabbah*, Shir haShirim, 5:2.

However, on Pesach one skips over the doors, and they are opened on their own, as Mochin d'Gadlus comes to us without any preparation.

The revelation of Pesach is beyond preparation, beyond 'order'. On Pesach night we can reach Gadlus Rishon without first experiencing the lower level of Katnus. We can gain higher maturity without the normal pattern of growth, moving from immaturity to maturity. Normally, we move from question to answer, from child to adult, from night to day, which is the normal course of reality. Yet, on Pesach night we are gifted Gadlus / greatness instantaneously, without any process of gradual development. We are immediately given clarity, higher awareness, and a deep sense of the interconnectivity of all life. Our whole life 'makes sense', not on a mere rational level, but on a level of *Deveikus* / unity with our deeper self, and absolute clarity in terms of who we really are and how we need to live our lives. This is all bestowed upon us from Above as we enter the Seder.

From the first moment of the Seder we are given Gadlus Rishon, which is the sense of being a *Melech* / sovereign, a master, a person who has everything they need and want. A Melech has self-mastery, freely flowing *Mochin* / higher awareness, and a sense of being chosen. We receive the state of the noble Cohen Gadol on Seder night. All of this occurs even before we experience Katnus Rishon.

In a state of Katnus, we feel *Katua* / broken, disjointed and immature, whereas in Gadlus there is a sense of unity.* In a Gadlus state, one has a global sense of clarity. In Katnus, things are mixed up and broken apart, like the paradigm of the Tree of Knowledge of Good and Evil, the world of duality. In this experience of life, everything seems partly good and partly, or potentially, bad, and thus there is never complete moral clarity. The perspective of Gadlus is the complete clarity of unity-consciousness, the wholeness of the Tree of Life. On Pesach night we receive a great *Tikkun* / healing, a rectification of the *Cheit* / sin of eating from the Tree of Knowledge. This inner Tikkun comes to us by means of the Gadlus that we are given to experience, so long as we open ourselves up to it.

In the normal course of events, first comes night, then day, as is the order of Creation, "It was evening, it was morning, day one." First comes darkness and then light, first Katnus then Gadlus, first question then answer. Similarly, in the course of human development, first comes childhood and then adulthood. First we are immature, guided by our emotions, and only when we become a *Gadol* / adult are we potentially guided by our rational faculties. A child is not just physically *Katan* / small, but is also without *Mochin* / higher capacities of awareness. A child's life is intensively guided by their parents; the child does not decide where to live or when to go to sleep. Within this parental container, they are guided by their emotional reactions. If, G-d forbid, a child is traumatized, they

* And the etymological root Gimel-Dalet represents a unit, a continuation.

can be trapped in their trauma, without an ability to see life from a more intellectual perspective, to make some sense of their experience and thus free themselves enough in order to choose their responses. They are stuck in 'smallness' without Da'as. Once they become mature, they can try to make sense of their past, learn new responses to life, and free themselves, G-d willing, from their trauma. Without Mochin d'Gadlus, one can remain in a perpetual state of Din, constriction, limitation, and exile.

This is true of all of life: first comes Katnus and only later, Gadlus. But on the night that we left Egypt, and from that point forward, every year on this night, the order is reversed. First we are lifted into utter Gadlus, the 'answer', and only then do we revisit Katnus, the 'question', the bitterness, the brokenness. In this way, when we do taste the bitterness of Maror it will be within a context of sweetness, wholeness and expansiveness. We experience the sting of lack and need within a state of luxuriant fullness. We feel *Cheser* / absence within a paradigm of *Sheleimus* / wholeness and completion.

LEAVING IN HASTE & KATNUS AFTER GADLUS

Now we can better understand the reason we left Egypt in great haste, as Hashem had "skipped" over the houses of Klal Israel, and we in turn experienced a leap "passing over" all spiritual and emotional levels, instantaneously attaining Gadlus. Since we were so steeped in the mire of Egyptian culture, of *Kelipah* / impurity, pagan practice and lore, we needed a radical unhinging in order to be lifted out. We needed to be 'blasted' out, as it were, especially since our Da'as and awareness itself was in exile, in Kelipah. The normal, gradual, progressive path from Katnus to Gadlus would not have allowed us to leave.

A person who is 'enslaved' to a negative pattern of behavior cannot escape his Katnus if he begins by slowly working out his issues or gradually reducing his indulgences. Rather, he needs to begin by going to extremes in removing himself from the behavior and its contexts and triggers. Only after sustaining his distance and transcendence for a little while does he have the inner support and equilibrium to descend and begin unlearning his Katnus behavior. For example, if a person finds himself becoming angry, he should try for a certain period of time to stay away from anger all together, being almost stoic or above life's dramas. Then, from this place of relative expansiveness, he can go back and explore the beliefs, fears and sufferings underlying his reactivity.

Spiritually, Klal Yisrael was sunk into the lowest depths of *Tumah* / impurity and *Avdus* / slavery, and to become free they needed a radical, dramatic shift. They needed to leave in haste, and to be suddenly catapulted into a taste of Gadlus, an awareness of their latent potential for freedom, clarity, faith and empowerment. This is Gadlus Rishon.

Klal Yisrael experiences this same dynamic every year on the night of Pesach. We start the night with Gadlus. Our first act is Kiddush, a term which comes from the word *Kodesh* / holy, separated. We stand up in the presence of this holy night, hold a beautiful cup of wine in our hands and declare that this night is the night of Gadlus, expansive freedom. On this night we are completely separated from exile, from *Mitzrayim* / Egypt, from any internal or external slavery.

We start with Gadlus. Only then do we go wash our hands to rid them of ritual impurity and plunge back into Katnus and constricted consciousness. We eat Karpas, a small piece of bitter onion or parsley dipped in salt water. This is a 'lowly' vegetable, plucked from the ground where people trod, too insignificant to nourish or energize us. Then, we proceed to break the middle Matzah, acknowledging the *Katua* / brokenness in our lives. Finally, the *Katan* / child, or our inner child, asks questions, raises uncertainties and seeming contradictions. We begin to answer by confessing our painful Katnus: "In the beginning, we were idol worshipers...."

On this night, we do not travel the normal route of beginning from lower states and progressively elevating ourselves. Rather, we leap to the very highest level of Gadlus and then abruptly descend and start dealing with extremely low levels — idolatry representing the most degraded state that a human being can reach. Starting with Gadlus and then 'dipping' into Katnus is actually the way to ensure that our transformation over the course of this night is complete. From the state of Katnus Rishon, we gradually step higher and higher until we are established in *Gadlus Sheini* / second level expansion, a place of deep clarity and answers, joy and connection, gratitude and ecstatic praise of HaKadosh Baruch Hu, our All-Powerful Redeemer.

Once we have already tasted the maturity of Gadlus, we can go back into the immaturity of Katnus and not be scared that we will stay stuck there. We will not end up simply wallowing in our *Tzaros* / hardships and indulging in our despair.

Indeed, in order to meet the needs of our confused inner *Katan* / child self, we need to have a foothold in the restful maturity of our inner *Gadol* / adult, our benevolent parental self.

The Arizal teaches a deep metaphysical and psycho-spiritual truth: if you start a process of growth with Katnus, there will always be a worry of *Yenikah* / leakage into the *Chitzonim* / external, unwanted forces. Inwardly, this means that if you attempt to deal with Katnus while you are still in a Katnus stage, you may end up dealing with Katnus for the rest of your life. People who think of themselves in a Katnus paradigm, as a failure, inadequate, powerless, and they speak and think all day about their Katnus, even though their intention of speaking about it is to get out of this stage, they can end up just living their whole lives in Katnus. For example, forms of psychotherapy that propose to heal people by having them repeatedly detail their experiences of trauma or conflict — what is wrong, what hurts, and 'what others did to me' — can end up perpetuating that same kind of experience for the rest of their lives. Higher consciousness is not accessed, so there is nowhere to go.

On Pesach night we are gifted freedom from Above. We are given immediate access to Gadlus without first working to climb out of the Katnus stage. When, after a sustained glimpse of pure, higher consciousness, we descend into our problems, pettiness and impurity, there is no fear of getting lost there.

And only when our Gadlus is secured, do we, and should we, go back into the normal course of development and start unpacking and speaking about our Katnus, so that we can be propelled to reach even higher and deeper levels of Gadlus.

KATNUS WITHIN GADLUS

What's more, if we know what it is to stand upon the roof of our being in such a way that we are no longer afraid to visit our 'basement' level, we can courageously begin to include our Katnus within the context of our Gadlus. Eventually, we will be able to experience feelings of lack or desire within a context of *Sheleimus* / wholeness and fullness, a sense of drive within a context of having arrived, a sense of yearning within settledness, a sense of questioning within a greater sense of 'the answer'.

Accordingly, we can understand also the Arizal's teaching about the order of the four cups going from higher to lower. What the Arizal is revealing is that on the night of Pesach we do not travel the normal route; we do not begin from lower and gradually move up higher. Rather, on this night there is a jump, a skipping over, and we start right away with Gadlus, a very high level, and then afterward we climb down and start dealing with the lower levels to ensure that our transformation is complete. Thus we start with the joy and luxury of Kiddush, and afterward move to acknowledge our pain, our questions, our immaturity and the alienation of idol worship, and then we gradually move back toward an even greater clarity, sensing answers to our questions, joy, and connection.

When we start with Gadlus and then move into Katnus, we realize we will get to an even higher, deeper and more inclusive Gadlus. The descent from our initial Gadlus hits the initial Katnus like a diving board, catapulting us into a higher Gadlus.

WE ARE GADLUS

The essential element in all of this is that in our initial Gadlus, we declare who we truly are: a chosen, free, and proud people, and individuals who are like royalty and High Priests, experiencing the greatness of the Source of Existence. Gadlus is who we are, and it is how we can manifest ourselves throughout the entire coming year, if we so choose.

As individuals and as a nation, we also have experiences of brokenness, sadness, bitterness, and nagging uncertainty. But when we know who we truly are, and what we can become, our collective and individual Gadlus will eventually shine forth. Because we *are* Gadlus, we can *start* from Gadlus, and we can and will always reclaim our status as Gadlus. Collectively, we know that Hashem will redeem us, and the Geulah will come, because Geulah is what we are in essence, and it is our destiny that this essence will be revealed.

People sometimes choose a path of spiritual constriction, lowliness, poverty, slavery, or even "idol worship," but Pesach night reveals to our hearts that anyone, at any time, can reclaim their birthright, their inner Gadlus.

WE START & WILL END WITH GADLUS

When we start with who we truly are and who we could be, then, when we descend to a place of Katnus or spiritual contraction, we are protected. Thus, after Kiddush, when we eat an onion dipped in salt water, we point out that there are poor and lonely people still in the world who need a place to eat or feel included; there is still brokenness throughout Creation. And then we start speaking about our history and the history of Klal Yisrael. Despite all the 'lows', the Katnus, the persecutions, pogroms, dispersions, exiles, and expulsions — while they may seem a total disgrace and sometimes even the end of the world, everything always turns around and ends well. We always return to some level of Gadlus, even following a devastating Katnus.

We were born as a proud people, the sons and daughters of Avraham, Yitzchak, Yaakov, Sarah, Rivkah, Rochel, and Leah, our majestic grandparents, but then we descended to Egypt, and even to a place of being lowly slaves. Even at the very beginning of our collective historical journey, we were in a state of peril when Lavan wanted to eradicate Yaakov. Yet we are

Gadlus, we are rooted in Gadlus, we will always reclaim Gadlus, Hashem will redeem us, Hashem will choose us as we truly are.

Sometimes, to deeply refine our way of living, the Omnipresent One guides us into a stage of bitterness, loss or Katnus, a place of spiritual constriction or physical descent, even to poverty or 'slavery'. But the true destination in all our journeys is to a greater level of Gadlus. For this reason, we tell our collective story of *Genus* / disgrace, and gently but steadily open into *Shevach* / glory.

Finally, we arrive at Nirtzah, the revelation of our timeless inner Gadlus, the stainless, changeless perfection of our Divine soul, the part of us which never descends into exile, our portion of eternal freedom. May we always remember this is who we truly are.

Part Three
The Seder Plate

Chapter One:
The Three Matzos:
Their Outer & Inner Meanings

W HAT IS THE SIMPLE HALACHIC REASON THAT WE use three Matzos when leading a Seder? It is so we will have two whole, unbroken Matzos over which to bless HaMotzi, as we do at every Shabbos and Yom Tov meal, as well as one Matzah to break at Yachatz. The two loaves of Shabbos and Yom Tov commemorate the two whole portions of *Mon* / Manna that miraculously appeared every Friday, allowing us to dedicate the day of Shabbos to being with Hashem, rather than to gathering the day's food. The third Matzah of the Seder is broken, symbolizing *Lechem Oni*, or the 'bread of poverty' (*Devarim*, 16:3). A poor person must ration his food, so even if he manages to obtain a full loaf of bread, he breaks it and hides a portion to eat later.

As such, we take three complete Matzos on Seder Night: two complete loaves as on every Yom Tov and Shabbos, and a third loaf which we break at the beginning of the Seder, so that we can recite the Haggadah over a broken Matzah.[*]

PESHAT / SIMPLE REASONS FOR THREE MATZOS

Overall, there are three reasons offered in the Torah, and thus the Haggadah, for why we eat Matzah:

1) To remind us of the bread of affliction we ate as slaves. As we say in the beginning of the Haggadah, "This is the bread of affliction that our ancestors ate in Egypt."

---

[*] From *Tosefos*, Berachos, 39b, it seems clear that on Shabbos we need to recite the blessing for bread over two whole loaves of bread (מיהו בשבת נכון להחמיר ולברך קודם שיחתוך שלא תשמט ידו לבצוע קודם שתכלה הברכה שאז לא יהיה לו לחם משנה). As such, the Rosh writes that on Pesach we need two whole Matzos (upon which recite HaMotzi) and one broken Matzah, which we break in the beginning of the Seder. This is also how the Shulchan Aruch rules. As Tosefos clearly writes on *Pesachim* 116b, we need to take three Matzos. The Rif (10th Century) and the Gra (18th Century) used only two Matzos for the Seder. See also *Seder Rav Amram Gaon. Machzor Vitri*, Hilchos Pesach, 60. *Ohr Zarua* 2, 252. They held like the opinion that we need only one unbroken Matzah, and one Matzah to break, as suggested by the simple reading of the Gemara, דאמר רב פפא: הכל מודים בפסח, שמניח פרוסה בתוך שלמה ובוצע. מאי טעמא? "לחם עני" כתיב. אמר רבי אבא ובשבת חייב אדם לבצוע על שתי ככרות. מאי טעמא? "לחם משנה" כתיב :*Berachos*, 39b. This suggests one broken Matzah and one whole, as the broken Matzah is 'within' a whole one. Perhaps Tosefos's version is different. This is the way Tosefos on *Pesachim*, ibid, quotes this Gemara: דקאמר הכל מודים לענין פסח שמניח פרוסה בתוך השלימות ובוצע — "a broken Matzah within the whole ones." The prevailing opinion today is to use three Matzos. The Tur brings down the Rif: כתב רב אלפס שאין צריך אלא שתי מצות, אחת פרוסה לשנים ומברך על חציה המוציא ועל אכילת מצה וחציה השני לאפיקומן והשלמה לכריכה, Yet, he continues, והתוס' כתבו שצריך לעשות ג' כדפרישית וכ"כ רב עמרם ולזה הסכים א"א הרא"ש ז"ל: Tur, *Orach Chayim*, 475.

2) Towards the end of Maggid we recite a Mishnah that teaches us, "This Matzah that we eat — for what reason? Because the dough of our fathers did not have time to become leavened before the King of kings, the Holy One, blessed be He, revealed Himself to them and redeemed them." We eat the Matzah as a reminder of the bread that we ate as we were leaving Egypt, as the dough did not have time to rise.

3) We eat Matzah as a remembrance of the Matzah that Klal Yisrael were commanded to eat on the night they were going to leave Egypt, long before they actually left. As the Pasuk says, "On the evening (of Pesach), you shall eat Matzos" (*Shemos*, 12:18).

In other words, there are three types of Matzah related to the going out of Egypt: Matzah as the bread of affliction, Matzah that was produced because they left in great haste, which is Matzah as the bread of freedom, and Matzah as the Mitzvah to eat Matzah with the Korban Pesach.

This closer reading of text is perhaps the *Peshat* / literal reason why we have three Matzos. The middle, and later broken, Matzah is a reminder of the bread of affliction, broken, not complete Matzah, the first reason we eat Matzah. The bottom, full Matzah serves as a reminder of the second reason, the flat bread that does not rise. Besides being flat, it also sits on the bottom of the stack, and this is a reminder of the bread that we ate in haste, as it did not have time to rise.

The top Matzah, which we recite the blessing over and eat as part of the Mitzvah of the night, corresponds to the third reason, the Mitzvah of eating Matzah.

REMEZ / THE HINTED REASON FOR THREE MATZOS

The Three Matzos of the Seder hint at the minimum three Matzos that were offered in the Beis haMikdash as a *Todah* / 'thanksgiving offering'. This offering was made when a person was saved from danger, for example, released from prison. On Pesach, we give thanks for the Exodus from Egypt, which was like being freed from prison, and so we eat three Matzos, as there were three types of baked Matzos in the Todah* (חלות רקיקין ורבוכה / cakes, wafers and cakes of flour saturated with oil, and one leavened bread; ideally ten of each, but even one of each is sufficient: *Menachos*, 76a-76b).

---

* The Mordechai, end of *Pesachim*. The Rosh (*Pesachim*, 10) writes that in the Korban Pesach, the total measure of flour used for each of the three Matzos was an Isaron, and thus, many in Ashkenaz have the custom to bake the three Matzos for the Seder also using one Isaron: See Tur, *Orach Chayim*, 475. אמר רב יהודה אמר רב: ארבעה צריכין להודות: יורדי הים, הולכי מדברות, ומי שהיה חולה ונתרפא, ומי שהיה חבוש בבית האסורים ויצא / "Rav Yehuda said that Rav said: Four must offer thanks with a thanks offering and a special public blessing. They are: seafarers, those who walk in the desert, and one who was ill and recovered, and one who was incarcerated in prison and went out": *Berachos*, 54b. All of these are learned from Chapter 107 in *Tehilim*. Interestingly, in leaving Egypt, Klal Yisrael experienced all these four: they were released from prison, they were spiritually sick and some were physically sick, and were healed at Matan Torah, and they traveled in the desert, and also 'passed over water' with the splitting of the sea.

The three Matzos also remind us of when Avraham is visited by the angels and he calls to Sarah, "Hurry! Three measures of the finest flour! Knead it, and make עֻגוֹת / *Ugos* / round breads" (*Bereishis*, 18:6). The Medrash (*Bereishis Rabbah*, 48:12) says this meal takes place on Pesach, and the Ugos are Matzos, made in a hurry so they do not become Chametz. We take three Matzos to be reminded of the "three measures" in the meal of Avraham.

DERUSH / THE EXPANDED REASON FOR THE THREE MATZOS

The three Matzos represent the three *Avos* / patriarchs, Avraham, Yitzchak, and Yaakov (Rokeach. Maharal, *Gevuros Hashem*, 36). They also represent the three categories of Jews: Cohen, Levi, and Yisrael (Arizal).

As described earlier, when we are preparing for the Seder, we stack the Matzos in this order: first the Matzah representing Yisrael on the bottom, then Levi above it, and finally the Cohen on top. In this order, their acronym is *YeiLeCh*, meaning 'going' or journeying. The Seder is a transformative process, a journey towards liberation (*The Rebbe's Haggadah*).

SOD / THE MYSTICAL REASON FOR THREE MATZOS

The Gemara says, "A child does not יוֹדֵעַ / know how to call 'father,' or 'mother,' until he tastes grain" (*Sanhedrin*, 70b). This implies that the consumption of wheat is associated with our intellectual development, specifically, the faculty of Da'as.

The Arizal teaches that the three Matzos symbolize the three forms of intellect: *Chochmah* / wisdom, *Binah* / understanding, and *Da'as* / awareness.

The Matzah on the bottom of the stack is the one that is combined with Maror to make the *Korech* / Hillel's sandwich. This Matzah specifically embodies the quality of Da'as, an intellectual potential that bridges right brain creativity and left brain analytics, connecting intellectual information in the mind with emotional responses in the heart. A similar dynamic is found in the Korech sandwich which brings together the intellect (Matzah) and emotions (Maror), as well as redemption (Matzah) and slavery (Maror).

Since the middle Matzah is broken into two, it is an expression of Binah, the left part of the brain and the capacity to break down creative ideas into finer details. The larger of the two pieces is itself broken into five smaller pieces before it is hidden away as the Afikoman. These five pieces represent the five levels of Gevurah, restriction and discipline (Chesed of Gevurah, Gevurah of Gevurah, Tiferes of Gevurah, Netzach of Gevurah, and Hod of Gevurah), another 'left-column' attribute, which is just below Binah on the Tree of Life.

In terms of the Four Letter Name of Hashem (Yud-Hei-Vav-Hei), Binah is connected with the 'upper' letter Hei. Hei is the fifth letter in the Aleph -Beis, and is composed of two parts — a right vertical line connected to a horizontal line above, and a left suspended line to the left — thus the middle Matzah is broken into two, and then further into five.*

The top Matzah is consumed together with the remaining piece of the middle Matzah, in fulfillment of the Mitzvah of eating Matzah. Fulfilling a Mitzvah, a Divine command, is a manifestation of Chochmah, a higher intuition or faith in what is above and beyond us. Since the top Matzah is connected with the letter Yud (in the Name of Hashem), a simple one-pointed letter, the Matzah is not broken and remains 'one'.

Also, since the idea of Matzah (in contrast to Chametz) is the letter Hei, symbolizing humility, simplicity, and unaffectedness, the three Matzos correspond to the three ways that we can write the letter Hei. Hei can be written as the combination of a Dalet and Yud, a Dalet and a Vav, or as three lines, which are three Vavs. ה.

Thus, the top Matzah, upon which we recite the blessing of HaMotzi, is at first a whole Matzah, but when we break off a small piece to eat, the small piece of Matzah broken off is shaped like a Yud, and the remaining part of the Matzah is shaped as a Dalet.

The middle Matzah, which is broken at the beginning of the Seder, is meant to be broken into the shape of a Dalet and

---

* The numerical value of the word *Matzah* is 135, which is the same as the combined values of the Divine Names AV (72) and SaG (63). AV is associated with the Sefirah of Chochmah, and SaG is associated with the Sefirah of Binah.

the smaller piece in the shape of a Vav (as it is nearly half a Matzah, bigger than the form of a Yud).

The bottom Matzah is used to make a sandwich of three items: meat from the Pesach offering (when offered), Matzah and Maror. This fact corresponds to the Hei made of three lines, three Vavs (*Pri Eitz Chayim*, Sha'ar Chag haMatzos, 3).

FIRST MATZAH	The Mitzvah	Avraham	Chochmah	Cohen
SECOND (BROKEN) MATZAH	Bread of Affliction	Yitzchak	Binah	Levi
THIRD MATZAH	Bread of Haste	Yaakov	Da'as	Yisrael

THREE AND FOUR

Now we have an understanding of why we use three Matzos. Another, more philosophical, question arises: why should there be three Matzos when the main numerical theme of the Haggadah is 'four', as in four sons, four questions, four cups of wine? What is the inner reason for having three Matzos but four cups of wine, and how can this understanding inspire our Seder?* (This is not a technical question demanding a technical answer, Halachic or otherwise. As explored above, a quantity of three is Halachically needed in order to have two full Matzos and a broken one, and so this is more of a philosophical question. See *Likutei Sichos*, 26, Va'era, to explore the below in more detail.)

The Gemara (*Shabbos*, 104a) says that the letters Gimel (numerically 3) and Dalet (numerically 4) together mean *Gomel Dalim* / giver to the poor. The letter Gimel is the *Gomel* / giver, and the letter Dalet, is the *Dalim* / poor people, thus the relationship between three and four is one of giving and receiving. 'Three' is the giver and 'four' is the receiver.

This relationship between 'giver', as three, and 'receiver', as four, can be more fully understood through an analogy of giv-

---

* Both the cups of wine and the Matzah are related to *Mochin* / mind. The three Matzos correspond to the three potentials of the mind. The upper Matzah is *Chochmah* / wisdom, the middle is *Binah* / understanding, and the lower is *Da'as* / knowledge, the place of choice. In contrast to the bland Matzah, the flavorful wine is connected with the world of mind that is internalized and savored, and relates to how intellectual ideas inform actual choices. Within the actual choice there is Da'as of Chesed, a choice to move forward, to do, and there is Da'as of Gevurah, a choice not to act, to refrain, and thus Da'as can be counted as two distinct faculties, bringing the potentials of the mind to a total of four, corresponding to the four cups of wine.

ing or transmitting an insight to another person. When the 'giver' is considering how to communicate a subtle insight to the 'receiver', the insight has three metaphorical dimensions within the mind of the giver: *Omek* / 'depth', *Orech* / 'length', and *Rochav* / 'breadth'.

'Depth' refers to the giver's deep understanding of the meaning of the insight. 'Length' refers to the giver's ability to articulate the insight, taking it out of abstraction and extending it outwards in an understandable form. 'Broadening' means the giver's ability to develop practical implications of the insight.

The receiver is 'poor' in terms of these three dimensions, as it were. He does not have the Omek, Orech, or Rochav of the insight, as of yet. However, when the giver finally communicates the insight, a fourth dimension is added to the three: the relationship with the receiver. Thus, when the insight of 'three' (Gimel) is received, it becomes 'four' (Dalet). The giver's insight now expands vertically and horizontally within the vessel of the receiver's mind, and now there can be a unity between giver and receiver, a 'fourth' dimension.

OUR REDEMPTION

In terms of Yetzias Mitzrayim, and in general, HaKadosh Baruch Hu is the 'Giver' in the relationship and we, the redeemed ones, are the 'receivers'. Eventually, we reach a mature relationship with HaKadosh Baruch Hu, but at first, this relationship must be developed so that we can receive what will be given. In the beginning of the unfolding of the Exodus narrative, as slaves, with no voice, dreams, or hope, with no inner identity and selfhood, we were an immature group of people, and we were not yet able to receive the gift of redemption. During the journey towards redemption, we slowly regained our voice, our inner core, and became ready to have a genuine relationship with our Redeemer. We developed a sense of selfhood, of being a person who could receive and assimilate Divine *Shefa* / abundance.

We drink four cups of wine in correspondence to the four expressions the Torah uses in reference to Yetzias Mitzrayim: "I will take you out," "I will save you," "I will redeem you," and "I will take you to Me." The first three expressions are like the three dimensions of insight within the giver, and they imply 'poverty' on the part of the receiver, for there is not yet an active receptivity or relationship. Thus, "take out," "save," and "redeem" all suggest a passive posture on the part of the one being taken out, the immature receiver. In this paradigm, it is all about the Giver. However, the fourth term, "...take you to Me," implies a relationship, a unity. This is when real communication between both parties is possible.

In the expression "I will take you to Me," the term 'take' / *l'Kicha*, alludes to the 'taking' of a marriage partner; כי יקח איש אשה / "when a man will 'take' a wife" (*Devarim*, 22:13). HaKadosh Baruch Hu takes us in marriage when we reach Mount Sinai. Under the 'wedding canopy' of the mountain suspended above us, we received the Torah like a gulp of wine, and internalized the depth, length, and breadth of the Divine insight it communicates. At Sinai, the 'fourth' dimension became revealed in the relationship and unification between the Giver and the receiver — this provides an inner reason why there are four cups of wine.

WINE IS FOUR, MATZAH IS THREE

The three Matzos, as the 'bread of poverty', are flat and relatively tasteless, representing the receiver in an empty, passive, open state. Therefore, the first three expressions of redemption, in which the receiver is passive, correspond to the three Matzos. They also correspond to the three levels of intellect, Chochmah, Binah and Da'as, before they are touched and ignited by Divine love.

Wine, in contrast to Matzah, is full of taste, color, and passion, representing the receiver fully present, alive, and engaged in a loving relationship. The four cups of wine thus represent the fourth expression of redemption, when we, the receivers, are mature enough to enter into intimate communication with HaKadosh Baruch Hu.

By the conclusion of the Seder, after the fourth cup, settling into the state of *Nirtzah* / 'desired', we achieve a vivid taste of the deepest sweetness of life: effortless intimacy with our Creator.

Chapter Two:
Meditations on the Seder Plate:
Lines, Circles, & Infinity

I N A SELF-CONTAINED AND RIGID PARADIGM OF CAUSE-
and-effect or action-and-reaction, the possibility of genuine freedom is merely an illusion. In a rigid, linear dimension of time, the past creates the present, the present gives
birth to the future, and everything is mechanically predetermined by its preceding causes, leaving no room for freedom. Yet, as we sit down to the Seder on Pesach night, we do
dream of genuine freedom, liberated from strict deterministic
causality. We aspire to what existentialists would call 'radical
freedom', in which we can choose something just because we
choose it, uninfluenced by precedents and non-reactive in the

face of possible results. But is such freedom truly attainable? Is not every choice determined by a previous choice? Is not our present a result of our past, and an impregnation of the future?

In an evolving universe, once something is set into motion, the ripple effects are interminable. Every effect can be traced to a cause, and the cause in turn is merely an effect of a previous cause. Such is the nature of a closed self-contained system, that which is referred to, in the language of the inner dimensions of Torah, as *Seder Hishtalshelus* / evolving order. On Pesach night, however, we are given the power to tap into a space beyond Seder Hishtalshelus, beyond the 'order' and 'mechanics' of the universe. We are empowered to transcend cause and effect and to *Pesach* / 'skip over' all linear processes. In the time of our Exodus, this quality is what thrust us out of Egypt, and its physical, mental, emotional, and spiritual slavery, and brought us to freedom. Opening up to this power of 'Pesach' allows us to articulate our 'beyond-Seder', beyond-order freedom, throughout the entire 'order' of the coming year.

Before leapfrogging to a place 'beyond order', we need to ensure that our vessels of 'order' are in place, as only "a filled vessel is able to receive." So we start Seder Night with a clear delineated regimen and display of *Seder* / order, before we even begin reciting the Haggadah, which speaks of freedom. We ensure that we are prepared for the experience, so that later on we are able to integrate the experience of going 'beyond order' in real time and space, within the workings of 'order' and the natural flow of life.

Appropriately, we first create an elaborate structure of the *Ka'arah* / Seder plate, a vessel holding a very defined and strict 'order' of elements — only to reach a point at the end of the Seder in which the Ka'arah is in total chaos and disarray. This image expresses the dynamic of Seder Night, assuming order upon ourselves and also transcending order.

COSMIC STRUCTURE OF THE SEDER PLATE

Let's begin by understanding the great unfolding of Seder Hishtalshelus on a cosmic level, which will help us better understand the structure of the Ka'arah.

Initially, there was (and is) only the *Ohr Ein Sof* — the endless, Infinite Light of Hashem. Finitude, the tapestry of time, space, and consciousness, could not emerge when all of reality was overwhelmed by the Infinite light. To create the possibility of 'otherness' and apparent separation, there 'needed', so to speak, to be a great *Tzimtzum* / contraction and concealment of the *Ein Sof* / Infinite within Itself. Only then could a finite existence come into focus.

The first 'otherness' that was formed was an abstract *Igul* / 'circle'. The image is of a circular space in which all potential reality was contained within as one, non-individuated, and non-distinct, no beginning and no end. Within the circle, a *Kav* / line was formed with distinct points and an up-and-down sequential structure with a clear beginning and a definite end.

In other words, the Tzimtzum caused the displaced Light to encircle the 'Vacated Space' in the 'shape' of an *Igul* / circle or sphere. Circularity is a metaphor for a non-physical paradigm of perfect equality, in which all potentialities are equal, without distinction, individuation or reification; without beginning or end. Next, a thin line or ray of *Ohr Yashar* / 'direct Light' called the *Kav* (a light still directly connected to the pre-Tzimtzum Infinite Light) beamed into the vacuum (the Kav immediately begins to illuminate the perimeter of the "empty space," forming concentric circles of Light as it moves inward).

It is important to realize that these physical metaphors, such as lines and circles, are not implying actual shapes or physical dimensions, rather they are poetically charged images that point to abstract spiritual realities. Nor are they really events in time, even though they are described as a sequence of events occurring at the genesis of our universe, rather they are ever-present dynamics of the continuous act of Divine creation.

On the line of the Kav, there are ten regressive grades, ten points. These original points are the ten *Sefiros* / 'Divine Attributes', which act as 'screens' in relation to the *Ohr Ein Sof* / Light of the Infinite, as the Light penetrates our defined reality through them. The distinctly formed and shaped Sefiros are like curtains or 'colored' containers through which the infinite, colorless, formless, unified light is reflected into our world, in such a way that it appears to be differentiated and colored.

The order of the *Sefiros* are as follows. First there are the three intellectual Sefiros: on the right side, *Chochmah* / intuition and wisdom, on the left, *Binah* / cognition and reason, and in the middle, *Da'as* / knowledge and awareness, the ability to assimilate wisdom and reason in a practical manner.

Next are the three primary internal emotions: on the right, 'expansive' column is *Chesed* / love and giving. On the left, 'constrictive' column is *Gevurah* / strength and restraint. In the middle is their synthesis, *Tiferes* / compassion and harmony. Compassion is the idea of the 'giver' giving with a sensitivity for how much the 'receiver' can and needs to receive.

Then there are the three primary 'outer' emotions, how we outwardly express our inner strivings. On the right, expansive column is *Netzach* / confidence and perseverance. On the left column is *Hod* / humility and devotion, and in the middle is the channel of unification, connecting the 'giver' and the 'receiver,' *Yesod* / relationship and intimacy.

Malchus / kingship is receptivity, as it is the vessel that receives from the preceding nine Sefiros and re-channels the energies downward, thus becoming the 'crown' for the subsequent *Partzuf* / persona and structure of Sefiros.

As we prepare the Ka'arah, we mimic this cosmic unfolding of Seder Hishtalshelus. We first take an *Igul* / circle, the Ka'arah itself, and place it on the table. Although not required, a Ka'arah is generally round like the shape of handmade

Shemurah Matzah (*Teshuvas Mahari*, Orach Chayim, 157. Note: *Medrash Rabbah*, Bamidbar, 13:14 with regards to the offerings of the Nesi'im. See also: Ramban, Rabbeinu Bachya on *Bamidbar*, 7:3).

We begin to assemble the structure by placing three round Matzos in a stack. These represent the three intellectual Sefiros of Chochmah, Binah, and Da'as, as the consumption of wheat is connected with our intellectual development. In the words of Chazal, "A child does not know how to call 'Father' or 'Mother' until he tastes grain." 'Father' / *Abba* is the name of the *Partzuf* / personalization of Chochmah, and 'Mother' / *Ima* is the name of Binah.

On the bottom we place the Matzah that will form the *Korech* / 'Hillel sandwich'. This Matzah embodies Da'as, a Sefirah which unites and synthesizes opposites. Hillel's sandwich represents a synthesis of our intellect (Matzah) and emotions (Maror).

In the middle we place the Matzah that will be broken in two, the larger half being hidden away as the Afikoman, while the smaller half remains in the stack. This Matzah represents the left column Sefirah of Binah, the idea of breaking down ideas into finer details. Thus it is broken in two, with the Afikoman itself broken into five smaller parts, reflecting the five levels of the left-column Sefirah of Gevurah.

On top we place the Matzah that will be consumed together with the smaller half of the middle Matzah when we fulfill our obligation to eat Matzah. This Matzah reflects Choch-mah, a higher intuition, supra-rational faith and connection to transcendence — and therefore this is the Matzah that will be eaten to fulfill the basically supra-rational Mitzvah of eating Matzah.

Next we arrange six items of food in two interpenetrating triangles which reflect our internal and outer emotions, respec-tively. These six items represent six points of light, the six emo-tional Sefiros.

Based on the literal words of the Arizal, the practice of the students of the Baal Shem Tov is to place the Ka'arah on top of the three Matzos (*Ba'er Heitev*, Orach Chayim, 473:4. Alter Rebbe, *Shulchan Aruch,* ibid, 26. *Shu'T Minchas Elazar*, 6:13. There are others who also follow the Arizal, but who place the Ka'arah near the Matzah, not on top: *Kaf haChayim,* ibid, 58. Note, Rama, *ibid,* 4). This order represents the *Midos /* emotional Sefiros on top of the intellectual Sefiros. Normally, in the flow of the Sefiros, first comes the *Mochin /* mind, then the Midos. According to this pattern, the Matzah should be on the top of the Ka'arah. Why is the order reversed here?

As explored earlier, throughout the year, in our spiritual, intellectual, emotional, and physical development and experi-ence, we first find ourselves in a state of *Katnus /* smallness, and then, only afterwards in a state *Gadlus /* expansiveness. On the night of *Pesach /* 'passing over', there was and is a leaping over of normal processes, and there is a revelation of Gadlus before any experience of Katnus. As the normal order of our reality is reversed, the Ka'arah of Midos is stationed higher than the Matzah of Mochin. This also reflects the truth that the Midos are in a 'redeemed' state and in total sync with their Mochin.

Let us return to the six items of the Ka'arah and their correspondence to the six lower Sefiros (*Pri Eitz Chayim*, Sha'ar Chag haMatzos, 6). The upper triangle of items reflects the three dominant and internal emotional Sefiros, and the lower triangle represents the three outer and more externally directed Sefiros. Additionally, the upper triangle on the Ka'arah is connected with Mitzvos of the Torah which were performed during the times of the Beis haMikdash: the two special *Korbanos* / offerings of Pesach (the Chagigah and the Pesach), and the Maror. The lower triangle represents three prominent Rabbinic Mitzvos and customs, (the Charoses, Karpas, and the Hillel sandwich).

Upper Right Side: On the upper right side of the plate is the *Zeroa,* a roasted chicken neck or shankbone symbolizing the Korban Pesach.* The Hebrew word *Zeroa* / זרוע reminds us of the *Zeroa haNetuya* /הנטויה זרוע the outstretched arm of Hashem, the Divine Chesed and lovingkindness that was shown to us, which brought us salvation. Thus the Zeroa is the attribute of Chesed.

---

* ומנהגו לעשות צלי מזרוע הבהמה זכר לזרוע נטויה :*Col-Bo*, 50. Simply, the Zeroa reminds us of the Korban Pesach / offering of Passover. צריך שני מיני בשר אחד זכר לפסח ואחד זכר לחגיגה / "Two types of meat, one as a remembrance of the Korban Pesach and one as a remembrance of the Korban Chagigah": *Pesachim*, 114b. And this is according to all opinions, both the opinion that we can use "beets and rice" for the Zeroa, and the opinion that we need to take two forms of meat, as the Ran explains.

Upper Left Side: On the opposite side, on the upper left column, we place the *Beitzah,* a boiled egg, symbolizing the Korban Chagigah. The egg is also a traditional food of mourning, as the oval shape represents a completed cycle of life. For this reason, the egg is associated with Gevurah, the 'constriction' felt in a time of loss, when there is an experiential 'concealment' of revealed Chesed.

Gevurah also means strength. Unlike most other items of food where cooking softens the food, the more you cook an egg the harder it becomes, hinting at the element of Gevurah. This is related to our hardships in Egypt; the harsher the conditions, the 'hotter' it got, the stronger we became. Thus the Beitzah is the attribute of Gevurah.*

---

* The Egg is to remind us of the *Korban Chagigah* / festival day offering, which we no longer bring because of the destruction of the Beis haMikdash: *Pesachim,* 114b. The word ביעה / egg in Aramaic, the language of the Gemara, means 'desires', as in "Hashem בעא / desires to redeem us with an outstretched hand": in the name of the Yerushalmi, *Col-Bo,* Siman 50:22. *Beis Yoseph,* Orach Chayim, 473.

Although the Gemara says, according to Rav Yoseph, we need to use מיני בשר / 'a type of meat' as a reminder for the Chagigah, which would mean that one should have a piece of meat on the Ka'arah instead of an egg, and indeed this is how the Rambam rules — ובזמן הזה מביאין על השלחן שני מיני בשר אחד זכר לפסח ואחד זכר לחגיגה: Rambam, *Hilchos Chametz uMatzah,* 8:1. Yet, the custom is nevertheless to use an egg, which is somewhat related to meat, perhaps at least like the "gravy" of the meat (*Bach,* Siman 473. Although see Hagahos Maimoniyos, *Hilchos Chametz uMatzah,* 8:2). And as mentioned, the egg is related to the word בעא, and the egg is connected to 'mourning', since the first night of Pesach falls out on the same day of the week as Tishah b'Av will, later that year.

In terms of the Sefiros, the egg embodies the Sefirah of Gevurah, as it is a 'closed' or rounded item, symbolizing limitation, restriction, and destruc-

Upper Middle: In the middle, at the third point of the upper triangle, the *Maror* / bitter herbs are arranged reflecting the attribute of *Tiferes* / mercy and compassion. Becoming aware of our own spiritual condition may arouse a *Merirus* / bitterness within us, creating a desire to change and stimulating a compassionate response. Merirus is not depression, in which we stop feeling altogether, rather, it is an overwhelming feeling of bitterness over our estrangement, realizing how disengaged we are, how far we are from living our truth and being connected with HaKadosh Baruch Hu. This inner stimulation of desire to

tion. As above, the oval image of the egg instills within us the idea of a complete life cycle, and thus the egg is a food of mourning. And so, this is an additional reason why an egg is used. *Beis Yoseph*, Ibid. Rama, *Darchei Moshe*, ibid. *Igros Moshe*, Orach Chayim 1, 156.

Additionally, the egg represents an embryonic or pre-birth state similar to the condition of Klal Yisrael in Egypt, before the going out of Egypt, their national, collective birth. This is similar to the Pesach Offering which they offered while still in Egypt which was roasted in a fetal position, with its head between its knees, to illustrate the same pre-birth state.

Another reason for an egg, says the Kotzker Rebbe, rather than a piece of meat, is that besides being loosely connected to meat, an egg contains the potential of new life (although the eggs we actually eat today are not fertilized). Thus it serves a double purpose: it reminds us of the past and the Chagigah of the past, and it also fills us with the hope of the 'new life' of the future, and the Chagigah that will be again offered with the building of the Third and final Beis haMikdash.

These "two cooked foods" (*Pesachim*, 114b) also correspond to Moshe and Aharon. *Sefer Rokeach*, Seder Leil Pesach, Siman 59. Accordingly, the Maror, which represents bitterness and whose root is *Mar* / bitter, corresponds to Miriam (whose name is also rooted in the word *Mar*). These are the three who help facilitate the Exodus from Egypt, as the *Navi* says, "I brought you up out of Egypt and redeemed you from the land of slavery. I sent Moshe to lead you, also Aharon and Miriam": *Michah*, 6:4. Based on this Pasuk, there was a custom from and in the times of Rav Sharira Gaon, to place three items on the Ka'arah, one for Moshe, one for Aharon, and one for Miriam. *Ma'aseh Rokeach*, ibid.

return to Hashem awakens *Rachamim Rabim* / Infinite compassion from on High.

When through external stimuli we feel discomfort or bitterness, we also awaken within ourselves our own ability to be empathetic to others who are in real pain. The eating of the Maror awakens such empathy and compassion, for the bitterness of our own lowliness arouses Compassion from on High (*Likutei Torah*, Shir HaShirim, Kol Dodi). Thus Maror is the attribute of Tiferes.*

* Maror is connected with Tiferes, compassion. Romaine lettuce is also used as Maror. Lettuce in Talmudic language (Aramaic) is called *Chasa*, which also happens to mean "compassion" in Aramaic. "מאי חסא — דחס רחמנא עילווין / What is the meaning of *Chasa* / lettuce? It refers to the fact that the All-Merciful One has mercy on us": *Pesachim*, 39a. Rabbeinu Yerucham writes (see *Beis Yoseph*, Orach Chayim, 473) that a person should endeavor to eat Chasa for Maror, even if it's expensive — טוב לחזר אחר חסא מטעם שאמרנו, אפילו לקנות בדמים יקרים. *Chok Yaakov* (ad loc, 473:2) writes, one should even spend a third more money on the Seder in order to buy Chasa. This is also the ruling of the Alter Rebbe (ibid, 30): 'אע"פ שכל ה מינים אלו נקראים מרור בלשון תורה, מ"מ מדברי סופרים מצוה לחזור אחר חזרת לקנותו אפילו בדמים יקרים, על דרך שיתבאר בסי' תרנ"ו לענין אתרוג הדור. See also *Shu'T Chacham Tzvi*, Siman 119.

We use horseradish as Maror even though it is 1) more *Charif* / sharp than *Mar* / bitter, 2) we eat the root of horseradish itself. However, horseradish is not clearly mentioned in the Mishnah as one of the five items that can be used for Maror; the reason for the use of horseradish seems to be due to the colder climate in Europe, where lettuce was not available during Pesach, only horseradish.

The *Tosefos Yom Tov* (on *Pesachim*, 2:6) and the *Hagahos Maimoniyos* (on *Chametz uMatzah*, 7:13) both mention the use of horseradish as Maror and identify "*Tamcha*" (one of the 5 items mentioned in the Mishnah) as horseradish. The Chasam Sofer writes that תמכ"א is an acronym for תמיד מספרים כבוד א-ל, thus in a place where it is difficult to have clean Chasa lettuce, we should use Tamcha: See *Chasam Sofer*, Orach Chayim, 132. *Mishnah Berurah*, 473:42.

Today most people use horseradish. The beauty of the horseradish is that the longer you chew on it, the less sharp it tastes and the sweeter it becomes. This is the opposite of the Chazeres (Chasa), which morphs from sweet to bitter. Chazeres, the romaine lettuce that we also use as Maror, is at first more sweet or soft, and then hard or harsh in the end. Speaking of the value of taking Chasa for Maror, the Gemara says, מה מרור זה שתחילתו רך וסופו קשה אף מצריים תחילתן רכה וסופן קשה / "Just as these bitter herbs (lettuce) are soft at first and harsh in the end, so too, the Egyptians were soft at first (when they paid Klal Yisrael for their work) but were harsh in the end (when they enslaved them)": *Pesachim*, 39a. This is specifically speaking about *Chazeres* / lettuce, as clear from the Gemara, and as the Yerushalmi adds, מה חזרת תחילתה מתוק וסופה מר כך עשו המצריים / "Just as Chazeres is first sweet then bitter, the same were the Egyptians": *Pesachim*, 2:5. What does תחילתו רך וסופו קשה mean? Rashi writes this means at first it grows as soft and then hardens. The Rivan writes that at first the Chazeres is sweet and then after chewing it for a while becomes bitter (thus, even if the Chazeres of today is not so bitter when you start eating it, still you fulfill your obligation by eating it).

The first choice for the Mitzvah of Maror is to use the Chazeres — this is the simple Peshat of the Mechaber, that we are allowed (in fact it is better) to use Chazeres, and although it is initially sweet, eventually there is a bitterness: See Alter Rebbe, *Shulchan Aruch*, Orach Chayim, 473:30.

The *KafhaChayim* also seems to be worried about the issue that the Chazeres of today is sweet (See also Ridbaz on *Yerushalmi*, 6:1. *Chazon Ish,* Orach Chayim, 124), and so he writes, ואעפ"י שהיא מתוקה ואין בה מרירות כ"כ כמו בשאר המינים מ"מ קים להו לרז"ל שידעו לדבר בלשה"ק יותר ממנו שעיקר שם מרור הכתוב בתורה חונה עליו תחלה: *Ibid*, 473:90. Yet, the Alter Rebbe clearly rules that the lettuce we eat today, although it is not so bitter, is the first choice. This is the opinion of the *Chacham Tzvi* (*Orach Chayim*, 119). *Shu'T Chavos Yair*. See also *Mishnah Berurah*, 473:34. But we obviously need to make sure to check properly for bugs.

Besides, it is important to note that people often confuse 'bitter' with 'sharp'. Horseradish is more 'sharp' tasting, while Chazeres has a more 'bitter' taste. As such, both items contain their opposites, moving from sweet to bitter or from bitter to sweet.

Chazeres is connected with the Hebrew word *Chozer* / return, and thus connected to the *Ohr Yashar* / direct light, and the *Ohr Chozer* / reflective light. This allows us to move 'directly' from sweet to bitter, and then 'reflecting' backward, to move from bitter to sweet (Numerically, *Chazeres* = 615, the same as *Chochmah* / 73, *Binah* / 67 and *Da'as* / 474, plus 1 for the word itself = 615).

Indeed, many people use both horseradish (what everyone calls Maror) and romaine lettuce or endives, and eat them together. This seems to be a prevailing custom.

The Mishnah (*Pesachim,* 39a) says, ואלו ירקות שאדם יוצא בהן ידי חובתו בפסח / "And these are the vegetables with which a person can fulfill his obligation to eat bitter herbs on Pesach: Chazeres, Tamcha, Charvina, Ulshin and Maror (a bitter vegetable)." (Although Rashi writes, כל עשב מר נקרא מרור / "Every bitter herb is called Maror": *Shemos,* 12:8. Perhaps Rashi is talking about the *Din* / law of the Torah). Then the Mishnah says that יוצאין בהן בין לחין בין יבשין אבל לא כבושין ולא שלוקין ולא מבושלין / "One fulfills his obligation with them whether they are fresh or dry, however, one does not fulfill his obligation if they are pickled, 'over-boiled' or boiled." The Mishnah concludes, ומצטרפין לכזית / "they form together to create a Kezayis," the amount required to eat. What do these last words in the Mishnah, ומצטרפין לכזית mean? Simply, that you can take all or some of the above five types, and mix them together, and fulfill your obligation if you eat a Kezayis of the mixture.

Yet, Rashi writes, אם אין לו מאחד מהן כזית אבל יש לו מזה חצי זית ומזה חצי זית מצטרפין זה עם זה כדי לצאת ידי חובתו, which means, that the Mishnah is talking about a case in which a person does not have a Kezayis of any of the above five foods. Yet, if he does have a Kezayis of each and still mixes them into one Kezayis to eat, perhaps he is only *Yotzei Bedi'eved* / discharged of obligation after the fact and not in the ideal way. This is the way the Ran understands Rashi: דה"ה דהוה מצי למיתני לענין כזית מצה דמצטרפין אלא לגבי מצה פשיטא לי' אבל הכא איצטריך סד"א כיון דאמרירותא קפדינן טעמא דחד מבטל בחבריו קמ"ל דכיון דיש לכולן טעם מרירות מצטרפים. In other words, with regards to the types of wheat one may use for Matzah, the previous Mishnah does not say ומצטרפין לכזית because of course they do, why would they not? However, with the types of Maror, one would think that they each taste a little different, and therefore they cancel each other out, and for this reason the Mishnah says that Bedi'eved, if you mixed them, you are Yotzei.

This seems to be what Rashi is saying (however, the Sefas Emes has a different understanding of Rashi, that Rashi is talking about the כבושין שלוקין מבושלין). According to this, some Poskim (such as Rav Shlomo Zalman, הליכות שלמה על מועדי השנה, ניסן-אב), write that one should not mix any of the types of Maror, so if you are eating lettuce for Maror, eat only lettuce without the horseradish. Yet, the Mechaber rules וכולם מצטרפים לכזית / "and they all combine for the measurement of a Kezayis": *Orach Chayim,* 473:5. And indeed, the *Aruch haShulchan* (ibid, 14) writes, חמישה מינים אלו מצטרפין לכזית. / "All these five ולכן יש אצלינו שלוקחין מעט חזרת עם מעט תמכא, שטוב לאכלן יחד combine for a Kezayis, therefore there are those among us who take a little of Chazeres with a little of horseradish (which some sources identify with בתמכא), as it is good (easier) to eat them together."

Next we arrange the lower triangle, reflecting the outer emotional Sefiros, and the Mitzvos of the sages and the customs of Seder Night.

Lower Right Side: On the lower right column we place the *Charoses,* a mixture of various fruits that are crushed with some wine into a liquid or paste. The Charoses corresponds to Netzach, as the Charoses is composed of fruits of trees, growing tall and mighty, mirroring the quality of power, confidence, and perseverance.

Besides neutralizing any harmful bitterness of the Maror / Chazeres, the Charoses reminds us of the mortar that we used when we laid bricks as slaves. Despite those harsh conditions, we persevered and built structures that lasted and survived the sands of time. The Charoses, with its dominant ingredient of apples, also reminds us of the words, "Under the apple tree I betrothed you." This verse alludes to the fact that despite the horrific hardships of slavery, we were resilient and flourished, and the more the Egyptians oppressed us, the more we multiplied. This is the quality of Netzach, self-confidence, resilience and perseverance — no matter the trials and tribulations that may come, *Chas v'Shalom* / Heaven forbid, we will always over-

---

In other words, there is such a Minhag Yisrael at least for the last couple of hundred years, and that is the Minhag Chabad — to eat *L'chatchilah* / initially and as the ideal practice, Chazeres and horseradish together.

This seems to be also the opinion of the Rambam, that even L'chatchilah you can mix the different types of Maror. ואם אכל מאחד מהן או מחמשתן כזית יצא: *Hilchos Chametz uMatzah,* 7:13.

come. Charoses is thus the attribute of Netzach.[*]

---

* Even if Charoses is not a 'Mitzvah', we eat it for a 'medical' reason, due to the 'poison' in the bitter herbs, which is neutralized by the sweet Charoses. Rebbe Levi, however, says that Charoses is a remembrance of the apple in the verse, "Who is this who comes up from the wilderness, reclining upon her beloved? Under the apple tree I betrothed you" (*Shir haShirim*, 8:5), which is an allusion to Klal Yisrael leaving Egypt. The women in Egypt also gave birth to their children under the apple trees: *Sotah*, 11b. Rebbe Yochanan says that the Charoses is in remembrance of the mortar used by Klal Yisrael in their slave labor in Egypt: *Pesachim*, 116a. So it is a Mitzvah, a ritual practice.

The word *Charoses* is Aramaic for a word that means a collection of things that are mixed up and crushed. There was in Yerushalayim a place called "the gate of trash" (*Nechemyah*, 3:14), a place where people literally threw all their garbage, and the Targum translates "gate of trash" as "the gate of *Charsis*": See also *Ohr Zarua haGadol*, Hilchos Pesach, 256. *Imrei Shefer*, Maror.

One of the main purposes of the pasty Charoses is a reminder of the brick and mortar the slaves used in Egypt: *Pri Chadash*. Alter Rebbe, *Shulchan Aruch*, Orach Chayim, 475:11. As such, the Hebrew word *Even* / stone, in German and Yiddish is an acronym for the basic three ingredients of the Charoses: *Epel* / apples, *Beren* / pears, and *Nisin* / nuts. Charoses embodies the Sefirah of Netzach, endurance and strength, as mortar 'cement' endures.

On the one hand, Charoses is a reminder of the cement and enslavement in Egypt, yet on the other hand, it is also a remembrance of the apple tree and leaving Egypt (although the apple tree can also serve as a reminder of the hardship of slavery, of needing to hide: *Derishah*, Orach Chayim, 473:2). In addition to the apples, pears, and nuts, we add a little wine to remind ourselves of the blood of the first *Makah* / Plague, which represents the beginnings of our redemption: *Yerushalmi, Pesachim*, 10:13. Alter Rebbe, *Shulchan Aruch*, Orach Chayim, 473:32-34. Perhaps for this reason (and this will answer the question of the *Manhig*, Hilchos Pesach, Siman 79. *Tur*, Orach Chayim, 475: ועוד הקשה בעל המנהיג לדבריהם שמצה היא זכר זה עם זה יתחברו והאיך לטיט זכר וחרוסת לחירות), there are some Rishonim who are of the opinion that we need to dip the Matzah (which represents our freedom) in Charoses (*Seder Rav Amram Gaon*. Rambam, *Hilchos Chametz uMatzah*, 8:8), as Charoses is also connected to freedom: ומן הדין עלינו

Lower Left Side: On the lower left column, we place the Karpas, either a piece of onion or potato. Karpas reflects the idea of *Hod* / humility, as vegetables, in contrast to fruit, grow within or in close proximity to the ground. Whereas the fruits of Charoses are Netzach, perseverance and confidence, Karpas is humility and wonderment. In fact, in the word Karpas[*]

להחמיר כדעת הגאונים הראשונים אלא שלא נהגו כן. Bach, *Ibid.*

The theme of Pesach is *Peh-Sach*, the liberation of speech. This is also related to Charoses. The word Charoses, teaches the Arizal, can spell the words *Sach* / speak, *Rus* / Ruth. "What is the meaning of the name Ruth?... She was privileged to be the ancestress of David, who saturated (in Hebrew, *Rava* / saturated is related to the word *Ruth*) the Holy One, blessed be He, with songs and hymns" (*Berachos*, 7b). In this way, *Charoses* can be translated as 'speech of song and praise'. And this is the highest or deepest form of speech, one that we reach at the climax of the Exodus narrative, with the singing of the Shirah at the Sea. On this night we reach this climax towards the end of the Haggadah, where we sing Hashem's praise.

Regarding these issues, the Rambam rules that we need to dip the Matzah in Charoses: ומטבל מצה בחרסת ואוכל. Yet the Ra'avad argues, זה הבל / *Zeh Hevel* / this is 'nonsense': *Hilchos Chametz uMatzah*, 8:8. Besides the simple meaning of this counter of the Ra'avad, it is possible to reinterpret the words זה הבל as 'this is according to Hevel.' The Arizal teaches that specifically someone whose *Shoresh Neshamah* / soul root is in Kayin needs to ensure that they have salt on the table, whereas one whose Shoresh Neshamah is from Hevel does not. In fact, perhaps this is what the words זה הבל can mean; only those souls whose root is Hevel do not need to dip the Matzah in salt and can do so in Charoses, whereas souls of Kayin need to dip it in salt: *Shulchan haTahor*, Siman 167, Zeir Zahav 3.

[*] Whereas the actual word *Karpas* comes from the Greek word *Karpos*, which means fruit of the soil, Chazal tease out meanings even from non-Torah words (Rav Yaakov Emdin, *Lechem Nikudim*, Avos, 2:14), and certainly once they have been adapted into Hebrew. כרפס spelled in reverse also stands for ס' פרך / 'sixty, harsh labor', alluding to the six hundred thousand slaves in Egypt: *Sefer haManhig*, 60. *Avudraham*, Haggadah. *Sifrei Maharil*, Liku-

one can find the words *Caf* / palm of the hand (and *Pas* also means hand: *Daniel*, 5:5) and the letter Reish (Rosh) is symbolic of someone who is impoverished, and Samach is related to the word *Somech* / support (*Berachos*, 4b. *Osyos d'Rebbe Akiva*, Samach), thus Karpas represents the hand of the poor open to receive in humility.

Additionally, the purpose of the custom of Karpas, which during the Seder will be dipped in salt water (or Charoses), is to elicit questions from the children (as Rashi, *Pesachim*, 114a writes). This, too, is related to Hod, awakening a sense of wonder, which is connected to humility, and standing in awe at the mysteries of Creation. In these ways, Karpas reflects the attribute of Hod.

Lower Middle: the Chazeres is placed in the lower middle column. The Chazeres is the bitter herb that will eventually be used in the Hillel sandwich. Chazeres reflects the Sefirah of *Yesod* / foundational connectivity, the middle column integra-

---

tim, Seder Haggadah, 14. *Shu'T Chasam Sofer*, Orach Chayim, 132. Karpas is also dipped into salt water, reminding us of the *Kesones Pasim* / Yoseph's multicolored cloak that was dipped in blood, and the sale of Yoseph, which is a harbinger and meta-cause of the eventual slavery in Egypt. The Medrash says, "Hashem tells the Shevatim, 'You have sold him to be a slave, as it says, "Yoseph was sold as a slave"' (*Tehilim*, 105:17), therefore, you too will read every year, *Avadim Hayinu* / 'We were slaves to Pharoh in Egypt': *Medrash Shocher Tov*, 10:3. Indeed, the word כרפס / Kar'**pas**, is an allusion to the words כתנת פסים / Kesones **Pas**im: Rabbeinu Menoach, *Hilchos Chametz u'Matzah*, 8:2. *Archos Chayim*, Hilchos Leil Pesach. The Ben Ish Chai adds: כר / *KaR* are the last two letters of the word מכר / *MaChAR* / 'sold', and פס / *Pas* are the first two letters of the word פסים / *Pasim*, thus *KarPas* is an allusion to the Kesones Pasim: *Ben Ish Chai*, Shanah Rishonah, Tzav, 32.

tive force which binds the Sefiros together. On the Ka'arah, the Chazeres 'sensitively' connects and integrates the entire system of seemingly polarized structures and dynamics of the Seder. For instance, it brings together freedom and exile, affliction and salvation, the Matzah of liberation and the Maror of pain.

Malchus, in this three dimensional depiction of the Sefiros, is the Seder plate, the Ka'arah itself, the vessel and container of all the points of light above it.

Having arranged the items in their appropriate locations, ensuring that its 'order' is in place, we can now be on our journey toward radical infinite freedom (As the Rebbe Rashab once said following arranging his Seder plate, "I have just saddled the wagon": *Reshimas haYoman*, p. 371). With our structure intact, we can receive the awe inspiring Koach / power of freedom by revealing the Infinity which is beyond the *Hishtalshelus* / order of Creation; beyond the worlds of *Asiyah* / actualization, *Yetzirah* / formation, and *Beriah* / creation. This will allow us to recognize and internalize a manifestation of, in the words of the Haggadah, "I, and not an angel...I, and not a Saraph...I, and not a messenger, but I, Hashem Alone."

THE SEDER PLATE

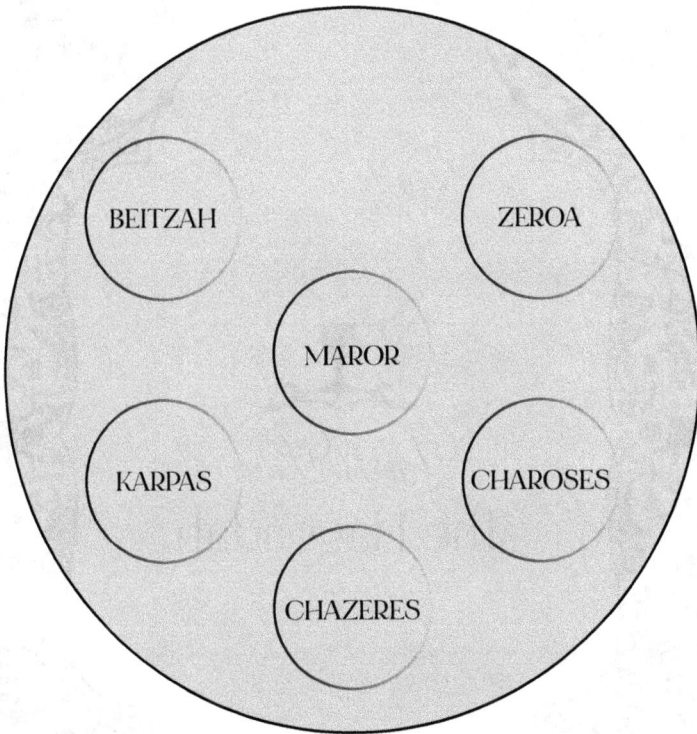

Part Four

The Haggadah

Chapter One:
The Essence of Pesach Night:
Remembering and
Speaking About the Miracles

THE RAMBAM (*HILCHOS CHAMETZ UMATZAH*, 7:1) BEGINS explaining the laws of the night of Pesach as follows: מצות עשה של תורה לספר בנסים ונפלאות שנעשו לאבותינו במצרים בליל חמשה עשר בניסן שנאמר זכור את היום הזה אשר יצאתם ממצרים כמו שנאמר זכור את יום השבת / "It is a Torah command to speak, on the night of the Fifteenth of Nisan, all about the miracles and wonders that were performed for our forefathers in Egypt, as it is stated, 'Remember this day that you went out of Egypt', just as it is stated: 'Remember the day of Shabbos.'"

Many scholars have wondered the obvious — why does the Rambam add that we should "remember the going out of Egypt, just as it is stated, remember the day of Shabbos?" What does the remembrance of Shabbos add to the definition of *Leil haSeder* / Seder Night? Let the Rambam just write that on the night of Pesach there is a Mitzvah to speak about the miracles of the Exodus, as it is stated, 'Remember this day that you went out of Egypt?'*

---

* The apparent source for this Rambam is the Gemara in *Pesachim*, 117b: אמר רב אחא בר יעקב: וצריך שיזכיר יציאת מצרים בקידוש היום. כתיב הכא: למען תזכור את יום. וכתיב התם: זכור את יום השבת לקדשו. However, as the *Yad Eisan* asks, the Gemara merely teaches that we draw a parallel between remembering Shabbos to the remembering of the going out of Egypt, but not the other way around. Thus, he suggests that the source is from *Medrash Rabbah*, Parshas Bo. The *Minchas Chinuch*, Mitzvah 21, explains that the Rambam brings in the remembrance of Shabbos, since, from the other Pasuk (*Shemos*, 13:14), which tells us to speak about the going out of Egypt, one would think that this Mitzvah is only if you have a son who asks you, but sitting alone, maybe there is no Mitzvah to "remember." As the Medrash, *Mechilta deRebbe Yishmael*, Bo, 2, teaches, והיה כי ישאלך בנך מחר לאמר יכול אם שאלך אתה מגיד לו ואם לאו אי אתה מגיד לו ת"ל והגדת לבנך אעפ"י שלא שאלך: אין לי אלא בזמן שיש לו בן בינו לבין עצמו, בינו לבין אחרים מנין ת"ל ויאמר משה אל העם זכור את היום הזה אשר יצאתם ממצרים. And as the Rambam, in Sefer haMitzvos, ולשון מכילתא מכלל שנאמר כי ישאלך בנך יכול אם ישאלך בנך אתה 157, writes, מגיד לו כו' תלמוד לומר והגדת לבנך אע"פ שאינו שואלך, אין לי אלא בזמן שיש לו בן בינו לבין עצמו בינו לבין אחרים מנין תלמוד לומר ויאמר משה אל העם זכור את היום הזה. Yet, this does not הזה, רוצה לומר שהוא צוה לזכרו כמו שאמר זכור את יום השבת answer the Rambam in *Hilchos Chametz uMatzah*, 7:1, as there, he does not yet bring the Pasuk in *Shemos*, 13:14, where one would have thought that it only applies if one has a son present at the Seder. And besides, the Mechilta does not bring זכור את יום השבת לקדשו to prove that we need to remember the going out of Egypt even if we do not have a child asking, rather, says, בינו לבין עצמו, בינו לבין אחרים מנין ת"ל ויאמר משה אל העם זכור את היום הזה אשר יצאתם ממצרים. And the only reason the Rambam in Sefer haMitzvos adds כמו שאמר זכור את יום השבת, since in *Sefer haMitzvos*, the main source for "remembering" is the Pasuk כי ישאלך בנך. See *Likutei Sichos*, 21, p. 68, at length, regarding the first answer of 'context'.

The source for connecting the remembrance of the going out of Egypt with the remembrance of Shabbos is from the Medrash (as the Yad Eisan suggests, *Shemos Rabbah*, end of Bo) which says, והזהר לישראל כשם שבראתי את העולם ואמרתי להם לישראל לזכר את יום השבת זכר למעשה בראשית, שנאמר זכור את יום השבת, כך היו זוכרים הנסים שעשיתי לכם במצרים וזכרו ליום שיצאתם משם, שנאמר זכור את היום הזה אשר יצאתם ממצרים / "HaKadosh Baruch Hu told Moshe, 'Go and inform Klal Yisrael that just as I have created the world and told them to remember the day of Shabbos as a remembrance of the creation (process), they should remember the miracles that I performed for them in Egypt, and they should remember the Exodus from Egypt.'"

True, there is a good source for the Rambam, but that does not answer the question, rather it just transposes the question on the Medrash.

When the Rambam writes that we need to remember the going out of Egypt as we remember Shabbos, it behooves us to see what the Rambam writes earlier in his book, in the laws of Shabbos, regarding remembering Shabbos.

In the laws of Shabbos (*Hilchos Shabbos*, 29:1) the Rambam writes, מצות עשה מן התורה לקדש את יום השבת בדברים שנאמר זכור את יום השבת לקדשו. כלומר זכרהו זכירת שבח וקדוש / "It is a Torah command to sanctify the day of Shabbos with words, as it is states, 'Remember the day of Shabbos to sanctify it,' meaning, remember it with praise and sanctity."

When the Torah tells us to remember the days of *Yetzias Mitzrayim* / the Going Out of Egypt, and that there is a Mitzvah to do so on the night of Pesach, perhaps the Torah just wants us simply, as stated, to remember that we left Egypt, i.e., to 'think about' Yetzias Mitzrayim. How do we know that the Torah wants us to do so verbally? Also, how do we know that on the night of Pesach we need to לספר בנסים ונפלאות שנעשו לאבותינו במצרים / "tell over the miracles and wonders that occurred to our ancestors in Egypt?" Maybe, even if we assume there is a Mitzvah to not only think about it but also speak about it, maybe the Mitzvah is to verbally mention just that we left Egypt on this night many years ago; how do we know that there is a Mitzvah to speak specifically about the miracles as well?

These are the two questions: why must we speak in general, and why must we speak about the miracles? This is what the Rambam, perhaps, is suggesting: regarding Shabbos we learned, זכור את יום השבת לקדשו. כלומר זכרהו זכירת שבח וקדוש / "'Remember the day of Shabbos to sanctify it,' meaning, remember it with praise and sanctity." That is to say, there is a very specific type of remembrance when it comes to Shabbos; it is a remembrance *'to'*, or for the purpose and objective of sanctifying it. זכור...לקדשו / "Remember...to sanctify." It is not simply to remember Shabbos, but to remember to bring oneself to a point of sanctifying Shabbos, and do so with words, explaining the 'context' of the creation story. And the 'remembrance' of Pesach follows the same principle: we need to remember the going out of Egypt, and to speak of the context, the miracles. We need לספר בנסים ונפלאות שנעשו לאבותינו במצרים / "to tell verbally of the miracles and wonders that were performed for our ancestors in Egypt."*

* Another answer to this puzzling Rambam is perhaps as follows. Speaking of Kiddush, the remembrance on Shabbos, the Rambam writes, מצות עשה מן התורה לקדש את יום השבת בדברים שנאמר זכור את יום השבת לקדשו. כלומר זכרהו זכירת שבח וקדוש. וצריך לזכרהו בכניסתו וביציאתו. בכניסתו בקדוש היום וביציאתו בהבדלה / "It is a positive Mitzvah of the Torah to express the sanctity of the Shabbos day in words, for it is written: 'Remember to sanctify the Sabbath day'; that is to say, remember it in terms of praise and sanctification. One should remember it at its beginning and its conclusion by reciting the Kiddush when Shabbos begins, and the Havdalah when it ends" (*Hilchos Shabbos*, 29:1). The Rambam clearly juxtaposes Kiddush with Havdalah, and that they are both part of the Mitzvah to remember Shabbos. On a deeper level, the Rambam is actually hinting to us that Kiddush and Havdalah are essentially part of the same *Geder* / quality, definition. The Gemara tells us that אין עושין מצות חבילות חבילות / "One does not perform Mitzvos in bundles": *Pesachim*, 102b. As such, if one uses a cup of wine to recite one blessing, such as *Bentching* / Grace After Meals, one should not double up and use the same cup of wine and recite Kiddush, for example. Yet, one may, and in fact, does, recite Kiddush and Havdalah on the same cup of wine. Why? This is because הבדלה וקידוש חדא מילתא היא / "Havdalah and Kiddush are one matter." But how are they "one matter" if Kiddush is to sanctify the seventh day and Havdalah is to separate the seventh day of Shabbos from the other six days of the week? The answer is, that in every act of Kiddush, dedication, sanctification there are two acts transpiring; one is dedicating and sanctifying Shabbos, and in the process it is also separating Shabbos from the other days (as in the act of *Kiddushin* / marriage, מקודשת לי, מיוחדת לי and thus, אסר לה אכולי עלמא כהקדש: *Kiddushin*, 2b, and *Tosefos*, ad loc). And the same can be argued in reverse: every Havdalah is an act of *Kiddush*. When we recite Kiddush on Friday night, we are remembering and declaring, sanctifying and making Shabbos holy in our experience, and in this act separating it from the other days of the week. In the words of the Rambam, *Sefer haMitzvos*, Mitzvah 155: היא שצונו לקדש את השבת ולאמר דברים בכניסתו וביציאתו נזכיר בם יציאת מצרים וקדוש היום ומעלתו והבדלו משאר הימים הקודמים ממנו והבאים אחריו / "...We are commanded to sanctify Shabbos and declare when it enters and exists...the sanctity of the day and its distinction and separation from the days of the week that come before and after it...." This is perhaps what the Rambam is hinting at when he writes that we need to remember the going out of Egypt as we remember Shabbos. Part of this

Just as Shabbos is all about *Kedushah* / sanctity, as it is called, "Shabbos *Kodesh*" — Pesach is all about the *Nisim* / miracles. The *Etzem* / Essence of Shabbos is Kedushah, as the Etzem of Pesach is the Nisim.

This is a night to recall the going out of Egypt and all the miracles, physical and spiritual, that occurred for our ancestors, as well as those that occur for us, as we need to envision ourselves as if we too left (and are leaving) Egypt in every generation, and in truth, every day.

This is a night to speak about, to describe, and expand upon the miracles. It was in order to fulfill this Mitzvah that the sages and rabbis of old formulated a text called *Haggadah shel Pesach*, which includes the basic narrative of the Exodus from Egypt, a recounting of the miracles and wonders, and passages offering praise and thanks.

---

remembrance — its Kiddush — is Havdalah; we need to declare and elaborate how this night is different "from all other nights of the year," as this is the night when Hashem chose us from all, and drew us closer. In the words of the Rambam, ומסים בדת האמת שקרבנו המקום לו והבדילנו מהאמות וקרבנו ליחודו / "And we conclude speaking about the true faith, that Hashem separated us from the other nations and drew us closer to His Unity": *Hilchos Chametz uMatzah*, 7:4. Incidentally, this also is true in reverse, Havdalah on Motza'ei Shabbos night is a type of Kiddush, a way to sanctify all the food we are going to eat in the coming week, and also (Havdalah in Maariv) a way to be *Mekadeish* / sanctify our entire work-week.

THE HAGGADAH

The core of the text of the Haggadah dates back to the time of the Mishnah, the era of the Second Beis haMikdash. In fact, parts of the Haggadah are even mentioned in the Mishnah, in the final tractate of Pesachim. For this reason, there are some sources that suggest that the Haggadah was first formulated by the *Anshei K'neses haGedolah* / the Men of the Great Assembly. An allusion to a text called The Haggadah is found in the Gemara (*Shavuos*, 46b). A full 'printed' version of the Haggadah is found in the *Siddurim* / *prayer books* of the Geonim, such as the *Siddurim* written by Rav Amram (9th Century) and Rav Saadia Gaon (10th Century). Clearly, there have been slight additions to the texts throughout the ages, mostly near the end of the Haggadah, after the drinking of the fourth cup of wine.

Later sages debate the actual title of the Haggadah. The Avudraham (14th Century) writes that it should be *Haggadah* beginning with a Hei, while the Mordechai (13th Century) writes that it should be *Aggadah*, beginning with an Aleph (*Mordechai*, Pesachim, 117a).

The word *Aggadah* has the numerical value of 13 (Aleph/1, Gimel/3, Dalet/4, Hei/5 = 13), this represents that during the month of Nisan, the sign of *T'leh* / Aries / the Lamb, we broke free from the influence of the lamb, which was an Egyptian deity, and in fact we offered lambs as offerings to HaKadosh Baruch Hu. With the going out of Egypt in Nisan, and eventually with the giving of the Torah, we reached beyond *Mazal* / zodiac influences, and reached the *Bechinah* / paradigm of 13, the level of *Echad* (also numerically 13) / Hashem's Oneness. The root of the word *Aggadah* is *Gad*, which means *Mazal* (see Rashi on *Bereishis*, 30:11, quoting *Medrash Rabbah*, 71:9. See also the *Targum Yonason Ben Uziel*).

Today, most people call it simply The Haggadah, and there are two possible reasons. The term הגדה / *Haggadah* is derived from the Torah's phrase והגדת לבנך / *v'Higadeta l'Vincha*, "You shall *tell* your child" about the Exodus from Egypt (*Shemos* 13:8). As such, it indicates this Mitzvah of 'telling'.

Haggadah can also be derived from the word *Hoda'ah* / 'offering thanks' or singing praise. Among the *P'sukim* / verses that are quoted at length in the Haggadah are the P'sukim regarding the *Bikurim* / First Fruit offerings: ואמרת אליו הגדתי היום לה' אלקיך כי־באתי אל־הארץ אשר נשבע ה' לאבתינו לתת לנו / (You shall go to the priest in charge at that time) and say to him, "I acknowledge this day before Hashem your G-d that I have entered the Land that Hashem swore to our fathers to assign us." The word הגדתי / "I acknowledge" in the *Targum Yerushalmi* translates as אודין ושבחין / "I will be thankful and offer praise" (Avudraham). As such, Haggadah means both a telling, and hints to a type of telling that is laced with gratitude and thanks to HaKadosh Baruch Hu.

BEING BIRTHED THROUGH THE HAGGADAH

As explored earlier, the Exodus is our collective birth, the birth of Klal Yisrael. Prior to Yetzias Mitzrayim, while still in Egypt, we were similar to a fetus within her mother's womb (*Mechilta*, Beshalach, 6. *Medrash Tehilim*, 114). As slaves, we were confined to merely being an extension of someone else's whims and wants. We were a voiceless, nameless, unexpressed, undefined people. As a fetus in her mother's womb, we were silent, unrevealed, and lacking any inner life, self-understanding or individual will. Yetzias Mitzrayim changed all of this.

Through the retelling of the story of Yetzias Mitzrayim, we tap into the *Koach* / power of 'rebirthing' ourselves. By telling the story of our going out of Egypt, we remember the past and relive in the present an exodus out of our own personal *Mitzrayim* / Egypt, our *Meitzarim* / constrictions, the states in which we lack a voice or self-understanding. The Haggadah facilitates a 'drawing out the heart', as our sages tell us, דברי אגדה המושכין את הלב / "Words of *Aggadah* draw the heart" (*Chagigah*, 14a).

In Hebrew, the root of *Haggadah*, the letters Gimel-Dalet, refers to a continuation, an extension from one (person) to the other (*Shabbos*, 104a). Generally, when the letters Gimel and Dalet are found in a word it represents continuation, such as in the phrase *Agudah Achas* / one congregation, or the prohibition of *Lo Tisgodedu* / do not create factions (separations within the community). Even in the language of Chazal, *Gad* means connecting, continuation, as in the phrase *Gud Asik* or *Gud Achis* /

walls of the Sukkah extending upwards or downwards. Essentially, the word *Gad* means connecting, extending, and continuing.

The Torah calls the *Mon* / Manna "a seed of Gad." Why? "Because the Mon is like a story, which draws the heart of man like water" (*Yuma*, 75a). Similarly, when we recite the Haggadah we are connecting 'what we know' to 'how we feel' — our hearts are being drawn and 'connected' into the narrative. *Haggadah* also refers to words spoken with "strength" and power (*Makos*, 11a. See also Rashi, *Shemos* 19:3). In this way, the words of the Haggadah draw us in with power, vigor, and excitement.

Our inner heart or inner knowing becomes revealed through the exciting, emotional recitation of the Haggadah. As a result, we become re-birthed and enlivened; we find our individual expressivity and animation. Our deepest true voice becomes revealed and manifest. As we draw from our deepest heart and reveal more of who we really are, we simultaneously draw down the supernal heart of Divine understanding into our life, heart, and mind.

We are not merely telling over a piece of history — 'his-story', meaning someone else's story, something that occurred to someone in a distant past — rather, we are reciting the Haggadah as a living, present, sacred memory of our own collective past and feeling it vividly in the present. These days are נזכרים ונעשים / "remembered and performed." By creatively remembering our suffering and liberation through animated words and symbolic actions, we create and relive that redemption in the present.

Turning the Haggadah 'inward' toward our own consciousness here and now, we recognize that all the characters in the story are aspects of us. There is a small part of us that is foolishly stubborn like Pharaoh, and a small part of us that is still enslaved, maybe not to another human being, but to money, power, fame, prestige, pain, or another transient phenomenon of this world. Reading the Haggadah in this way, we begin to 'draw the heart' and reveal the deepest layers of our soul. This is not an intellectual exercise of cold, detached remembrance and recollection. When we contemplate our own inner slaveries and redemptions, and when we are present with the Koach of Geulah that is gifted to us on this night, we can affect our 'rebirth' and our own personal redemption. And in truth, activating our *Geulah Peratis* / personal redemption adds light to the dawning redemption of all of Klal Yisrael and of the whole world. Drawing out our spark of Moshiach within helps us all usher in a world of Moshiach, peace, harmony, healing and unity for all humanity. May this come to be, speedily, in our days.

Chapter Two:
Reciting the Haggadah in Hebrew:
The Root Language of Redemption

W HEN WE RECITE THE HAGGADAH, IT IS ESSENTIAL that we understand what we are saying and the story we are telling over. Nevertheless, everyone should try to recite at least a portion of the Haggadah in the original *Lashon haKodesh* / holy tongue, the Divine language of Hebrew, if possible. The Hebrew blessings, for example, are good selections to focus on for those who are in the process of learning to read and resonate with these Divine sounds.

Just as *Galus* / exile manifests in space, namely as our geographical Galus from our Homeland, the Holy Land of Israel — and Galus manifests in consciousness, as our dissociation or alienation from our most authentic self, there is also a manifestation of Galus in language.

Lashon haKodesh, specifically meaning Biblical Hebrew, is the language of creation, revelation, and redemption. In this way, it is our most authentic language, and the medium through which we most readily receive redemption and revelation.

Lashon haKodesh is our indigenous language, our original means of communication. Our collective dreams, hopes, longings, and yearnings are articulated in Lashon haKodesh; our prophets prophesied in Lashon haKodesh, and our set prayers are written in Lashon haKodesh. It is both our national language and the meta-language of all languages. In fact, all other languages are called the *Achorayim* / 'posterior', the back or outer expressions, of Lashon haKodesh. Any *Targum* / translation of Lashon haKodesh is an 'exiled' version of the original. Lashon haKodesh is direct from the Source and it is the resonance of redemption.

If we want to fully re-experience *Yetzias Mitzrayim* / the Going Out of Egypt, we need to speak about it in the language that it was experienced in, the language through which it has been reenacted and re-experienced throughout all the ages in all the Seders throughout history, from Rebbe Akiva to Rashi, from Rambam to the Arizal. When we translate the Lashon haKodesh into another language, we dilute our experience of Yetzias Mitzrayim. Lashon haKodesh is the primordial language of redemption.

When we recite the story of Yetzias Mitzrayim, with its miracles and wonders, in the language of the Torah, we draw the dynamics of that story into the world. In the words of the Chozeh of Lublin (*Divrei Emes*, Beshalach), "Through the recitation of the letters in the Torah — that speak about the miracle — we awaken the source of the miracle" (וכן שמעתי מהרב המגיד (מזלאטשוב ז"ל שבאותיות הסיפור מעוררים השורש של הנסים כי הכל באותיות).

The metaphysical source of everything that occurs, and all of life, is the Torah, the Divine blueprint of Creation. Every letter, word and Pasuk of the Torah has spiritual and physical creative power. In fact, the Creator looked into the Torah and only then created the world (*Medrash Rabbah*, 1:1), meaning that the Torah is the blueprint of all of reality. Everything first exists in the Torah and only then does it appear in actuality (*Asarah Ma'amaros*, Ma'amar Chikur Din, 3:22). Torah is the very root of existence and the Divine intelligence through which all phenomena come into existence.

To simplify this idea, imagine you are a developer and you want to build a building. Initially, the idea of the building exists in your mind, then you create the plans as the blueprint, and only afterwards do you go ahead and build the structure. The

Torah is the way the structures of the world exist in the blueprint stage. Our natural, physical reality is thus a derivative of a deeper spiritual reality.

As the Shaloh haKadosh writes, the Torah is a *Roshem* / impression of Divinity, and man (and by extension, all of Creation) is a Roshem of the Torah. In the words of the Gaon of Vilna "All that was, is and will be, until the end of time is included within the Torah. Not only the general ideas, but all the details of every type of creation, and specifically every individual person, from the day of his birth to the moment of death, all incarnations and all details of details..." (*Sifra deTzniusa*, Chap. 5. Ramban on *Devarim*, 32:40).

When the Torah describes the splitting of the sea, for example, the Torah is not just describing an event, rather it is also speaking of the spiritual source of the event, and how this spiritual, metaphysical source was expressed in the natural world. As a result, when we recite verses of the Torah about the Splitting of the Sea, we contact the source of this event, and draw to ourselves the power to 'split a sea', whatever that may mean, in our own lives. Reciting the Torah's verses about Yetzias Mitzrayim gives us the strength to go out of our own 'Mitzrayim' and draws into the world the power of redemption from oppression (See also *Chasam Sofer*, Torah, Ekev, 7:17).

This helps explain the fact that the *Segulah* / 'positive omen' for *Parnasah* / livelihood is to read the Torah portion of the Manna (*Shulchan Aruch*, Orach Chayim, 1:5. *Yerushalmi, Berachos.* כל האומר

פ'. המן בכל יום מובטח לו שלא יתמעטו מזונותיו *Perishah,* (on the Tur), ad loc. *Shu'T Tashbatz,* 189, ואני ערב. Although see *Aruch haShulchan,* 1:25). Likewise, to help draw a Shiduch / proper wedding partner into one's life, one may read about the creation of Adam and Chavah or the story of the Shiduch between Rivkah and Yitzchak, because the sources of Shiduchim are present in the deepest spiritual vibrational realms.

This is why we recite the Haggadah out loud, in Lashon haKodesh; these Torah words are where our power to leave Egypt lies. When we activate the original frequencies of the Torah's narration of the going out of Egypt, we are tapping into the power to initiate a Geulah / redemption or exodus from our own personal enslavements and limitations. We are drawing down redemption from its supernal source Above into this world.

Chapter Three
All Dualities Allude to Oneness:
The Numerical Inner Structure
of the Haggadah

W E LIVE IN A WORLD OF DUALITIES AND OPPOSITES.
Everything is created זֶה-לְעֻמַּת זֶה / *Zeh l'Umas Zeh*
/ "one opposite the other" (*Koheles*, 7:14), and in the
language of the Gemara, "Everything has both a male and female counterpart" (*Bava Basra*, 74b). This dual quality of Creation stems from the first letter in the Torah, Beis, meaning
'two'. Our world is called *Alma d'Piruda* / world of separation' or two-ness, although it emerges from the *Alma d'Yechuda*
/ world of unity. The Torah begins with the letter Beis, the

second letter of the Aleph-Beis, as our world is created from the world of 'two' and (apparent) 'separation'. This is because the original *Ein Sof* / Infinite Light of Hashem's Oneness was 'contracted' and 'concealed' to make space for Creation, otherness, two-ness, to exist. This contraction, withdrawal within Itself, is called Tzimtzum.

As we are formed within a world of duality, we function in a mode of duality. Much like computers, our brains are binary systems. The brain automatically categorizes all our perceptions as good or bad, inside or outside, light or dark, etc., but never both at once. Since our brains operate through dichotomies, so does our language. With words, we attempt to diffuse any sense of ambiguity by defining objects and experiences in contrast to their opposites. Every time we make a certain statement, we are silently invoking an opposite counterstatement.

Even our concept of time is a dualistic paradigm of past and future. The idea that now we are in exile and we are aspiring to a future Redemption is inherently dualistic. Thus it appears that there is nothing but duality and separation, and in this state of consciousness we desperately seek answers, redemption, and a future state of total freedom. On the other hand, we have a deep, perhaps subconscious intuition that underlying all of this duality is *Yichud*, 'non-duality', or oneness without an opposite. From the comprehensive perspective of the Ein Sof there is only Yichud, and the world of separation is enfolded *within* the Alma d'Yechuda. A deep, 'beyond Tzimtzum' part of us knows that Redemption is already here, within us, right now.

NUMERICAL STRUCTURES IN THE HAGGADAH

2 / TWO

Just like our experience of the dualistic universe, the Haggadah appears to be composed of a series of dichotomies. It guides us through an intricate meditation on opposites such as freedom and slavery, questions and answers, child and adult, wise and foolish, hidden and revealed, bitter and sweet, Chametz and Matzah, affliction and healing, pain and joy. We speak of and eat foods that represent our slavery, and we also speak of freedom and eat foods in a way that demonstrates our liberation. There is a child who asks, and an adult who answers. There is the bitter Maror and sweet Charoses.

We also focus on complex rituals that include precise measurements and timings, struggling to do everything 'properly'. Finally, in the last section called Nirtzah, we affirm that our ritual has been 'accepted', everything is already perfect and there's nothing more to 'do'. It seems to be a night that highlights dualities.

A simple reason why the Haggadah is in a question-answer format is because that is the way the Torah hints to the idea of a Seder Night: "And it will be when your child will ask you…"

(*Devarim*, 6:20-21). But why does the Torah choose a process of question and answer? On one level, this is how the binary brain learns. A question and answer format helps us to ingrain and retain a lesson; growth comes through curiosity, challenge, and discovery.

Without the tension of questions, there would be no motivation to receive answers. The greater the tension of not knowing, the greater the impact when the knowledge is revealed. Similarly, the greater the exile, the greater the potential redemption; the greater the bitterness, the greater the potential sweetness. Humility brings greater elevation, and the child brings greater understanding to the adult. Through the mode of questions, the Haggadah uses our perception of duality to guide us on a path to discover deeper and deeper layers of freedom.

3 / THREE

'Three' is also a major numerical theme of Pesach and the Seder. The three Matzos is one prominent example. Indeed, there are also three *types* of Matzah related to Yetzias Mitzrayim: Matzah as the bread of affliction, the Matzah of the Mitzvah to eat Matzah along with the Korban Pesach, and the Matzah that was produced due to their leaving Mitzrayim in great haste. Similarly, we find three in terms of the Korban Pesach, the offering of Pesach, which when performed, was brought in three groups (*Mishnah Pesachim*, 5:5: הפסח נשחט בשלש כתות, שנאמר ושחטו אתו כל קהל עדת ישראל, (שמות יב) קהל ועדה וישראל. The Korban Pesach was slaughtered in three groups, meaning those bringing the offering were divided into three separate sets, as it is stated: "And the whole *assembly* of the *congregation* of *Israel* shall slaughter it in the afternoon" (*Shmos,* 12:6). The verse is interpreted as referring to three groups: the assembly, the congregation, and Israel).

There are three Mitzvos of eating on Pesach: the Korban Pesach, the Matzah, and the Maror. And today, "Anyone who did not mention these three matters on Pesach night has not fulfilled his obligation." Furthermore, the Geulah from Egypt was activated through the actions of three people, as the Navi says, "I sent Moshe to lead you, also Aharon and Miriam" (*Michah,* 6:4). And Moshe is in general referred to as the 'third' (על ידי תליתאי: *Shabbos,* 88a), as he was born after Aharon and Miriam.

Three is symbolic of unity. At certain moments in the Haggadah, two opposites are combined in the creation of a third entity. For example, there is often a thesis or statement, then an antithesis or challenge to that statement, and finally a synthesis or resolution which includes both the thesis and its antithesis. In the section of Korech, 'Hillel's sandwich' unifies the Maror (exile) with the Matzah (redemption). The third entity, the sandwich, is more than a combination of the two. It is a new state in which exile and redemption paradoxically co-exist.

Another combination of opposites is in the fact that Matzah is called "the Bread of Poverty (of a slave)" and yet it is also called "the Bread of Freedom." The fact that there are three Matzos under the Seder plate also hints to the power of three to unify opposites, and this can be illustrated through *Gematria* / numerical value. Three times the words *Lechem Oni,* 'Bread of Poverty' equals 624 (*Lechem*/78 + *Oni*/130 = 208. 3 x 208 = 624). This is the same value as the word *Cheirus*, 'freedom' (Ches/8 + Yud/10 + Reish/200 + Vav/6, Tav/400 = 624). The 'third entity' revealed between the two paradigms paradoxically contains and transcends both poverty and freedom.

In fact, all the items of the Seder contain opposites. Again, the Matzah is both a poor man's bread and bread of freedom; a bread connected to 'mourning'*and of course a bread of joy and Hallel and gratitude.

Maror is bitter and reminds us of our bitter state in exile and yet, the simple reason that we eat Maror with the Korban Pesach, as the Pasuk says, ואכלו את-הבשר בלילה הזה צלי-אש ומצות על-מררים יאכלהו / "They shall eat the flesh that same night; they shall eat it roasted over the fire, with unleavened bread and with bitter herbs" (*Shemos*, 12:8), is, as the Ohr haChayim writes: "The plain meaning of the Pasuk seems to be that the roasting of the lamb whole is a symbol of freedom. Freedom means wholeness. The requirement to eat bitter herbs with it is natural; the Egyptians used to eat roast meat with something pungent as this enhanced the taste of the meat and enabled the person who ate it to thoroughly enjoy his meal. Letting the bitter herbs precede the meat in his mouth made one more conscious of the contrast, and of how something which by itself had tasted bitter would suddenly transform the whole

---

* *Pesachim*, 36a. Lechem 'Oni, with an Ayin, as in poor, but similar to *Oni*, with an Aleph, meaning bread of acute mourning. The Mitzvah must be fulfilled with a Matzah that can be eaten during a period of acute mourning.

meal into an enjoyable experience. The unleavened bread also contributed to that feeling. We therefore find that there were three components which combined to make the meal enjoyable." So Maror is eaten with the meat to make it taste better.*

* Here are the words of the *Ohr haChayim*: לפי פשט הכתוב לפי מה שראינו שאמר ה' שצריך צלי אש ושיהיה שלם כו' זה יגיד שדעת עליון הוא להראות בחינה הגדולה והחירות ואין רשות אחרים עליהם, ולפי זה גם המרורים שיצו ה' הוא לצד כי כן דרך אוכלי צלי לאכול עמו דבר חד כי בזה יערב לחיך האוכל ויאכל בכל אות נפשו. גם בזה יוכר גודל העריבות כשיקדים לפיו מרורים. גם מה שהזכיר המצות הוא פרט אשר יכונן חיך אוכל יטעם לו הצלי. Interestingly enough, in the language of the Mishnah, עד שמגיע לפרפרת הפת / "before he reaches the dessert of the bread" (*Pesachim*, 114a), thus Chazal call the Maror a פרפרת / 'dessert' or appetizer.

There is a *Din* / law that a Korban has to be eaten in a manner of למשחה לגדולה (*Chulin*, 132b). אמר רב חסדא מתנות כהונה אין נאכלות אלא צלי ואין נאכלות אלא בחרדל מאי טעמא אמר קרא (במדבר יח, ח) למשחה לגדולה כדרך שהמלכים אוכלים / "Rav Chisda says, 'Gifts of the priesthood may be consumed only when they are roasted, and they may be consumed only with mustard seasoning.' What is the reason? Since the Pasuk says 'I have given them for prominence'. The term "for prominence" means as a mark of greatness, meaning it should be eaten in the manner of kings (roasted and with mustard).

This principle of למשחה לגדולה seems to apply as well to the Korban Pesach, which is eaten by all, not just the Cohanim.

The Brisker Rav, in *Stencil*, Menachos, 21a, argues that according to Tosefos, למשחה לגדולה is only regarding the part of the Korban that is eaten by the Cohanim, not regarding the other meat, like Shelamim which were eaten by the owner of the Korban. For this reason, Tosefos offers another reason (other than Rashi's) for why the Korban Pesach needs to be eaten with a slightly full stomach. In *Pesachim*, 70a, Tosefos writes, ואומר ריב"א דמשמע בירושלמי דהא דפסח נאכל על השבע היינו מדרבנן גזירה משום שבירת עצם שאם לא היתה באה על השבע מתוך שהוא רעב לאכול הבשר שסביב העצמות היה בא לידי שבירתן. Rashi, however, writes a different reason: so that the eating of the Korban Pesach should be more pleasurable: *Pesachim*, 70a. Later, Rashi (*Pesachim*, 86a) writes clearly, שהוא נאכל באחרונה על השבע שכן חובת כל הקרבנות כדקיימא לן (חולין דף קלב:) למשחה לגדולה כדרך שהמלכים אוכלין.

And, as explored earlier, when Maror is chewed long enough it becomes sweet.

In this way, Maror itself — although today it is eaten to remind us of the hardship of slavery — contains its opposite, sweetness, within itself. This can help us understand the ruling of the Beis Yoseph (*Orach Chayim*, 475): שאם רצה לאוכלו בהיסיבה רשאי / "If one wishes to eat the Maror reclining, one is permitted." This seems puzzling; how may one recline when eating foods that represent their slavery? In fact, the Magen Avraham writes a similar Halacha: ואם אכלו בהסיבה יצא / "if one ended up eating (the Maror) reclining, then he has fulfilled his obligation nonetheless" (*Orach Chayim*, 475:5). This suggests that he should not recline, but if he did he has 'nonetheless' fulfilled his obligation. What is the reasoning of the Beis Yoseph? Perhaps it is that Maror contains its own opposite — the 'sweetness' and repose of freedom.

The Charoses reminds us of the cement with which they labored in Egypt, and yet, also reminds us of the "apple trees" (רבי לוי אומר: זכר לתפוח. ורבי יוחנן אומר: זכר לטיט) *Pesachim*, 116a). We also add red wine to be reminded of the blood of the first *Makah* /

This seems to suggest that Rashi holds that the principle of למשחה לגדולה applies even to Korbanos that are not eaten by the Cohanim. Yet, we could also argue that Rashi, with regards to all other Korbanos, holds like Tosefos, that למשחה לגדולה only applies to the Cohen's *Achilah* / eating, but since we find that the Torah wants everyone to eat the Korban Pesach in a royal way, not to break the bones, for example (as poor people do), so the Din of למשחה לגדולה applies only to the Korban Pesach.

Plague which was the beginning of our redemption (*Yerushalmi*, *Pesachim*, 10:13. Alter Rebbe, *Shulchan Aruch*, Orach Chayim, 473:32-34).

The four cups of wine, which we drink to celebrate our freedom, are also red wine (better to use red wine: *Tur* and *Shulchan Aruch*, Orach Chayim, 472:11. Red wine also intoxicates more: Ramban, *Pesachim*, 108b. Rashbam on *Bava Basra*, 97b), thus the reason for drinking good wine on this night is to assist us in viscerally sensing our freedom, and yet it is also to remind us of our blood that was spilled in Egypt (Taz, *ad loc.*). Additionally, red wine reminds us of the 'positive' blood of the Mitzvah of Milah, and also the blood of the Pesach offering, which we painted on the *Mezuzos* / doorposts of our houses. It is also connected with the blood of our oppressors that was spilled (Riva, *Bava Basra*, ibid).

We break the Matzah in half, before we begin to tell the story of the descent and elevation from Egypt, to remind us of our brokenness, and because we should recite the Haggadah over 'poor man's bread'. And yet, breaking the Matzah in half also reminds us of the sea that split for us, as we left Egypt (*Da'as Zekeinim*, Tosefos, *Shemos*, 12:8: ובציעתה זכר לקריעת ים סוף וירדן שנבקע בפסח. *Kaf haChayim*, 477:6). Indeed, everything in the Haggadah, as in life, contains its opposite.

Such paradoxes invite further questions. What exactly does it mean that exile and redemption can co-exist? And once we understand this, how can we grow to the point that we realize it in our own experience? Such questions lead us from 'three' to 'four'; as 'four' is a number that expresses a process of growth through stages.

4 / FOUR

The Haggadah is filled with fours, from the four cups of wine to the four children and the four questions* (and the four items from which we eat the volume of a Kezayis: Matzah, Maror, Korech, and Afikoman). These correspond to the four expressions the Torah uses with regards to Hashem remembering us in Egypt, "And Hashem *heard* their cries" (Shemos, 2:24), "And Hashem *saw*" (2:25), "and Hashem *knew*" (2:25), "and Hashem *remembered*" (2:24).

Four is two times two, an expanded expression of 'two-ness'. So whereas in the Torah itself we find pairs of two: the child asking and the adult responding, our sages expanded upon the pairing of two and emphasized fours. The expanded diversity and interconnectedness of 'four' allows for room within the realm of duality to engage in a process, a path of ascending through different levels, a journey in the direction of unity.

---

* The number of questions in the Mishnah is four: *Pesachim*, 116a. This number seems to be precise, as one of the questions in the Mishnah is, "Why on every night of the year do we eat roasted, cooked, stewed meat, and on this night we eat only roasted meat (the latter referring to the Korban Pesach)?" This question is no longer applicable, as we do not offer the Korban Pesach, yet, instead of just eliminating that question and having only three questions, another question was added (which was not applicable in more ancient times, as everyone reclined when they dined every night): "Why all nights of the year do we eat either sitting or reclining, while on this night we all recline?" The point of adding this question is that we want to ask specifically four questions.

This is illustrated by the fact that prior to the Exodus, we needed four days to prepare and ascend to the level of redemption. On the Tenth of Nisan, we took the lamb for the Pesach sacrifice and tied it to the bedpost for four days before offering it to HaKadosh Baruch Hu on the Night of Pesach.

5 / FIVE

There is an additional dimension to the Haggadah. Even as we focus on the progressive structure of 'four', we can see, as if out of the corner of our eye, that each 'four' subtly alludes to a 'five' that transcends, includes, and unifies the 'four'. Whereas 'four' is a dualistic path of ascent through the world of separation and pairs, 'five' includes and pervades each point along the path.

The fifth level alludes to the World to Come, where there is only *Yichud* / Divine unity. The oneness of 'five' is similar to 'three' in that it includes and unifies opposites, questions and answers. However, 'five' also includes and transcends all paradoxical answers and all processes or paths of ascent. This is the deeper unity symbolized by the fifth cup, the Cup of Eliyahu haNavi.

FOUR WORLDS

Our reality is composed of four distinct 'worlds', or progressive stages of spirituality. They are *Asiyah* / the physical world, *Yetzirah* / the emotional world, *Beriah* / the intellectual world, and *Atzilus* / the transcendental world. Each 'four' in the Haggadah corresponds to these four worlds. The Haggadah leads us upward through these four stages, toward greater and greater levels of unity and inner freedom.

Here are some examples of the pairs of 'fours' in the Haggadah, and their correspondence with the Four higher / inner Worlds. Following the exploration of the Four Cups, we will attempt to reveal the fifth dimension that is hidden within the 'four'.

Four Stages of the Seder and the Four Worlds

1. The first stage of the Seder is composed mostly of *Ma'aseh* / action. This stage includes the steps of *Kadeish* / reciting Kiddush, *Urchatz* / washing the hands, *Karpas* / eating the vegetable dipped in salt water, and *Yachatz* / breaking the middle Matzah. All of these steps occur in the world of physical action, Asiyah.

2. The second stage is composed mostly of *Dibbur* / speech. This is the step of Maggid, where we speak at length of slavery and redemption. Maggid stimulates and draws out our emotions, as explored earlier, as such, Maggid occurs in the emotional world of Yetzirah.

3. The third stage is composed mostly of *Mach'shavah* / thought or intention. This stage includes the steps of Motzi-Matzah, Maror, and Korech, when we eat Matzah and Maror hopefully focused on the intention and intellectual understanding of what and why we are eating these items of food. This occurs in the intellectual world of Beriah.

4. The fourth stage of the Seder is connected to *Chochmah* / wisdom or *Hirhur* / higher subtle intuition. As we sing Hallel and other praises that are normally recited only during the day, we can have an intuitive sense of the dawning of Redemption and of transcending the darkness of all exiles. This occurs in the spiritual, transcendent, brilliant world of Atzilus.

The Four Torah-Mitzvos of Pesach

1. The Korban Pesach offering is an animal offering which was brought to the Beis haMikdash on Erev Pesach, the 14th of Nisan. The meat of the offering was eaten later on, that evening at the Seder. This Mitzvah consists of physical acts, and occurs in the world of Asiyah (as all *Korbanos* / offerings are connected to the world of Asiyah).

2. Maggid is the Mitzvah of telling the story of the Exodus,

utilizing speech, which in turn arouses our emotion. This Mitzvah is enfolded within the inner world of Yetzirah.

3. Maror is the Mitzvah of eating bitter herbs (with the Korban Pesach) hinting to a form of mental sharpness (Note, Tosefos, *Pesachim*, 114a: פרפרת קרי המרור שאוכל אחר המצה ופרפרת כלומר ממשכת המאכל כמו פרפראות לחכמה). This Mitzvah is connected to the world of Beriah.

4. Matzah is the Mitzvah of eating unleavened bread, which is a simple, pure food, transcendent of any 'outside' and extraneous ingredients. This Mitzvah occurs in the inner world of Atzilus, pure transcendence.

It is interesting to note that regarding the words לחם עוני, literally 'poor man's bread', which is the way the Torah describes Matzah, *Chazal* / our sages have teased out four possible interpretations of what exactly עוני means, and some practical applications of what type of bread constitutes Matzah (*Pesachim*, 36a. *Pesachim*, 115b, 116a). These practical definitions of Matzah are: 1) 'Poor' bread, meaning simply flour and water without any wine, oil or honey (a bread that even one in mourning, an *Oni*, can eat). 2) Not whole or 'important' bread, rather broken bread. 3) Just as a poor person heats the oven and his wife bakes their bread quickly before the small amount of wood they have is used up, similarly here; when baking Matzah, he heats the oven and his wife bakes the Matzah quickly so the dough does not rise.* 4) It is a bread upon which many words

* The Rosh brings down from Rav Hai Gaon that a person should endeavor to bake (or at least help bake) his own Matzah: ובעלי מעשה וחסידים והתמימים

and 'answers' are spoken, meaning the Haggadah is said over the Matzah. These four interpretations correspond to the four stages of development of Creation which the *Chokrim* / philosophers speak about (Gra, *Pesachim*, 115b): there is the *Poel* / Maker, the *Chomer* / substance, the *Tzurah* / form, and the *Tachlis* / culmination and ultimate objective (*Moreh Nevuchim*, 1, 69. Maharal, *Derush l'Shabbos haGadol. Pirush haGra*, Mishlei, 1:1). For example, a carpenter, the Poel, takes a piece of wood, the Chomer, and shapes the wood into a table, a Tzurah, so that he can eat at the table, the Tachlis. The Chomer of the Matzah needs to be poor, simple bread, just flour and water. The Tzurah of the Matzah is that it needs to be thin and broken. The Poel needs to bake the Matzah quickly, and the Tachlis of the Matzah is to have it at the Seder and recite the Haggadah upon the broken Matzah.

These four dimensions are parallel to the four inner worlds that the *Mekubalim* / Kabbalists speak of: Atzilus is the *Poel* / the Maker, the Creator. Beriah is where the *Chomer* / undefined substance of Creation is created, the first emergence of Creation. Yetzirah is where creation assumes *Tzurah* / form, definition and borders. And Asiyah is the *Tachlis* / the actualization, finalization, and objective of the entire process.

מחמירין על עצמן כגאונים המחמירין ולשין ואופין בעצמן כההיא דאמרינן מה דרכו של עני הוא מסיק ואשתו אופה. *Rosh*, Pesachim, 2:26. See also *Tur* and *Shulchan Aruch*, 460. Not only because מצוה בו יותר מבשלוחו / it is better to perform a Mitzvah (albeit baking Matzah is not the actual Mitzvah, rather a *Hachanah* / preparation for a Mitzvah) by yourself than to send a messenger (*Magen Avraham*, ad loc, דקדושין מצוה בו יותר מבשלוחו ב"דאמרי' רפ), but because of this definition of poor man's bread — "Just as a poor person heats the oven and his wife bakes their bread": Netziv, *HaAmek Sha'alah*, 168:1.

Four Unusual Rituals of the Seder

Chazal mention four acts and rituals of the Seder that are designed to invite wonder and arouse the children present to ask questions.

1. חוטפין מצות / Grab the Matzah: This can either mean to eat the Matzah very quickly, or literally to grab it, i.e., allow the children to grab the Afikoman from the Seder leader, in order to hide it for later on (*Pesachim*, 109a; Rashbam, Rashi, Meiri, *ad loc*; Rambam, *Hilchos Chametz uMatzah*, 7:3). To a child's estimation, it is extraordinary that we are allowed or even encouraged to eat something very quickly, or to grab a piece of food and play hide-and-seek with it. Eating or grabbing are physical acts, hinting at the world of Asiyah. Besides, the Afikoman is hidden during the step of Yachatz, within the first of the four stages of the Seder, which corresponds to the world of Asiyah.

2. עוקרין את השולחן / Moving aside the table: At some point during Talmudic times, when people sat on the ground with short tables in front of them, they would move aside these tables for the reading of the Haggadah (*Pesachim*, 115b). To the child, it seemed that they were about to be served a meal, but instead the tables were removed and the adults began reciting passages and singing songs. This aroused an emotion of won-

der, which is part of the step of Maggid, the world of Yetzirah.

3. מזגו לו כוס שני וכאן הבן שואל אביו / Fill the Second Cup of wine. The filling and eventual drinking of the second cup of wine is done before we begin to eat the festive meal (*Pesachim*, 116a, Rashbam. כאן במזיגת כוס שני הבן שואל את אביו אם הוא חכם מה נשתנה עכשיו שמוזגין כוס שני קודם אכילה). For the child, this is peculiar, since we have already made Kiddush, so why do we fill another cup of wine. And why, instead of eating, as we would normally do on every Shabbos or Yom Tov, do we fill another cup? We drink this second cup at the culmination of Maggid, when we are transitioning from the world of Yetzirah into the world of Beriah.

4. טיבולי, כי היכי דליהוי ביה היכירא לתינוקות / Dipping Maror into Charoses (*Pesachim*, 114b): It surprises the child when we dip bitter herbs into a sweet paste, and then for no apparent reason, shake the sweet paste off, and eat the bitter Maror. This dipping represents a 'sweetening the Din' or neutralizing of the negativity in our lives, which alludes to the perfect world of Atzilus. From an Atzilus perspective 'all is good', always.

The Four Blessings of Baruch haMakom

In the Maggid section, the word 'blessed' appears four times within the sentence of *Baruch haMakom*. These can be read as four individual blessings: *Baruch haMakom*, 'Blessed is the Omnipresent.' *Baruch Hu*, 'Blessed is He.' *Baruch sheNasan Torah l'Amo Yisrael*, 'Blessed is the One who bestows Torah upon His People Israel.' *Baruch Hu*, 'Blessed is He.'

1. Baruch haMakom: *HaMakom* means 'the Omnipresent' and also 'the Space'. Both meanings allude to the Divinity present in the physical space of this material world of Asiyah; haMakom is the context, the Ultimate Space, that contains all the content of life.

2. Baruch Hu: Hu is a third person pronoun, indicating that it is outside of our immediate sphere. This hints at a hidden spiritual reality above the physical layer of reality, the world of Yetzirah.

3. Baruch sheNasan Torah l'Amo Yisrael: In this blessing, we acknowledge the Torah, the Divine intelligence, which resides in the world of Beriah.

4. Baruch Hu: Here, *Hu* refers to the highest hidden reality, the Transcendent, mysterious world of Atzilus.

FOUR CUPS, FOUR STEPS TO FREEDOM

There are four cups of *Cheirus* / freedom, and when we drink each of them, they incrementally increase our level of inner freedom. In *Gematria* / numerical value, four times the words כוס יין / *Kos Yayin* / 'cup of wine' equals 624 (*Kos* (86) + *Yayin* (70) = 156, and 4 x 156 = 624).

This is the same value as the word חירות / *Cheirus* / freedom (Ches/8 + Yud/10 + Reish/200 + Vav/6 + Tav/400 = 624).*

Each time we recite the blessing for wine over one of the cups, we raise it off the table. Each cup should raise us to a higher spiritual state of freedom, corresponding with a higher inner world, from Asiyah to Yetzirah, to Beriah, and finally to Atzilus.

This is another reason why we drink wine, and not for example drinking orange juice, or symbolizing the four expressions of redemption by eating four oranges: the nature of wine is the more one drinks the more intoxicated one becomes, and the more joyous and open one should become. There is a unique, palpably cumulative effect to wine (*HaAmek Davar*, Shemos, 6:6. *HaAmek Sha'alah*, Sha'alah 77:4). The four terms of redemption are not merely four distinct expressions, rather they too imply four progressive stages of redemption, one leads into the next, and one moves forward in every stage.

---

* Cup is כוס / *Kos* in Hebrew and numerically 86, which is the same value as the Name *Elokim*, the vessel, the concealment, the element of Hashem's judgment (86 is also the Name *Eh'yeh* / 21 plus Ado-nai / 65). The cup is filled with wine, which represents the Name of Hashem 26 (Yud/10, Hei/5, Vav/6, Hei/5 = 26), as it is connected and revealed in the name of Ado-nai 65 (Aleph/1, Dalet/4, Nun/50, Yud/10 = 65) 26 + 65 = 91. 4 times 91 = 364, which is the same as the word *haSatan* / the Satan. There are 365 days of the solar year, say our sages, one day of the year is free of Satan, the 365th day, Yom Kippur. On Pesach night we have the power to break 'Satan', all constrictions and limitations, and reach real inner freedom.

Four Cups and Four Worlds

1. We recite Kiddush over the first cup. *Kiddush* or *Kadeish* means 'separation', alluding to the physical world of Asiyah, where separation from its Source is most vivid.

2. Maggid is recited over the second cup. Speech and story-telling, arousing the heart, correspond to the emotional world of Yetzirah.

3. We fill the third cup at Beirach, the culmination of the meal. The meal began with Matzah and Maror, which were eaten with thoughtful intention.* We therefore enter intellectual discussions of the Exodus, and reflections on Maggid, during Shulchan Orech. This is the cup of the intellectual world of Beriah.

4. We sing Hallel over the fourth cup and reach transcendent levels of consciousness corresponding to the world of Atzilus.**

---

* However, אכל מצה בלא כונה כגון שאנסוהו עכו"ם או לסטים לאכל יצא ידי חובתו: Rambam, *Hilchos Chametz uMatzah*, 6:3. Yet, המתעסק בתקיעת שופר להתלמד לא יצא ידי חובתו: *Hilchos Shofar*, 2:4. And the reason why by Matzah one fulfills the obligation, is not because one does not need Kavanah at all, rather, because when a person eats there is some level of Kavanah of eating (one is not merely a מתעסק), even when the eating is done by force.

** A similar teaching is found in the Gra, who speaks of the four cups corresponding to the four worlds, in an ascending order. *Pirush haGra*, Haggadah. The Gra writes that the four cups move in progressive order. The first cup is *Olam haZeh* / this physical world, the second cup is *Yemos* *haMoshiach* / world of Moshiach, the third cup is *Techiyas haMeisim* / the resurrection of the dead, and the fourth cup is *Olam haBa* / the future (perfect) world.

The holy Arizal teaches that the four children and the four cups proceed from a higher level to a lower level. In a roundabout descending order, Chochmah, the first cup and the Chacham, are Atzilus, Kedushah, and transcendence. The Rasha and the second cup are Asiyah, and thus we begin Maggid the story with the lowest level — serving idols. The Tam and the third cup are Beriah, in which there is nothing overwhelmingly negative anymore. The She'eino Yodei'a Lishol and the fourth cup are Yetzirah: *Pri Eitz Chayim*, Sha'ar 21:6-7.

The Arizal writes that the first cup is Chochmah, as on this night, we first begin with *Gadlus* / expansiveness, the second cup is Binah, the third is Chesed, and the fourth is Gevurah: *Pri Eitz Chayim,* Sha'ar haMitzvos, 2. See also *Shaloh,* Maseches Pesachim, p. 188.

The four cups correspond to the Name of Hashem, from Yud to Hei: the first cup Yud and the fourth cup the final Hei: *Rabbeinu Bachya,* Parshas Bo.

The *Zohar* (see Rav Yaakov Tzvi Yallish, *Kehilas Yaakov* 1, p. 732) writes that Chochmah is associated with Kiddush and Kedushah, Binah is associated with going out of Egypt, as well as *Yovel* / complete freedom, Tiferes is associated with the *Mon* / Manna, and Malchus is associated with the first blessing of Birchas haMazon, which was initiated by Moshe, the embodiment of Malchus. Finally, the section of *Shefoch Chamascha*, corresponds to the lower Hei of Hashem's name, which is also Malchus.

The structure that is explored within the present essay is based on the movement of the Seder from lower to higher, which is founded on Chazal and many later sources, and of course, all *b'Derech Efshar* / permissible methods of interpretation, at least for the purpose of Derush and to tease out some meaning for Avodas Hashem.

Four Cups,
Four Letters of Hashem's Name &
Four Partzufim or Divine Personae

1. The first cup corresponds to the final letter Hei of the Divine Name (Yud-Hei-Vav-Hei). This is *Nukva*, the mystically feminine persona, otherwise known as the *Shechinah*, or the Sefirah of Malchus, which includes and is most connected to the physical, the manifest world.

2. The second cup corresponds to the Vav of Hashem's name. This is *Zeir Anpin*, the mystically masculine persona. *Zeir Anpin* / 'Small Face' is the collective term for the Six Emotive Sefiros.

3. The third cup corresponds to the upper Hei of Hashem's name. This is *Ima* / 'Mother', which is the Sefirah of *Binah* / higher understanding.

4. The fourth cup corresponds to the Yud of Hashem's name. This is *Abba* / 'Father', the Sefirah of *Chochmah* / Divine 'wisdom' and intuition.

Four Cups and Four Senses

1. The first cup corresponds to the sense of touch, the most physical of the senses.

2. The second cup corresponds to the sense of sight. This cup is filled for Maggid which is to be recited "...when the Matzah and Maror are *Munachim Lefanecha* / set before you," i.e., when we see them. Also, we start Maggid by saying, "This is the bread...," at which point we uncover or lift the Matzah so it will be visible.

3. The third cup corresponds to the sense of taste. This cup is filled before Beirach, the blessing after the meal, after we have eaten the Matzah, Maror, and the feast. We have also just eaten the Afikoman, whose taste should remain in our mouths the rest of the night.

4. The fourth cup corresponds to the sense of hearing. This cup is filled before Hallel, the songs of praise. Hearing is the highest sense, as it is the means through which we receive transcendent wisdom, beyond what the eyes can see.

Four Cups and Four Matriarchs

The Shaloh and the Maharal write that the four cups correspond to the Four Mothers of Klal Yisrael — Sarah, Rivkah, Rochel, and Leah.

1. The first cup is Sarah. The *Bechirah*, the Divine chosen-ness of Klal Yisrael, began with Sarah. This is reflected in the Kiddush, when we say *Ki Vanu Bacharta...*, "for You Hashem have chosen us...."

2. The second cup is Rivkah. We begin Maggid with our genealogy, beginning with the 'negative' and concluding with the positive. This is like Rivkah, who gave birth to the negative character of Eisav first and the positive character of Yaakov last.

3. The third cup is Rochel. It was she who gave birth to Yoseph the sustainer who gave sustenance to the entire family of Yaakov and to all of Egypt, and thus we recite *Birchas haMazon* / the Blessing after Meals over this cup.

4. The fourth cup is Leah. She gave birth to Yehudah, the ancestor of David, who sang praises to Hashem and who became the composer of the Book of *Tehilim* / Psalms. As such, we too sing the psalms of Hallel over this cup.

Four Cups and Four Levels of Self

There were four grand exiles revealed to the minor prophet Daniel in a dream, in the form of four wild beasts. These four exiles were inflicted at the hands of four kingdoms, as the Maharal explains (*Ner Mitzvah*) — four nations that wrestled power and kingship from Klal Yisrael, delaying our ultimate redemption. In terms of personal exile, these four cups can be seen as representing four stages of becoming free.

There are exiles and constrictions that can occur on various levels of our being. There can be an exile of the *Guf* or 'body', or an exile of the *Nefesh* or 'spirit', which is emotional and psychological. There can be an exile of the *Seichel*, 'intellect', a philosophical and theological alienation, and there can be an exile of *haCol*, 'the totality', an ontological and existential alienation.

1. The first cup brings redemption from exiles of the body. The literal act of stepping up to the table.

2. With the second cup we have already moved away from physical constrictions, and we now aspire to attain psychological and emotional freedom. This cup helps us attain it, as Maggid is all about arousing one's spirit and emotions.

3. With the third cup we move into a more mindful state as explored at length earlier, and begin the process of freeing our intellect.

4. With the fourth cup we tap into the level of total existential freedom.

Four Cups and
Four Terms of Redemption

The *Yerushalmi* explains that the four cups of wine represent the four terms or expressions the Torah employs with regard to Yetzias Mitzrayim:

1. וְהוֹצֵאתִי / "I will take you out."

2. וְהִצַּלְתִּי / "I will save you."

3. וְגָאַלְתִּי / "I will redeem you."

4. וְלָקַחְתִּי / "I will take you to Me."

When we drink the cups at the Seder, we are invoking these four terms, which together comprise the full process of redemption.*

---

* The Meiri (*Pesachim*, 99b) adds that each of the four expressions signifies a redemption within itself: *V'Hotzeisi* refers to the redemption from the physical servitude of Mitzrayim (this can be related to the world of Asiyah). *V'Hitzalti* refers to redemption from the 'normal' subjugations of kingdoms, such as taxes and tributes to the king (this can be related to the world of Dibbur and Yetzirah). *V'Ga'alti* teaches that HaKadosh Baruch Hu will bring about our complete domination over our foes (this is complete understanding, and is connected with Beriah). *V'Lakachti* alludes to the giving of the Torah, which is the *Tachlis haCol* / the 'ultimate purpose of everything' (this is 'transcendence' and connected with Atzilus).

Four Cups & Four Stages of Personal Development and Redemption

The four cups and the four expressions of Redemption can also be seen as four stages in personal development: birth, adolescence, engagement, and marriage.

1. The phrase והוצאתי / "V'Hotzeisi / "I will take you out," alludes to birth. Egypt was like a womb and the process of the Exodus was akin to labor and birth (*Mechilta*, Beshalach, 6. *Medrash Tehilim*, 114). The First Cup is called *Kadeish*, meaning 'separation' — suggesting the separation from exile in the birth of Klal Yisrael. At this stage we are pre-verbal and 'pre-personal'.

2. The phrase והצלתי / *V'Hitzalti* / "I will save you," alludes to adolescence, when we develop our individual personalities. At this stage of development, many people encounter a sense of desperation and a need to be 'saved'. The second cup is Maggid, meaning 'spoken', and this also suggests adolescence, when we develop a capacity to express ourselves and to 'have a voice'.

3. The phrase וגאלתי / *V'Go'alti* / "I will redeem you," alludes to the stage of maturation in which one can become engaged to a future spouse. *Go'alti* comes from the word *Geulah* or 'redeem', which can also mean 'acquire', a Tal-

mudic term for engagement.

4. The phrase ולקחתי / *V'Lakachti* / "I will take you," alludes to the mature stage in which one can actually join with another in marriage. *L'kuchin* comes from the word *Yikach*, which refers to taking a marriage partner.[*]

FIVE: THE END OF THE PATH

Within the paradigm of opposites represented by 'four', we cannot reach a permanent state of freedom, for when we assert freedom, the opposite of freedom is automatically invoked. While we may gain clarity from questions and answers, such answers invariably lead to new questions. Redemptions, also, lead to new exiles, in a perpetual movement toward a fulfillment that is never fully attained. It seems as though the path never ends. Yet, we still instinctually yearn for a redemption that will be eternal and irreversible, a state of oneness and unity without an opposite.

---

[*] The *Yerushalmi* teaches that someone who eats Matzah on Erev Pesach is similar to someone who has relations with his future wife before the wedding, in his in-laws' home: *Pesachim*, 10. *Tosefos*, Pesachim, 99b. And just like in marriage we first recite the seven blessings and then get married, the same is with Matzah, we recite seven blessings before we eat the Matzah: *Zohar*, Raya M'hemna 3, p. 251b. *Ohr Zarua, Shibolei haLeket*, Siman 208:600, see also: *Rokeach*, Siman 32 (The seven blessings are counted up until the blessings on the actual Matzah, when we 'reveal' the Matzah / the 'bride'). This means that at the peak of the Seder, after the seven blessings, there is an inner marriage between ourselves and HaKadosh Baruch Hu, the idea of *V'Lakachti* — full intimacy. This is supported by the fact that 'eating bread' is sometimes used by the sages as a euphemism for marital relations.

The truth is, eternal freedom does exist in a realm beyond the paradigm of 'four', beyond *Seder* or order, beyond duality, and beyond path or process. This is the paradigm of 'five', the end of the progressive path. In terms of the Haggadah, the fifth level is (the fifteenth step) *Nirtzah*, or 'acceptance', which reveals the perfect unity already present in our lives, the deepest levels of our soul, and thus the realization of *Dayeinu* / 'It is sufficient.'

As we mentioned above, 'five' does not obliterate 'four', rather it includes and unifies 'four'. Even though it is the end of the path, it does not end the useful function of the path, within its context of growth and change. That is, when we realize the changeless essential freedom symbolized by 'five' we still seek spiritual progress, but for a different reason and from a radically different place.

While we realize that we have the answer and everything is already perfect (on some level), we also realize that in appearance and in actuality, all is *not* yet perfect. There is still much pain and suffering in this world, the world is not redeemed, and it is not sufficient for us to attain some private Geulah consciousness. We want all of reality and all of life to experience Geulah and ultimate redemption. Also, even if the current exile does not obstruct for us the reality that redemption already exists in the here and now, exile does continue to appear in the world, at least in this moment. We therefore continue to ask questions and to strive, yearn, long, for the Ultimate Redemption of the entire world, with the coming of Moshiach, speedily in our days.

REDEMPTION 'FROM' OR 'WITHIN' EXILE

Just as there is a world of duality and a world of unity, there is the world of movement and progress, and a world of ever-present stillness. There is a type of *Geulah* / redemption that can manifest within the world of duality and *Tenuah* / movement, and there is a type of Geulah that manifests within the world of Yichud, beyond Tenuah. There is a redemption connected with 'angels and messengers' including the 'messenger' Moshe, and a redemption that is connected with Hashem Alone.

Our world, and even angels, operates in a world of Tenuah. The world is created by Divine movements — utterances — and our world is defined by movement. Yaakov sees in his dream angels ascending and descending the ladder, in a state of perpetual movement. But above the ladder, as it were, Hashem is present, beyond movement.

With regards to the source of the four cups and the four expressions of redemption, the Torah says, והוצאתי אתכם מתחת סבלת מצרים והצלתי אתכם מעבדתם וגאלתי אתכם בזרוע נטויה ובשפטים גדלים ולקחתי אתכם לי לעם / "I will *take* you out *from* the labors of the Egyptians and *deliver* you *from* their bondage. I will *redeem* you with an outstretched arm and through extraordinary chastisements. And I will *take* you to be My people" (*Shemos*, 6:6-7). The delivery and redemption is "from" the place of bondage, a movement out of slavery to freedom. This is connected with the four cups of wine. Yet, there is the hidden fifth 'level', one that is beyond (although includes) all the movements and dualities.

At the peak of the Exodus unfolding, Moshe tells Klal Yisrael, כה אמר ה' כחצת הלילה אני יוצא בתוך מצרים / "Like this Hashem has said: 'Toward midnight I will go forth *among* the Egyptians'" (*Shemos*, 11:4). Hashem says, "I alone, not an angel or messenger," but I Alone will be present בתוך מצרים / among the Egyptians. Here HaKadosh Baruch Hu alone is present 'within' Egypt; this revelation does not function in a dualistic paradigm in which Klal Yisrael "leaves" Egypt in order to be "redeemed," but rather it is a revelation of utter *Yichud* / unity, 'Hashem Alone', beyond all (and including all) dualities and dichotomies, beyond all movement. Thus, there is a paradoxical revelation of redemption from *within* Egypt.

The fifth cup is connected with this world of Unity, and thus we do not need to drink it or even to move the cup from the *Mashpia* / giver, to one's mouth, the *Mekabel* / receiver. In fact, the wine is poured back into the original bottle, representing Hashem Alone, beyond movement. This is the fifth dimension and one connected to the fifth 'level' of our soul, Yechidah. The four lower levels of our soul are connected to the world of movement, duality and thus the possibility of a shadow side. Our Yechidah is one with the *Yechidah Shel Olam* / the Oneness of the World; it is always present and has no counterpoint or opposite (*Yevamos*, 122a: בבואה דבבואה לית להו. Yechidah has no opposite force: *Likutei Torah*, Teitzei, 37c).

FIVE IN THE HAGGADAH

Towards the end of the Seder, we fill the fifth cup. Today this cup is known as the *Kos Eliyahu haNavi*, or 'Cup of Elijah the Prophet', and as such it alludes to the presence of the Future Redemption as it already exists and is nested within each of the four levels. This is the non-duality that includes and permeates every stage along the path toward unity.

For example, in the Maggid section, five sages gather in Bnei Brak to discuss the Exodus, and there is an argument between Rebbe Eliezer and Rebbe Akiva regarding how many plagues there were.* There were ten plagues according to all opinions,

---

* There is a hint to the fifth level when the Haggadah says, "Hashem took us out with (1) a mighty hand, (2) an outstretched arm, (3) awesome greatness, (4) signs, and (5) *wonders*." The end of the first part of the Haggadah also alludes to 'five' when it says, "We give thanks, we praise..." — using ten descriptions of praise and thanks that Hashem is taking us out (1) "from slavery to freedom, (2) from sorrow to joy, (3) from mourning to Yom Tov, (4) from darkness to great light, and (5) from oppression to Redemption." These are five levels of freedom, which also correspond to the four exiles and the exile of Egypt, which is the root of all four exiles. "From slavery to freedom" refers the exile of Egypt and the Exodus. "From sorrow to joy" is the Babylonian exile, the destruction of the Beis haMikdash and eventual building of the Second Beis haMikdash and the communal return to Eretz Yisrael (which brought great joy: *Nechemya*, 8:17). "From mourning to Yom Tov" is the Persian exile and the story of Purim, when at first there was *Eivel* / mourning, and later a Yom Tov was established (*Megilas Esther*, 4:3, 8:17). "From darkness to light" is the story of the Greek exile; the darkness of Greece (*Medrash Rabbah*, Bereishis, 3:4) and then the light of Chanukah. "From oppression to Redemption" is our present exile, the Roman exile — and the ultimate Redemption, may it come speedily, in our days. The Maharal points out in *Gevuros Hashem*, Chap. 61, that there are versions of the Haggadah that do not say "...from darkness to great light." Therefore, there are some versions that stress the dimension of 'four', while other versions allude to 'five' as well.

but the question is how deep each plague penetrated reality, penetrating all four or five levels, thus 40 or 50 plagues. This is essentially a debate about the nature of oneness and redemption, and the level of consciousness of each sage is evident in his words. Rebbe Eliezer says that the root and the effect of the plagues is on the level of 'four', as in the four elements, while Rebbe Akiva feels that the root and the effect of the plagues is on the level of 'five', present even on the hidden 'fifth' level, which lies beyond and is what maintains the divergent four elements.*

THE FIFTH CUP

The Gemara offers the opinion of Rebbe Tarfon that we should drink a fifth cup at the Seder, and say the Great Hallel.** While in practice the law does not follow this opinion, we still have a custom to fill a 'fifth cup', but not to drink it

---

* *Likutei Sichos,* 16, 87. See also: *Tzafnas Paneach,* Torah, Shemos, 7:17. 19:21. Rav Yitzchak Chaver, *Haggadah,* ad loc. See for earlier sources about this argument, the four elements or even the fifth; the *Col-Bo,* the *Avudaraham* and the Ritva in their commentaries to the Haggadah. *Akeidas Yitzchak,* Beshalach, Sha'ar 40, and many other sources. It was precisely Rebbe Akiva who saw the 'fifth' level deep within the Makos. Rebbe Akiva is the one who would דורש על כל קוץ וקוץ תילין תילין של הלכות / "derive from each and every thorn of these crowns mounds upon mounds of Halachos": *Menachos,* 29b. The crowns of the letters of the four-letter name of Hashem, the Yud-Hei-Vav-Hei, are connected with the 'fifth dimension'.

** *Pesachim,* 118a, according to many of the Geonim and the version of the Rambam. According to Rashi and the Rashbam the Gemara does mention this fifth cup, thus the ruling of the Tur, Siman 481: כוס חמישי לא הוזכר לגירסת רשב"ם ואין לעשותו.

(ויש לו למזג כוס חמישי ולומר עליו הלל הגדול): Rambam, *Hilchos Chametz uMatzah*, 8:10. The Rambam does not mention drinking it, just filling the cup). This has become known as the 'Cup of Eliyahu'.*

The later Halachic codes continue the Talmudic debate whether or not there should be a fifth cup. It seems we should fill an additional cup over which we recite the Hallel. As with other unresolved arguments, the sages said that 'the Tishbi' (Eliyahu) will resolve the issue when he returns to earth. This is the origin of the term 'Cup of Eliyahu'. Until Eliyahu comes, as a compromise, the fifth cup shall be poured but not consumed.

---

* In other words, the fifth cup is connected with the cup of Eliyahu. This seems to be the opinion of the Maharal, the Gra, and many others. Once speaking about the Cup of Eliyahu, the Rebbe said that by Chassidim this interpretation was not accepted, and rather, the reason for the Cup of Eliyahu is its connection to our faith in Moshiach, and not connected to a 'fifth cup' (in the category of the other cups). The Alter Rebbe writes in his *Shulchan Aruch* (*Orach Chayim*, 480:5), ובקצת מקומות נוהגין שלא לנעול החדרים שישנים שם בליל פסח כי הוא ליל שמורים לכל בני ישראל לדורותם להוציאם מגלות הזה ואם יבא אליהו ימצא פתח פתוח ונצא לקראתו במהרה ואנו מאמינים בזה ויש באמונה זו שכר גדול ובמקומות שמצויין גנבים אין לסמוך על הנס כמו שנתבאר בסי' תל"ג. ונוהגין במדינות אלו למזוג כוס אחד יותר מהמסובין וקורין אותו כוס של אליהו הנביא. Thus it seems that from the Alter Rebbe the reason for the Cup of Eliyahu is to show our Emunah, faith in the coming of Eliyahu and Moshiach, unrelated to the idea of a 'fifth' cup, and wine is used to fill it because wine is a Davar Chashuv, much like the reason that wine is used for Kiddush: The Rebbe, *HaMelech b'Mesibo* 1, pp. 136, 144. Either way, this cup is certainly connected to Moshiach and Redemption. The Ra'avad and Tosefos connect this cup with the phrase והבאתי אתכם אל-הארץ / *V'Heiveisi* / "and I will bring you (into Eretz Yisrael): *Archos Chayim*, Leil Pesach, 79. *Da'as Zekeinim*, Shemos, 12:8. This cup is connected with the final Redemption: the Levush on *Orach Chayim*, 481.

The deeper reason for the Cup of Eliyahu is that Eliyahu is the *Meveser haGeulah*, the harbinger of the ultimate redemption. The 'term of redemption' connected to this cup is *V'Heiveisi* / "and I will (future tense) bring you to the Land." At this point in the Seder, we are no longer contemplating the past redemption from Egypt, but rather the imminent or 'future' redemption. Like Eliyahu, the fifth cup ushers in the ultimate freedom for all eternity. This 'future' is now.

The fifth cup is beyond *Seder* / order, levels and stages, beyond path and process, and beyond duality — and therefore we do not drink it. We do not *need* to internalize this cup, for the Messianic Era is of another paradigm altogether, beyond a world of opposites, such as internal or external. Ultimately, we cannot make Nirtzah into our reality, nor strive for a future Nirtzah, we can only *be* Nirtzah in the present moment. Nirtzah is totally imminent — it is already all-pervasive — and so striving only perpetuates the illusion of not being there yet.

- **In terms of the letters of Hashem's Name,** the fifth cup is the *Kotzo Shel Yud* / the tiny tip which crowns the Yud of Hashem's Name. The truth is, every letter is crowned with an identical tip. This also corresponds to the Yechidah, the fifth level of soul, which transcends and includes all other levels.

- **In terms of relationship,** the fifth cup is the Fifth term of redemption and intimacy with Hashem: *V'Heiveisi* / 'I will bring you to the Holy Land.' The term *V'Heiveisi* comes from the word *Bi'ah* which connotes a full marital unification. This will be fully achieved with the revelation of Moshiach.

• **In terms of the Partzufim,** the fifth cup is *Atik*, the innermost level of the Sefirah of Keser. Metaphorically, this is both a crown above the head, transcending the body, and yet it includes the whole body.

• **In terms of the Worlds,** the fifth cup is Adam Kadmon. Adam Kadmon is essentially beyond the definition of 'world'.

• **In terms of the senses,** the fifth cup is the sense of smell, which is higher than the dualistic realm of the Tree of Knowledge. In other words, this sense was not damaged with the eating of the fruit of the Tree of Knowledge (*Bnei Yissaschar,* Adar 1). It is said that Moshiach will judge spiritual matters using the sense of smell.

There have been (and maybe there are even today) some Chassidim, such as the Ishbitzers, who did drink the fifth cup. Most people refrain from drinking this fifth cup, but not because we are 'not there yet' (in the future, as it were), rather because we do not view it as a separate cup. It is like the Kotzo Shel Yud, which is present in every letter, as every letter of the Aleph Beis begins with a small dot, like the Kotz of the Yud. The fifth cup is similarly present in every cup, and not even just the four cups of the Seder. We could even say that because we pour the fifth cup back in the bottle, we *do* drink Eliyahu's wine, but at another time, perhaps, at lunch the next day ('beyond Seder'), and we do so without even thinking about it ('beyond intellect').

Since the fifth cup is not a separate cup, it is not a separate level, and it can be found within all levels. In this sense, 'four' alludes to 'five'; all dualities allude to non-duality; exile alludes to the presence of Redemption, even here and now, and there is some measure of the fifth level of Geulah within all four dimensions of exile.

WAYS TO EMBODY REDEMPTION IN OUR LIVES

The Seder is a potent ritual that makes embodying redemption possible. However, we still need to apply and practice its lessons in our lives throughout the year. Let us use the Four Questions and the Four Children as two practical models for tapping into the fifth level at all times.

THE FOUR INNER CHILDREN

The Four Children and their respective needs also epitomize the four levels of consciousness and redemption within us.

In progressive order, it can be said that the *Chacham* / 'Wise Child' reflects the world of Asiyah because his cynical intellect introduces the concept of the pointlessness of having a Seder. Because he is passionate about his questions, the *Rasha* / 'Wicked Child' exists in Yetzirah, the emotional universe. The *Tam* / 'Simple Child' paradoxically exists in Beriah because by asking questions which are unassuming in their simplicity, he receives knowledge through a dialectical process. The *She'eino Yodei'a Lishol* / 'Child that Doesn't Know to Ask' exemplifies Atzilus because he does not feel the need to ask a question — he is already at the fourth level, close to a place beyond all questions.

Then there is a fifth child who does not even come to the Seder. This can obviously be interpreted in a negative way: he is so far removed from spirituality that he does not even know to show up. He is a living question, a seemingly unsolvable spiritual problem. But everything has both an outer appearance, or 'vessel', and an inner Divine expression or 'light'. Only according to his 'vessel' reality, does he 'not know to come to the Seder'.

According to his 'light' reality, the fifth child does not come to the Seder because he is higher than *Seder* / 'order'. He does not need answers, for he is a living answer. He is, of course, beyond being a 'child'; he represents a reality where there is no longer a higher person teaching a lower person. He is, rather, a fulfillment of the Messianic prophecy; *Lo y'lamdu od ish el rei'eihu...kulam yeidu osi* / "No one will teach his friend anymore...for all will know Me."

We have all of the four children within us, and in our essence, we are the fifth child as well. Realizing this fact is the first step toward embodying redemption. To manifest the fifth child, we should keep asking questions appropriate to our level of 'process', but at the same time, we should remember that in our essence we are already one with the unspeakable answer.

As the fifth child we are beyond all levels; our not-knowing transcends both knowledge and ignorance. We are beyond need and the fulfillment of need. We are above the duality of exile and redemption, for we ourselves are, so to speak, like Eliyahu, the eternal harbinger of Redemption, as by revealing the Yechidah within ourselves, we are revealing a spark of Moshiach within the world (*Meor Einayim*, Pinchas. *Likutei Sichos*, 20, p. 522. 2, p. 599).

ASKING THE FOUR QUESTIONS

The four questions of *Mah Nishtanah* reflect our progress through the Four Worlds. From the added perspective of the Fifth World of *Nirtzah*, where all is already accepted, answered and unified, our questions are not filled with anxiety or ego-based striving. Having a question is no longer an exile, nor a descent for the sake of ascent. The 'fifth question', rather, emanates from a place where question and answer are one.

Our only real questions are these: Why is this night, this exile, different from all other exiles? Why, in this state of internal redemption and completion, are there still people who still appear to be suffering alienation and estrangement from the Source of all Life? And what can I do to help?

The first question of *Mah Nishtanah* concerns 'dipping' and reflects the world of Asiyah. Dipping the Karpas in salt water reminds us of the tears of affliction, and the dipping of the Maror in Charoses reminds us of the sweetness of our physical liberation from Mitzrayim. *From the fifth level we should also ask ourselves: what can I do to bring liberation and a sweetening of reality to all who are physically afflicted?*

The second question concerns Matzah and brings us to the world of Yetzirah. The flat, simple bread of poverty is a reminder that we must transcend our inflated egos and attain humility before we can activate emotional healing and inner redemption. *From the fifth level, we should also ask ourselves: do I have the humility to speak to others in ways that will bring them emotional freedom and healing?*

The third question concerns Maror and brings us to the world of Beriah. The sharpness of Maror clears our minds, preparing our consciousness for higher understanding. *From the fifth level, we should also ask ourselves: do I have the intellectual clarity to communicate and transmit to others the higher understanding of redemption?*

Finally, the fourth question concerns reclining, and brings us to the world of Atzilus. Reclining is peaceful repose and stillness, in comparison to the agitation and effort of striving symbolized by standing or sitting erect. *From the fifth level, we should also ask ourselves: in my presence, are others allowed to experience the perfect stillness of their own being?*

BLESSINGS FOR PESACH

This is a night to give Hoda'ah for all the *Nisim* / miracles HaKadosh Baruch Hu performed for Klal Yisrael, and for us. May we thank Hashem for all the Yetzias Mitzrayims of our lives, in unconstricted *Dibbur* / speech and in abundant detail.

This night, the Seder of Nisim, is the great opening of the *Tzinor* / channel of all the miracles of the future. Therefore, may we also create the *Cheshek* / desire for what we need in *Gashmiyus* / physicality and *Ruchniyus* / spirituality, and to articulate them *b'Dibbur*, telling our Creator about everything that we want for our new lives, starting tonight. May we know that we are reborn, and that we are loved with an Infinite Love.

On this night, HaKadosh Baruch Hu gives us the gift of גדלות / Gadlus, we just need to truly have Emunah and act as if we are the כהן גדול / Cohen Gadol serving the Supreme Beloved One in the white garments of גדלות רוחני / spiritual expansiveness. We should know that we are all royalty, reclining amid the finery of גדלות גשמי / material expansiveness. When we do this, the night becomes the foundation and *Tzinor* / conduit for all spiritual and material blessings throughout the entire year.

Even if, Chas v'Shalom, we may fall from the heights we were gifted on this night, we can recall a mental picture of

Seder Night and our inner *Reshimu* / imprint of the great light and Gadlus of the Seder. This will help reconnect us to this timeless light and give us the strength to get up again and return to our true state of priestly royalty.

The *Ikar* / main point is that this should be the last Seder in Galus for all of Klal Yisrael and we should be *Zocheh* / have the merit of bringing the Korban Pesach in the year that is presently unfolding; *l'Shanah haBa'ah b'Yerushalayim* / "This coming year in Jerusalem."

	LEVEL ONE	LEVEL 2	LEVEL 3	LEVEL 4	NON-LEVEL 5
CUPS	KIDDUSH	OVER MAGGID	OVER BENTCHING	OVER HALLEL	UNDRUNKC UP OF ELIYAHU
TERMS OF REDEMPTION	I WILL TAKE YOU OUT	AND DELIVER YOU	AND REDEEM YOU	AND TAKE YOU TO BE MY PEOPLE	AND BRING YOU TO THE LAND
LETTERS OF DIVINE NAME	LOWER HEI	VAV	UPPER HEI	YUD	KOTZO SHEL YUD (ALSO IN EVERY LETTER)
WORLDS	ASIYAH	YETZIRAH	BERIAH	ATZILUS	ADAM KADMON
PARTZUFIM	SHECHINAH / MALCHUS	ZEIR ANPIN / TIFERES	IMA / BINAH	ABBA / CHOCHMAH	ATIK / KESER
CHILDREN	CHACHAM	RASHA	TAM	SHE'EINO YODEI'A LISHOL	MISSING AT THE 'SEDER' / BEYOND ORDER
QUESTIONS	DIPPING	MATZAH	MAROR	RECLINING	HOW CAN I MANIFEST MY SPARK OF MOSHIACH?

Other Books by Rav Pinson

RECLAIMING THE SELF
The Way of Teshuvah

Teshuvah is one of the great gifts of life. It speaks of a hope for a better today and empowers us to choose a brighter tomorrow. But what exactly is Teshuvah? How does it work? How can we undo our past and how do we deal with guilt? And what is healthy regret without eroding our self-esteem? In this fascinating and empowering book, the path for genuine transformation and a way to include all of our past in the powerful moment of the now, is explored and demonstrated.

THE MYSTERY OF KADDISH
Understanding the Mourner's Kaddish

The Mystery of Kaddish is an in-depth exploration into the Mourner's Prayer. Throughout Jewish history, there have been many rites and rituals associated with loss and mourning, yet none have prevailed quite like the Mourner's Kaddish Prayer, which has become the definitive ritual of mourning. The book explores the source of this prayer and deconstructs the meaning to better understand the grieving process and how the Kaddish prayer supports and uplifts the bereaved through their own personal journey to healing.

UPSHERNISH: The First Haircut
Exploring the Laws, Customs & Meanings of a Boy's First Haircut

What is the meaning of Upsherin, the traditional celebration of a boy's first haircut at the age of three? Why is a boy's hair allowed to grow freely for his first three years? What is the deeper import of hair in all its lengths and varieties? What is the meaning of hair coverings? Includes a guide to conducting an Upsherin ceremony.

A BOND FOR ETERNITY
Understanding the Bris Milah

What is the Bris Milah – the covenant of circumcision? What does it represent, symbolize and signify? This book provides an in depth and sensitive review of this fundamental Mitzvah. In this little masterpiece of wisdom – profound yet accessible —the deeper meaning of this essential rite of passage and its eternal link to the Jewish people, is revealed and explored.

REINCARNATION AND JUDAISM
The Journey of the Soul

A fascinating analysis of the concept of Gilgul / Reincarnation. Dipping into the fountain of ancient wisdom and modern understanding, this book addresses and answers such basic questions as: What is reincarnation? Why does it occur? And how does it affect us personally?

INNER RHYTHMS
The Kabbalah of MUSIC

Exploring the inner dimension of sound and music, and particularly, how music permeates all aspects of life. The topics range from Deveikus/ Unity and Yichudim/Unifications, to the more personal issues, such as Simcha/Happiness and Marirus/ sadness.

MEDITATION AND JUDAISM
Exploring the Jewish Meditative Paths

A comprehensive work encompassing the entire spectrum of Jewish thought, from the sages of the Talmud and the early Kabbalists to the modern philosophers and Chassidic masters. This book is both a scholarly, in-depth study of meditative practices, and a practical, easy to follow guide for any person interested in meditating the Jewish way.

———

TOWARD THE INFINITE

A book focusing exclusively on the Chassidic approach to meditation known as Hisbonenus. Encompassing the entire meditative experience, it takes the reader on a comprehensive and engaging journey through this unique practice. The book explores the various states of consciousness that a person encounters in the course of the meditation, beginning at a level of extreme self-awareness and concluding with a state of total non-awareness.

———

THIRTY – TWO GATES OF WISDOM
into the Heart of Kabbalah & Chassidus

What is Kabbalah? And what are the differences between the theoretical, meditative, magical and personal Kabbalistic teachings? What are the four paths of interpreting the teachings of the ARIzal? What did Chassidus teach? These are some of the fundamental issues expanded upon in this text. And then, more specifically, why are there so many names of G-d and what do they represent? What are the key concepts of these deeper teachings?

The book explores the grand narrative of the great chain of reality, how there was and is a movement from the Infinite Oneness of Hashem to a world of (apparent) duality and multiplicity.

THE PURIM READER
The Holiday of Purim Explored

With a Persian name, a masquerade dress code and a woman as the heroine, Purim is certainly unusual amongst the Jewish holidays. Most people are very familiar with the costumes, Megilah and revelry, but are mystified by their significance. This book offers a glimpse into the hidden world of Purim, uncovering these mysteries and offering a deeper understanding of this unique holiday.

EIGHT LIGHTS
8 Meditations for Chanukah

What is the meaning and message of Chanukah? What is the spiritual significance of the Lights of the Menorah? What are the Lights telling us? What is the deeper dimension of the Dreidel? Rav Pinson, with his trademark deep learning and spiritual sensitivity guides us through eight meditations relating to the Lights of the Menorah, the eight days of Chanukah, and a fascinating exploration of the symbolism and structure of the Dreidel. Includes a detailed how-to guide for lighting the Chanukah Menorah.

PASSPORT TO KABBALAH
A Journey of Inner Transformation

Life is a journey full of ups and downs, inside-outs, and unexpected detours. There are times when we think we know exactly where we want to be headed, and other times when we are so lost we don't even know where we are. This slim book provides readers with a passport of sorts to help them through any obstacles along their path of self-refinement, reflection, and self-transformation.

THE FOUR SPECIES
The Symbolism of the Lulav & Esrog

The Four Species have inspired countless commentaries and traditions and intrigued scholars and mystics alike. In this little masterpiece of wisdom both profound and practical - the deep symbolic roots and nature of the Four Species are explored. The Na'anuim, or ritual of the Lulav movement, is meticulously detailed and Kavanos,, are offered for use with the practice. Includes an illustrated guide to the Lulav Movements.

THE BOOK OF LIFE AFTER LIFE

What is a soul? What happens to us after we physically die?

What is consciousness, and can it survive without a physical brain?

Can we remember our past lives?

Do near-death experiences prove immortality?

What is Gan Eden? Resurrection?

Exploring the possibility of surviving death, the near-death experience and a glimpse into what awaits us after this life.

(This book is an updated and expanded version of the book; Jewish Wisdom of the Afterlife)

THE GARDEN OF PARADOX:

The Essence of Non - Dual Kabbalah

This book is a Primer on the Essential Philosophy of Kabbalah presented as a series of 3 conversations, revealing the mysteries of Creator, Creation and Consciousness. With three representational students, embodying respectively, the philosopher, the activist and the mystic, the book, tackles the larger questions of life. Who is G-d? Who am I? Why do I exist? What is my purpose in this life? Written in clear and concise prose, the text, gently guides the reader towards making sense of life's paradoxes and living meaningfully.

BREATHING & QUIETING THE MIND

Achieving a sense of self-mastery and inner freedom demands that we gain a measure of hegemony over our thoughts. We learn to choose out thoughts so that we are not at the mercy of whatever belches up to the mind. Through quieting the mind and conscious breathing we can slow the onrush of anxious, scattered thinking and come to a deeper awareness of the interconnectedness of all of life.

Source texts are included in translation, with how-to-guides for the various practices.

VISUALIZATION AND IMAGERY:
Harnessing the Power of our Mind's Eye

We assume that what we see with our eyes is absolute. Yet, beyond our ability to choose what we see, we have the ability to choose how we see. This directly translates into how we experience life. In a world saturated with visual imagery, our senses are continuously assaulted with Kelipa/empty/fantasy imagery that we would not necessarily choose. These images can negatively affect our relationship with ourselves, with the world around us, and with the Divine. This volume seeks to show us how we can alter that which we observe through harnessing the power of our mind's eye, the inner sanctum of our imagination. We thus create a new way to see and experience the world. This book teaches us how to utilize visualization and imagery as a way to develop our spiritual sensitivity and higher intuition, and ultimately achieve Deveikus/Unity with Hashem.

SOUND AND VIBRATION:
Tuning into the Echoes of Creation

Through our perception of sound and vibration we internalize the world around us. What we hear, and how we process that hearing, has a profound impact on how we experience life. What we hear can empower us or harm us. A defining human capacity is to harness the power sound -- through speech, dialogue, and song, and through listening to others. Hearing is primary dimension of our existence. In fact, as a fetus our ears were the first fully operating sensory organs to develop.

This book will guide you in methods of utilizing the power of sound and vibration to heal and maintain mental, emotional and spiritual health, to fine-tune your Midos and even to guide you into deeper levels of Deveikus

/ conscious unity with Hashem. The vibratory patterns of the Aleph-Beis are particularly useful portals into our deeper conscious selves. Through chanting and deep listening, we can use the letters and sounds to shift our very mindset, to induce us into a state of presence and spiritual elevation.

THE POWER OF CHOICE:
A Practical Guide to Conscious Living

It is the essential premise of this book that we hold the key to unlock many of the gates that seem closed to us and keep us from living our fullest life. That key we all hold is the power to choose. The Power of Choice is the primary tool that we have at our disposal to impact the world and effect change within our own lives. We often give up this power to outside forces such as the market, media, politicians or peer pressure; or to internal forces that often function beyond our conscious control such as ego, anger, lust, greed or jealousy. Making conscious, compassionate and creative decisions is the cornerstone of living a mature and meaningful life.

MYSTIC TALES FROM THE EMEK HAMELECH

Mystic Tales of the Emek HaMelech, is a wondrous and inspiring collection of stories culled from the Emek HaMelech. Emek HaMelech, from which these stories have been taken, (as well as its author) is a bit of a mystery. But like all good mysteries, it is one worth investigating. In this spirit the present volume is being offered to the general public in the merit and memory of its saintly author, as well as in the hopes of introducing a vital voice of deeper Torah teaching and tradition to a contemporary English speaking audience

INNER WORLDS OF JEWISH PRAYER
A Guide to Develop and Deepen the Prayer Experience

While much attention has been paid to the poetry, history, theology and contextual meaning of the prayers, the intention of this work is to provide a guide to finding meaning and effecting transformation through the prayer experience itself.

Explore: *What happens when we pray? *How do we enter the mind-state of prayer? *Learning to incorporate the body into the prayers. *Discover techniques to enhance and deepen prayer and make it a transformative experience.

This empowering and inspiring text, demonstrates how through proper mindset, preparation and dedication, the experience of prayer can be deeply transformative and ultimately, life-altering.

WRAPPED IN MAJESTY
Tefillin - Exploring the Mystery

Tefillin, the black boxes and leather straps that are worn during prayer, are curiously powerful and mysterious. Within the inky black boxes lie untold secrets. In this profound, passionate and thought-provoking text, the multi-dimensional perspectives of Tefillin are explored and revealed. Magically weaving together all levels of Torah including the Peshat (literal observation), to Remez (allegorical), to Derush, (homiletic), to Sod (hidden) into one beautiful tapestry. Inspirational and instructive, Wrapped in Majesty: Tefillin, will make putting on the Tefillin more meaningful and inspiring.

SECRETS OF THE MIKVAH:
Waters of Transformation

A Mikvah is a pool of water used for the purpose of ritual immersion; a place where one moves from a state of Tumah; impurity, blockage and death— to a place of Teharah; purity, fluidity and life.

In SECRETS OF THE MIKVAH, Rav Pinson delves into the transformative powers of the Mikvah with his trademark all-encompassing perspective that ranges from the literal, Pshat observation and Halachic implications of the texts, to the allegorical, the philosophical, and finally, to the deep secrets of the Mikvah as revealed by Kabbalah and Chassidus.

This insightful and inspirational text demonstrates how immersion in a Mikvah can be a transformative and life-altering practice, and includes various Kavanos—deep intentions—for all people, through various stages of life, that empower and enrich the immersion experience.

———————

THE MYSTERY OF SHABBOS
Shabbat Rediscovered

Delving into the transformative power of Shabbos. With an all-encompassing perspective that ranges from the literal, Pshat observation and Halachic implications of the texts, to the allegorical, the philosophical, and finally, to the deeper secrets as revealed by Kabbalah and Chassidus, creating an elegant tapestry of thought and experience. THE MYSTERY OF SHABBOS is a profound meditation on the meaning of Shabbos and demonstrates the physical, emotional, mental and spiritual possibilities available and given to us with the gift of Shabbos. Studying and contemplating this inspired text on the depths of Shabbos will unveil a redemptive light in your experience of the Seventh Day -- and by extension, every day of your life.

THE SPIRAL OF TIME:
A 12 Part Series on the Months of the Year

VOL 1: THE SPIRAL OF TIME:
Unraveling the Yearly Cycle

Many centuries ago, the Sages of Israel were the foremost authority in the fields of both astronomical calculation and astrological wisdom, including the deeper interpretations of the cycles and seasons. Over time, this wisdom became hidden within the esoteric teachings of the Torah, and as a result was known only to students and scholars of the deepest depths of the tradition. More recently, the great teachers, from R.Yitzchak Luria (the Arizal) to the Baal Shem Tov, taught that as the world approaches the Era of Redemption, it is a Mitzvah / spiritual obligation to broadly reveal this wisdom.

"The Spiral of Time" is volume 1 is a series of 12 books, and serves as an introductory book to the basic concepts and nature of the Hebrew calendar and explores the special day of Rosh Chodesh.

VOL 2: THE MONTH OF NISAN:
Miraculous Awakenings from Above

The month of NISAN is the first month of the lunar cycle of the year, a month that brings in the spring and a month of redemption. Spring represents a time of plenty, abundance, sunshine, hope, and possibility. Redemption, on whatever level, feels palpable and accessible. In spring, the world is redeemed from the cold winter, the flower is redeemed from the tree, the grass from the earth, and we too feel that redemption is possible. A whole complex of ideas, including newness, redemption, going out of Egypt, and being freed from slavery, is intricately bound with the idea of Aviv / spring and the powerful month of Nisan.

VOL 3: THE MONTH OF IYYAR: EVOLVING THE SELF
& The Holiday of LAG B'OMER

The month of IYYAR is the second month of the spring, a month that connects the Redemption from Egypt in Nissan with the Revelation of Torah in Sivan. The Chai/ Eighteenth day of the Month is the day we celebrate the Rashbi (Rabbi Shimon Bar Yochai) and the revealing of the hidden aspects of the Torah. This is the 'Holiday' of Lag b'Omer. The book explores the unique quality of this special month, a month that has a Mitzvah of counting the Omer every day. In addition, the book explores the roots and significance of the mystical 'holiday' of Lag b'Omer. Including the customs & Practices of Lag b'Omer, such as, bonfires, bows & arrows, parades, Upsherin, and more.

VOL 4: THE MONTH OF SIVAN:
The Art of Receiving: Shavuos and Matan Torah

Sivan is the third month of the lunar cycle. One is a singularity. Two is division. Three is harmony, a unity that synthesizes individuality and multiplicity, Heaven and Earth, Spirituality and Physicality. During this month we celebrate Shavuos and the giving of the Torah, the ultimate expression of the unity of the Above and Below and we aspire to connect with the Keser/Crown of Torah that Transcends and yet includes all Worlds. Learning how to truly receive Higher wisdom in our Lower faculties is the mental, emotional, and spiritual exercise of the month.

VOL 5: THE MONTHS OF TAMUZ AND AV:

Embracing Brokenness –
17th of Tamuz, Tisha B'Av, & Tu B'Av

Each month and season of the year, radiates with distinct Divine qualities and unique opportunities for growth and Tikkun.

The summer month of Tamuz and Av contain the longest and hottest days of the year. The raised temperature is indicative of a corresponding spiritual heat, a time of harsher judgement and potential destruction, such as the destructions of the first and second Beis HaMikdash, which began on the 17th of Tamuz and culminated on the 9th and 10th of Av.

A few days later, on Tu b'Av, the darkness is transformed and reveals the greatest light and possibility for new life. During these summer months of Tamuz and Av we embrace our brokenness so that we can heal and transform darkness into light.

VOL 6: THE MONTH OF ELUL:

Days of Introspection and Transformation

Each month of the year radiates with a distinct quality and provides unique opportunities for growth and personal transformation. Elul, as the final month of the spring/summer season is connected to endings. Elul gives us the strength to be able to finish strong, to end well. Elul also serves as a month of preparation for the New Year/Rosh Hashanah.

We inhale our past year, ending with wisdom and then we also gain the wisdom to begin anew and exhale a positive year into being. The mental, emotional, and spiritual objective of this month is introspection and the reclaiming of our inner purity and wholeness.

VOL 7: THE MONTH OF TISHREI:
A Time of Rebirth & Upward Movement

Each month of the year radiates with distinct Divine qualities and unique opportunities for growth and spiritual illumination. As Tishrei begins the new yearly cycle, it is an appropriate month to introspect, reflect and resolve to move forward and preserve moving forward into the more inward months of the winter. This month creates the space to unburden ourselves from our negativities, and enter a more sacred, grounded sacred space. In Tishrei we are given the gift of forgiveness and then the ability to truly regain our space and inner joy.

VOL 8: THE MONTH OF CHESHVAN:
Navigating Transitions, Elevating the Fall

Directly on the heels of the inspiring and holiday-filled month of Tishrei, Cheshvan is a month that is quiet and devoid of holidays. In the month of Cheshvan we use the stored up energies of the previous months to self-generate our inspiration and creativity and provide ourselves with the strength to rise up after a fall. In Cheshvan we are entering into a stormier, wetter and colder season. It is a month of transition. The mental, emotional and spiritual objective of this month is to weather the transitions, learn to self-generate and stand tall. And if we do fall, we use the quality of this month to get back up and do so with more conviction, strength, wisdom and clarity.

VOL 9: THE MONTH OF KISLEV:
Rekindling Hope, Dreams and Trust

Kislev is the final month of the fall. Throughout this month, daylight progressively shortens, and the temperatures drop. Towards the end of the month, at the darkest hour, the winter solstice arrives and we begin the celebration of Chanukah. We commemorate the miracle of a small jug of oil that burned for eight nights, and as we celebrate, daylight expands. In the month of Kislev-despite the darkness, or perhaps because of it-we have the ability to tap into the Ohr HaGanuz, the hidden light of hope that rekindles our dreams and aspirations.

VOL 10: THE MONTH OF TEVES:
Refining Relationships, Elevating the Body

The quality of Teves is generally harsh—much like its counterpart Tamuz in the summer, thus the tendency for many is to hunker down, retract, curl up and wait for the month to pass by, only to reemerge when the harshness has dissipated. Think for a moment about the 'easier' months of the year, which, like gentle waves in the ocean, carry us where we want to go. We can ride these energies easily and they can propel us forward effortlessly, we just need to go with the overall flow, so to speak. The harsher months, on the other hand, can be compared to the more powerful waves that emanate from the belly of the ocean, which come forcefully crashing down and can easily drown a person before they even realize what has happened. However, those who want to utilize the momentum of the powerful energy that is available during such times can, with caution and creativity, harness these intense waves and ride them higher and farther than other, more gentle circumstances may allow. However, harnessing the power of Tohu, the raw energy of the body, does in fact need to be approached with great care and attention.

VOL 11: THE MONTH OF SHEVAT: ELEVATING EATING
& The Holiday of Tu b'Shevat

Each month of the year radiates with a distinct Divine energy and thus unique opportunities for growth, *Tikkun* and illumination. According to the deeper teachings of the Torah, all of these distinct qualities, opportunities and natural phenomena correspond to a certain data set. That is, the nature of each month is elucidated by a specific letter of the Aleph Beis, a tribe, verse, human sense, and so forth. The month of Shevat is particularly connected to food and our relationship to bodily intake. During this month we celebrate Tu b'Shevat, the New Year of the Tree, and aspire to create a proper and physically/emotionally/spiritually healthy relationship with food.

VOL 12: THE MONTH OF ADAR:
Transformation Through Laughter & Holy Doubt

Each month of the year radiates with distinct Divine qualities and unique opportunities for growth and spiritual illumination. As Adar concludes the monthly cycle of the year, as well as the solar phenomena of the winter, it is an appropriate month to think about our essential identity, before moving out to meet the world come spring. This month we strive to create a healthy relationship with holy humor, unbounded joy, and a general sense of lightness of being. Through the work of Adar we transform negative, crippling doubt and uncertainties into radical wonderment and openness.

ILLUMINATED SOUND:
The Baal Shem Tov on Prayer

In the year 1698 a great light was revealed to the world with the descent of the holy soul of the Baal Shem Tov. In time, the Baal Shem Tov became one of the most important and influential teachers of Torah in all of history, and the founder of Chassidus.

Amongst the vast repository of profound and revolutionary teachings of the holy Baal Shem Tov, the teachings on the path of Tefilah / Prayer are the most elaborate. The teachings of the Baal Shem Tov on Tefilah include some of his most innovative expressions, or Chidushim. Tefilah is the essential and central tenet from which all other teachings flow.

In this masterful and practical text, Rav Pinson revives the awe-inspiring and transformational teachings of the Baal Shem Tov, and illuminates his unique path to Tefilah.

A CALL TO MAJESTY:
The Mysteries of Shofar & Rosh Hashanah

The Shofar is the preeminent symbol of Rosh Hashanah, waking us up to a time of deep introspection and celebration. But why do we blow the Shofar on this most special of days? While the Torah decrees that the Shofar must be blown, it does not provide a reason. On the deepest level, the Shofar is of course beyond reason altogether, and yet, from within its shape, sound and story, a constellation of "reasons" emerge. Rebirth. Responsibility. Radical Amazement. On a primal vibrational level, the Shofar calls each of us to a place of deeper consciousness and community as we crown the King of All Creation.

THE CALL TO MAJESTY delves deeply into the world of Rosh Hashanah and its primary Mitzvah, the sound of the Shofar. Weaving together a multi-dimensional tapestry of practical, allegorical, philosophical, and mystical ideas and implications, the teachings collected herein empower us all to answer the higher calling of the Shofar.